Confusion of Tongues

OXFORD MORAL THEORY

Series Editor
David Copp, University of California, Davis

Confusion of Tongues

A THEORY OF NORMATIVE LANGUAGE

Stephen Finlay

OXFORD
UNIVERSITY PRESS

OXFORD
UNIVERSITY PRESS

Oxford University Press is a department of the University of Oxford.
It furthers the University's objective of excellence in research, scholarship,
and education by publishing worldwide.

Oxford   New York
Auckland   Cape Town   Dar es Salaam   Hong Kong   Karachi
Kuala Lumpur   Madrid   Melbourne   Mexico City   Nairobi
New Delhi   Shanghai   Taipei   Toronto

With offices in
Argentina   Austria   Brazil   Chile   Czech Republic   France   Greece
Guatemala   Hungary   Italy   Japan   Poland   Portugal   Singapore
South Korea   Switzerland   Thailand   Turkey   Ukraine   Vietnam

Oxford is a registered trademark of Oxford University Press
in the UK and certain other countries.

Published in the United States of America by
Oxford University Press
198 Madison Avenue, New York, NY 10016

CIP data is on file at the Library of Congress.

ISBN 978–0–19–934749–0 (hardcover); 978–0–19–064963–0 (paperback)

{ CONTENTS }

{ ACKNOWLEDGMENTS }

Work on this book began in 2008 with the support of a Charles A. Ryskamp Research Fellowship from the Mellon Foundation and American Council of Learned Societies, and finished in 2013 with the support of a fellowship from the National Endowment of the Humanities. Without this generous funding it's hard to imagine how it could have been written. But the ideas proposed here have been developing since at least 1999 and my Ph.D. dissertation at the University of Illinois, Urbana-Champaign, under the guidance of James Wallace, Gary Ebbs, Jeff McMahan, and Richard Schacht. I have therefore benefited from many more people than I could possibly remember or name, and I apologize to those whose assistance isn't acknowledged below.

Those to whom I am indebted for their comments on this manuscript include Matthew Chrisman, Brian Coffey, David Copp, Janice Dowell, Daan Evers, Joanna Klimczyk, Karen Lewis, Mike Ridge, Jake Ross, Mark Schroeder, Kadri Vihvelin, Ralph Wedgwood, David Wolfsdorf, Gideon Yaffe, an anonymous reviewer for Oxford University Press, audiences of numerous talks over the last few years (particularly the philosophy department at Umeå University for inviting me to present the 2012 Burman Lectures in Philosophy), and the participants in graduate seminars I taught at the University of Southern California in the fall of 2009 and the spring of 2012: Rima Basu, Josh Crabill, Justin Dallman, Ryan Gillespie, Rishi Joshi, Nick Laskowski, Ben Lennertz, Alida Liberman, Matt Lutz, Michael Milona, Shyam Nair, Caleb Perl, Abelard Podgorski, Jason Raibley, Indrek Reiland, Sam Shpall, Kenneth Silver, Justin Snedegar, Ryan Walsh, and Aness Webster. I have also benefited from conversations with Gunnar Björnsson, Kenny Easwaran, Allan Gibbard, Jim Higginbotham, Angelika Kratzer, and Barry Schein. Thanks to Nicky Drake for pointing out typos in the hardcover edition, and to Peter Ohlin, Emily Sacharin, and Andrew Ward at Oxford University Press for all their assistance. The appendix to Chapter 3 is based on a paper cowritten with Justin Snedegar, "One Ought Too Many", *Philosophy & Phenomenological Research* 89:1, (2014), pp. 102–24. An earlier version of some sections of Chapter 4 was published as "Explaining Reasons" in the *Deutsches Jahrbuch für Philosophie*, vol. 4, 2012. The material in Chapter 8 partly draws on an earlier paper cowritten with Gunnar Björnsson, "Metaethical Contextualism Defended", *Ethics* 121 (2010), pp. 7–36.

Special thanks are due to Mark Schroeder for constant encouragement and advice, which kept me going whenever I began to doubt myself, Gideon Yaffe for many years of friendship and organizing a one-day workshop on the manuscript, David Copp for inviting it for the Oxford Moral Theory series, and Mike Ridge for reading the entire manuscript and providing extensive comments not once but twice. Perhaps needless to say the many flaws that remain are nobody's fault but mine. I don't consider this project as finished so much as having run out of time. It's rightly been said that a metaethicist is a jack of all trades: this book has an ambitiously wide scope, wading amateurishly into many issues (at least in semantics, pragmatics, moral psychology, and probability, not to mention in metaethics) on which there are now large and sophisticated literatures. If I had attempted to master all these literatures this book would never have been completed or published. I sincerely apologize to all those whose work I ought to have read or cited but haven't, and hope any errors or oversights aren't too serious.

My greatest debts are to my wife Sarah and my daughters Ashleigh, Jorja, and Alex, for their patience, sacrifices, and love. They are my Reasons for everything, and I dedicate this book to them.

{ 1 }

Introduction

This book is about the meaning and use of normative language, in particular the words 'good', 'ought', and 'reason', which are of central interest to moral and practical philosophy. In the first half of the book I take a linguistic approach, arguing that the evidence from various ordinary uses consistently points toward a unifying semantics for normative words as *end-relational*. According to this theory, normative words refer to probabilistic relations in which things stand to particular "ends" or potential states of affairs that vary from context to context. In the second half, I address the distinctive features of peculiarly moral and deliberative uses of this language in speech and thought. These are broadly classifiable as forms of either "practicality" or "objectivity", and largely comprise the central problems of metaethics. I demonstrate that the end-relational theory accommodates and explains these features systematically by appeal to basic principles of conversational pragmatics, concerning the way we use normative language in pursuit of our purposes.

The myth of the Tower of Babel provides allegories for the book's two major themes. This is a tale of vain human ambition foiled by disagreement that arises from misunderstandings of language, the proverbial Confusion of Tongues. The first allegory concerns *ethical* or normative disagreement: I argue that our most fundamental disagreements over what things are good, what one ought to do, and what reasons there are to do it involve a "confusion of tongues" in the sense that we are talking past each other, using the same sentences and words to refer to different facts and properties. The second allegory concerns *metaethical* (or "metanormative") disagreement: I'll argue that philosophical disputes over (inter alia) the nature of normative facts and properties are due to a "confusion of tongues" in the different sense of a failure to understand our own use of normative language. In this chapter I first explain these themes and why I believe the meaning of normative language matters, then introduce my method and strategy.

1.1. The Big Picture

From a naturalistic perspective, human beings are simply animals motivated by contingent desires for varying ends, which inevitably bring us into conflict. Basic desires are "ultimate ends" which are "never referred to any other object", in Hume's words, and practical thought is just the "slave of the passions", the arena in which they vie for control and calculate means. But the practice of normative speech and thought has been the object of a grand philosophical ambition to elevate humanity above "mere" animality. On the basis of our normative judgments we are able to act or refrain from acting rather than simply being moved by the strongest impulse of the moment. Practical speech and thought are viewed as answering to an independent normative reality to which desire properly defers. To Hume's claim that no reason can be given why we hate pain, it can be replied that pain is *bad*. We treat others with kindness and respect because we judge it to be what we *ought* to do. Call the various ways the normative is independent from individuals' subjective attitudes its *objectivity*.

This objectivity has been viewed by many philosophers as raising us from the natural to the divine, from "brutes" to beings created "in the likeness of God", from desire to reason, from causal determination to freedom, and from arbitrary mores to universal law. In the ancient world, Plato identified the Idea of the Good as the divine itself and prime cause of all motion, a view also embraced by Augustine in late antiquity and by Aquinas in the medieval era. In the early modern era, Joseph Butler proclaimed moral sensibility a compass implanted in us by God with authority over our passions, while Immanuel Kant identified it as the sole and conclusive proof that we aren't mere animals driven by desire and trapped in the natural order of inexorable cause and effect, but free beings existing also in a divine realm of pure reason.[1] Even in our era of scientific naturalism, many moral philosophers claim to see in normative speech and thought the twinkle of something beyond the natural world accessible to our animal senses. The turn of the twentieth century saw in the work of Henry Sidgwick and G. E. Moore a revival of the Platonic doctrine of a sui generis realm of value accessible only to our intellect. After decades of disfavor this "nonnaturalism" now seems the dominant faith among contemporary moral philosophers.[2]

Like the Tower of Babel, however, normative speech and thought haven't raised us to a utopia of peace and happiness. Instead they play a central role

---

[1] Kant attributes objectivity to the structure of agency rather than to the external world. See also Watson 1975 on the link between normative judgment and freedom.

[2] Recent champions include Robert Audi, Frithjof Bergmann, Roger Crisp, Terence Cuneo, Jonathan Dancy, Ronald Dworkin, David Enoch, William FitzPatrick, Jean Hampton, Chris Heathwood, Michael Huemer, Colin McGinn, John McDowell, David McNaughton, Thomas Nagel, Graham Oddie, Derek Parfit, T. M. Scanlon, Russ Shafer-Landau, John Skorupski, Phillip Stratton-Lake, and David Wiggins. Oddly, many claim the view is unpopular.

in ugly conflicts, often at levels of violence not found among the animals we've called "brutes". In Plato's *Euthyphro* Socrates asks, "What differences are there which...make us angry and set us at enmity with each other?" and himself proposes the answer that "these enmities arise when the matters of disagreement are the just and the unjust, good and evil". Thousands of years later this observation is no less apt, with the first decade of the new millennium dominated by the "war on terror", a vicious conflict which has both sides claiming to be fighting a battle of "good" versus "evil". Socrates lays the blame on our lack of a method for settling the truth about the normative facts. We seem unable to settle normative disagreements empirically by observation and experiment, and so quarrel because we can't establish which of our opposing opinions is true.

Philosophy attempts to help resolve these disagreements through normative ethics, the "science" of morality, but because Socrates' problem of method remains unsolved the scientific credentials of ethics are widely scorned. Unable to settle normative disagreements, philosophy turns to scrutinize the concepts with which the issues are framed, shifting from ethical to metaethical enquiry. Instead of asking "What things are good?", "What ought I to do?", and "What are the reasons for doing it?", we begin to ask, "What does it mean for something to be *good*, or what I *ought* to do, or a *reason*?" Many philosophers have attempted to help resolve normative disagreement by clarifying what these disagreements are about; for example, Jeremy Bentham and John Stuart Mill believed that by establishing that *good* means nothing but *utility* they had given ethics a scientific basis, and laid the foundation for moral agreement and a better society.

But lack of a method couldn't be more than half of the story. Being unable to settle normative questions wouldn't bring us into conflict if we were indifferent to them. We also have no means of establishing how many hairs were on Plato's head when he wrote those passages in the *Euthyphro*, but this doesn't lead us to quarrel. Socrates neglects to mention the remarkable degree to which the "good" matters to us. We care not only that we ourselves pursue the good, avoid the bad, and act as we ought, but generally that others do also, which is why our normative disagreements are often so vehement. Call the special connection of the normative to motivation its *practicality*.

Contrary to the hopes described above, many naturalistic philosophers interpret this practicality (along with the extent and intractability of normative disagreement) as indicating a different kind of truth: that normative speech and thought are instead simply another manifestation of our animal nature.[3] These disagreements are consequences not so much of epistemic limitations as of normative speech and thought being merely expressions of conflicting desires. As Hobbes wrote,

---

[3] Such views are attributed (correctly or incorrectly) to Protagoras, Mandeville, Hobbes, Spinoza, Hume, Darwin, Nietzsche, and Dewey, for example.

Whatsoever is the object of any man's appetite or desire, that is it which he for his part calleth *good*.... For these words of good, evil, and contemptible are ever used with relation to the person that useth them: there being nothing simply and absolutely so; nor any common rule of good and evil to be taken from the nature of the objects themselves. (1651/1994: Ch. 6)

Normative thought doesn't seek a common objective truth, on this view. Instead, we are using our seemingly shared words to express incompatible things, in a sense talking past each other. Normative disagreements involve a confusion of tongues, like that which thwarted the construction of the Tower of Babel, and the hope to raise ourselves above animality with a scientific resolution of these disagreements is in vain.

Here we confront a fundamental controversy, which Michael Smith has even called "the Moral Problem": how to reconcile the objectivity of the normative with its practicality. The battle lines are roughly captured by Aristotle's version of the "Euthyphro Question": *Do we desire things because they are good, or are they good because we desire them?*[4] The theory of normative language advanced in this book suggests answers to this and other questions about the metaphysics, psychology, and epistemology of ethics. While both horns of the dilemma have elements of truth, it ultimately supports the priority of desire over normativity, implying that at least our fundamental normative disagreements involve a confusion of tongues, in the sense of my ethical allegory.

1.2. A Method for Metaethics

The primary theme of this book is that the puzzles of metaethics arise largely from failure to understand the meaning and use of our own normative language. Metaethical disagreement is itself due to a confusion of tongues, or more accurately, a confusion *about* tongues, which is my second, metaethical allegory. This suggests a method: if our puzzles are due to confusion about normative language, then they might be solved by studying it. I shall employ an *analytic* method, seeking a metaphysical analysis of normative facts, properties, and relations by means of a conceptual analysis of the meanings of the normative words by which we refer to them. The result will be a form of *analytic reductionism* (or "analytic naturalism"), an explanatory reduction of normative properties (etc.) into complexes of non-normative properties by reductively defining normative words and concepts in entirely non-normative terms.

Analysis is *reductive* if it aims to identify the nature or essence of something by revealing how it is composed out of more basic components; it "reduces" a complex whole into simpler parts and their relationships.[5] What it is to be (pure,

---

[4] *Metaphysics* 1072a29.
[5] See also Schroeder 2007: Ch. 4.

grain) *alcohol* is to be CH_3CH_2OH, for example, an ionic compound of carbon, hydrogen, and oxygen. What it is to be an *aunt* is to be either a sister-of or a wife-of-a-sibling-of a parent of somebody. Carbon, hydrogen, and oxygen ions, and the relation of ionic bondage are all simpler and more basic components of the complex structured substance alcohol; the relations being-a-sister-of, being-a-parent-of, being-a-sibling-of, and being-married-to are all more basic components of the complex structured property of being somebody's aunt.[6]

A reductive analysis of some kind of object, property, or relation can help answer various questions about it. If we have better epistemic access to some of its constituents, then we may be able to settle controversies over what lies in its extension. Whether Clara is Alex's aunt can be settled by investigating Alex's family and discovering if Clara indeed stands in either the sister-of relation or the wife-of-a-sibling-of relation to somebody who stands in the parent-of relation to Alex. If we're unsure whether the liquid in some bottle is alcohol, this could at least be ruled out if we're in a position to determine that it isn't carbon-based.

Having a reductive definition of the property of goodness might therefore be hoped to provide an empirical method for determining what possesses it, helping settle normative disagreements and perhaps laying the groundwork for a scientific ethics. It might also reveal whether normativity has priority over desire or vice versa, just like reductive analysis of the property of being Alex's aunt reveals that its instantiation depends upon one of Alex's parents having a sibling.

While some analyses of normative properties might be fairly obvious and plausible—those reducing them to more basic normative properties (like analyses of goodness into facts about *oughts*, reasons, rationality, or vice versa)—these are no better than circular with regard to the central puzzles of metaethics, which concern the nature of the normative as such. This book controversially seeks definitions that are "reductive" in a stronger sense, which I'll henceforth assume: "naturalistic" reductions of the normative into entirely *non-normative* components. Contrary to some claims, this isn't to deny the existence of the normative, any more than reducing alcohol to a structured complex of carbon, hydrogen, and oxygen ions is to deny the existence of alcohol.[7]

---

[6] Might some essential definitions be nonreductive? What it is to be a US $1 bill involves a relation to the US Treasury, but the Treasury isn't a part of any $1 bill (Mele 2003: 52); see also Moore's bizarre claim that a horse can be defined by its anatomical parts. A reduction of what it is *to be a US $1 bill* (or an instance of the kind *alcohol*, or *horse*) mustn't be confused with a reduction of a particular $1 bill, or what it is to be that particular bill (alcohol sample, horse, etc.). The US Treasury mightn't be a part of any US $1 bill any more than Alex is a part of her aunt, but it plausibly is part of the *property* of being a US $1 bill.

[7] E.g., Nagel 1986: 138, McNaughton 1988: 44, Oddie 2005: 18; see Schroeder 2007: 73 for discussion.

A reductive analysis is "analytic" if it proceeds via the analytic method, seeking to reductively analyze our concept of the property as composed out of simpler conceptual parts, as represented by a description (e.g., the concept of the relation *aunt of* is roughly the concept of *a sister-of or wife-of-a-sibling-of a parent of*). This takes the composition of the concept as revealing the metaphysical composition or essence of the property itself. Whereas we needn't commit to any particular view of what concepts are, I suggest they shouldn't be regarded as additional entities between us and the world, but rather as properties, etc. *as conceived of*; to "have the concept" *aunt* is just to conceive of the relation of being a sister-of or wife-of-a-sibling-of a parent of.[8]

While I presume we can have concepts for which we lack words, I've promised an enquiry into the meanings of words as fixed by the linguistic conventions of a community, a *semantic* analysis. (To avoid confusion, note that my use of 'semantics' throughout this book, as referring to the branch of semiotics dealing with conventional *meanings* of words, diverges from a common use among philosophers as referring rather to the study of the *truth conditions* of claims or sentences.)[9] A semantic analysis is analytic if it identifies a word as having a conceptual meaning, and defines it by reductively analyzing that concept.

According to a classic description theory of meaning, a speaker uses a word to speak or think about something by virtue of associating the word with a descriptive concept that picks that thing out. Her semantic competence with the word ("knowing its meaning") is constituted by her using and interpreting it with its conventional concept (or concepts, in cases of lexical ambiguity). Full competence with or knowing the meaning of the word 'aunt', for example, requires associating it with the concept *sister-of or wife-of-a-sibling-of a parent*. (Competence comes in degrees; my four-year-old daughter has only partial competence or a vague concept of 'aunt'. She understands that it applies to a person A in relation to B only if A is a female relative of B, and can therefore deduce that a car can't be an aunt, but doesn't yet grasp a sufficient condition.) My method is therefore to reductively analyze what it is to be good, a reason, or what ought to be, by reductively analyzing the concepts with which the words 'good', 'ought', and 'reason' are conventionally used.

So far we've talked about words, concepts, and objects, properties, and relations, but we'll also need to talk about what are constructed out of these.

---

[8] The very existence of concepts is also controversial. While I'll assume them here, the theory advanced in this book should be translatable into rival models of (or vocabularies for) linguistic competence.

[9] Contemporary expressivists (e.g., Ridge 2014) sometimes claim to offer "metasemantic" theories (i.e., of how normative sentences have truth conditions) rather than "semantic" theories (i.e., of what those truth conditions are), but these are still semantic theories in my sense. I take this other use of 'semantic' to be an influence of the discredited theory that the meaning of a linguistic expression just is its truth conditions.

I assume the following model. Linguistically, words compose in structures of grammatical syntax to form *sentences*. Conceptually, concepts compose in structures of logical syntax to form *thoughts*. Metaphysically, objects, properties, and relations compose in logical structures to form *states of affairs*. To call a state of affairs a "fact" is to represent it as actual rather than merely possible, while to call it a "proposition" is to represent it merely as possible, or "proposed". Sentences in different grammatical moods (declarative, interrogative, imperative, etc.) are used by semantic convention to advance propositions with different illocutionary forces, such as to assert, enquire, prescribe, and so forth.

Propositions and derivatively sentences that correspond to the facts are *true*, others are generally false. But a grammatically complete sentence can still be *logically incomplete*, in which case it fails to express a proposition by semantic convention, and therefore lacks a truth value. It may still be used to communicate a proposition by virtue of the audience's ability to identify from contextual cues intended elements of the logical form that the speaker has left implicit. In such cases, we'll say that the logically incomplete sentence is used as *elliptical* for another, logically complete sentence in which the intended proposition is fully explicit. If somebody says 'She put her shoes on', for example, he is most likely using it as elliptical for 'She put her shoes on *her feet.*'

The analytic method faces a classic puzzle. If competent users of normative language possess concepts that pick out normative properties by their essences, then apparently they must already know the nature of these properties. Here normative language is importantly different from words like 'aunt', 'triangle', and 'yesterday'. Arguably every speaker competent with 'aunt' knows that to be an aunt is to be a sister-of or a spouse-of-a-sibling-of a parent, sufficiently to be able to explain this upon a little reflection. But clearly not every speaker competent with 'good' is able to explain what it is to be good, or it wouldn't be a topic of ongoing metaethical debate. This is the Paradox of Analysis: either an analysis is correct, so it must already be known by all competent speakers and thereby be trivially uninformative, or else it is informative, so it must be incorrect since competent speakers don't already know it.[10]

The solution is that analyticity can be opaque or unobvious, because there are different ways of knowing a concept. Ordinary competence is a form of *tacit* knowledge or *know-how*: a disposition or ability to follow a rule R that functions unconsciously and typically doesn't rise to the level of explicit knowledge or theory (i.e., *knowing that* one follows R), just as knowing how to ride a bicycle or play a composition on the piano doesn't entail any ability to describe or explain how you do it. This ability manifests itself in our dispositions to use words and produce sentences and in our intuitions about whether a word or sentence is correctly or incorrectly used in particular contexts. Conceptual

---

[10] Langford 1942.

competence doesn't involve associating a word with a description (string of words) per se; rather, a descriptive definition is a linguistic representation of the complex concept. Competent speakers can therefore fail to recognize a correct definition.

Conceptual analysis seeks explicit, reflective knowledge that R is the rule one follows across different contexts. With simpler concepts like *aunt* a minimal amount of reflection on our practices suffices for theoretical understanding, but more complex concepts are more difficult to analyze, and are the objects of *philosophical* analysis.[11] The analytic project therefore views metaethical puzzles as arising from ignorance or confusion about our own practices of normative speech and thought, and views metaethical enquiry as an exercise in self-comprehension and an attempt to raise to explicit theory that which we already know implicitly.

Conceptual analysis is commonly understood to be an a priori rather than empirical exercise: to identify what it is to be somebody's aunt we need only examine our concepts, "from the armchair", and needn't go find a bunch of aunts to examine. But it is debatable how much direct access we have to our unconscious and implicit mental processes. In my opinion it is possible to analyze concepts directly through introspection (although mastery of this skill varies), but while I'm hopeful that some readers may recognize the truth of my theory directly through introspection, many others won't be so swayed. I therefore pursue a less subjective method of proof: to demonstrate that the end-relational theory provides the best explanation of our linguistic intuitions. As manifestations of our conceptual competence, these intuitions provide reliable empirical data about it.[12] This method blurs the distinction between a priori and empirical enquiry: it gathers observational data, but because these consist in intuitions of competent speakers, and we are ourselves competent speakers, we can each conduct it from the armchair.

1.3. A Defunct Method?

This sketch of a method may be thought to blunder naively across a minefield of serious problems. Once assumed uncritically, reductive semantic analysis in metaethics faced a series of challenges over the course of the last century that have resulted in its almost universal repudiation.[13] Most books published in the

---

[11] See King 1998, although he rejects talk of "concepts".

[12] Cf. Brandt 1979: 4 ("the method of appeal to linguistic intuitions...makes clear how normative enquiries can have a firm scientific basis. For how certain words are used...can be known by observation. There is no more reason to deny that these questions can be answered by the methods of science than there is to deny that descriptive grammar, or descriptive semantics, is an empirical science"); see also Williamson 2007: 285.

[13] Jackson 1998 is a notable exception. Many of my methodological claims echo his, but I reject his approach to conceptual analysis. Jackson identifies a concept with a cluster of "input"

field in recent decades include a perfunctory dismissal of it from the ranks of serious contenders; a sample:

> It is surely a quite remarkable feature of the history of moral philosophy that attempts at giving naturalistic definitions have all been such failures...Surely the most plausible explanation of these failures is that such analyses are impossible. (Smith 1994: 55–56, also rejecting nonanalytic reductions)
>
> The narrowly conceived subject-matter and methodology of analytic metaethics has all but disappeared from the philosophical scene. (Timmons 1999: 9)
>
> It is easy to see that normative concepts... are probably not plausibly analyzed in terms of non-normative concepts. (Schroeder 2007: 65)

Each challenge can be formulated as a possibility that would if it obtained make the project of analytic reduction futile.

First, attempting to reduce normative properties into simpler, non-normative components presupposes that no normative property is itself among the simple or primitive elements of the world that can't be reduced or explained any further, contrary to the views of G. E. Moore and many contemporary metaethicists, like Derek Parfit, who writes that "normativity is either an illusion, or involves irreducibly normative facts".[14] This is the *primitivist's* challenge.[15]

Second, an even more basic presupposition of the reductive project is that the semantic function of normative language is descriptive, and that it refers to properties, relations, objects, and facts in the world. But some parts of language have other, nondescriptive kinds of semantic or conceptual role; consider performatives like 'hello' and 'please', the imperative mood ('Go now!'), ejaculatives like 'ouch' and 'hooray', and perhaps logical connectives like 'or'. To understand the meaning of these is not to know what they refer to, but what they are conventionally used to do: perform speech acts of greeting, request, and command, express pain and delight, and so on. Normative language is indeed characteristically used for nondescriptive purposes, such as to express speakers' motivational attitudes, to influence others' motivations, and to perform acts of commending, recommending, prescribing, etc. (this is part of its practicality), and so many philosophers claim it is "expressive" instead of (or

---

and "output" platitudes, picking out a property by its position in a network of other properties and dispositions, which can then be investigated empirically to identify the property. I think this puts the cart before the horse, and to disregard the lesson from the Paradox of Analysis: we accept the platitudes because we have an implicit concept that identifies the property—essentially.

[14] Parfit 2011b: 267.

[15] I prefer the term 'primitivism' over the more usual 'nonnaturalism', as the latter is used ambiguously for primitivism and also as a label for the epistemological doctrine that some normative truths can be known nonempirically.

perhaps, as well as) descriptive by semantic convention. This is the *expressivist's* challenge.[16]

Third, the analytic method presupposes that the structure of normative properties, etc. is reflected in the structure of conceptual meanings of those words. But words don't need to be semantically associated with such concepts in order to have meaning and refer, as illustrated by 'alcohol' and the usual example of 'water'. We use 'water' to talk about water, which is H_2O, an ionic compound of hydrogen and oxygen. Yet prior to discovery of its composition in the eighteenth century, people competently used 'water' to refer to water without having any idea they were referring to a compound, indeed commonly believing it to be an element. These speakers therefore can't have had a concept of water with a structure reflecting the metaphysical structure of water itself, and so couldn't have discovered the essential nature of water by semantic or conceptual analysis. Nonetheless, 'Water is H_2O' is a true reductive definition. It is *synthetic* rather than analytic, not knowable a priori from the philosopher's armchair on the basis of the conceptual meaning of 'water' alone, but requiring empirical investigation into water itself.

Over the last fifty years reductionists have embraced the hypothesis that the essential definitions of normative properties are also synthetic, and so have largely abandoned the analytic method. (A more radical form of this challenge objects to the presupposition that normative words have conceptual meanings at all. Semantic externalism, as captured in Putnam's slogan that "meaning ain't in the head", rejects the description theory of reference, appealing instead to mechanisms like causal chains.)[17] Call this the *synthetic realist's* challenge.

Fourth, the analytic method proposes to provide metaphysical knowledge about normative facts or properties by analysis of our normative concepts, but this may seem to presuppose that these concepts aren't defective in some way. Call this the *revisionist* challenge. Not all kinds of conceptual "defect" pose genuine threats, however. Sometimes it's claimed that ordinary normative speech and thought is conceptually committed to something that doesn't

---

[16] Not all practical roles assigned to normative language are accurately labeled 'expressive'—hence Chrisman 2015 argues for a third alternative to "descriptivism" and "expressivism"—but I'll retain this label for convenience.

[17] Cf. Durrant 1970, Putnam 1975, Kripke 1980. Descriptivists respond with a *causal description theory* (e.g., Searle 1983, Jackson 1998), but no such causal description seems plausibly "the meaning" of such words (see Soames 2004). Strictly, Putnam claimed that *if meaning is what determines reference, then* it ain't in the head; I believe we should reject the antecedent: the lesson to draw from indexicals like 'I' is that sometimes meaning and the external world *together* determine reference, and the lesson to draw from names and natural kind terms is that some words are used to refer without having a conventional meaning. But externalists never proved (nor generally claimed to prove) that no words have conventional conceptual meanings (cf. Hacking 1983), and there are numerous reasons to expect that normative words do, including extensive allegedly a priori truths (see, e.g., Pigden 2011), their "narrow cosmological role", philosophers' inability to explain how ordinary speakers use the words, the instinctive tendency to the armchair, and the fact that expressivism is a contender.

actually exist, like a particular kind of freedom, authority, and so on. In this case, our concepts may pick out properties or relations that are uninstantiated, requiring an error theory on which our positive normative judgments are all untrue, and the only "normative facts" are negative ones such as that nothing is really good. But this isn't a problem for the method, which aims merely to discover what these properties and relations are.

Others argue that our normative words and concepts are obsolete or redundant (perhaps because they are uninstantiated), in that we'd be better served by embracing new concepts and "reforming definitions" of these words.[18] This also doesn't challenge the method as a way of investigating the nature of goodness, reasons, etc.: it's merely a proposal or recommendation to change the subject, to goodness*, reasons*, etc., and a shift from descriptive to prescriptive metaethics—a shift I believe this book proves to be unduly hasty.

But two other kinds of alleged "defect" (often behind these other suggestions) do present a genuine challenge: first, that normative concepts may be *idiosyncratic*, varying either between communities and languages, or even between individuals—an extreme kind of "confusion of tongues".[19] In this case, armchair analysis can at best uncover what the investigator herself, and perhaps others in the same language community, mean by 'good', 'ought', or 'reason', but will not have universal or general application to the normative speech and thought of others. Or worse, they might just be *vague* or *inchoate*—maybe nonsensical, self-contradictory, or malformed—and therefore we wouldn't have any determinate concepts to analyze.[20]

Each of these challenges identifies a possibility that threatens the project of analytic reduction, and that shouldn't be overlooked. But I don't believe that any have been proven true (or even very likely), and so for all its critics have shown, analytic reduction may yet turn out to be a viable method for metaethics. The primary source of skepticism is the perceived force of G. E. Moore's "Open Question Argument" (OQA), the core of which can be summarized as follows (I'll assume for the sake of argument that 'good' is the basic normative term):

(OQ1) If a description '*D*' is a correct definition of (synonymous with) a term '*F*' then questions of the form (i), 'Granting that *a* is *F*, is *a D*?' and 'Granting that *a* is *D*, is a *F*?', will be *closed*.

(OQ2) For any description '*D*' that could be proposed as a noncircular definition of 'good', the corresponding questions of form (i) won't be closed.

---

[18] E.g., Mackie 1977, Brandt 1979, Railton 1986; see also Harman 1996.
[19] E.g., Moore 1903, Brandt 1979: 6–7, Parfit 2011b.
[20] E.g., Wittgenstein 1930/1996, Anscombe 1958, Brandt 1979: 6, Joyce 2001.

(OQ3)   Therefore, the word 'good' is not correctly defined by
(synonymous with) any description.

A "closed question" is often interpreted, following Moore, as having an
answer that can't be sensibly or intelligibly doubted by anyone who understands
it, like questions of the form (ii) 'Granting that *a* is *D*, is *a D*?' If '*D*' provides a
correct analysis of the concept expressed by '*F*', the thought goes, then '*D*' and
'*F*' will be synonymous, and questions about *D* of form (i) will be equivalent in
meaning or significance to questions of form (ii). The questions 'Granting that
t is the day immediately before today, is *t* yesterday?' and 'Granting that *t* is
yesterday, is *t* the day immediately before today?' are plausibly closed (affirma-
tively) in this sense, for example, indicating that 'yesterday' is correctly defined
by *the day immediately before today*. If a question of form (i) isn't closed—that
is, it's an "open question"—this supposedly indicates that '*D*' isn't a correct definition of '*F*'. However, this interpretation doesn't allow for opaque concepts
and unobvious analyses.[21] This can be fixed by understanding a question to be
"closed" just in case it's *possible* to know whether an answer is correct merely
on the basis of understanding the question.

Moore took these considerations to prove that the basic normative properties are primitive, but his reasoning was fallacious, and they can and have
instead been taken to support the hypotheses that normative words are semantically expressivist, that their essential definitions are synthetic, or that they are
conceptually defective. But it's widely agreed that the argument through OQ3
succeeds, disqualifying analytic reduction. Most philosophers accept that normative words like 'good', 'ought', and 'reason' express concepts that differ fundamentally in kind from any expressible with strings of entirely non-normative
terms. Yet this argument rests on an apparently rash and unprovable premise: OQ2 denies the possibility that any definition that could ever be proposed
would pass the open question test, although nobody has considered every possible candidate.

Sometimes OQ2 is defended by appeal to intuitions: the normative is said
to be self-evidently "too different" to be composed of non-normative parts, as
vividly expressed by Wittgenstein:

> I at once see clearly, as it were in a flash of light, not only that no
> description that I can think of would do to describe what I mean...but
> that I would reject every significant description that anybody could
> possibly suggest, *ab initio*.[22]

---

[21] Lewy 1964, Frankena 1973: 99, Lewis 1989. See Pigden (2007, 2011: 8–9) for a different
way of strengthening the notion of an open question, which yields a merely inductive argument.
[22] Wittgenstein 1930/1996. See also Parfit 1997: 121–22, 2011, Dancy 2005, Enoch 2007: 44,
2011, Huemer 2005: 94–95, 229, FitzPatrick 2008: 180.

It's hard to see why these intuitions should be taken seriously as perceptions of ineffable truth rather than simply failures of imagination. Convictions about irreducibility (as of the "elements" of water, earth, air, and fire, or "atoms" of gold, carbon, oxygen, etc.) have proven highly unreliable. Composite things often have characteristics totally different from any of their components: alcohol and water are both liquids at room temperature but are composed entirely out of ingredients that aren't liquids in isolation; alcohol is intoxicating and water is thirst-quenching, unlike any of their components.[23]

An account is also owed of what characteristic of the normative is just "too different" for reducibility to non-normative parts. The usual answer is simply *its normativity*, but this begs the question since analytic reductionism itself entails that none of the proper parts of the normative is itself normative, just as none of the proper parts of a molecule of alcohol is itself a molecule of alcohol. I will ultimately argue that the distinguishing characteristics of normativity are actually predicted by the end-relational theory.

OQ2 is usually justified more circumspectly, with a modest inductive argument: since all the different attempts considered so far have failed the open question test, it can be inferred that all other theories would also fail and so analytic reduction is impossible.[24] This induction can't guarantee its conclusion, of course, and is refuted by a single counterexample like the one I propose to provide. But observe also how weak this induction is: it infers from a limited number of failures not merely that the *next* attempt will fail, but that *all possible* attempts would fail—even though at most only one reductive theory could be correct.[25] Even if there is some inductive basis for pessimism about the reductive project in general, these past failures cannot be an objection against any new theory, which itself entails that all other (genuinely distinct) theories are false and so will fail the open question test.[26] A result that a theory predicts can't be evidence against it.

The sample hasn't been selected randomly from all possible analyses, of course, but from the best efforts of brilliant minds over many years. This point provides an *abductive* argument for OQ2: the best explanation of the failure to find a successful analysis to date is that no such analysis is waiting to be

---

[23] Similarly, circles are spatially extended though composed entirely of extensionless points (Schroeder 2007).

[24] E.g., Shafer-Landau 2003, Wedgwood 2007, Pigden 2011: 9.

[25] Contrast regular (strong) inductive arguments. If none of the first ten balls drawn from a barrel of 100 are red, we can be fairly confident that the next ball drawn won't be red. But we shouldn't be very confident that no remaining balls are red. While the ratio of sample to population matters, plausibly far more feasible reductive theories are possible than have been considered. (OQ2 is sometimes even inferred from observation of a single failure; e.g., Moore 1903, Schroeder 2007, Enoch 2011.)

[26] A close antecedent of the end-relational theory (Ziff 1960) is conceded to meet the test by one opponent, James Griffin (1992: 308).

found.[27] While this may be the strongest basis for the premise, it encounters another induction problem. To be the "best explanation" is to be better than all alternatives, but how can we be confident of this? The possibility remains that a better explanation of the long history of futility may be found that doesn't support OQ2; I'll propose a pragmatic one in the next chapter. The OQA is often observed not to be an argument, strictly speaking, but rather a *challenge*, against which any aspiring reductive analysis must be tested. I will argue that the end-relational theory draws this particular sword from its stone.

The objection remains that I might only succeed in analyzing idiosyncratic concepts. My method consists largely in examining my own intuitions about the uses of English words, and it indeed can't be known a priori that other languages have words with the same meanings, or even that all other competent speakers of English use these words with the same meanings. These are just empirical hypotheses: I believe our results will go some way to confirming them (because these analyses will accommodate and explain the way others use these words, and identify basic concepts that can be expected to occupy a central role in any human language), though they certainly invite further empirical testing.

Other kinds of arguments against the method's presuppositions might be offered, but I won't engage further in abstract methodological arguments here. My proof that the analytic method is viable will be "in the pudding": its successful execution in the following chapters.

1.4. Simply the Best

My case for the end-relational theory will be that it provides the best explanation of our practices of normative speech and thought. Proving such a claim might seem to require investigating all rivals and cataloging their advantages and disadvantages, which would make a longer, boring, largely negative, and unoriginal book. Instead I will draw comparisons mostly with primitivism and expressivism, which provide useful foils as dialectical extremes respectively emphasizing objectivity and practicality. I will argue, more ambitiously, that the theory wins by default as the *simplest and most conservative* theory that accommodates and explains our practices. This also is a comparative claim, of course, but I will justify it by providing an account that is simple and conservative in absolute terms. If another theory's claim to this distinction is proven superior, then we should prefer it, but this seems unlikely.

However, I'll also suggest, more ambitiously but more tentatively, that this is the *only* theory that can accommodate and explain substantially all relevant

---

[27] E.g., Smith 1994: 55–56. Ridge 2008 also proposes an abductive reading of the OQA: the best explanation why questions of form (i) seem open is that they are open. This still requires an induction to the conclusion that *all* questions of this form are open.

data, and satisfactorily reconcile objectivity with practicality. By contrast, metaethicists often advertise their views as merely the least difficult to swallow from a choice of bitter pills, as exemplified by Bertrand Russell's remark that "while my own opinions as to ethics do not satisfy me, other people's satisfy me still less".[28] Primitivism is quietistic, for example, denying even the possibility of explanatory answers to such basic questions as what goodness or normativity is, or how it is perceived.

By "simplest", I mean that the theory accommodates the data in the most parsimonious way, requiring fewer basic entities, properties, meanings, attitudes, and principles than other, more complex theories. By "most conservative", I mean it is least revisionary of naive or common-sense views people are disposed to accept prior to grappling with metaethical puzzles, contrasting with more radical or exotic theories. In comparison with the extravagances of its rivals, the end-relational theory is sober and austere.

One might wonder whether this strategy fetishizes these qualities, and whether they are legitimate criteria for evaluating theories. A complex phenomenon might be expected to require a complex theory, and conservatism might seem a dubious constraint given how many naive views have been refuted by revolutionary discoveries, like those of Copernicus, Galileo, Darwin, Einstein, et cetera. My reply is that the simpler and more conservative theory *that accommodates and explains all the data* (as well as any rival) is the better theory, precisely because it is more likely correct.

The simpler explanation is more likely to be correct for the reason that simpler theories are less likely to generate correct predictions by accident. There is less probative value in a complex theory generating correct predictions, since this can be due to its ad hoc origin rather than either correctness or coincidence. This doesn't provide any reason to expect that a simple theory can generate correct predictions, but if it is found that one does (as I'll argue), this will be strong confirmation for it. Similarly, conservative views enjoy the authority of the intuitive, unconscious mind, which is vastly superior to the reflective, conscious mind at processing large amounts of experience. Although intuitions can be mistaken, they provide a high degree of prima facie justification.[29]

I make this claim to maximal simplicity and conservatism with regard to multiple dimensions—metaphysics, logic, psychology, epistemology, ethics, and especially linguistics—and holistically; that is, the theory isn't simpler and more conservative than every rival in every single dimension, but all things considered. No view can be metaphysically simpler than expressivist views that deny normative language refers to any properties at all, for example, but simplicity or conservatism in one dimension often entails a commitment to more complex or

---

[28] Russell 1944; see also Gibbard 1990: "all analysis strains its concept", and Enoch 2011, who argues for primitivism by tallying "plausibility points" for and against.

[29] See the case in Talbot 2009, for example.

radical views in another: the metaphysical simplicity of these expressivist views comes at the cost at least of complex and radical treatments of semantics and logic. We'll take stock in the conclusion, but here I'll briefly sketch the basis for my case.

(A) In particular, I'll pursue the desideratum of a maximally simple *semantics*. Whereas metaethicists have generally been bad linguists, offering definitions of normative words based on narrow focus on particular kinds of use, these words are used in a much broader range of ways, which commits rival theories to extensive lexical ambiguities. But by following the clues from language itself we'll identify single, shared, unifying meanings for these words that accommodate virtually all their uses, and explain the meaning of normative sentences compositionally by simple and general rules of grammar. (Simplicity is a desideratum for semantics and grammar not only for the general reasons observed above, but also because a language that permits more to be done with less is easier to learn and more flexible to use, and therefore more likely to have evolved.)

(B) As this semantics is descriptivist, it conservatively analyzes normative words as referring to genuine facts, properties, and relations, incurring greater *metaphysical* commitments than nondescriptivist views like expressivism, and error theory. But unlike metaphysically extravagant theories (postulating mysterious primitive normative properties or supernatural entities), as a form of "reductive naturalism" this theory identifies these with properties already recognized by a common-sense and broadly scientific metaphysics. (My analysis won't limit itself to a narrowly physicalist ontology, however, which itself breaks radically with common-sense views about what exists.)

(C) We'll therefore also require only conservative *epistemological* commitments to uncontroversial sources of knowledge, unlike primitivism (for example), which commonly appeals to an unexplained, seemingly magical ability to acquire knowledge of substantive or nonconceptual truths by intellectual intuition independently of experience, or "synthetic a priori" propositions.

(D) As a form of descriptivism, the theory is maximally conservative with respect to *logic*: it needs nothing more than the common-sense theory of truth as correspondence with the facts, and the traditional view of logic as governing the truth relations between sentences. By contrast, expressivist theories are committed to radical and complex treatments of truth and logic (which I confess to having difficulty even understanding). Much attention has therefore been devoted to the nature of logical validity in recent metaethics; whether or not these approaches can be made to work, this is an issue our theory avoids altogether.

(E) With respect to *psychology*, we'll require nothing beyond the simple and conservative view that human beings are animals motivated by desire for various contingent ends, and the naive Humean theory of motivation that appeals only to contingent beliefs that function to reflect the world and contingent desires that function to shape it. By contrast, rival theories sometimes advance more extravagant hypotheses, such as that certain kinds of facts or beliefs are necessarily or intrinsically motivating by themselves, that some desires are necessarily possessed by all agents, or that there are hybrid attitudes of "besire"—a notion that didn't occur to anybody until a use was found for it in addressing a philosophical puzzle.

(F) Finally, metaethical theories often have radical *ethical* or normative implications, which conflict with common-sense beliefs about what is good or bad, or ought to be done, etc.; the most extreme case may be error theories which predict that all positive moral claims are untrue. By contrast, our theory will be ethically conservative: predicting uncontroversial normative truths, vindicating our general confidence in our ability to have normative and moral knowledge, while also being substantively neutral on controversial questions about what is good or ought to be done either morally or all things considered.

This may all sound too good to be true. How could a maximally simple and conservative account be correct, when the puzzles of metaethics have resisted resolution for so long and inspired so many complex and radical theories? Indeed, these puzzles largely consist in special features of practicality and objectivity found in moral and deliberative uses of normative language that are widely seen as posing insurmountable challenges for theories that are simple and conservative in just these ways.[30] But I shall argue that philosophers have missed one important dimension or piece of the puzzle, and that the solutions have been hidden from view by the richness of the *pragmatics* of normative language.

To clarify my second, metaethical allegory, I claim that metaethical puzzles and disagreements arise from confusion about how we use normative language in different contexts to do and communicate more than it strictly means. We'll see that when supplemented with a maximally simple and conservative account of the basic principles of pragmatics the end-relational theory answers all these challenges, fully accommodating and explaining the practice of normative speech and thought. The solutions to these puzzles have been inaccessible to philosophical reflection because of the richness of this pragmatic dimension and the poverty of our theoretical grasp of it, but recent advances in our understanding of pragmatics have left them exposed, just as shifting sands sometimes uncover a shipwreck that has eluded years of expert searching.

The first part of the book (Chapters 2–4) examines the meaning of 'good', 'ought', and 'reason' in their various mundane uses, finding in each case that the linguistic evidence points consistently to an end-relational semantics. I'll set aside the moral and deliberative uses that generate the special puzzles

---

[30] Close relatives of the end-relational theory, which also relativize normative concepts or properties to something like norms, standards, goals, desires, etc., have been offered by Ziff 1960, Harman 1975, 1996, Mackie 1977, Wong 1984, Railton 1986, and Copp 1997.

of metaethics until the second part (Chapters 5–8), where I'll argue that the end-relational semantics accommodate and explain these uses too, when combined with the basic principle of pragmatics I'll introduce in Chapter 5, thereby answering challenges about their various forms of practicality and objectivity. Readers impatient to reach the discussion of metaethical puzzles may choose to read just one of Chapters 2 or 3 before turning to Chapter 5, but I ask you not to forget that the simplicity, conservatism, and predictive power of this semantics constitutes my primary evidence that the end-relational theory is not only consistent with our practices of normative speech and thought, but also correct.

A Good Word to Start With

As our most general normative adjective, 'good' is a primary focus of metaethical enquiry. It is a good word for us to start with, as we'll eventually vindicate G. E. Moore's claim that it expresses the simplest normative concept. Whereas denials of its analyzability have largely been motivated by features exemplified by peculiarly moral uses, 'good' is used all the time in mundane ways, to talk about good handwriting or commutes, being good at stealing, good for unblocking drains, good to read to children, etc. These ordinary uses don't so plausibly attribute a primitive, unanalyzable property or merely express attitudes, and even many who are skeptical of analytic reduction of the moral 'good' happily allow it has another ordinary meaning susceptible to analysis.

The default hypothesis should be that 'good' has a single, unified semantics, however, especially since the moral/nonmoral distinction is both systematic across general normative vocabulary and robustly cross-linguistic.[1] Before positing lexical ambiguity we should determine exactly what 'good' means in these ordinary uses.[2] Since even these uses exhibit great grammatical variety, a unifying analysis may seem improbable. I'll first search for a common logical form underlying the diverse grammar, then offer a unifying semantics that reductively analyzes the conceptual meaning of 'good' in terms of comparisons of probability, setting aside metaethically troublesome uses until Chapter 5.[3]

2.1. Incomplete Predicates

Identifying properties of ordinary goodness can seem easy when looking at particular cases. Boats are good if they have a complex property of seaworthiness,

---

[1] Cf. Mackie 1977: 51.

[2] As also counseled by (e.g.) Perry 1926, Ziff 1960, Mackie 1977, Thomson 1992, 1997, 2001, Foot 2001.

[3] This develops the view in Finlay 2001, 2004.

combining buoyancy, maneuverability, etc., carrots are good in part because of their high vitamin A content, and the goodness of a drain cleaner consists in its being highly corrosive of organic matter while noncorrosive of metals and plastics. Would-be synthetic definitions often appeal to such properties.[4] But "the meaning" of 'good' would need to be something all good things have in common.

This may seem a wild goose chase, since the properties constituting good-ness for one kind of thing are sometimes exactly contrary to the properties con-stituting goodness for another—compare good buoys and good anchors, good sedatives and good stimulants. But 'good' couldn't have a different meaning in every case, as we easily apply it to indefinitely many kinds of objects. Somehow conceptual competence enables us to apply it in these different ways. Since there apparently isn't any definable property that all good things have in common, it might be tempting to infer that they share an indefinable property or are the objects of a common attitude. This assumes that since 'good' is an adjective, unless it is lexically ambiguous it must refer to a common property—which over-looks the flexibility and relativity in the meanings of many words that permits adjectives to be used with a common meaning to predicate different properties.

Indexicals like 'I', 'now', and 'here' are one kind of word with this flexibility. Their conventional meaning is a conceptual "character", consisting in a crite-rion that determines a reference from the context of use;[5] the character of 'I' is *the actual speaker in the context of use*. Indexicals are used with constant mean-ings to refer to different people, places, times, etc. in different contexts. Some (hybrid) expressivists favor an indexical semantics for a secondary descriptive meaning of normative language. On one version 'good' has a character that selects whichever property the speaker approves of in the context; if one is cut-ting steak and in such contexts approves of knives being serrated, for example, then to say a knife is "good" is to say it is serrated.[6]

But indexicality isn't the only source of semantic flexibility: another is *logi-cal incompleteness*, as illustrated by the adjectives 'old', 'tall', 'fast', 'cold', and 'eager'. These logically incomplete predicates are used to refer to *relational* properties of standing in some relation R to some other thing. Unlike com-plete relational predicates, involving a relation to one particular thing (as being "terrestrial" consists in a relation to Earth), these have one or more open argument-places in their logical form. Nothing can be old, tall, fast, cold, or eager simpliciter, but only in particular ways or relative to particular classes of objects. A 1974 Ford Capri might appropriately be deemed old *for a car still on*

---

[4] E.g., Sturgeon 1985, Boyd 1988, Railton 1989 (the boat example is his), Brink 1989.
[5] Kaplan 1989.
[6] See Hare 1952 (the steak-cutting example is his), Stevenson 1944, Edwards 1955, Dreier 1990, Barker 1999, and for criticism Finlay 2005, Schroeder 2009b. Phillips 1998 describes 'good' as "quasi-indexical"; his contextualist account has a number of affinities with mine.

the road, for example, but not old *for a classic car*, and fast *for a car of its age* but not fast *for a sports coupe*. You might be eager *to drive it*, but not eager *to buy it*. Although each of 'old', 'fast', and 'eager' has a common conventional meaning, it is used to refer to different relational properties, as qualified with *adjunct propositional phrases* like 'for a car still on the road' and 'to drive the car'. It would be absurd to infer from the fact that the things we call "old" don't have any analyzable property in common that 'old' must either refer to a primitive property or function nondescriptively to express speakers' attitudes.

An incomplete predicate semantics is more natural for 'good' than an indexical semantics, because it shares the characteristic features of other incomplete predicates.[7] Like many words of this class 'good' is a gradable adjective: to be "good" is to exceed some degree of value, just as being "old", "tall", and "fast" are respectively to exceed some degree of age, height, and velocity. 'Good' has a comparative, 'better', and a superlative, 'best', as 'old' has 'older' and 'oldest', 'tall' has 'taller' and 'tallest', etc. It has a gradable inverse, 'bad', as 'old' has 'new' and 'young', 'tall' has 'short', etc.[8] More importantly, like other words in this class, we commonly qualify 'good' with adjunct prepositional phrases, which supply the extra arguments needed for logical completeness. We talk about what is good *for a used car*, good *as a hammer*, good *to drive*, good *at stealing*, etc. The natural hypothesis is therefore that 'good' is a member of this family of incomplete predicates, implying that the various kinds of goodness are relational properties.[9]

By this hypothesis, a sentence of the form '*n* is good' can be used to express any number of different propositions according to how 'good' is relativized. This has implications for the OQA, providing a first illustration of the pragmatic origin of metaethical puzzles. If 'good' is used to predicate different properties, this explains why a competent speaker can always coherently ask of any logically complete predicate D_1 proposed as a definition of 'good', 'I grant that *x* is D_1, but is *x* good?' Even if D_1 correctly and transparently defines one property to which a use of 'good' can refer, there will always be another property defined by a different predicate D_2 to which 'good' can also be used to refer.[10]

The openness of these questions can then be explained pragmatically. Because we expect people not to waste their own and others' time by asking obviously trivial questions, we can justifiably infer merely from the speaker's asking the question that she is using 'good' to express a predicate other than D_1. Consider a speaker who asks, 'I grant that this car was manufactured longer ago

---

[7] See also Szabo 2001.

[8] Unlike age and height, the value spectrum extends into negative integers (disvalue), and therefore 'good' has two different kinds of inverse, 'bad' (having significant disvalue) and 'poor' (lacking significant value); cf. Ziff 1960.

[9] See also Ziff 1960, Mackie 1977, Thomson 1992, 1997, 2001, Kraut 2007.

[10] Cf. Prior 1949, Mackie 1977: 60.

than most cars still on the road, but is it *old?*' She would naturally be assumed to mean something other than *old for a car still on the road.* Since the hypothesis that 'good' is an incomplete predicate predicts OQ2, the argument is further undermined. What needs to be seen is whether *logically complete* predications of goodness can be defined in ways that yield closed questions.

Our default hypothesis should be that 'good' has just one ordinary, flexible meaning as an incomplete predicate. To test it, three questions need to be addressed: (i) What kinds of arguments does 'good' require for completeness? (the logical form of basic predications of goodness); (ii) What is the category of objects to which 'good' logically applies? (the basic bearers of goodness); and (iii) What relation between object and arguments does 'good' signify? (the semantic contribution of 'good'). Answering the first question about logical form will lead to an answer to the second question about the basic bearers of goodness, and ultimately to an answer to the third question, and a semantic analysis of 'good' itself.

The linguistic data relevant to the first question consist in the kinds of prepositional phrases used to relativize 'good'. At first glance the prospects for finding a unified logical form may seem dim, because 'good' is relativized in an exceptionally and bewilderingly diverse variety of ways. At least the following grammatical forms can be observed (using 'φ' for verb phrases, 's' and 'n' for noun phrases referring respectively to individuals and objects, 'K' for predicates, and 'p' for sentences):[11]

PP1:   'good to φ'

PP2:   'good for s'

PP3:   'good for φ-ing'

PP4:   'good with n'/ 'good with Ks'

PP5:   'good at φ-ing'

PP6:   'good as a K'

Additionally, 'good' takes different kinds of complements or grammatical objects:

C1:   'n is good'/ 'Ks are good'

C2:   'good that p'

C3:   'good K'

Superficially these three complementizations suggest (C1) that 'good' is a predicate of ordinary objects n, (C2) that it's a predicate of states of affairs (a propositional operator), and (C3) that it's a predicate-modifier, which combines with predicates 'K' to form new complex predicates of objects.

---

[11] See also Thomson 1997, Shanklin 2011; some are discussed in Finlay 2001, 2004.

We could say simply that there are different *ways* of being good, individuated grammatically by different prepositional phrases of the forms in PP1–6. These different ways of being good include being good *for catching cold*, good *to drink with pasta*, good *at fencing*, good *for Sarah*, good *to Lexy*, good *with small children*, and good *as a bookend*. Judy Thomson holds that all goodness is goodness in a way, so that understanding any use of 'good' requires some such relativizing phrase to be understood. But what is it to be good "in a way"? Relativization by grammatical phrase is superficial, and doesn't get us any closer to a semantics, especially a unifying theory. The forms in PP1–6 seem to supply very different kinds of arguments, and it may seem difficult to imagine how they could all be supplementing the same incomplete predicate.

If 'good' does have a unified meaning, then any kind of argument required for its logical completion in one case will be required for every meaningful use of 'good'. So if a phrase of the form 'for s' functions to relativize goodness to an agent, for example, then 'good' can only have a unifying semantics if all goodness is agent-relative. Since we often use sentences of the simple form (C1) 'n is good', any such argument must sometimes not be explicitly represented in the grammar, and be implicit; that is, the sentence must be logically incomplete and used as elliptical for another in which the argument is represented. If the proposition expressed by a use of 'good' involves some implicit argument, then it will be clarified and explicated, rather than modified, by making that argument explicit.

My strategy will therefore be to examine each type of relativizing phrase to see what kind of argument it supplies, and whether making such an argument explicit seems to explicate or modify the propositions expressed by the use of sentences omitting them.[12] I'll therefore begin with the grammatically simplest sentences, C1, in which 'good' superficially appears logically simple, predicating a property of goodness to an object (or objects); for example:

(1) 'Chocolate is good.'

(2) 'Isaac Albéniz's piano compositions are good.'

(3) 'Friends are good.'

(4) 'Jim's escape plan is good.'

(5) 'Voting is good.'

(6) 'Pleasure is good.'

I'll now investigate whether ordinary use of these sentences expresses propositions relativized in the various ways represented by PP1–6.

---

[12] Not all adjunct prepositional phrases supply arguments to other predicates; consider '*t* was good *on Sunday*.' It isn't plausible that 'on Sunday' supplies a logical argument of 'good'.

2.2. Good for *s* to φ

These simple sentences naturally invite the query, "Good in what way?" Their ordinary uses can plausibly be explicated by PP1, 'to φ' phrases. Chocolate is good *to eat*, Albéniz's compositions are good *to listen to*, friends are good *to have*, Jim's escape plan is good *to follow*, voting is good *to do*, and pleasure is good *to experience*.

These are evidently explications rather than modifications of the intended propositions, since we can't make sense of calling these things "good" except in relation to verb phrases of this kind. A person who reacts to being told that chocolate is good by framing some to display on her living-room wall, or by smearing some on her wrinkles, has failed to understand that the value of chocolate lies in its consumption rather than its visual appreciation or cosmetic application. Conversely, if Hannibal's reaction to (3) is literally to have his friends for dinner, then he has failed to understand that the value of friends lies in their friendship rather than their consumption. If a speaker were to continue, 'I didn't mean to say that chocolate is good *to eat*', or 'I didn't mean to say that friends are good *to have*', then we would generally be puzzled and ask what he did mean to say.

The uses of 'good' in (1)–(6) are therefore plausibly interpreted as relativized to particular *action-types*, understood loosely as any reference of a verb phrase 'φ'. The relevant values for φ are automatically assumed in these cases because obvious, so this part of the logical form can be omitted from the grammar and left implicit. But the same objects can also be judged good in different ways, relative to other values for φ. Chocolate is also good *to bribe children with*, Albéniz's compositions are good *to train pianists with*, and friends are good *to play jokes on*. Given the right contexts these simple '*n* is good' sentences can also be interpreted in other less obvious ways. So in its ordinary uses 'good' apparently has an argument-place for action-types, and sentences of the form '*n* is good' are used as elliptical for '*n* is good to φ'.

These '*n* is good to φ' sentences invite further clarification, however, and still seem incomplete. We can naturally ask, "Good *for whom or what* to φ?" Verbs require subjects and actions require agents: there is no eating without an eater, no experiencing without an experiencer.[13] An agent can be specified grammatically with a PP2, 'for *s*' phrase:

(1a)   'Chocolate is good *for people* to eat.'

(2a)   'Albéniz's compositions are good *for people with an ear for expressionist music* to listen to.'

(5a)   'Voting is good *for eligible voters* to do.'

---

[13] Shanklin 2011 discusses similarities between 'good' and what linguists call "experiencer verbs".

Although (1)–(6) are naturally taken to express truths, they are only plausibly true relative to restricted classes of individuals as values for *s*. Chocolate isn't good *for dogs* to eat, and voting isn't good *for children, noncitizens, or the insane* to do.

Sometimes *s* is a universal class: arguably pleasure is good *for any creature* to experience. Analysis of some '*n* is good' sentences also requires a generic quantifier such as *all typical people*. For convenience I'll assume that the impersonal pronoun 'one' functions this way; a use of (1) might therefore be interpreted as asserting that chocolate is good *for one* to eat. But even in these generic cases, 'good to φ' is still understood as relativized to a restricted class of "agent". Pleasure is arguably good for any creature to experience, but (6) presumably isn't used to mean that it's good even for rocks or plants to experience.

Caution is needed in describing 'for *s*' as specifying an "agent". This place in the logical form of 'good' sentences can be occupied by things that aren't properly agents at all, needing merely to be the subject of the φ-ing. Consider a parent coloring pictures with a toddler who says,

(7) 'Green is good for leaves.'

This can be interpreted as 'Green is good for leaves [to be colored].' Or consider 'Strong walls are good for castles [to have].' Here leaves and castles are the "agents" of the "action-types" *being colored* and *having strong walls*.

Simple '*n* is good' sentences are plausibly interpreted as relativized not simply to particular action-types but to pairs of agents and action-types: that is, '*n* is good' and '*n* is good to φ' sentences are elliptical for sentences of the form

G1: '*n* is good *for s to φ*.'

Because relevant values for *s* in (1)–(6) are so obvious, this part of the logical form can also be omitted and left implicit. But the same objects can also be judged good relative to other less obvious agents, which can be specified with 'for *s*'. Consider:

(8) 'Torment is good.'

(8a) 'Torment is good to suffer.'

Asserting these sentences seems preposterous, but many people would happily assent to

(8b) 'Torment is good *for murderers* to suffer.'

Sentences like (8b) will emerge below to conceal a significant logical ambiguity. But the lesson here is that individuating ways of being good by prepositional phrase isn't sufficiently fine-grained. Otherwise being good *for Sarah* and being good *to experience* would have to be identified as different ways of being good. But these relativizing phrases of forms PP1 and PP2 aren't mutually exclusive, as they complete different parts of the logical form of 'good'. Being good *for Sarah* to experience is one way of being good to experience; another is being good *for Lexy* to experience. Likewise, being good for Sarah *to experience* is one way of being good for Sarah; another is being good for Sarah *to do*. But these also will turn out to be incomplete.

2.3. Bearers of Value: From Objects to States of Affairs

What is the logical form of 'good for s to φ'? Rather than distinguishing two separate argument-places for an agent s and an action-type φ, we might wonder whether 'for s to φ' expresses some single kind of argument. As these phrases are composed of a subject and a predicate we're close to having all the components of a *sentence*, which suggests a further unification. The grammatical contrast between C1, 'n is good', and C2, 'good that p', feeds a controversy over whether the fundamental bearers of value are ordinary objects or states of affairs. But if 'n is good' sentences implicitly contain an embedded sentence, or *prejacent*, this suggests that perhaps a common logical form can be identified for 'n is good' and 'good that p' by analyzing claims about the goodness of an object as concerning the goodness of some state of affairs involving that object.

This unifying hypothesis faces two grammatical obstacles. First, 'n is good for s to φ' still has an noun, 'n', as its subject. Second, 'for s to φ' phrases don't yet provide all the necessary components of a sentence, because here 'φ' is itself an incomplete predicate with the logical form $\varphi(s, a)$. This is especially obvious for sentences with hanging prepositions like 'Albéniz's compositions are good to listen *to*', 'Chocolate is good to bribe children *with*', and 'Friends are good to play jokes *on*.' These prepositions indicate that the predicates ('listen', 'bribe children', 'play jokes') logically require completion by some object a, grammatically calling for a noun phrase.

Taken together these two "obstacles" add up to a solution, because the predicates are evidently completed by the object n in each case: a is n. Good to listen to *what*? To Albéniz's compositions, of course. Good to bribe children with *what*? With chocolate, of course. This holds equally for sentences without hanging prepositions. In 'Chocolate is good to eat', 'to eat' is a two-place predicate, and the answer to 'Good to eat *what*?' is: *chocolate*. Plausibly therefore, 'n is good for s to φ' exhibits deletion of the noun phrase 'n' after the predicate 'φ': '...good for s to φ [n]'. 'Chocolate is good to eat chocolate' doesn't make sense, of course, and the repetition of the noun is redundant. These 'n is good for s to φ' sentences exhibit *subject movement*: the object of the verb 'to φ' moves up from its usual position after the verb to the subject position before the main verb, 'is'.[14]

---

[14] See also Shanklin 2011.

Subject movement is a common feature in English, an artifact of the grammatical rule that a verb must always have a grammatical subject. So although the modal verb 'might' is a sentential or propositional operator rather than a predicate of objects, for example, we cannot correctly say 'Might be that he is in Auckland', but rather either (i) '*He* might be in Auckland', or (ii) '*It* might be that he is in Auckland.' The grammatical subject 'he' in (i) exhibits subject movement, while in (ii) 'it' is a dummy subject, a grammatical placeholder that doesn't represent anything in the logical form. This is also seen in 'good that *p*' sentences, which require the dummy subject in order to be grammatical: '*It* is good that *p*.'

This implies that '*n* is good [for *s* to φ]' sentences can be transformed with a dummy subject into sentences of the form,

G2:   'It is good for *s* to φ *n*.'

So 'Chocolate is good [for one] to eat' becomes 'It is good [for one] to eat chocolate', 'Green is good for leaves [to be colored]' becomes 'It is good for leaves to be colored green', and 'Friends are good [for one] to have' becomes 'It is good [for one] to have friends.' From here it is a short step to understanding 'good' as expressing a propositional operator and moving from 'It is good for *s* to φ *n*' to 'It is good that *s* φ's *n*', that is, to sentences of the form 'It is good that *p*':

(1b)   'It is good that one eats chocolate.'

(7a)   'It is good that leaves are colored green.'

(3a)   'It is good that one has friends.'

These generic sentences presumably involve a wide-scope quantifier; for example, *for every typical person x it is good that x has friends.*

There are some reasons to doubt that these analyses of '*n* is good' sentences are explications that leave truth conditions unchanged, however. First, 'It is good that one has friends' seems factive in a way that 'Friends are good for one to have' or 'It is good for one to have friends' don't: it implies one actually has friends. This problem is easily solved by distinguishing between its being good *that p* (e.g., *that* one has friends), and its being good *if p* (e.g., *if* one has friends), and can be attributed to the factiveness of 'that' in extensional contexts. But there is a more serious obstacle. Plausibly, friends are good to have and pleasure is good to experience regardless of who one is. So friends are good to have and pleasure is good to experience even if the agent in question is (e.g.) a serial murderer or child molester. While it mightn't be true that Albéniz's compositions are good for just anybody to listen to, or that chocolate is good for just anybody to eat, still it seems true that they are good to listen to or eat for many murderers and child molesters.

Even if Peter is a serial child molester, we can still correctly say,

(9)   'Pleasure is good for Peter to experience.'

But many people who would grant this would adamantly deny it is good if serial child molesters have friends, experience pleasure, eat chocolate, or listen to Albéniz's compositions, and so would reject

(9a)   'It is good if Peter experiences pleasure.'

They would deny these things precisely because friends are good to have, pleasure is good to experience, etc., even for many child molesters. On this popular view it's bad if good things happen to undeserving people. So 'good for s to φ' doesn't seem to entail, let alone mean, 'good if s φs'.[15]

The idea that value is fundamentally a property of objects is also intuitively appealing. Plausibly it's because Albéniz's compositions are good that it's good to listen to them, and it is because it's good to listen to them that it's good if one listens to them. It is because (the taste of) chocolate is good that it's good to eat it, and good if one eats it. Nonetheless, I shall argue that this analysis can be vindicated by identifying some further logical structure. (The appendix to this chapter shows how it can be reconciled with the intuition that some value is fundamentally a property of objects.)

2.4. Good for Whom or What?

Some pieces of grammatical data have yet to be fitted into our jigsaw puzzle. 'Good for s' is logically ambiguous, as illustrated by (8b), 'Torment is good for murderers to suffer.'[16] An utterance of this may be taken to say something true, while taking an utterance of

(8c)   'Torment is good *for murderers*',

to say something false. In its most prominent sense, 'good for s' seems to mean roughly *beneficial for s*, but can't mean this in a sentence like (8b). Because torment presumably isn't beneficial for murderers, (8c) is naturally interpreted as false, although it can also be read as elliptical for (8b) and thereby true. A common reason for saying that torment is good for murderers to suffer is that suffering torment is *bad* for murderers. A parent saying 'Green is good for leaves [to be colored]' wouldn't be asserting that it's beneficial for leaves, to be colored

---

[15] 'n is good for s to φ' also has the same grammatical form as 'n is tough for s to φ', but we can't transform (e.g.) 'Rejection is tough for Johnny to get over' into 'It is tough that Johnny gets over rejection', which may seem problematic (see Shanklin 2011 for exploration of similarities between 'good' and what linguists call "tough adjectives"). I attribute this to a difference in the logical form of 'tough' which requires 'for s' always to function as a relativizer rather than a complementizer; to be tough is always to be tough for somebody, but we'll see the parallel fail for 'good'.

[16] As also observed in Kraut 2007.

green. Consider also 'Chocolate is good [for one] to eat', which presumably isn't usually used to mean that eating chocolate is beneficial.

Some uses of 'good' are explicitly relativized to subjects by means of a 'for *s*' phrase. An intercepted pass in a game of football might be good *for the home team* but not good *for the visiting team*. The political mood in the United States late in 2008 was good *for Barack Obama*, but not good *for John McCain*. Philosophers commonly call this "agent-relative value", but as this terminology would here be both confusing and misleading I'll call it *patient-relative*. While it's controversial whether all value is patient-relative, or whether there is also patient-neutral (or "agent-neutral") value, it's hardly ever denied that 'good' is sometimes used in patient-relative ways. A unifying semantics for 'good' may therefore seem to require that every meaningful use of 'good' be relativized to the kind of argument represented by these 'for *s*' phrases, that is, that every sentence of the form '*n* is good' or '*n* is good for *s* to φ' is used as elliptical for a sentence of the form,

G3: '*n* is good for s_p, for s_a to φ.'

(I'll use 's_p' for "patients" or beneficiaries and 's_a' for "agents".)

Use of at least some simpler 'good' sentences can plausibly be explicated by sentences of this form; for example (3) is plausibly used elliptically for 'Friends are good for one, for one to have.' Ellipsis is predictable in common cases like this where the patient and agent are identical, to avoid grammatical repetition. Sentence (5) is plausibly used as elliptical for something like 'Voting is good for the nation, for eligible voters to do.' Given the platitude that (retributive) justice is sought for the sake of the victims, use of (8b) can reasonably be interpreted as elliptical for 'Torment is good [for their victims,] for murderers to suffer', or less awkwardly, 'It is good [for their victims,] for murderers to suffer torment.' If a speaker who uttered (3) continued, '...but I don't mean to say that friends are good for one, for one to have', she is likely to be asked what she meant instead.

Observing this logical ambiguity removes the obstacle to analyzing '*n* is good' into 'It is good that *p*.' If 'good' logically requires a *for s_p* argument, then sentences of the form G2, 'It is good for *s* to φ *n*', will always be used elliptically for sentences of the form

G4: 'It is good for s_p, for s_a to φ *n*.'

A significant logical ambiguity will therefore be concealed in G2, 'It is good for *s* to φ *n*' sentences, which must be interpreted as either

G2a: 'It is good [for s_p], for *s* to φ *n*.'

G2b: 'It is good for *s*, [for s_a] to φ *n*.'

The most natural readings of (8b) and (9) can then be logically disambiguated as

(8d) 'It is good [for s_p], for murderers to suffer torment.'

(9b) 'It is good for Peter, [for s_a] to experience pleasure.'

For (8d), s_p is naturally identified as somebody like *victims*, as indicated by context. For (9b), s_a is naturally identified as Peter, as a result of the earlier reference to him in the sentence. Sentence (9b) is plausibly true, and there are no semantic obstacles to interpreting it as assigning value to a proposition, since this is explicitly qualified as being merely value for Peter; that is, as

(9b*)   'It is good for Peter, if Peter experiences pleasure.'

By contrast, the unacceptable sentence (9a), 'It is good if Peter experiences pleasure', can't be interpreted as equivalent to (9b), because it contains 'if Peter...', which is unambiguously a complementizer (rather than 'for Peter...', which is ambiguously either a complementizer or relativizer) and must rather be interpreted as

(9a*)   'It is good [for s_p], if Peter experiences pleasure.'

Since it isn't plausibly good for us, or his victims, or justice (etc.) that Peter experiences pleasure, to explain the unacceptability of (9a) it only needs to be explained why s_p is here naturally interpreted as referring to some patient other than Peter.

Semantics alone doesn't explain why s_a in (9) or (9b) is naturally identified as Peter while s_p in (9a) or (9a*) can't be, but while a full pragmatic answer will emerge in Chapter 5, a simple answer can be offered here. Pronouns characteristically refer *backwards* ("anaphorically"), whether they are explicit or implicit. So (9) is naturally interpreted as 'It is good for Peter, [for s_a] to experience pleasure', taking the omitted element to point backwards to the reference of 'Peter'. But since the use of 'if' or 'that' forces a reading of (9a) on which the reference to s_p precedes 'Peter', grammar gives no indication that s_p is Peter. On the contrary, the explicit reference to Peter by name *after* the implicit pronoun positively indicates that it doesn't refer to him, since otherwise the speaker wouldn't later need to name him. 'It is good [for s_p],...' is therefore naturally read as relativizing value to a patient other than Peter who is somehow salient in the context. Since the pleasure of child molesters isn't generally good for people other than themselves, use of (9a) can be expected to express a false proposition.

Our present hypothesis is that 'n is good' sentences are always used as elliptical for 'It is good for s_p, for s_a to φ n' sentences, which are simply grammatical variants of 'It is good for s_p, if p.' To determine the plausibility of all goodness being patient-relative we need to investigate the class of "patients" or values for s_p that are semantically acceptable in this argument-place. Limiting patients to agents proper or even to persons is far too narrow, as we've seen. We talk about what is good or beneficial for animals, plants, institutions like governments and banks, and artifacts like cars, computers, and scissors. We can as intelligibly talk about what was good for Barack Obama's presidential campaign as about what was good for Obama, and what was good for the campaign needn't always have been good for Obama, like the death of his grandmother. It may also be more appropriate to say that the torment of murderers is good for *justice* than that it's good for victims. Although the class of patients is evidently very broad, there are constraints: while talk about what is good for a spider, a fern, a book, or a reputation is easily understood, without a special context it's hard to make sense of talk about what is good for a rock, a piece of lint, a shadow, or Wednesdays.[17]

Making sense of 'good for s_p' is often said to require identifying an *interest* associated with s_p in some way. What is good for a person or creature is what is in her interest, and where s_p isn't a person or creature (e.g., 'good for the pool') an interest must be saliently related to s_p in another way, like an interest some-body has in its state. It's natural to say that the interest of Obama's campaign was in his winning the 2008 presidential election, that the suffering of criminals serves the "interests of justice", and that the home team has an interest in win-ning the football game. By contrast, things that aren't natural candidates for being patients, like rocks, lint, shadows, and Wednesdays, aren't associated by default with any interests.

Some philosophers therefore advance *interest-relational* theories: that to be "good" in some way is always to be related to an interest of some patient.[18] Paul Ziff proposes "a relatively simple hypothesis about the meaning of the word 'good', viz. that 'good' has associated with it the condition of answering to certain interests".[19] But the hypothesis faces a difficulty: some ordinary uses of 'good' aren't naturally understood as relativized to any patient's interests.[20]

Suppose a perverted genius creates a Doomsday Device; we can appropri-ately say, 'This device is good for destroying the universe', although it needn't serve the interests of any patient, even its inventor or the device itself. Similarly, a piece of wood might be considered good *for whittling* without it's being sup-posed that it's good for anyone or anything that it be whittled—for example if whittling is a worthless activity that only fosters sloth and other vices. Or sup-pose a speaker asserts, 'Chocolate is good to eat', or 'Green is good for leaves to be colored', to which it's responded, 'Whose interests are you saying it's good for?' The speaker can resist: "I didn't mean to say it is good *for anybody's inter-ests* for them to eat chocolate. It's just good to eat. It isn't good *for* you." Not all uses of 'good' seem to involve such a 'for s_p' relativizer, even implicitly.

Perhaps if we try hard enough a candidate might always be found for some inanimate or hypothetical "patient" with a relevant interest: for example, the "interest" of destruction or vice. But these sentences resisting 'for s_p' relativizers are more naturally explicated with a further kind of relativizing phrase, PP3,

---

[17] Cf. also the examples in Ziff 1960: 210–11.

[18] E.g., Perry 1926, Dewey 1939, Ziff 1960, Mackie 1977, Railton 1986.

[19] Ziff 1960: 218f. He contrasts interests with needs or passionate desires, pointing out that 'good' seems oddly weak in relation to these, but this seems rather to be pragmatic (by the maxim of quality), since it's odd to deny that something is good if it "answers" to salient needs or desires.

[20] Cf. Thomson 2008: Ch. 2.

'for φ_e-ing'—for example, 'good for destroying the universe'.[21] 'Green is good for leaves' is plausibly used elliptically for

(7b)   'It is good *for drawing realistic pictures*, for leaves to be colored green',

and ordinary use of 'Chocolate is good to eat' may be explicable as

(1c)   'It is good for *having pleasure*, for one to eat chocolate.'

If a speaker continued after uttering the simple '*n* is good' sentence by saying '...but I don't mean to say that it's good for drawing realistic pictures/for having pleasure', then we'd be puzzled and ask what she did mean.

As with 'good to φ', it can sensibly be asked, 'Good for *whose* φ-ing?' Sentences (1)/(1c) can be explicated further as elliptical for 'It's good for *one's* having pleasure, for one to eat chocolate', since one person's eating chocolate isn't clearly good for anybody else's pleasure. So these 'good for φ_e-ing' sentences can be analyzed as elliptical for sentences of the form

G5:   'It is good for *s*'s φ_e-ing, for s_a to φ_m *n*.'

To say that something is good for [*s*'s] φ_e-ing is to provide an answer to the familiar question, "What is it good for?", naturally interpreted as asking after its *instrumental value*.

To be good for φ_e-ing is roughly to be good as a *means* to φ_e-ing, so these relativizers are naturally described as identifying an *end*. As 'φ_e-ing' is in the progressive tense it indicates movement toward a potential outcome or end state of affairs, that *e*. *Destroying* the universe is moving toward the state of affairs that the universe is destroyed; *winning* the election is moving toward the state of affairs that the election is won. Such an end or outcome can also be specified by a noun phrase; for example, instead of 'good for destroying the universe' we can say 'good for the destruction of the universe'. So 'good for [*s*'s] φ_e-ing' can be analyzed as relativizing goodness to an end *e*—as *end-relational*—using 'end' as a term of art for any proposition conceived as a potential outcome. While calling something an "end" may commonly imply it is *somebody's* end, or a desired or intended goal, I'll use it more broadly to include merely possible goals; to say 'This device is good for destroying the universe' needn't imply that anybody actually desires or intends that end.

Identifying both patient-relative and end-relative uses of 'good' may appear to put the prospects for a unified logical form in jeopardy. If 'good' sometimes has a patient-argument and sometimes has an end-argument, then it only has a unified logical form if every proper use of 'good' is relativized

---

[21] 'for φ-ing' phrases are also ambiguous, as 'good for eating' can be equivalent to 'good to eat'.

to both a patient and an end. But these two kinds of relativizer rather seem to exclude each other. If s_a's φ_m-ing n is good for [s's] φ_e-ing, there doesn't seem to be any incompleteness requiring a relation to some patient s_p who is benefited. "For *whom* is it good for one's drawing realistic pictures, that leaves are colored green?" isn't an intelligible question. But a unified form might still be identifiable if one kind of relativization is reducible to the other. End-relativity seems unlikely to be reducible to patient-relativity since we've already observed that some end-relative sentences resist analysis as patient-relative. The prospects for the opposite reduction, of patient-relativity into end-relativity, appear better.

'Good for s_p' might simply be taken as elliptical for 'good for s_p's φ_e-ing'; the two kinds of relativizers would then result from omitting reference alternatively to the "agent" or the "action" components of the end proposition e. This yields plausible results: 'good for justice' is naturally explicated, for example, as 'good for justice's being served'. Whereas 'good for s_p' has restrictions on natural values for s_p, 'good for s_p's φ_e-ing' (or 'good for e') isn't similarly restricted, and is intelligible for any value of e. Acceptable values for s_p appear to be precisely those that suggest natural candidates for an omitted 'φ_e-ing'. A patient's "interest" can be identified with an end or outcome saliently desired or desirable on behalf of that patient. The interest saliently related to justice is in the state of affairs *that justice is served*, for example, while the interest saliently related to victims is *that they receive justice*, and the interest related to a reputation is *that it remains untarnished*. By contrast, 'good for a rock' and 'good for a piece of lint' don't naturally suggest candidates for φ_e-ing, because no kind of future state of affairs is generally made salient by mention of rocks or lint.

Sometimes providing both kinds of relativizing phrase isn't unintelligible but merely redundant. We can say either that the political mood late in 2008 was good for Obama (i.e., for s_p), or that it was good for Obama's defeating McCain (i.e., for s_p's φ_e-ing). It seems redundant to say,

> (10) 'The political mood late in 2008 was good for Obama's defeating McCain, for Obama.'

But there is an asymmetry here, because it seems *less* redundant to say,

> (10a) 'The political mood late in 2008 was good for Obama, for Obama's defeating McCain.'

Compare also:

> (11) 'The intercepted pass was good for the home team's defeating the visitors, for the home team.'

> (11a) 'The intercepted pass was good for the home team, for their defeating the visitors.'

In 'good for s_p's φ_e-ing, for s_p' the second relativizer seems gratuitous, while in 'good for s_p, for s_p's φ_e-ing' it helpfully explicates the first relativizer. The 'for φ_e-ing' phrases expand on the vaguer 'for s_p' phrases. Being good for defeating McCain is one way something can be good for Obama, but not vice versa, while being good for defeating the visiting team is one way something can be good for the home team. But these aren't the only ways of being good for those patients; contrast

(10b)   'The political mood late in 2008 was good for Obama, for his raising funds.'

(11b)   'The intercepted pass was good for the home team, for their salvaging a little pride.'

Our hypothesis is therefore that 'good' sentences are fundamentally end-relational, and that patient- and interest-relativity are merely special cases of this.[22] All simple predicative uses of 'good' would therefore be elliptical for sentences of the form

G-LF: 'It is good for e if p',

or more explicitly 'It is good for s_p's φ_e-ing, for s_a to φ_m n.' This hypothesis can be tested against our simple 'n is good' sentences (1)–(6) by considering the question "What is it good for?" One's eating chocolate is good for *one's having gustatory pleasure*. One's having friends is good for *one's having a happy and fulfilling life*, at least. Following Jim's escape plan is good for *escaping prison*. Listening to Albéniz's compositions is good for *having aesthetic pleasure*. Voting is good for *maintenance of a healthy democracy*, inter alia. Anybody uttering one of these simple sentences who continues by saying that he doesn't mean it's good for *that* would immediately invite queries about what he did mean.

Some simple 'good' sentences don't appear so amenable to this treatment, of course, like (6): what is one's experiencing pleasure good for? Speech and thought about "final" value, or what is "good for its own sake", poses a challenge addressed in Chapter 7. The remainder of this chapter examines the prospects for a unifying end-relational semantics for ordinary uses of 'good'. I'll argue that G-LF explicates the logical form of 'good': it expresses a propositional operator $G_e(p)$ which takes an object or complement proposition p and has an argument-place relativizing to an end-proposition e.

---

[22] Ziff (1960: 218–19) favors "interests" over "ends" due to the implication I've canceled that an "end" is *somebody's goal*, but we've seen that appeal to interests also fails to accommodate all ordinary uses of 'good'. By canceling instead the implication that an "interest" is *something's interest* (as in Finlay 2001, 2004) "end-relational" and "interest-relational" theories may become merely terminological variants.

2.5. Good as a *K*, Good *K*s, etc.

While a variety of ways of being good can be analyzed as sharing the underlying logical form G-LF, we haven't yet investigated many other ways of qualifying or relativizing 'good', such as (PP4) 'good with *K*s', (PP5) 'good at φ-ing', and (PP6) 'good as a *K*'. If our semantics is to be completely unifying, all these also must be explicable by sentences of this same form.

To avoid taxing the reader's patience further I won't attempt an exhaustive investigation, but it seems plausible that at least many of these further kinds of qualifiers also function to make explicit particular components of either an end or complement proposition, where the remaining components are left implicit. 'Good with *K*s' can be explicated by 'good [for *e*, for *s* to φ_m] *with K*s', for example, with salient default values for *e* and φ_m. For *s* to be "good with children" is for it to be good for some salient *e* (e.g., children's being happy or entertained) for *s* to interact in some salient way φ (e.g., play, talk) with children. 'Good at φ-ing' can be explicated by 'good [for *e*, for *s* to be the person engaged] at φ-ing'; for example, for *s* to be "good at fighting" is for it to be good for *e* (e.g., a fighter's being defeated) for *s* to be the one engaged at fighting him. G-LF can accommodate the great majority of ways 'good' is used, even if some outlying polysemy or idioms can be found which it doesn't assimilate.[23]

It is important that we consider one other kind of grammatical use, (C3) 'good *K*', as it motivates a competing theory of the logical form and semantics of 'good' with a lineage going back to Plato and Aristotle. In these uses 'good' is a grammatically "attributive" adjective, attached to a noun phrase '*K*' to form a complex predicate 'good *K*' (e.g., 'good paper airplane', 'good anchor', 'good joke') rather than a "predicative" adjective, predicated of the noun as in '*K*s are good'/'*n* is good.' This grammatical difference doesn't entail a difference in logical form, as for any adjective '*A*' we can switch without change of meaning between 'This is an *A K*' and 'This *K* is *A*'; for example, 'This is a black cat' and 'This cat is black.' But Peter Geach postulated an imperfectly corresponding distinction in logical form, so that in 'good *K*', 'good' is logically a predicate-modifier rather than a predicate. This would have a single argument-place for a kind of object *K*, and refer to a function from the property of being a *K* to a different property, of being a *good K*. Some philosophers, including Geach, further suggest that 'good' has a unified semantics as logically attributive:that *every* meaningful use of 'good' must be understood as completed by some intended noun phrase.[24] The Aristotelian tradition in

---

[23] The occurrence of 'good' in 'goodbye' is semantically unrelated, for example (Ziff 1960: 209, Shanklin 2011), apparently a corruption of 'God be with ye'. Shanklin (2011) argues that 'good to *s*' also involves at least polysemy, since somebody can be good to *s* without doing anything good for *s*, or for any salient interests or ends. Perhaps to be "good to *s*" is to do to *s* things that are generically good, i.e., which it is good for one to receive.

[24] E.g., Geach 1956: 65, Foot 1985, Thomson 2008.

moral philosophy interprets the moral use of 'good' accordingly as meaning *good person* or *good human being*.[25]

Perhaps ordinary predicative uses of 'good' can always be naturally paraphrased by introducing noun phrases. 'Pleasure is good' might be explicated as 'Pleasure is a good *sensation*', for example, and 'It's good that Obama won the 2008 presidential election' as 'It's a good *state of affairs* (or simply a good *thing*) that Obama won the 2008 presidential election.' But if 'good' has a unified meaning as a predicate modifier then it must modify predicates in some systematic way. Is there a satisfactory general story about what is meant in moving from talking about *K*s to talking about *good K*s?

This question suggests looking at the intelligibility constraints on values for '*K*'. It isn't clear what might be meant by saying that something is (e.g.) a "good rock", or a "good piece of lint", or a "good shadow".[26] Although these can be intelligible in the right contexts, combining 'good' with these noun phrases doesn't determine any predicate by semantic convention. So what is the relation that good paper airplanes, anchors, and jokes bear to paper airplanes, anchors, and jokes in general, and that no subclass of rocks, lint, or shadows bears to rocks, lint, or shadows in general? While attributivists don't always answer this question, Plato and Aristotle provide an influential response.

Understanding 'good paper airplane', 'good anchor', and 'good joke' only requires knowing what those kinds are *for*: their "telos" or *function*.[27] Good members of different kinds *K* have in common the disposition to perform the function of their kinds well.[28] So 'good rock', 'good lint', and 'good shadow' leave us puzzled because these values for *K* aren't functional classifications, and don't make any particular function salient. This observation inspires moral functionalism, the idea that to be a good person or human being is to be disposed to perform the function of persons or human beings well.

Unfortunately, 'person' and 'human being' don't seem to be functional nouns, as persons and humans as such don't appear to be *for* anything. "Our existence precedes our essence", in Sartre's slogan. This may be disputed, but the problem is more general. 'Good *K*' is intelligible for many *K*s with no plausible function; consider 'good sunset', 'good day', 'good boy', 'good feeling', 'good behavior', as well as the abstract cases 'good thing', 'good event', and 'good state of affairs'. Or consider the intuitively true sentences 'Pleasure is a good sensation' and 'Pain is a bad sensation.' Sensations of pleasure and pain

---

[25] E.g., Foot 2001, Bloomfield 2001, Casebeer 2003, Thomson 2008.

[26] These aren't identical with the restrictions on *good for* s_p, even in the same examples: e.g., what makes somebody a good bodyguard/is good *in* a bodyguard (e.g., willingness to take a bullet for a client) needn't be good *for* the bodyguard. Conflating *what x is good for* and *what is good for x* is a fundamental error in the Ergon argument of Plato and Aristotle.

[27] Thomson (2008: 20–21) argues that the relevant class is *standard-setting* rather than functional kinds.

[28] This is circular, since 'well' is the adverbial form of 'good', but I won't worry about this here.

indeed have a natural function: to motivate pursuit of what is beneficial and avoidance of what is harmful to the organism. So functionalism would seem to predict incorrectly that the pleasure from heroin abuse isn't a good sensation while the pain from self-mutilation is.

While functionalist attributivism only works for a limited range of data, the end-relational semantics isn't similarly restricted. First, the cases of 'good K' that resist attributivism present no difficulty, because wherever K isn't a functional kind, 'n is a good K' can be interpreted simply as a grammatical variant of 'n is a K that is good', or more explicitly 'n is a K such that it is good for e, for s to φ it.' 'That's a good sunset' can be explicated as 'That's a sunset such that it's good for one's having aesthetic pleasure if one views it.' Second, the functional uses of 'good K' that motivate attributivism are easily accommodated.

Since having a function is simply to serve some end, any functional noun-phrase 'K' makes salient an end e. Consider relativizing phrases of the form PP6, 'good as a K'. If the function of Ks corresponds to the end e_K then to be good as a K is to be good for e_K. The function of anchors is to stop ships from floating away, for example, and to be good as an anchor is to be good to use for stopping ships from floating away. So 'This is good as an anchor' can be explicated by 'This is good [for stopping ships from floating away, for one to use] as an anchor', while 'This is good as a joke' can be explicated by 'This is good [for making people laugh, for one to tell] as a joke.'[29] The functional uses of 'good K' can then be understood as equivalent to 'good as a K'. Something is a good anchor, paper airplane, or joke in the functional sense just in case it is good *as* an anchor, paper airplane, or joke.[30] Our theory therefore suggests that 'n is a good K' is logically ambiguous between

C3a: 'n is a K, such that it's good for e, for s_a to $\varphi_m n$',

C3b: 'It's good for e_K, for s_a to $\varphi_m n$ as a K.'

This ambiguity has significant implications for moral functionalism. A way of testing whether a particular instance of 'good K' conceals the form of C3a or of C3b is to consider whether in this instance being a good or bad K entails being a K. This holds for the non-functional, C3a sentences: nothing can be a good or bad sunset in the usual sense without being a sunset, a good or bad day without being a day, a good or bad sensation without being a sensation, or a good or bad state of affairs without being a state of affairs. But it doesn't hold for functional, C3b sentences.[31] Something can be a good or a bad anchor

---

[29] This fits awkwardly with vocational nouns, as in 'good teacher' and 'good president', as it's jarring to say (e.g.) that teachers are for educating students with. Saying n is "for φ_e" suggests n is an instrument used in φ_e-ing, but these nouns refer rather to agents. Instead of 'good for φ_e-ing', the right kind of phrase here is PP5, 'good at φ_m-ing'.

[30] 'Good K' can be used non-functionally even if K is a functional kind; see Szabo 2001. Consider the humor in Sherlock Holmes's joke about a serial-killing cab driver (in the television series *Sherlock*): "He was a bad cabbie...you should have seen the route he took to get here."

[31] I owe this point to Shyam Nair.

without being a real anchor, a good or a bad paper airplane without being a paper airplane, etc. Observe that 'good person' and 'good human being' behave like the non-functional cases with the logical form in C3a: one can't be a good or a bad person in the usual sense without being a person, or a good or a bad human being without being human. Moral functionalism therefore provides another illustration of philosophy led astray by confusion about language.

2.6. The Meaning of 'Good'

A wide grammatical variety of 'good' sentences can be attributed the same logical form G-LF, by which the word expresses a relational property schema $G_e(p)$, predicating of a proposition p a property of standing in some as-yet unidentified relation R to an end-proposition e. To identify the conceptual meaning or semantic contribution of 'good', or what it means to say that it's *good* for e if p, we therefore need only to identify a relation R that intuitive instances of goodness have in common: between eating chocolate and having gustatory pleasure, the home team's intercepting a pass and their winning the game, the economic mood late in 2008 and Obama's winning the presidential election, leaves being colored green and drawing realistic pictures, etc. This doesn't seem particularly difficult, and philosophers who have considered the question have all given rather similar answers, for example, that p "promotes", "serves", "answers to", "satisfies", or "is conducive to" e.[32] Plausibly, being able to recognize some such answer as roughly correct is necessary for knowing what it means to be "good" for something.

While philosophers have generally been content with some such answer as sufficiently elucidating, some variety and vagueness remains here, and each is merely a proposed synonymy rather than a reductive analysis. I think 'promotes' or 'is conducive to' may be closest—being good for e is approximately *being promotive of e*—but we'll see it isn't sufficiently general.[33] A natural hypothesis is that p is good for (or promotes) e just in case *p increases the probability that e*. One's eating chocolate increases the probability of one's having pleasure, the home team's intercepting a pass increases the probability of their winning, and the economic mood late in 2008 increased the probability of Obama's winning

---

[32] E.g., Wittgenstein 1930/1996, Perry 1926, Ziff 1960, Thomson 1992, 1997, 2001, Schroeder 2007. My previous treatments are in Finlay 2001, 2004, 2006.

[33] Note we can't substitute '*n* is promotive' for '*n* is good'. The difference may be primarily grammatical; compare 'complete' and 'finish' (Jim Higginbotham's example; consider also 'select' and 'choose'), which both have a logical argument-place for an object: one completes or finishes *something*. Yet while 'I finished' is a grammatically well-formed sentence like '*n* is good', 'I completed' isn't, like '*n* is promotive.' An explanation why this would give 'good' a more normative sense can be derived from the results of Chapter 5.

the election. Here then is a first, informal statement of an end-relational semantics for 'good':

G-ERa: 'It's good for *e* if *p*' means that *p* increases the probability of *e*.[34]

This is still vague, and its two key conceptual components of *probability* and of *increasing* need to be clarified. I begin with the second task.

"Increase" is an essentially comparative notion: something is increased just in case it is made greater or larger. So the other term in the comparison needs to be identified: greater *than what*? The most obvious answer may be temporal: to increase something is to make it greater than it previously was. This seems to work for some cases: plausibly the pass being intercepted is good for the home team's winning the game just in case it makes the probability of their winning greater than it was immediately prior to the interception. But it fails to accommodate other cases: consider 'It's good for blasphemers' well-being that a vengeful god doesn't exist', which expresses a coherent thought but can't mean that the nonexistence of a vengeful god makes the probability of blasphemers' well-being greater than it was prior to the nonexistence of any such god. This case calls instead for a modal comparison, between the actual probability of *e* and some counterfactual probability of *e*, that is, in some counterfactual world-state or states: the nonexistence of a vengeful god makes the probability of blasphemers' well-being greater than it *otherwise would be*.

This modal analysis is more general, since the former case can also be understood as a comparison with the probability of the home team's winning were the pass not intercepted. This suggests that 'It's good for *e* if *p*' means, a bit more precisely, that the probability (*pr*) of *e* is greater if *p* than if *not-p*,[35] or

G-ERb: 'It's good for *e* if *p*' means that $pr(e|p) > pr(e|{\sim}p)$.

Any use of 'good' would then involve comparisons where at least one term is counterfactual. (For convenience I'll focus on cases where *p* is actual and *not-p* is counterfactual, though it can be judged either that it *is good that p* or that

---

[34] This hypothesis may seem to have problematic implications for children's acquisition of competence with 'good', given Piaget's classic finding that a mature conception of probability doesn't develop until around twelve (Piaget & Inhelder 1951/1975). But (i) more recent research in developmental psychology challenges these claims, finding that even babies employ surprisingly advanced probabilistic reasoning (e.g., Sobel et al. 2004), and (ii) young children may use the word passably well with only partial competence; e.g., at six, my daughter explained that calling something 'good' means *you like it*, which we'll see in Chapter 5 isn't far from the truth. (This might help explain why young children are seldom impressed by being told that eating broccoli or getting shots is good, or that eating lots of candy isn't.)

[35] Finlay 2006. Schroeder 2007 offers an alternative analysis of promotion (in analyzing reasons) comparing probabilities conditional on φ-ing with probabilities conditional on "doing nothing", which (inter alia) implies that doing nothing is never good/something there is a reason to do; see discussion in Evers 2009, Behrends & DiPaulo 2011.

it *would be good if p*, and in some cases both terms will be counterfactual; i.e. what would be good because of what otherwise would be the case.)

This introduces difficult issues. In drawing these comparisons we aren't concerned with just the propositions *p* and *not-p*. There are many different ways of being the case that *not-p* (and also that *p*, though here I'll assume this is made concrete by the actual world-state). Consider the claim that it's good for his team's winning their baseball game that Aramis draws a walk from his at-bat. G-ERb holds that the truth of this depends on the probability of winning if Aramis *hadn't* drawn a walk, but the many different ways for Aramis not to draw a walk include his striking out, hitting a home run, being ejected by the umpire, grounding into a double play, or the game being called off due to rain, etc. The probability of a win had Aramis not drawn a walk by striking out may be very different from the probability of a win had he not drawn a walk by hitting a home run instead. Which of these alternative possibilities is relevant to the claim that it's good Aramis drew a walk?

At opposite extremes are the views (i) that such claims always compare one particular counterfactual world-state w_{-p} in which *not-p*, and (ii) that they compare the set W_{-p} of all counterfactual world-states in which *not-p*.[36] Both of these can be ruled out. Speakers can't have in mind a particular counterfactual world-state, because their interests aren't so fine-grained as to be sensitive to every detail like the exact number of hairs on each person's head.[37] In judging whether it's good that Aramis drew a walk, it's relevant both that he might otherwise have hit a home run and also that he might otherwise have struck out. But we're also not interested in every possible way of its being true that *not-p*. Evaluations of Aramis's walk won't generally be sensitive to world-states in which the rules of baseball are different, or he became a hockey player instead and somebody else drew a walk in his place.

A narrower interest can be presumed, in a set of possibilities consistent with a background the speaker has in mind, which we can identify with a proposition *b* constituting a partial description of a world-state, and make explicit with a 'given *b*' relativizing phrase. A semantic theory could accommodate this in various ways, but I'll assume here another argument-place in the logical form of 'good': $G_{e,b}(p)$. Typical backgrounds include *given the actual state of the world at time t*, for example, and *given that the world-state doesn't perceptibly differ from its actual state at t*; in our example it presumably includes at least that the rules of baseball and the current state of the game remain the same. The *not-p* term of the comparison will therefore be the conjunction

---

[36] Bradley 1998 suggests view (i). These correspond roughly to "actualist" and "possibilist" theories about the semantics of 'ought'; see Jackson & Pargetter 1986.

[37] See also Oddie & Milne 1991.

(*not-p* & *b*), while the *p* term can be identified as (*p* & *b*);[38] this provides our final definition:

G-ER: 'It's good for *e* if *p*, [given *b*]' means that $pr(e|p \ \& \ b) >$
$pr(e|{\sim}p \ \& \ b)$.

The relevant probability of *e* conditional on *not-p* will involve some kind of *balancing* of the various relevant ways of *not-p*; that one of the many ways Aramis might have not drawn a walk is by hitting a home run instead doesn't preclude its being good that he drew a walk, for example, though the probability of a win given a home run is presumably greater. Something doesn't have to be best to be good.

Before tackling the question of how to understand these probabilities, consider the implications of G-ER for the gradability of 'good'. Whereas goodness or value comes in degrees, 'makes more probable than otherwise' isn't similarly gradable: either *p* makes *e* more likely than *not-p* does, or it doesn't. But the analysis suggests a natural extension: that degrees of value are degrees of probability-increasing. To be *more good (better) than x for e* is to increase the probability of *e* more than *x* does; to be *most good (best) for e* is to increase the probability of *e* most of all the relevant alternatives.

'Good' has a contrary in 'bad', of course, and value contrasts with disvalue. Our analysis naturally suggests that being *bad for e* is decreasing the probability of *e*, and that degrees of badness or disvalue are degrees of probability-decreasing. But something can also be "better" by being less-bad-than; instead of complicating these definitions of 'better' and 'best', degrees of probability-decreasing can simply be identified with *negative* degrees of probability-increasing. Being *worse than x for e* is therefore to increase the probability of *e* less (decrease it more) than *x*; being *worst for e* is to increase the probability of *e* least (decrease it the most) of all the alternatives. (Not all comparisons of value are made relative to the same end, of course; we'll consider comparisons involving different ends in Chapter 6.)

This analysis implies a natural equilibrium point of value neutrality (relative to a background *b*), dividing what is good to some degree from what is bad to some degree. This arguably contrasts with most pairs of gradable adjectives: 'hot' and 'cold', 'heavy' and 'light', and 'short' and 'tall', for example, respectively grade degrees of temperature, weight, and height apparently without a natural point of neutrality, and orthodox semantic treatments of these posit an additional argument-place in the logical form for a *degree* parameter, which can vary by context. It might therefore be complained that the most conservative semantics for 'good' would model after other gradable adjectives in this respect. But we can remain neutral on controversial issues about gradability.

---

[38] This may be an oversimplification, since the *p* and *not-p* terms could require distinct backgrounds *b* and *b'*. Alternatively, '*p*' (and '*not-p*'?) might underspecify the object of evaluation, and be elliptical for (e.g.) *Aramis draws a walk* [*in the way he actually does*].

On one hand, some theories of gradability analyze the degree parameter as determined by a contextually selected comparison set (e.g., as the *average* temperature, weight, or height), in the same way that our analysis generates the point of value neutrality from the comparison set determined by the background *b*, so there mightn't really be any difference.[39] On the other hand, a degree argument only seems necessary for scales that lack natural neutral points. Contrast 'hot' and 'cold' (etc.) with 'left' and 'right', which are also gradable (e.g., *slightly* versus *sharply* left) but are naturally separated by *straight ahead*, making a semantic degree parameter gratuitous. Value and disvalue are intuitively conceived as being separated in a similarly natural way; I suggest it is a platitude that it's *good* if something exists just in case it's better that it exists than that it doesn't.[40]

The second major issue needing clarification concerns the notion of *probability* involved in speech about goodness. A distinction is commonly drawn between at least *objective* probability (or "chance") and *subjective* probability (or "rational credence").[41] To contrast these in a rudimentary way, objective probability is based on the state of the world at a time, while subjective probability is based on (and so relative to) sets of evidence or beliefs about the state of the world. So if *p* is in fact the case at t_1 then its objective probability at t_1 is 1, for example, but its subjective probability relative to our evidence may yet be anything between 0 and 1.

Many ordinary uses of 'good' clearly seem to involve objective probability: if the objective probability of *e* is greater if *p* than if *not-p*, then it's intuitive that *p* is good for *e*, whereas somebody who has no idea of the objective probabilities can naturally say that he doesn't know whether *p* is good for *e*. It's less clear whether subjective probability is also relevant to goodness. Arguably the notion of promotion requires analysis in terms of objective rather than subjective probability.[42] Suppose Chuck is a marooned castaway ignorant about whether Obama won the 2008 US presidential election. News that Obama gave the 2009 State of the Union Address would therefore be evidence that increases Chuck's subjective probability (i.e., relative to his beliefs) that Obama won in 2008. But it wouldn't be correct to say that Obama's giving the address

---

[39] There is a large technical literature on these issues; see, e.g., Kennedy 2007.

[40] Two objections: (i) it's sometimes appropriately judged that *none* of the alternatives are good, and (ii) saying that something is "good" seems stronger than saying it's "good to some degree". In reply: first, our flexibility about how relevant *not-p* world-states are selected allows comparisons with counterfactual alternatives that aren't among the available alternatives. Second, pragmatic explanations are available for why something wouldn't normally be called "good" without qualification unless it was thought good to a significant degree, just as something wouldn't normally be described as "to the left" without qualification unless significantly to the left.

[41] See the survey in Hájek 2011, for example.

[42] Behrends & DiPaolo (2011) argue that that 'promotes' isn't properly analyzed in terms of probability at all; if their examples succeed I think they also show promotion of *e* without goodness for *e*, providing another reason why 'promotes' isn't exactly synonymous with 'good for'.

"promotes" his winning the election. Or consider the information that the polls prior to the election show Obama with a lead (not to be confused with actually leading in voter support); this is evidence that may raise our subjective probability that he wins, but it needn't itself promote his winning.

However, some ordinary uses of 'good' do seem to involve subjective rather than objective probabilities, or promotion. Ben Bradley observes a kind of "signatory" value.[43] Upon learning about Obama's 2009 SOTU address, Chuck may (if hoping for an Obama victory) say, 'That's good!' A campaign adviser might react similarly to a positive poll. These might be suspected really to be judgments about what is evidenced rather than about the evidence itself, and Bradley himself suggests that news is only *correctly* judged good if what it evinces actually obtains.[44] But consider this variation on one of his scenarios:

> *Good Test*:   Carl goes into hospital with suspected cancer. The doctor runs an initial diagnostic test, which gives no false positives and so can conclusively confirm cancer, but gives false negatives in 70% of cases where cancer is present. She reports that the test is negative.

Carl can appropriately respond to the doctor's news by saying, 'That's good.' While the result may slightly increase Carl's subjective probability that he is cancer-free, it doesn't affect its objective probability. Neither can Carl's response be elliptical for 'That [I don't have cancer] is good', since the result doesn't prove any such thing, and Carl's subjective probability he is cancer-free could still be far below the threshold for justified belief.

Other ends may be proposed,[45] but in any case Carl seems able to say explicitly, 'It's good for my not having cancer that the test is negative', as Chuck seems able to say, 'It's good for Obama's having won the election that he gave the 2009 SOTU.'[46] But not all evidence for an (epistemically) subjective use of 'good' concerns merely signatory value. Observe also that confidence in predicating goodness often outstrips confidence and warrant for claims about objective probability. If determinism is true then nothing has ever increased the objective probability of any end *e* that doesn't actually eventuate, for example,

---

[43] Bradley 1998.

[44] His argument is that the news wouldn't be called "good" if other evidence proved the presence of cancer. But then it also wouldn't increase the subjective probability of *e* relative to the overall evidence, so this can be explained by the sensitivity of goodness/probability judgments to the fullest available information, explored in later chapters.

[45] Neither *knowing whether he has cancer* nor *knowing he is cancer-free* works; the former implies that a positive test confirming cancer would be better news, while the latter shares the problem of the original. *Raising his credence he is cancer-free* may be more promising.

[46] However, by Grice's maxim of quality saying *p* merely "increases" the probability that *e* is pragmatically odd when it's known to *guarantee* that *e*.

which was always zero.[47] But I'm far more confident that some events are good for (e.g.) our slowing the progress of global warming than I am of the disjunction: (we'll succeed at slowing global warming or determinism is false). 'Good' sentences therefore seem to harbor the same ambiguity as 'probability' sentences, making this a better definiens than 'promotion'.[48]

These different types of "probability" are sometimes taken to indicate a basic ambiguity in the word, which threatens the prospects for a unifying semantics for 'good'. But unifying treatments of objective and subjective probability are possible, and for expository purposes in this book I'll assume a simple and conservative model of this kind, though an end-relational semantics should be compatible with other models. Intuitive *classical* or *logical* theories analyze probability as a measure of a possibility-space,[49] a set of possibilities W_b defined by consistency with a partial description of a world-state which can be identified with the background b. I'll assume that every background also determines a unique measure function, or probability distribution over propositions. Rather than identifying possibilities as individual possible worlds (or completely specified world-states), I'll treat them as alternative world-state *types*, mutually exclusive partial properties of a world as individuated by b (or partitions on the set of all possible worlds consistent with b).[50] Given a finite possibility-space we can therefore talk more plainly of a *proportion* or *count* of possibilities. The probability that a die comes up 6 on a single roll is 1/6, for example, because that's the proportion of the possibilities in which that proposition is true.[51]

On this model, different kinds of probability are distinguished by how their possibility-spaces are defined.[52] Objective probabilities are measures of spaces

---

[47] By our analysis probabilities of ends can be increased even given determinism, as the compared term is counterfactual.

[48] Another reason is provided by analytic connections with 'ought' and 'reason' (e.g., what you *ought* or have *most reason* to choose is also the *best* choice), which we'll see have both objective and subjective senses too.

[49] E.g., LaPlace 1814, Carnap 1950, and see discussion in Hájek 2011.

[50] (Or partitions on the set of possible worlds consistent with b.) The thought is that a background determines how finely the possibilities are individuated; e.g., an objective background such as *given the actual state of the world at t* generates a set of maximally fine-grained possibilities, while a subjective background such as *given what s believes* generates a set of possibilities individuated only as finely as s's beliefs permit. So if A knows only that B is going to choose a number between two and twelve, then her epistemic probability that B chooses seven is 1/11, as each choice occupies an equal portion of possibility-space. But if she knows that B is going to choose by rolling two six-sided dice, then the probability is 1/6, because B's dice rolls add to seven in 6 of the 36 different possibilities she can discriminate. This model relies on the Principle of Indifference; wherever there is reason to think some possibilities are more likely than others they can be individuated more finely with unidentified variables.

[51] Relative to information that the die has a specific bias the proportion is no longer 1/6, though relative to information merely that the die isn't fair the proportion remains 1/6.

[52] This implies a contextualist account of speech about probability as implicitly relativistic, which faces objections analogous to those discussed for normative language in Chapters 5–8; parallel pragmatic solutions will apply.

defined by reference to the objective state of the world; for example, the ways things could unfold from time t given the world's actual state at t. Subjective probabilities are measures of spaces defined by reference to what somebody knows (epistemic probability) or believes (doxastic probability)—and are distinct from her *credences*, which are her perceptions or estimations of subjective probability.

By our theory, a use of 'It's good for e if p, given b' compares the measure of (b & p) possibilities in which e against the measure of (b & $\sim p$) possibilities in which e, whether these are objective or subjective probabilities. Judgments of objective goodness typically involve comparison with the probability of events unfolding in certain ways (e.g., the home team's winning the game) had some event not occurred (e.g., the pass not being intercepted), however the relevant counterfactual space is conceived (e.g., allowing causal indeterminacy, minimal changes to history, or local miracles). Judgments of subjective goodness involve comparisons with the subjective probability of states of affairs (e.g., Carl's being free of cancer) given different evidence or beliefs (e.g., if the test result were positive). The unified meaning of 'It's good for e if p' can be illustrated as in Figure 2.1.

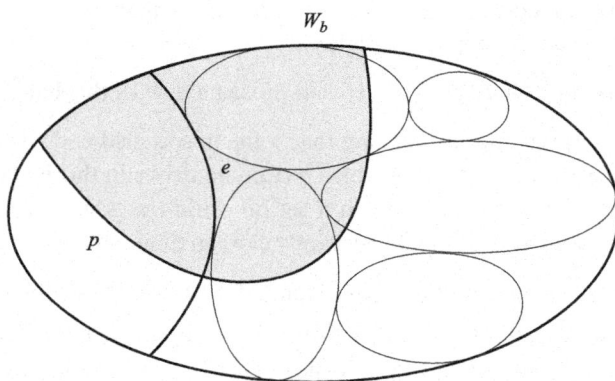

FIGURE 2.1 'p is good for e'

Shading represents possibilities in which e, and the smaller circles in the *not-p* space are included (optionally) to represent different possible ways of realizing *not-p* consistent with b. This diagram's essential feature for illustrating the meaning of 'good' is that e holds in a greater measure of the p space than of the *not-p* space, even if not of all *not-p* partitions: p needn't be best to be good.[53]

Examining the various ways 'good' is relativized and complementized leads to a unifying logical form $G_{e,b}(p)$ that accommodates many different ordinary uses. Identifying this form made it easy to identify and analyze a unified

---

[53] Formally, the definition G-ER is equivalent to $|W_{(b\&p\&e)}| / |W_{(b\&p)}| > |W_{(b\&\sim p\&e)}| / |W_{(b\&\sim p)}|$.

conceptual meaning that is plausibly constitutive of semantic competence with the word: that p increases the probability of an end e relative to a background b. This end-relational theory is only fully unifying, of course, if it can also be extended to the philosophically important uses of 'good' we've so far ignored, which may be reasonably doubted. Before addressing these challenges we'll investigate the ordinary uses of some other central normative words.

Appendix: The Goodness of Objects

The comparative character of our end-relational semantics for 'good' provides resources for accommodating the common intuition that the goodness of objects is often prior to and explanatory of the goodness of states of affairs, despite my claim that 'good' is fundamentally a predicate of propositions p rather than of objects n. On this theory, 'good that p' semantically compares a set of p world-states with a set of *not-p* world-states, which must be restricted somehow. It appears that speakers ordinarily exploit the subject movement and ellipsis exhibited by 'n is good' sentences to indicate intended dimensions of comparison.

Take the awkwardly explicit sentence,

(12)   'It is good that Ronald drives in those nails with this hammer.'

The theory interprets this as meaning that some unspecified end e is more likely relative to a set of world-states in which p (Ronald drives in those nails with this hammer) than it would be relative to a set of world-states in which *not-p*. But world-states in which *not-p* can be relevantly close in different ways. Contrast

(12a)   'This hammer is good, [for Ronald to drive in those nails with].'

(12b)   'Those nails are good, [for Ronald to drive in with this hammer].'

(12c)   'Ronald is good, [for those nails to be driven in by with this hammer].'

(12d)   'Driving in those nails is good, [for Ronald to do with this hammer].'

Is the speaker comparing world-states where Ronald drives in the nails with something other than *this hammer*? This is the natural reading of (12a), which has 'this hammer' as the grammatical subject. Is she comparing world-states where Ronald drives in something other than *those nails* with the hammer? This is the natural reading of (12b), with the grammatical subject 'those nails'. Sentence (12c) suggests comparison with world-states where someone other than *Ronald* drives in the nails with the hammer, and (12d) suggests comparison with world-states where Ronald does something with the hammer other than *driving in those nails*.

Consider (12a) as an instance of the form C1, 'n is good.' Since the world-state w_p differs from the relevantly contrasting *not-p* world-states only in the involvement of the hammer rather than other possible tools, there is an important truth in the claim that the goodness is here a property of the hammer itself. If the state of affairs p is better than a state of affairs q that contrasts merely by the use of some other tool, then the greater value of p over q is entirely due to properties of the hammer, like its weight, dimensions, and balance, which are here the *good-making* properties.[54] These ordinary non-normative properties of the hammer can therefore be helpfully described as its "goodness"; so too can the good-making properties of boats, chocolate, Albéniz's compositions, etc. be described as their "goodness". This is the kind of substantive use that at the start of the chapter we observed leading synthetic naturalist and indexical theories astray.

---

[54] A distinction between *intrinsic* and *extrinsic* value (as distinct from the final/instrumental distinction; see Korsgaard 1983, and further discussion in Chapter 7) might be accommodated by contrasting good-makers that are intrinsic properties of objects (e.g., melodic and harmonic qualities of Albéniz's compositions), from those that are extrinsic properties (e.g., being a gift from a deceased grandmother).

{ 3 }

The Probable Meaning of 'Ought'

Whereas 'good' is our most general normative adjective, 'ought' is our most general normative verb. Skepticism about analytic reduction in metaethics is therefore often expressed by denying the analyzability of 'ought': "no definition can break out of the normative circle, a circle of ought-like terms."[1] A related doctrine is known as "Hume's Law" due to the famous passage,

> As this ought, or ought not, expresses some new relation and affirmation, 'tis necessary that it shou'd be observ'd and explain'd and at the same time that a reason should be given; for what seems altogether inconceivable, how this new relation can be a deduction from others, which are entirely different from it. (*Treatise* III.i.1)

This skepticism is motivated primarily by the kinds of use characteristic of moral speech, in so-called categorical imperatives like 'Children ought to respect their elders.' But the word also has many other, ordinary kinds of uses, including *epistemic* or "predictive" uses (e.g., 'It ought to rain tomorrow'), *functional* uses (e.g., 'Anchors ought to be heavy', 'Jokes ought to be funny'), and *instrumental* uses or so-called hypothetical imperatives, (e.g., 'If Max wants to evade arrest, then he ought to mingle with the crowd'). When noticed at all, one or another of these is commonly dismissed as merely due to lexical ambiguity, and so irrelevant to metaethics.

However, the simplest semantics would identify a single meaning underlying all uses. This chapter seeks a unifying compositional semantics for ordinary uses of 'ought', as well as kindred verbs like 'should', 'must', 'have to', 'may', 'might', 'could', and 'can', deferring discussion of the metaethically puzzling uses. My strategy will be to focus on instrumental uses as key to a unifying reductive analysis, since they have widely been considered to be both normative in some way and reducible. I'll argue that the linguistic evidence leads to a unifying modal semantics for 'ought' in terms of comparative probability.

---

[1] Gibbard 2003: 6.

Normative senses of these words aren't due to lexical ambiguity but are generated compositionally from use of the same verbs in end-relational sentences.

3.1. The Problem with Instrumental Conditionals

Consider an instrumental conditional like

(1)   'If Max wants to evade arrest, then he ought to mingle with the crowd.'

(These are commonly called "hypothetical imperatives" by philosophers and "anankastic conditionals" by linguists, but both labels are misleading.)[2] Even while rejecting reductive analysis of the categorical 'ought', philosophers haven't traditionally been skeptical about the analyzability of this instrumental 'ought'. Kant, Wittgenstein, and J. L. Mackie all accepted that instrumental 'ought' sentences express "natural" facts, for example, while holding that moral or categorical uses of 'ought' have an irreducibly "nonnatural" meaning. But because these instrumental uses are agreed to be intuitively normative, a skepticism about their analyzability has recently emerged. Reversing the traditional view, writers comfortable with a categorical normative 'ought' (perhaps expressing a primitive relation or an imperative) today sometimes view the instrumental use as the puzzling case due to its stubborn resistance to assimilation by the categorical 'ought'.[3]

The basic difficulty consists in a *detaching problem*. Instrumental conditionals like (1) have the grammatical form

IC1:   'If *s* wants to ψ, then *s* ought to φ',

and so on their surface appear to be ordinary indicative conditionals of the form *if p then q*. But if they were, they should license inference by modus ponens: accepting the conditional together with the antecedent *p* commits one to accepting the detached consequent, *q*. Compare (1) with 'If Max wants to evade arrest, then he ought to consider how it would hurt his family.' As naturally interpreted this sentence does license modus ponens, but despite having the form IC1 it isn't an instrumental conditional, since φ-ing doesn't stand in an instrumental relation to ψ-ing. By contrast, genuine instrumental conditionals like (1) apparently don't license such inferences as generally valid, as illustrated by cases where φ-ing would be either unwise or wicked. Somebody who asserts

---

[2] After Kant and G. H. von Wright, respectively. (a) Their mood is declarative rather than imperative; contrast 'Max ought to mingle with the crowd' with 'Mingle with the crowd, Max!'; I discuss their credentials as imperatives in Chapters 5 and 7. (b) 'Anankastic' is from the Greek for *necessity*, but a necessity verb isn't necessary or sufficient for a conditional to be instrumental.

[3] E.g., Hampton 1998, Shafer-Landau 2003, Beardman 2007.

(1) and then discovers that Max indeed wants to evade arrest needn't necessarily accept 'Max ought to mingle with the crowd', because she may know that Max's evading arrest would hurt his family, for example, and therefore that Max ought not to evade arrest or take any steps toward it. Philosophers have attempted to solve this detaching problem by dismissing some part of the linguistic data as misleading. Here I'll canvass four different strategies offered in the literature.

First, some writers deny there really is any detaching problem: instrumental conditionals do license modus ponens.[4] Speakers may often assert instrumental conditionals when p is true and q is false, like (1), but these conditionals are simply false. An instrumental conditional is only true when φ-ing and ψ-ing themselves are neither unwise nor wicked, or else an intolerable form of "bootstrapping" would follow: given that modus ponens is a universally valid law of inference, and that doing whatever one ought to do is always justified, an agent could make any action justified just by desiring an end for which it is the means, regardless of how unwise or wicked either means or end is. A first criterion for successful analysis of instrumental conditionals is therefore:

> *No Bootstrapping*:   Desiring an end isn't sufficient to justify action
> aimed at it.

This strategy dismisses ordinary practices of asserting and accepting instrumental conditionals even when φ-ing or ψ-ing is unwise or wicked, as mistaken. They are suggested to be just careless talk resulting from incorrectly assuming that ψ-ing or φ-ing aren't unwise or wicked.[5] But this is implausible; the following sentence seems no less assertable than (1), for example, if an instrumental reading is stipulated:

> (2)   'If Henry wants to become a famous mass murderer then he ought to
> kill as many people as he can.'

An ordinary speaker asserting (2) surely isn't overlooking the wickedness of this desire. Somebody could intelligibly say,

> (2a)   'Henry ought not to want to become a famous mass murderer, of
> course. But if he wants to become one then he ought to kill as many
> people as he can.'

Even after conceding that s ought neither to φ nor to ψ (or want to ψ), we still recognize instrumental conditionals like (1) and (2) as expressing some kind of truth. This provides a second criterion for a successful analysis:

---

[4] E.g., Hill 1973, Korsgaard 1997, Hampton 1998, Thomson 2008: 179–85.

[5] Thomson 2008: 183. Another suggestion is that these claims are all understood suppositionally; i.e., 'Supposing it wasn't unwise or wicked, . . .'

Moral Insensitivity: For all agents *s* and all ends of ψ-ing however unwise or wicked, if *s* is able to ψ there is some (possibly disjunctive) action φ of which the instrumental conditional 'If *s* wants to ψ, then *s* ought to φ' is true.

Combining this with *No Bootstrapping* requires rejecting this first response to the problem, and so a third criterion can be derived:

Nondetachability: Instrumental conditionals don't license inference by modus ponens.

This isn't to deny that the consequent can be inferred in some contexts, only that modus ponens holds for instrumental conditionals as a general law of validity.

A second response dismisses the grammar of instrumental conditionals as deceiving us about logical form. Whereas the grammatical form IC1 suggests 'ought' has narrow scope relative to the conditional, logically it has *wide scope:* instead of

NS: $p \to O(r)$

at the level of logical form we have

WS: $O(p \to r)$.[6]

I'll assume, controversially, that 'ought' expresses a propositional operator (this is defended in the appendix). WS is logically equivalent to $O(r \lor \sim p)$, so (1) is thereby interpreted as meaning that it ought to be that either Max mingles with the crowd or he doesn't want to evade arrest. This accommodates *Nondetachability*; from (i) it ought to be that either Max mingles with the crowd or he doesn't want to evade arrest, and (ii) Max wants to evade arrest, it doesn't follow by modus ponens that (iii) Max ought to mingle with the crowd, since he could also comply with (i) by not wanting to evade arrest. As it is precisely in cases of unwise or wicked desires that we balk at detaching from instrumental conditionals, this is an attractive result.

An initial problem is that this predicts that ordinary instrumental conditionals like (1) and (2) are likely false. Everybody has conflicting desires, and since desiring something doesn't compel any attempt to get it, it's far from evident that agents ought not to want ends whenever they fail to adopt the means. Suppose the only way Max can be at his daughter's wedding is by evading arrest; it doesn't plausibly follow that if he wisely chooses not to evade arrest he ought to stop *wanting* to be at the wedding. If he did he'd rather be defective as a father and a human being; he ought rather to continue wanting it, and consequently regret his absence. On the other hand, if Max doesn't pursue the

---

[6] E.g., Hill 1973, Greenspan 1975, Dancy 1977, Gensler 1985, Broome 1999, 2001, 2002, 2005, Wallace 2001, Way 2010. Here '*r*' is the prejacent of '*q*'.

means, then intuitively he ought not to continue *intending* the end. Many writers therefore dismiss an additional piece of the linguistic data, claiming that by 'wants' we here really mean *intends*.[7]

Even with this modification, wide-scope accounts don't provide plausible analyses of ordinary instrumental conditionals.[8] WS has a symmetry that instrumental conditionals lack: it offers two options without favor (either φ or don't want/intend to ψ), whereas an instrumental conditional seems rather to recommend φ-ing (in some weak manner) on condition of having the goal of ψ-ing.[9] The wide-scope interpretation therefore seems too *weak*. Consider again the intelligibility of (2a), which read as wide-scope has the logical form $O(\sim p)$ & $O(r \lor \sim p)$. The second conjunct (e.g., that Henry ought either to get an automatic weapon or not want to become a famous mass murderer) is weaker or less informative than the first, which makes it peculiar both that the speaker appropriately uses the conjunction 'but' (which semantically indicates tension between the conjuncts), and that the speaker goes on to utter the conditional at all. This provides a fourth criterion:

Logical Strength: 'If *s* wants to ψ, then *s* ought to φ' isn't logically weaker than '*s* ought not to want to ψ.'

A third response offers a variation on wide-scoping, by appealing to ambiguity in the categorical 'ought' between a practical sense (what ought to be *done*) and an "epistemic" or *doxastic* sense (what ought to be *believed*).[10] This turns on the "cognitivist" theory that intending to φ is or involves a special kind of belief that one will φ.[11] Kieran Setiya proposes the following interpretation of instrumental conditionals:

'You ought (if you intend to ψ and believe that you will ψ only if you φ-because-you-now-intend-to-φ, believe that you are going to φ because you now intend to φ).'[12]

This is inspired by the observation that if you believe both that you will ψ and that you will ψ only if you φ, then you rationally ought to believe that you will

---

[7] But see Condoravdi & Lauer 2014.

[8] They may rather be taken as merely concerning the logical form of abstract principles of practical rationality, in which guise they aren't relevant here. I argue against principles of instrumental rationality in my 2009c.

[9] For this and related concerns see, e.g., Schroeder 2004, Kolodny 2005, Setiya 2007, Price 2008. Another objection raised is that wide-scoping fails to escape the detaching problem because absurd 'ought' claims can be detached from WS in certain conditions, e.g., when *s* is unable to not want to ψ. But as Mike Ridge observes, wide-scopers could explore pragmatic solutions.

[10] 'Epistemic ought' is used ambiguously to refer either to what I've called the *predictive* 'ought', or to what I'm here calling the *doxastic* 'ought'.

[11] See Harman 1976, Velleman 1989, Wallace 2001, Ross 2009.

[12] Setiya 2007: 669; for clarity I've substituted 'ought' for 'should', and 'φ' and 'ψ' for 'do E' and 'do M'.

φ. Besides disregarding the grammatical narrow scope of 'ought' and the use of 'wants', this strategy also dismisses the datum that ordinary instrumental conditionals address what agents ought to do (e.g., '...Max ought to *mingle with the crowd*') rather than what they ought to believe or intend, and postulates a second psychological condition in the antecedent ('...if you intend to ψ *and believe that you will ψ only if you φ*...') of which there is no trace in ordinary instrumental conditionals.

This doxastic interpretation avoids the wide-scoper's problem with *Logical Strength*; if 'ought' means something different in (2) than in 'Henry ought not to want to become a famous mass murderer', this explains why (2a) isn't oddly redundant. It may also fare better with *No Bootstrapping*, as it doesn't involve the practical sense of 'ought' relevant to justifying action. But as well as depending on a controversial theory of intention, it fails in two crucial respects as a plausible analysis. First, because it turns essentially on φ-ing being believed to be a *necessary* means to ψ-ing, it fails to account for more common cases concerning merely the instrumentally *best* means. Max's believing he will successfully evade arrest doesn't necessarily put him under pressure to believe he will mingle with the crowd if he believes this to be only one of many means. Second, because it conditionalizes on the agent's *believing* φ to be a necessary means to ψ-ing, it yields wrong predictions about the use of these sentences. If Max falsely believes that hiding in the cloak closet is the only means to evading arrest, while we know that mingling with the crowd is actually the only means, then we'd say (1), and not 'If Max wants to evade arrest, he ought to hide in the cloak closet.' If someone were to say the latter to Max as he tries to evade arrest, he could later justly accuse them of deceiving him. This yields fifth and sixth criteria:

Necessity Isn't Necessary: It's sufficient for the truth of an instrumental 'ought' sentence that φ-ing is merely the instrumentally best means to ψ-ing and not also a necessary means.

Belief Insensitivity: The truth of instrumental conditionals needn't be sensitive to *s*'s beliefs about the means to ψ-ing.

A fourth response seeks to avoid the problems facing wide-scoping by dismissing instead the use of 'ought' in instrumental conditionals. By 'ought' we allegedly mean a weaker normative relation, like *has some reason to*, which must be weighed against other reasons to determine what ought to be done.[13] So (1) is used to mean that if Max wants to evade arrest then he has some reason to mingle with the crowd. This view supposedly has the virtues of respecting *No Bootstrapping*, since merely having some reason to φ is too weak to imply justification to φ, and thereby also respecting *Nondetachability*, since nothing

---

[13] See Mackie 1977: 74–75, Schroeder 2004, van Roojen ms.

about what an agent genuinely ought to do follows by modus ponens from such conditionals. This strategy treats wanting something as a sufficient condition for having some reason to adopt means to it, and therefore has the logical form NS and avoids the problems of wide-scoping.

This solution is also unsatisfactory, however. First, it may merely exchange one bootstrapping problem for another, as it's reasonably doubted whether wanting something is sufficient for having a reason to pursue it.[14] Second, the detaching problem mightn't genuinely be evaded. If speakers are happy to use 'ought' in this loose way in instrumental conditionals, it's odd that they would suddenly become scrupulous when asserting the consequent. More signifi-cantly, this strategy misses the normative *stringency* of instrumental condition-als, which seem to indicate that there is something inadvisable (in a weakly instrumental sense) with s's not φ-ing if s wants to ψ.[15] Failing to do what one has some reason to do isn't sufficient for acting inadvisably; the reason must also not be outweighed. When φ-ing is a necessary means to ψ-ing, even stron-ger language is naturally used (e.g., 'If Max wants to evade arrest, he *has to* mingle with the crowd'), but it's even less plausible that 'have to' or 'must' is used to mean *has some reason*.[16]

These ordinary instrumental uses of 'ought' therefore pose a difficult puz-zle. But following rather than dismissing the linguistic evidence will lead to a semantically unifying and reductive solution that satisfies all six criteria we've derived.

3.2. Semantics for Modals

Attending to the linguistic data, we should notice immediately that 'ought' is only one of a family of verbs, including 'should', 'must', 'have to', 'may', 'might', 'could', and 'can', which can meaningfully be substituted into instrumental conditionals (as well as the other kinds of 'ought' sentences we observed); for example,

(3)   'If Max wants to evade arrest, then he could mingle with the crowd.'

(4)   'If Max wants to evade arrest, then he has to mingle with the crowd.'

A semantic analysis of instrumental conditionals must also account for these other words, which therefore provide clues to the meaning of 'ought'. I'll

---

[14] Schroeder (2007: 92–97) argues that denials of reasons are unreliable, since admitting 'some reason' pragmatically indicates *significant* reasons (i.e., worth mentioning). But then it's odd that there is no similar reticence with instrumental conditionals despite use of the stronger 'ought'.

[15] Schroeder 2009a makes this point in disowning his 2004 view.

[16] See also Setiya 2007.

temporarily shift focus to 'must', 'may', and their near synonyms like 'has to' and 'might', which are simpler to analyze.

These words are used with a wide variety of different surface senses. The senses of 'must', for example, include the *logical* (what is entailed), the *epistemic* (what is guaranteed by the evidence), the *nomic* (what is dictated by the laws of nature), the *circumstantial* (what is inevitable given the state of the world at some time), the *legal* (what is prescribed by law), the *prudential* (what is vital for one's well-being), and the *moral* (what is obligatory). A unifying semantics for this family of verbs must therefore identify a core meaning for each with the flexibility to generate the full range of its different senses

There are compelling reasons to expect that a substantially unifying theory is correct. First, the senses are too numerous for lexical ambiguity. 'Must' seems to have indefinitely many possible senses, since even some of the types listed are indefinitely divisible: what must epistemically be the case varies relative to different people or evidence, what must legally be the case varies relative to legal codes, what must inevitably be the case may vary relative to times, and so on. Second, these differences in sense are systematic across this vocabulary, indicating an underlying unity.[17] Third, this systematicity isn't peculiar to English but is robustly cross-linguistic.[18]

By orthodoxy and with great success, these different senses have been identified as involving different kinds of modality, or possibility and necessity. In the case of 'must', being *entailed, guaranteed, dictated, inevitable, prescribed, vital,* and *obligatory* are all different ways of being necessary. Linguists and logicians therefore treat normative senses of these modal auxiliary verbs as expressing some normative kind of modality, which is the unifying, simple, and conservative hypothesis we should pursue. Arguably the most conservative course would be just to adopt the influential theory in linguistics due to Angelika Kratzer and David Lewis.[19] However, we'll see that the Lewis-Kratzer semantics encounters problems, including with instrumental conditionals, that can be avoided by an even simpler theory.

Following standard treatments, these modal verbs can be analyzed as quantifying over possibilities (which I'll again view as world-state types). Necessity modals like 'must' and 'have to' mean roughly *in all possibilities*, while possibility modals like 'may', 'might', 'can', and 'could' mean roughly *in some possibilities*. The simplest way of generating different senses of modality is then by defining or restricting the possibility-space in different ways; to be nomologically

---

[17] Some of these verbs have lexically dedicated modal senses; 'needs to' seems restricted to normative uses, 'would' mostly to counterfactual uses, etc. But virtually any can have normative use, including ability verbs (like 'can') and epistemic verbs; while 'might' is often said to be exclusively epistemic (e.g., Portner 2009, Hacquard 2011), observe the normative flavor of mild advice available for 'If Max wants to evade arrest, he might mingle with the crowd.'

[18] See Palmer 1986, and comparative data in von Fintel & Iatridou 2008.

[19] Lewis 1975, Kratzer 1977, 1981.

(scientifically) possible is to be true in some possibilities consistent with the laws of nature, to be epistemically possible for s is to be true in some of the possibilities consistent with s's evidence, and so on. Normative modalities would therefore also be distinguished by how their domains are defined.

The simplest semantics with this combination of unity and flexibility would be *dyadic*, positing just one more argument-place in the logical form of modal verbs that functions to define a possibility-space. Following the simple model from Chapter 2, this can be identified again as a background b; the general logical form of modal auxiliary verbs can then be represented as $verb_b(p)$. The common semantic contribution of any modal auxiliary will be the quantificational operation it performs on the space W_b with p. This provides simple definitions for the necessity and possibility verbs 'must' and 'may':

$must_b(p)$:   In all possibilities in W_b, p.

$may_b(p)$:   In some possibilities in W_b, p.

Different *kinds* of backgrounds can be specified with adverbial modifiers like 'logically', 'epistemically', 'legally', 'counterfactually', and 'morally', but at least many of these are vague, as there are many different ways of being (e.g.) epistemically, legally, or counterfactually possible. As before, backgrounds can be explicated more precisely with a 'given...' phrase; for example, 'given the Pomona city bylaws', 'given what we then believed'.

Some kinds of modality are defined by systems of laws or rules; for example, nomological modality ('given the laws of nature'). The classic "Kanger-Anderson reduction" analyzes deontic (i.e., moral and legal) modality as quantifying over domains defined by consistency with a set of moral or legal laws; that is, over possibilities in which all the laws are obeyed.[20] But modals are commonly restricted also by particular states of affairs; for example, in circumstantial modalities (what *could* happen tomorrow, given what happened today). This also holds of most ordinary normative claims: whether you may drive home from work depends on whether you've been drinking, for example, and whether you ought to apologize depends on what you've done.

Both kinds of background restrictions can be accommodated together by identifying laws or rules as *general* propositions. The natural law of the conservation of motion, for example, is just the proposition that for every object x, the momentum of x remains the same unless subjected to an external force, and the Pomona city ordinance requiring registration of cats is the proposition that if x is a resident of Pomona, then if x owns a cat it is registered. The background b is an (often complex) partial description or sketch of a world-state; informally, $must_b(p)$ simply means that p is true in all ways of filling in the remaining details, and $may_b(p)$ simply means that p is true in some of those ways.

---

[20] Kanger 1957, Anderson 1958; see discussion in McNamara 2006. Like Kratzer's, this account isn't reductive in our strong sense, defining normative spaces with normative terms.

This yields an extremely flexible semantics for modals, supporting speech or thought about possibilities defined by whatever consistent set of propositions or incomplete sketch of the world one has in mind. We'll appeal to this flexibility to avoid various problems that motivate the greater complexity of other semantics, like Kratzer's, which are designed partly to address cases involving *inconsistent* restrictions on a possibility-space. Consider for example the Good Samaritan Paradox, concerning the moral truth that one ought to aid a victim of robbery.[21] Our semantics won't interpret this as meaning that in all possibilities where the moral laws are obeyed one goes to the aid of a robbery victim (since given such a background there are no robberies), but rather as assuming a consistent background like *given the actual state of the world at t_1 and that you yourself act at t_2 as the moral law prescribes.*

This flexibility raises issues about how an audience successfully interprets a modal claim when the background isn't explicit, but notice that even explicit qualifiers typically underdetermine the intended background and rely heavily on an implicit or assumed background, b_0. Explicit 'given b_1' qualifiers are generally used as elliptical for 'given b_1 [and b_0]'. Counterfactual uses illustrate this clearly; consider 'His baseball team couldn't have won, if Aramis hadn't reached base.' We previously saw that 'if Aramis hadn't reached base' underdetermines the intended set of counterfactual world-states, which presumably don't include possibilities where Aramis isn't even on the team. We'll begin to explore the pragmatic answers to these issues in earnest in Chapter 5.

An immediate benefit of this flexible semantics is a simple, unifying solution to a controversy over whether what an agent ought to do depends on the *facts* or on her *beliefs* (or *evidence*). Consider:

> *Deal or No Deal*: A game show contestant holds a suitcase that he knows contains either $1 or $1,000,000. He has to choose between taking its contents or accepting the Banker's miserly offer of $50,000. The case actually contains $1.

What ought the contestant to do? On one hand, it's intuitive to say that he ought to take the suitcase. It would be crazy to give up an even chance at $1,000,000 for merely $50,000, after all. On the other hand, it's intuitive (for anyone who knows the contents of the suitcase) to say that he ought to accept the offer, which is what anyone in a position to offer advice should tell him. The presence of such an adviser may change the contestant's subjective situation, of course, but this doesn't account for the insensitivity of appropriate advice to the agent's beliefs or evidence. Even if the adviser thinks that the agent's beliefs/evidence will continue to favor φ-ing despite her intervention, she still should base her 'ought' claims on the facts if she knows them; for example, 'I know

---

[21] Åqvist 1967.

you don't have any reason to believe me, but you really ought to φ.' In any case, if the contestant takes the suitcase he may well himself say, after discovering he has won a measly $1, 'I ought to have accepted the offer.' (We'll examine such cases more closely in Chapter 8.)

A common and natural response to this dilemma is to postulate an ambiguity between an objective sense of 'ought' that is sensitive to the facts, and a subjective (or "rational") sense of 'ought' that is sensitive to what an agent believes (or knows).[22] But a variation on the scenario shows these two senses to be insufficient:

> *Deal or No Deal—Revised*: The contestant holds two suitcases, one of which contains $1 and the other $1,000,000. He has to choose between taking either one of these cases or the banker's offer, which he has been told is $50,000 but the audience knows to be actually $750,000.[23]

Subjectively, the contestant ought to choose one of the two cases. Objectively, he ought to choose whichever case contains $1,000,000. But the audience can plausibly judge, and if possible advise him, that he ought to accept the banker's offer, even though they know this isn't what he subjectively or objectively ought to do. Rather it seems to be a different subjective sense sensitive to *their* beliefs or evidence.

This suggests a need for a different sense of 'ought' for every different background of information, what Frank Jackson calls an "annoying profusion" of senses:

> I think that we have no alternative but to recognize a whole range of oughts—what she ought to do by the light of her beliefs at the time of action, what she ought to do by the lights of what she later establishes..., what she ought to do by the lights of one or another onlooker who has different information on the subject, and...what she ought to do by God's lights.[24]

These words couldn't have indefinitely many distinct meanings, and our simple dyadic semantics provides a straightforward way of unifying the different senses by appealing to different values for *b* (as we did with 'good'). Circumstantial modalities are defined by reference to some factual background (e.g., *given what actually happened before*). Epistemic and doxastic modalities are defined

---

[22] Ewing 1953. Kolodny & MacFarlane's survey (ms) identifies Moore 1903, 1912, Thomson 1986, 1990 as arguing for a univocally objective 'ought', and Ross 1939, Pritchard 1949, Scanlon 2001, and Jackson 1991, 1997 as arguing for the existence of a subjective 'ought'.

[23] Structurally similar scenarios are discussed by Regan 1980, Jackson 1991, Ross 2006, Kolodny & MacFarlane ms, and others.

[24] Jackson 1991: 472–73.

by reference to a subjective background (e.g., *given what is known or believed by s*). A detective who says of a missing person, 'He might still be alive' can be speaking the truth even if the person is in fact, and so by circumstantial necessity, already dead.

Differences between objective and subjective normative 'ought' claims can therefore be explained without lexical ambiguity by interpreting objective senses of 'ought' ('must', 'may', etc.) as relativized to a mixed circumstantial-normative background, and subjective senses as relativized to a mixed epistemic- or doxastic-normative background. But we still need an explanation of what makes a background, and thereby a modal sentence, normative.

3.3. Modal Analysis of Instrumental Conditionals

If 'ought' and its relatives are modal verbs, then instrumental conditionals are apparently some kind of modal conditional. This suggests the conservative approach of applying the standard Kratzerian analysis of modal conditionals of the form 'If p then *verb q*.' According to this, the conditional 'if p' updates an implicit preliminary background b_0, making the background b the conjunction $(p \ \& \ b_0)$, which restricts the space of possibilities to those consistent with both p and b_0.[25] In other words, 'if p' is just a variant on 'given p', and a way of qualifying modal claims by partially specifying a background.

At first glance this approach to IC1 sentences like (4), 'If Max wants to evade arrest, then he has to mingle with the crowd', doesn't seem to fare much better with our criteria than the other strategies we surveyed. By *Moral Insensitivity*, an instrumental conditional is true whenever the action of φ-ing is a necessary means to the desired end of ψ-ing, but from no plausible background assumption b_0 does it follow that merely *desiring* an end necessitates taking the means to it. Since these conditionals are intuitively normative it might be suggested that b_0 includes some instrumental norm requiring agents always to take means to their desired ends. But as agents commonly have conflicting desires that preclude joint satisfaction, no such norm is plausible even as a merely instrumental principle, and would imply an absurd violation of *No Bootstrapping*. The criterion of *Nondetachability* also seems to be violated: since b_0 must be contextually salient, accepting (4) should license detaching 'Max has to mingle with the crowd' in a context upon learning that he indeed wants to evade arrest.

However, looking at a wider range of linguistic data should make us notice that IC1, 'If s wants...' sentences aren't the only ordinary ways of formulating instrumental conditionals. Consider:

---

[25] Kratzer 1979, 1986, developing a suggestion in Lewis 1975.

(5) 'If Max is going to evade arrest, then he has to mingle with the crowd.'

(6) 'In order to evade arrest, Max has to mingle with the crowd.'

These express intuitively very similar thoughts; at least, their modal consequents have the same instrumentally normative sense.[26] A thorough account of
instrumental conditionals must therefore also account for the forms,

IC2: 'If s is going to ψ, then s ought to φ.'

IC3: 'In order to ψ, s ought to φ.'

I'll argue next that our semantics supports a simple compositional analysis of
IC2 sentences in particular, which provides a reductive explanation of their
normative sense in terms of their distinctive *temporal* structure. I'll then argue
that this is a key to analyzing also IC1 and IC3 sentences. After that we'll
address the troublesome reference to desires in IC1 sentences like (4), and then
return to the issue of what 'ought' means in particular.

Many writers have observed that IC2 sentences are amenable to analysis as
ordinary modal conditionals, the antecedent functioning normally to update
an ordinary (circumstantial or epistemic) background with the antecedent's
proposition.[27] Sentence (5) can be read as meaning roughly that in all possibilities where Max evades arrest he mingles with the crowd, for example, or as
equivalent to

(5a) 'Max only evades arrest if he mingles with the crowd.'

Similarly plausible readings are available for possibility verbs. If mingling
with the crowd is merely one of many possible means to evade arrest then one
can say,

(7) 'If Max is going to evade arrest, he may/could/might mingle with the
crowd',

which is naturally read as meaning that in some possibilities in which Max
evades arrest he mingles with the crowd.

This approach faces a couple of objections that are easily addressed. First,
a necessity conditional like (5) might be accepted despite the existence of other
possibilities, for example, if Max could alternatively evade arrest by jumping
out an open window and falling to his death. But we can simply appeal to the
implicit assumptions b_0 and the ordinary imprecision or ellipsis in describing
the intended background.[28] A speaker asserting (4)–(6), or (5a) itself, may just

---

[26] Other forms are 'If Max *is to* evade arrest ...', a contraction of (5), and '*To* evade arrest ...',
a contraction of (6).

[27] E.g., Bech 1955, von Wright 1963: 10f, Sloman 1970, Sæbø 2001, Broome 2001, von Stechow
et al. 2006, von Fintel & Iatridou 2005, Huitink 2005.

[28] Cf. Kratzer 1979, 1986.

assume further restrictions such as '...without seriously injuring himself', or could just be ignoring some less salient possibilities. As this predicts, somebody asserting (5) does seem obliged to qualify or retract her claim if pressed with such possibilities.

Second, a possibility conditional like (7) (or a necessity conditional) might be accepted despite various *psychological* barriers. Suppose Max is disposed not to mingle with the crowd, for example; perhaps he believes incorrectly that hiding in the cloak closet is the only possible means of evading arrest, or has severe agoraphobia, in which case it mightn't be true that he mingles with the crowd in some possibilities in which he evades arrest. This violates *Belief Insensitivity*, which is plausibly generalized into a criterion of *Psychological Insensitivity*: dispositions of this kind don't in general affect the truth-conditions of instrumental conditionals. But as instrumental claims are generally concerned only with what is possible or necessary *given an agent's external circumstances*, the backgrounds can be expected to exclude information about the agent's psychology (though not necessarily in every case).[29]

This analysis has the virtue of satisfying several of our criteria: *No Bootstrapping* (this 'must' doesn't entail any robust kind of justification), *Moral Insensitivity* (necessary conditions on ψ-ing hold regardless of their wisdom or morality), and *Belief Insensitivity* (whether s believes φ-ing is necessary for ψ-ing is irrelevant, unless a background defined by s's beliefs is assumed). But it remains incomplete. So far we've invoked only general features of modal conditionals, but as most modal conditionals don't have the intuitively normative sense of IC2 and other instrumental conditionals, this sense remains unexplained. Additionally, instrumental conditionals have distinctive grammatical features that need explaining. I'll now argue that compositional analysis of these features identifies what is missing from the analysis, and that the normative sense of these conditionals is explained by the same features (of temporal structure) that distinguish them as instrumental.

3.4. Tense and Sense

Grammatically, instrumental conditionals require special characteristics of *tense* on the modal verb in the consequent, and *aspect* in the antecedent,

---

[29] Kratzer makes a similar point regarding ability modals like 'can' (1981: 53). Another objection, about irrelevant necessities (e.g., 'If Max is going to evade arrest, then the square root of 4 has to be 2'), receives a standard pragmatic solution: speakers are expected not to utter a conditional if they can say something logically stronger (and more efficient), so it indicates that the speaker takes the consequent's truth to depend on the antecedent somehow, and is infelicitous otherwise.

distinguishing them from other modal conditionals.[30] Consider first the consequent. The availability of normative senses (both instrumental and noninstrumental) of modal auxiliaries is partly controlled by tense. Contrast

(8a) 'Macbeth had to slay Duncan.'

(8b) 'Macbeth has to have slain Duncan.'

The difference in tense is sufficient to distinguish (8a) as intuitively normative from (8b) as intuitively epistemic.

This role of tense might be thought merely an arbitrary linguistic convention, of a kind that is commonplace.[31] But competent speakers are evidently sensitive to some systematic relationship between modal tense and modal sense. Observe that although practically any modal auxiliary verb can have a normative reading, modal *adverbs* like 'necessarily' and 'possibly', which are tenseless, resist normative readings unless lexically dedicated (like 'permissibly' and 'obligatorily'); compare 'Macbeth necessarily slays/slayed Duncan.' Also, tenses that yield epistemic senses in some contexts yield normative senses in others. For example, (8b) becomes more naturally interpreted as normative when embedded in an instrumental conditional: 'If he is going to become king, then Macbeth has to have slain Duncan.'

In investigating this relationship I'll focus on the necessity verb 'has to', as it takes tense in regular ways and therefore provides more systematic data. By contrast, linguists describe 'must' and 'ought' as "defectively tensed"; we'll return to them later. A tensed modal verb like 'has/had to' naturally suggests a temporalized modality: necessity or possibility *at a time t*, or *belonging to somebody/something at t*.[32] Our modal semantics suggests an obvious analysis of this, as many backgrounds are temporally located, providing "snapshots" of the world at a particular time; for example, 'given the state of the world at t' (circumstantial), 'given what we knew at t' (epistemic). Necessity or possibility at t can be defined by what is true in all or some possibilities consistent with such a background, b_t. Note that as these possibilities or world-states are temporally extended, it's coherent to say that an event occurring at t_1 is necessary at some earlier or later time t_2.

---

[30] As Portner (2009) also observes, Kratzer doesn't examine the interaction between modals and tense.

[31] While 'must' is generally interchangeable with 'have to', for example, 'have to have' can be normative but 'must have' requires an epistemic (or at least non-normative) reading, which I assume to be a purely conventional rule.

[32] Many tensed modal auxiliaries across a variety of languages are etymologically derived from past-tense forms of verbs *to possess*, including 'have to', 'got to', and 'ought' itself, which formerly meant *owned* (e.g., 'He ought a castle': OED). Philosophers sometimes note the derivation of 'ought' from 'owe' without realizing this was itself a verb of possession, not obligation. Nordlinger & Traugott (1997) report data that I think suggest a shift from 'I have a debt to pay' (a still recognizable turn of speech using 'have' as a possession verb) to the modalized 'I have to pay a debt'.

Now consider the antecedents. To get a reading of a modal conditional as instrumentally normative, distinctive grammatical constructions are needed here. Rather than using a simple finite tense (e.g., 'If Max *evades* arrest', 'If Max *evaded* arrest') we need a more cumbersome construction: either the *prospective aspect* or progressive + infinitive (e.g., 'If Max *is going to evade* arrest') found in IC2 sentences, or the *to be* + infinitive ('If Max *is to* evade arrest'), or the 'in order to' in IC3 sentences. I'll continue to focus on IC2, 'If s is going to φ' antecedents, but we'll see that the other constructions function the same way.

An explanation is needed for the use of the prospective aspect. In light of the similarity with IC1, 'If s wants...' sentences, it is often claimed that the basic meaning of 's is going to ψ' in instrumental conditionals is that s has the *desire or purpose* to ψ. If so, the simple analysis above is mistaken, and all the puzzles raised by IC1 sentences rear their heads again. This hypothesis may also seem to have strong linguistic support, as 's is going to ψ' does indeed clearly have a common function of indicating an agent's purpose. But it's also easy to find ordinary uses where the construction doesn't have this function; for example, 'It's going to rain tomorrow', or 'One day that boulder is going to fall.' Significantly, this includes some apparent instrumental conditionals, like

(9) 'If the boulder is going to fall, then somebody has to push it.'

Perhaps it may be argued that (9) isn't correctly classified as an instrumental conditional, but the significant point here is that its modal verb intuitively has the same instrumentally normative sense as in our previous examples. Interpreting this antecedent as meaning *if the boulder wants to fall* is obviously absurd.

Philosophers commonly make the ad hoc and noncompositional response that the antecedent is really about the desires of an unmentioned agent; that what is meant is *if somebody wants the boulder to fall*... But while it isn't absurd to say, 'If p is going to happen, even though nobody wants it to happen, then it has to be that q', it is absurd to say, 'If somebody wants p to happen, even though nobody wants it to happen, then it has to be that q.'[33] Following rather than dismissing the surface grammar will lead to a better, simpler, and more unifying analysis.

On an orthodox and transparently compositional analysis, the progressive construction 'is going to φ' differs from finite verb phrases like 'evades arrest' or 'slayed Duncan' in being about two different times,[34] which I'll call the *aspect-time* and the *event-time*. To say at the present time t_1 'The boulder is going to fall' is to say that the boulder has at t_1 the property of falling at some future time t_2. Although the sentence concerns a falling event occurring at some (event-) time t_2 in the future, it isn't directly about the future but about

---

[33] Some association with an agent's purpose may however be necessary for a *full-fledged* normative sense, as I'll discuss below.

[34] E.g., Comrie 1976: 64–65.

the present (aspect-) time t_1. It attributes the world at t_1 a future in which the boulder falls. This is to grammatically represent the boulder's falling as an outcome or *end*, in my technical sense. By contrast, 'The boulder will fall' expresses a proposition simply and directly about the future: its aspect-time is identical to its event-time t_2. The future tense ('will') locates this time relative to the speaker's present (the *utterance-time* t_1), but the sentence doesn't express a proposition about that present.

The grammatically transparent basic function of 'is going to' is therefore to describe the world or an object at an earlier time as possessing some future, which I'll call *temporal shifting*. The basis for attributing a future is some feature of the earlier, aspect-time that places a claim on that future, "the already present seeds of some future situation".[35] This provides an explanation why 'is going to' often functions to indicate purpose: an obvious way a person can come to possess a particular future is by desiring or intending it. A speaker can therefore communicate that an agent has a particular purpose by ascribing him that future as his present possession. (This is supported by the standard grammarian's account of the difference between 'I am going to' and 'I will' as ways of communicating intention: 'I am going to' is used when one already had the intention, while 'I will' is used to express a new intention upon forming it.) But other features of the present can also lay claim to a future, as in 'The boulder is going to fall' (e.g., in virtue of a weakened hillside) and 'It's going to rain' (e.g., in virtue of looming storm clouds). Here the present possesses this future in virtue of some property that makes it all but inevitable.[36]

Since some modal conditionals with an intuitively (instrumentally) normative sense concern nonagents (like (9)), the simplest hypothesis is that the prospective aspect is performing its basic function of temporal shifting, and not necessarily indicating any agent's purpose. This has significant implications for the interaction between these distinctive grammatical features of antecedents and consequents. Compare the following forms:

(10a)   'If s is going to ψ, then s has to φ.'

(10b)   'If s ψs, then s has to φ.'

(11a)   'If s was going to ψ, then s had to φ.'

(11b)   'If s ψ-ed, then s had to φ.'

While various readings of these forms may be possible (determined partly by the values for ψ and φ), (10a) and (11a) are naturally read as instrumentally normative, while (10b) and (11b) aren't. Possible readings of the second pair

---

[35] Comrie 1976: 65.

[36] 'Going to' also differs from 'will' in sometimes leaving open the possibility of noneventuality (Comrie 1976: 65). Hence 'He is going to get away. We have to stop him!' My analysis below assumes this feature to be inactive in instrumental conditionals.

include circumstantial senses (e.g., 'If the boulder falls, then it has to crack'), and noninstrumentally normative readings (e.g., 'If Macbeth becomes king, then he has to defend his crown against Malcolm').

The instrumental conditionals (10a) and (11a) support the following compositional analysis. By the temporal shifting induced by the prospective aspect, the antecedent ('*s* is/was going to ψ') describes the world at an earlier aspect-time t_1 as having a future in which s ψs at t_2 (e.g., 'If Max is going to evade arrest' describes the world at a time before the evading, as having that future). Next, notice that the consequent's modal verb has the same tense as the antecedent ('is going to...has to'/'was going to...had to'). In the absence of other cues, this naturally suggests that the consequent describes the world at the same aspect-time t_1 as the antecedent. The consequent therefore says that it is necessary at t_1 that s φs (at some time). This will be relative to an assumed preliminary background b_0, such as *given the actual state of the world at t_1*, which the antecedent updates in the normal way with the proposition that s is going to ψ at the future time t_2. Since the consequent's prejacent has an infinite tense ('...to φ'), it describes an event that happens at some time t_m *after, or at least not before*, the aspect-time t_1.

Sentences (10a) and (11a) can therefore be analyzed as meaning that in all possibilities consistent with the world at t_1 as described by the background b_{t1} *including* that it has a future in which s ψs at t_2, s φs at some time t_m *not before* t_1. So for example: sentence (5), 'If Max is going to evade arrest, then he has to mingle with the crowd', expresses the proposition that in all possibilities consistent with the background at t_1 including that Max evades arrest in the future, he mingles with the crowd at some time t_m not before t_1. This time t_m is most naturally interpreted as being *between t_1 and t_2* (inclusive);[37] hence (5) grammatically represents the following timeline:

$\leftarrow t_1$ (Aspect/Necessity)—t_m (Max mingles)—t_2 (Max evades arrest)$\rightarrow$

Consider now the composition of the noninstrumental conditionals (10b) and (11b). The only grammatical difference from their instrumental counterparts is the simple finite tense in the antecedent ('ψs', 'ψ-ed') replacing the prospective aspect. So the aspect-time of these antecedents is identical to their event-time, t_2. For example, 'Max evades arrest' describes the world at the time of the evasion event. But this also alters the reading of the consequent. By virtue of the modal verb's tense agreement with the antecedent ('ψs...has to',

---

[37] A pragmatic explanation: if t_m is later than t_2, this could be represented by the simple finite tense, 'if s ψs' (see below). So unless another explanation for the clumsier prospective aspect is salient, it suggests the order that can't be represented more simply. When an alternative explanation is salient, noninstrumental readings are available. Since indicating purpose is such an alternative, it actually encourages a *noninstrumental* reading; e.g., 'If he is going to evade arrest, we have to be ready to chase him.'

'ψ-ed . . . had to'), the consequent is naturally read as also describing the world at t_2, for example, as meaning that it is necessary at t_2 that Max mingles with the crowd (at some time t_n). This is relative to an implicit preliminary background b_0, such as *given the actual state of the external world at t_2*, which the antecedent updates in the normal way with the proposition that s ψs at that time t_2. Because of the infinitive tense of the consequent's prejacent ('to φ'), it describes a φ-ing event that happens at some time t_3 that is *after, or at least not before*, the aspect-time t_2.

Sentences (10b) and (11b) can therefore be analyzed as saying that in all possibilities consistent with the background at t_2 when s ψs, s φs at some not-earlier time t_3. So for example, 'If Max evades arrest, then he has to mingle with the crowd' expresses the proposition that in all possibilities consistent with the background at t_2, when Max evades arrest, he mingles with the crowd at a not-earlier time t_3. Our timeline:

$\leftarrow t_2$ (Aspect/Necessity: Max evades arrest)—t_3 (Max mingles)$\rightarrow$

The most obvious difference here is that the two pairs of sentence-forms are most naturally read as representing different temporal orders for their two events. Ordinary conditionals of the forms (10b) and (11b) represent the consequent's event as occurring after, or not before, the antecedent's event. On (10b) and (11b), Max mingles with the crowd after or not before he evades arrest. (Observe that the word 'then' also has an ordinary use as meaning *afterwards*; for example, 'I ate dinner, then I ate dessert.') By contrast, the temporal shifting function of the prospective aspect ('is going to ψ') in the antecedents of (10a) and (11a) enables representation of the events with a reversed temporal order.[38] It does this by pushing the antecedent's event into the relative future, so that the consequent's event happens before it. On (10a) and (11a), Max mingles with the crowd before or not after he evades arrest.

A tempting diagnosis of this difference is that this reversed order in (10a) and (11a) represents the temporal relationship of *ends* and *means*, as opposed to the relationship of *causes* and *effects*. (Not all means do occur before their ends, of course, nor do all consequences occur after their causes; sometimes they're simultaneous, as with constitutive means. In these cases the priority is metaphysical rather than temporal, but temporal order is apparently often used as a grammatical device for representing metaphysical order. To simplify discussion I'll start omitting the qualifications 'or not before/after', as implicitly understood.) However, explaining instrumentally normative senses of modal conditionals by the temporal order of their events isn't quite correct.

Consider sentences of the forms

---

[38] See also Sæbø 2001.

(10c) 'If s ψs, then s has to have φ-ed.'

(11c) 'If s ψ-ed, then s had to have φ-ed.'

These are most naturally read as epistemic rather than as instrumentally normative. But grammatically they represent the same reversed temporal order. Like (10b) and (11b), their simple finite antecedents describe the world at the event-time t_2 when s ψs. So by tense-agreement ('ψs...has to'/'ψ-ed...had to'), by default their consequents describe what is necessary at that same time t_2. They differ from the noninstrumental (10b) and (11b) only in the perfect infinitive tense in the consequents' prejacents, which represent the consequent's event (s's φ-ing) as having occurred at some *earlier* time t_1, before the aspect-time t_2. So for example, 'If Max evades arrest, then he has to have mingled with the crowd' represents the mingling as having occurred at some time before the evading. This is the same reversed temporal order of events represented by an instrumental conditional like (5); sometimes later events are treated as *evidence* for earlier events.

Grammatically, the epistemic sentences (10c) and (11c) are like the other noninstrumental conditionals (10b) and (11b), and unlike the instrumental conditionals (10a) and (11a), in just one respect: the temporal relation of the antecedent's event-time (of s's ψ-ing) and the *necessity* of the consequent's event (s' φ-ing). Whereas the instrumental conditionals (10a) and (11a) locate the necessity of the event at t_1, some time before the event itself occurs at t_2, these epistemic conditionals locate it rather at t_2, the time of the event itself. The following principle can be inferred:[39]

Prior Modality: Modal conditionals allow an instrumentally normative sense iff they represent the modality of the consequent's event as prior to the antecedent's event.

For independent support, compare the following pair of sentences:

(12a) 'Before I give you a license you have to have filled out an application.'

(12b) 'Since I gave you a license you have to have filled out an application.'

Sentence (12a) explicitly locates the necessity prior to the giving of the license, and the modal verb 'have to' prefers an instrumentally normative sense. Sentence (12b) explicitly locates the necessity subsequent to the same event, and the same modal verb 'have to' now prefers an epistemic sense.

---

[39] In Finlay 2010a I suggested rather that this condition was *jointly* sufficient for an instrumental conditional together with the *Temporal Ordering* condition that the consequent's event be represented as prior to the antecedent's event.

This analysis extends to and is corroborated by the other formulations of instrumental conditionals. The origin and significance of the IC3, 'in order to ψ' construction plausibly involves exactly this reversal of the usual order of antecedent and consequent.[40] Other modal words also provide supportive evidence. First, *Prior Modality* explains why tenseless modal adverbs like 'necessarily', 'possibly', and 'only' would generally resist normative readings (at least in the instrumental case). Second, 'have to' is relatively unusual among modal verbs in being regularly tensed, unlike 'must', 'ought', and 'should', which are present-tense verbs lacking past-tense forms, and we have no words 'musted', 'oughted', or 'shoulded' corresponding to 'had to'.[41] Accordingly, speakers must generally substitute 'had to' for these other modals when talking about normative necessities in the past, in order to conform with *Prior Modality*; for example, instead of saying, 'If Max was going to evade arrest, he must / ought to mingle with the crowd', one would say 'If Max was going to evade arrest, he had to mingle with the crowd.'[42]

What is the philosophical significance of these differences? In the epistemic conditionals (10c) and (11c), their normal temporal order locates the necessity at the antecedent's event time (when s ψs), which is later than the consequent's event time (when s φs). This is necessity at the time of various *consequences* of s's φ-ing, including that s ψs, which comprise *evidence* of the consequent's event (that s φ-ed). In 'If Max evaded arrest, then he had to have mingled with the crowd', the necessity is located at the time t_2 when Max evades arrest, for example, which is part of the evidence that Max had mingled with the crowd at some earlier time t_1. So we can conclude that epistemic necessity of p is just necessity at the time of evidence that p, or what the evidence makes necessary.[43]

The circumstantial conditionals (10b) and (11b) have the same normal temporal order, locating the necessity at the antecedent's event-time. But because the consequent's prejacent has a nonperfective tense ('had *to φ*'), this necessity

---

[40] "The phrase *in order to* (1655) preserves [the] etymological notion of "sequence"" (http://www.etymonline.com). 'In order to ψ' can also indicate purpose (e.g., 'In order to evade arrest, Max mingled with the crowd'), but getting this reading when it qualifies a modal sentence requires changing the grammatical order; contrast 'In order to evade arrest, Max ought to mingle with the crowd' and 'Max ought to mingle with the crowd in order to evade arrest'; see Ch. 8, note 57.

[41] Etymologically, all these were past-tense forms of regular nonmodal verbs that became present-tense modal verbs, leaving them with no past-tense forms of their own.

[42] While 'had to have' can't be replaced by 'must have' (i.e., 'has to have'), it *can* be replaced by 'ought to have', apparently violating *Prior Modality*. I speculate grammar tolerates this because of the lack of any regularly tensed verb synonymous with 'ought', which may also carry a presumption of normative over epistemic use; cf. Nordlinger & Traugott 1997, who argue that epistemic uses develop late.

[43] Epistemic conditionals don't require tense agreement, and the following form is common: 'If s ψ-ed, then s *has* to have φ-ed.' I interpret this as what is made necessary by evidence in the speaker's present (e.g., documents, remains), contrasting with '…s *had* to have φ-ed', about what is made necessary by evidence in the speaker's past (e.g., past events).

is before the consequent's event-time. This is necessity at the time of various *causes* for s's φ-ing, including that s ψs. In 'If Max evades arrest, then he has to mingle with the crowd', the necessity is also located at the time t_2 when Max evades arrest, for example, but now this is represented as a cause of Max's mingling with the crowd at some later time t_3. So we can conclude that the circumstantial necessity of p is just necessity at the time of causes for p, or what the causal conditions make necessary.

By contrast, the reversed temporal order of instrumental conditionals locates the necessity at some time t_1 (the antecedent's aspect-time) before the antecedent's event of s's ψ-ing at t_2. The antecedent restricts the possibility-space to only those world-states where the antecedent's event (the end e) subsequently comes to obtain, but otherwise the only relevant restrictions come in the form of (actual, known, or believed) background states of affairs at t_1 that could *prevent e* from later occurring at t_2. In other words, the necessity is located at the time of prior *obstacles* to e. We can therefore conclude that the instrumental necessity of p is a necessity at the time of obstacles to p, or what the state of the world at t_1 makes necessary before p can occur at t_2; that is, the necessary conditions for p.[44]

Compositional analysis therefore leads to what might seem like an incredibly obvious result: for an instrumentally normative reading of a modal conditional, it's necessary to interpret it as representing an end-means or instrumental relationship between events. The really significant result here, however, is that this also seems *sufficient* for generating an instrumentally normative sense of a modal verb. This analysis satisfies all the criteria that confound other accounts (except so far for *Necessity Isn't Necessary*). Wherever the implicit background isn't *given what s believes*, *Belief Insensitivity* is accommodated. As the analysis makes no reference to s's desires, *No Bootstrapping, Nondetachability*, and *Logical Strength* are straightforwardly met,[45] and as this is merely the 'must' of necessary conditions, so is *Moral Insensitivity*.

---

[44] A substantive difference between evidence at t_3 that s ψs at t_2 and obstacles at t_1 to s ψ-ing at t_2 is that for the former, s's ψ-ing is determinate, happening in a particular location, time, and way, while for the latter it is still indeterminate, and could be realized differently. Different propositions are therefore evidentially relevant than are instrumentally relevant; e.g., whether a particular person witnesses Max in the crowd.

[45] Might we face a different detaching problem? E.g., 'Max *is* going to evade arrest. Therefore he has to mingle with the crowd.' This inference is good so long as the conclusion is read evidentially rather than normatively. Modal conditionals don't always license detachment because their consequents depend on the antecedents not only for their truth but also for their sense, the background b being an argument of the modal. Conditionalizing explicitly on p can make a background salient that wouldn't otherwise be. Warrantedly asserting the antecedent p of an instrumental conditional (e.g., that Max *is* going to evade arrest) requires some kind of evidence, making an evidential rather than an instrumental background salient. Any necessity inferred from such evidence won't have a normative sense by our analysis.

It's therefore plausible that we've identified necessary and sufficient conditions for an instrumental conditional. As these are intuitively normative, we potentially have a unifying reductive analysis, on which ordinary modal auxiliaries acquire an instrumentally normative sense by having their backgrounds restricted by the eventuation of some state of affairs in the relative future—that is, by an end. This extends the end-relational theory from normative adjectives like 'good' to normative necessity verbs like 'must' and possibility verbs like 'may', but two remaining pieces of data about instrumental conditionals still await explanation: the use of 'If *s* wants…' antecedents and of 'ought'.

3.5. "Hypothetical Imperatives": Taking the Biscuit

The only grammatical data from instrumental conditionals not yet accounted for is the troublesome 'If *s* wants…' construction in IC1 sentences. We've seen reason to suspect this reference to agents' desires doesn't make a truth-conditional contribution to the propositions asserted with these sentences. However, if instead of dismissing this construction as misleading we look more broadly at linguistic practice, it should be noticed that 'If *s* wants…' has a common kind of non-truth-conditional use, in *relevance* (or "biscuit") conditionals like

(13)   'If you want biscuits, there are some on the table.'

As naturally interpreted, this sentence doesn't mean that the *truth* of the consequent *q* depends on the truth of the antecedent *p* (that whether there are biscuits on the table depends on *s* wanting some) but rather that the conversational *relevance* of *q* depends on the truth of *p*. It's therefore reasonable to hypothesize that instrumental IC1 sentences are relevance conditionals.

The proper linguistic analysis of relevance conditionals is controversial, but presumably the simplest and most unifying account analyzes them compositionally as involving ellipsis, so that (13) is used as elliptical for something like

(13a)   'If you want biscuits, [then this will be relevant information:] there
         are some on the table.'[46]

This avoids any semantic ambiguity between relevance and ordinary indicative uses of the conditional 'if', and provides everything needed for a complete compositional analysis of IC1 instrumental conditionals. Sentence (4) would be elliptical for

(14)   'If Max wants to evade arrest, [then this will be relevant
         information: If Max is going to evade arrest,] then he has to mingle
         with the crowd.'

---

[46] Cf. Siegel 2006.

Plausibly, (14) preserves the truth conditions of (4), and the relevance of an instrumental conditional does generally depend on an interest in (and not necessarily any intention for) the end, as we'll discuss further in Chapter 5.

As well as being compositional, unifying, and extensionally correct, this analysis also explains an anomaly that has prompted others to reject the hypothesis that IC1 sentences are relevance conditionals.[47] A known grammatical marker of relevance conditionals is their resistance to linking the antecedent and consequent clauses with 'then': consider the mild oddity of 'If you want biscuits, then there are some on the table.'[48] But a linking 'then' seems natural in instrumental conditionals. This peculiarity of relevance conditionals is straightforwardly explained by the ellipsis theory, according to which the consequent clause doesn't in general express a real (logical) consequent; 'There are some biscuits on the table' is just asserted as true. In the case of (14), however, the consequent clause ('he has to mingle with the crowd') is in fact also a logical consequent, albeit of an omitted antecedent, providing an explanation why instrumental conditionals are anomalous in this way.

Perhaps this isn't enough by itself to explain the use of 'then' when the clauses aren't truth-conditionally related, but observe additionally how similar 'if s wants to ψ' and 'if s is going to ψ' are. The former construction introduces s as an agent and ψ-ing as an end, and the verb 'wants' induces the same temporal shifting as 'is going to', satisfying the *Prior Modality* condition for an instrumental conditional. The antecedent of the relevance conditional therefore provides a functional substitute for the antecedent of the instrumental conditional. This makes it redundant to utter 'if s is going to ψ', so given the pressure towards efficiency in speech and thought it isn't surprising that (4) would ordinarily be used as elliptical for (14).

This treatment of IC1 sentences as hybrid relevance-instrumental conditionals preserves our previous solutions to the various problems arising from the use of 'wants'. An 'ought' can't correctly be detached from these sentences upon acceptance of the antecedents, because they don't really mean that s's *wanting* to ψ entails that s ought to φ. Although our analysis implies that a true IC1 sentence always has a true consequent, this isn't an 'ought' claim that is properly *inferred* from the antecedent, which rather functions to indicate its sense and relevance. The end-relational theory therefore provides a complete compositional explanation of the grammatical features of these formulations of instrumental conditionals.

---

[47] von Stechow et al. 2005, 2006 (who conclude that IC1 sentences are *similar* to relevance conditionals), von Fintel & Iatridou 2005, and Dreier 2009.

[48] Also compare 'If you want to have biscuits, you can't' (okay) with 'If you want to have biscuits, then you can't' (odd). This difference also influences the acceptability of past-tense antecedents; e.g., 'If you wanted biscuits, there were some on the table' (okay), 'If you wanted biscuits, then there were some on the table' (odd).

3.6. A Probabilistic Semantics for 'Ought'

If normative verbs like 'have to', 'must', 'may', 'could', and 'might' are reductively analyzable (at least in their instrumental senses) as end-relational uses of ordinary non-normative modals, what about 'ought'? Although philosophers often treat 'ought' as expressing obligation or normative necessity, it clearly means something different than 'must', which linguists mark by describing 'ought' as a "weak necessity" verb in contrast to "strong necessity" verbs like 'must'. But what is "weak necessity"? Clearly it lies between (genuine) necessity and mere possibility; '*s* must φ' entails '*s* ought to φ', which entails '*s* may φ', while the reverse entailments don't hold. A common and intuitive gloss is that while '*s* must φ' means that φ-ing is *s*'s only option, '*s* ought to φ' means that φ-ing is *s*'s *best* option, admitting other possibilities.[49] It may therefore be tempting simply to apply Chapter 2's analysis of 'best' here, but this would build merely a house of cards.

The simplest, most unifying hypothesis is that 'ought' works the same way all other modal auxiliaries do. Might the 'ought' of instrumental normativity just be an end-relational use of an ordinary non-normative 'ought'? It indeed has a non-normative use, exemplified in epistemic sentences like 'It ought to rain tomorrow.' Additionally, it has a synonym in 'should' (as I'll assume),[50] which exhibits the same ambiguity between normative and non-normative senses. So an underlying semantic unity should be expected, especially as the ambiguity is also found in expressions in other languages.[51] This non-normative 'ought' is widely but casually interpreted as meaning roughly *probably*, suggesting the hypothesis, which I'll defend, that the normative 'ought' can also be analyzed in terms of probability.[52] 'Probably' is appropriately weaker than 'necessary' ($pr = 1$) and stronger than 'possible' ($pr > 0$).

A couple of preliminary points: first, 'probably' (and 'likely') doesn't itself have an intuitively normative sense—like other tenseless modal adverbs such

---

[49] E.g., Sloman 1970, Williams 1981a: 125.

[50] 'Ought' is sometimes said to be more formal or moralistic (see Chapter 7) than 'should', but I find them fully intersubstitutable in my idiolect.

[51] von Fintel & Iatridou (2008) report that English is unusual in having a dedicated word for *ought*, which in many other languages is expressed by constructions compositionally representing counterfactual "strong" necessity (i.e., 'would have to')—with the same epistemic/normative ambiguity. As those constructions are accordingly ambiguous between "weak" necessity and genuine counterfactual necessity readings, this is apparently a conventionalized, noncompositional device.

[52] Wheeler (1974 & 2013) analyzes '*s* ought to φ' as roughly *s probably φs given it's a member of its kind*. Many others attempt to reduce the non-normative to the normative 'ought', roughly as *what ought to be expected* (Sloman 1970, von Fintel & Iatridou 2005, Thomson 2008: 204), but analysis in this direction isn't compositional, truth-preserving (e.g., 'It ought to have rained, but it didn't'), or unifying, and is ad hoc, not generalizing to other modals. For other attempts at unifying analyses see Wertheimer 1972, White 1975, Phillips 1998, Ridge 2014, Chrisman 2015.

as 'possibly' and 'necessarily'—which can be explained similarly by the *Prior Modality* requirement.[53] Second, 'ought' is accordingly more flexible than 'probably'. Contrast 'It probably rained, but it didn't' (odd) with 'It ought to have rained, but it didn't' (okay). Whereas 'probably' is tied to total present evidence, 'ought' like other auxiliaries can be relativized to any background, such as evidence at some previous time t, some subset of evidence at t, or what some agent s believes, and so on.

Many philosophers have observed that 'ought' seems essentially contrastive, like 'best', and I'll adopt a *contrastive probabilistic* semantics for the non-normative 'ought' as having an argument-place for a set R of relevant alternatives, which is usually implicit.[54] I propose the definition,

$ought_{b,R}(p)$: p is more likely relative to W_b than any r in R.

(On the classical model of probability we might say equivalently that p is true in *more* of the possibilities in W_b than any r is.) When applied to (1), 'If Max wants to evade arrest, then he ought to mingle with the crowd', this sentence is interpreted as meaning that given the preliminary background b_0 and e (Max is going to evade arrest) it's more likely that he first mingles with the crowd (p) than any relevant alternative r;

$pr(p|e \ \& \ b_0) > pr(r|e \ \& \ b_0)$, for all $r \in R$.

This analysis may seem unpromising, since its being most likely that Max mingles with the crowd seems very different from its being best that Max mingles with the crowd. But recall that our analysis of instrumental 'must' and 'may' required a preliminary background b_0 which excluded any information about the agent's dispositions to choose one means over another. Relative to such a background each alternative has equal probability; call this *symmetry of choice*.[55] As before, the modal's background b is formed by updating b_0 with the end e, restricting the possibility-space W_b to those possibilities consistent with b_0 in which e also eventuates.

Relative to this background b characterized by symmetry of choice, the alternative most likely to be performed will be the one on which the end e would be most likely to eventuate; that is,

---

[53] 'Probably' and 'likely' may also be strongly, even lexically, associated with epistemic use. On the classical theory of probability, a common, neutral (alethic) core can be identified in terms of *more* possibilities. Horn 1972 considers defining 'ought' as *in most possibilities*, ultimately rejecting it as incompatible with normative uses.

[54] E.g., Sloman 1970, Jackson 1985, Cariani 2013, Snedegar 2012a. An additional argument-place isn't the only way to accommodate contrastivity, and is assumed here noncommitally.

[55] This can be seen as a naturalized version of Kant's assumption of transcendental freedom. Strictly these results hold for symmetry of *performance* rather than of *choice* of means (Evers 2011), but usually only alternatives safely within the agent's power are relevant (explaining the intuition that 'ought' implies 'can'), so sometimes the appropriate alternative is merely to *try* to φ.

Equivalence: $\forall r \in R: pr(p|e \& b_0) > pr(r|e \& b_0)$ iff $pr(e|p \& b_0)$
$> pr(e|r \& b_0)$.

Our hypothesis therefore predicts that the means that *ought* to be taken relative
to an end *e* is just that which most increases the probability of the end, or the
most reliable means. In order to evade arrest, for example, Max ought to mingle
with the crowd just in case doing so makes his evading arrest more likely than it
would be if did something else instead. This result seems much more promising.

Observe that the right-hand side of *Equivalence* reproduces the analysis
derived for 'best' in Chapter 2, making *Equivalence* just a formal statement of
the widely accepted platitude that 'ought' is equivalent to 'best'. We therefore
have two independent paths to the same result, one by way of the platitude
linking normative 'ought' and 'best', the other by way of the meaning of the
non-normative 'ought'. This is either a highly improbable coincidence, or else
our unifying hypothesis is substantially correct. The linguistic evidence leads to
a unifying end-relational theory of the instrumental 'ought': what ought to be
done in order that *e* is just what would most likely be done given symmetry of
choice and that the end *e* subsequently obtains. This account satisfies all our
criteria, now including *Necessity Isn't Necessary*.

This analysis faces objections, however. First, it might appear to ascribe
an implausible level of mathematical sophistication to ordinary speakers
(*Equivalence* is a consequence of Bayes' theorem, for example). But it merely
requires ranking conditional probabilities rather than measuring them, which
is a skill learned at a young age, and recent research finds even preschoolers
reasoning in Bayesian ways.[56] To see how intuitive *Equivalence* is, suppose Max
has only two options for evading arrest—mingling with the crowd with .9 probability of success, and hiding in the cloak closet with .1 probability of success—and that you initially assign equal probability (.5) to his choosing either
option. If you then learn that Max successfully evaded arrest you should naturally conclude that he most likely (epistemically "ought to have") mingled with
the crowd.

More seriously, reliability is only one of indefinitely many grounds on
which a means may be evaluated as "best" and what ought to be chosen: others include cost, agreeability, moral permissibility, safety, etc. I might tell you,
for example, that if you want to drive to San Francisco from Los Angeles then
you ought to take the Pacific Coast Highway—not because it's the most reliable
route (that would probably be the I-5), but because it's the most scenic. Unlike
with 'must' and 'may', our semantics can't account for these factors simply by
appeal to other restrictions assumed in the preliminary background b_0, because
often 'ought' judgments involve *balancing* various desiderata or ends against
each other.

---

[56] See, e.g., Sobel et al. 2004.

These cases of *multiple ends* present a significant challenge to our end-relational semantics, and are central motivations for the greater complexity of rival semantic theories like Kratzer's. I'll defer discussion of this challenge of multiple ends until Chapter 6, where I'll argue that our simpler semantics is superior even for these more difficult cases. Here I limit my attention to what I'll call "pure" instrumental conditionals, concerning a single end or desideratum, and argue that this simpler theory better accommodates these basic cases.

3.7. Contra Kratzer

As it isn't feasible to compare all rival semantics for modals, my case for having the best theory depends on its maximal simplicity. But in view of the wide acceptance and thereby conservatism of the Lewis-Kratzer semantics it's worthwhile showing that ours isn't only simpler but also accommodates the data better. While a thorough comparison would have to involve all kinds of use (epistemic, counterfactual, etc.), here I can focus only on the instrumental uses we're examining, which have proven problematic on the Lewis-Kratzer approach.

That semantics is *polyadic* rather than dyadic:[57] in addition to a background functioning to restrict the domain of possibilities (the "modal base", which I'll label 'b' for consistency and clarity), it posits another argument-place in the logical form of modals for a secondary background, the "ordering source", which I'll label 'o';

$$verb_{b,o}(p).$$

The ordering source selects a set of propositions that function not to restrict the domain, like the modal base, but to order or rank the possibilities in the domain W_b, roughly according to their degree of consistency with o. (We'll get more precise in Chapter 6.) The modal then quantifies over a selection of these ordered possibilities; for example, 'must' means *in all the best/highest-ranked possibilities*. For Kratzer, sources of normativity like ends (ideals, rules, laws, etc.) go into the ordering source, rather than into the modal base b as in our analysis.

The ordering source performs a number of different functions in Kratzer's semantics. First, it accounts for gradability (e.g., "weak" vs. "strong" necessity)—which our semantics explains rather by different kinds of quantificational force for different terms (e.g., analyzing 'ought' as a probability rather than necessity operator).[58] Second, it marks backgrounds that are "irrealis",

---

[57] We posited an additional argument for 'ought', R, but this was an exception; we'll also see below that Kratzerian treatments have commonly appealed to even more arguments to accommodate the distinctive behavior of 'ought'.

[58] Kratzer is particularly concerned to account for degrees of *possibility* and *necessity*, but concedes that at least in English possibility operators aren't generally gradable (2012: 42).

or potentially nonfactual (e.g., in normative and counterfactual modalities), whereas the modal base b is stipulated to be "realis" and consist only of propositions taken as factual in the context. By contrast, our semantics has just one, flexible background for any kind or combination of consistent propositions a speaker might have in mind. Third, it accounts for modalities sensitive to inconsistent sets of propositions, like multiple ends (cases we'll address in Chapter 6). Finally, it functions to flag a use as normative, while (some) non-normative modalities have a null or empty ordering source. On our semantics, at least instrumentally normative uses are generated and flagged instead by including an end (or proposition about the relative future) in an ordinary non-normative background.[59]

Instrumental conditionals present a series of problems for Kratzer's semantics. First, since their antecedents clearly describe ends or ideals, and as they clearly have a normative sense, a Kratzerian approach apparently must interpret the antecedents as updating the *ordering source o* rather than the modal base b. This is anomalous on the standard Kratzerian analysis of the conditional, 'if p', as updating b and restricting the domain, and so it is suggested that the conditional 'if p' is ambiguous.[60] By contrast, our analysis has required only the standard account of modal conditionals.

Second, the supposition that the antecedent updates an ordering source seems to yield some absurd predictions. Since even the highest-ranked possibilities needn't satisfy *every* end in the ordering source, it might be expected that a sentence like 'If Max wants to evade arrest, then he has to get arrested' could turn out true by virtue of other, assumed ends. To block these results, it is suggested that instrumental conditionals must give p priority over all other ends in some way.[61] One suggestion is that here (again anomalously) 'if p' exhaustively specifies rather than merely updates the ordering source.[62] (This is functionally equivalent to our analysis which puts the end in b, the modal base, making the ordering source effectively redundant.)[63] But this would sacrifice the supposed advantage of accommodating "impure" instrumental conditionals sensitive to other ends.

---

[59] This triple duty of generating/marking at once gradability, nonfactuality, and normativity raises difficulties, since not all gradable or nonfactual modality is normative (e.g., counterfactual and epistemic), etc. Since there can't be mixed epistemic-normative ordering sources, this semantics can't so easily accommodate subjective normative modalities; e.g., what s ought to do *given what he believes*. In contrast to our simple and parallel treatment of objective and subjective 'ought', Kratzer now favors (in conversation) interpreting the latter as having a (realis) modal base of *facts about what s believes* and an ordering source of rules of rationality.

[60] Sæbø 2001, von Fintel & Iatridou 2005.

[61] Pragmatic explanations may be available here.

[62] Huitink 2005.

[63] von Stechow et al. 2005, 2006.

Another relevant difficulty is that the Kratzerian account of graded modality struggles to explain the difference between 'ought' and 'must'. Interpreting 'must' as meaning *in all the highest-ranked possibilities* threatens to collapse the intuitive distinction between 'must' and 'ought' as that between *only* and *best*. A leading strategy to address both this and the previous problem appeals to Kratzer's idea of multiple, *nested* ordering sources: to say that if s wants e then s *ought* to φ is to say that s φs in all possibilities in W_b ranked highest by a set of primary ends (including e) that are *also* ranked highest by some other set of secondary ends or ideals.[64] So the logical form of 'ought' includes a secondary ordering source o_2 which takes the possibilities in W_b that are highest-ranked by the primary ordering source o_1, and ranks these in turn. In other words, 'ought' means *in the best$_2$ of the best$_1$ possibilities*. This logical form can be represented as:

$$ought_{b,o1,o2}(p).$$

I must defer until Chapter 6 the question of whether introducing this further complexity into modal semantics is the right approach to normative claims sensitive to multiple ends, like impure instrumental conditionals. But we can here observe that this multiple-index approach fails to accommodate the simplest cases of the use of 'ought' in *pure* instrumental conditionals, which suggests that this hypothesis about the difference between 'ought' and 'must' is incorrect. Consider this scenario:

Single-Minded Theseus: Theseus is rushing through the labyrinth concerned with nothing but finding and slaying the Minotaur before it slaughters his compatriots. He reaches a room with three doors, and determines the following probabilities. If he takes door A, his likelihood of success is .5, if door B, it is .3, and if door C, zero.

The following judgments seem natural. In order to save his compatriots, Theseus *must* choose either A or B, he *ought* to choose A, but he doesn't *have to* choose A, because he *could* rather choose B—albeit ill-advisedly. Our simpler semantics predicts exactly these results: both A and B are possible means to his end, but because taking A is the means on which success is most likely, it is

---

[64] von Fintel & Iatridou 2005; see also Price 2008. Kratzer doesn't advance a semantics for 'ought', but endorses (in conversation) the view in Rubinstein 2014 that 'ought' contrasts with 'must' by indicating conversational controversy over how to prioritize the relevant ends. This hypothesis faces clear counterexamples: the Theseus case below illustrates 'ought' without controversy, and moral disagreements illustrate 'must' with controversy. A pragmatic explanation of Rubinstein's evidence can be derived from Chapter 6.

what he *ought* to do. The multiple-index theory predicts instead that if the only salient end is saving his compatriots, then saying he ought to choose A would be false. If there's anything he ought to do, it's to choose *either* A or B (in virtue of an empty secondary ordering source o_2).

To generate the intuitive results, multiple-indexed views must hold that *reliability* is a secondary, auxiliary end.[65] But this seems artificial and ad hoc. If Theseus chooses door B and is lucky enough to succeed, does he have any cause for regret? "Yes I saved my compatriots, but it would have been nicer if I had also taken the most reliable means!" Reliability doesn't seem optional in the way that "other" secondary ends are; we might as plausibly consider "success" a secondary end.[66] If Theseus is concerned about nothing other than saving his compatriots, that seems sufficient to make the action that maximizes his likelihood of success be what he *ought* to do. Our semantics correctly predicts this result, but the more complex Kratzerian semantics doesn't. For this and its other advantages the simpler semantics should be preferred, unless we find in Chapter 6 that the problem of multiple ends necessitates the additional complexity.

3.8. Conclusion

The linguistic data from ordinary use of 'ought' and other modal verbs leads to a simple and unifying semantics as expressing probability (necessity, possibility) relative to a background. The grammatical clues from instrumental conditionals suggests they are end-relational applications of these ordinary non-normative modal verbs, quantifying over possibilities in which certain ends eventuate. Since this instrumental 'ought' has an intuitively normative sense, we seem to have reductively analyzed a normative 'ought'.

As necessary and sufficient conditions aren't the same as meaning, this conclusion may be resisted in the manner of Henry Sidgwick:

> When (e.g.) a physician says, 'If you wish to be healthy you ought to rise early,' this is *not the same thing* as saying 'early rising is an indispensable condition of the attainment of health.' This latter proposition expresses

---

[65] As von Fintel & Iatridou 2005 and Price 2008 both suggest. This has other counterintuitive results our theory avoids. Suppose two trains go to Harlem, but only on the A-train will you have the opportunity to kiss Pedro Martinez, which you desire to do; von Fintel & Iatridou then predict the truth of 'If you want to go to Harlem, you ought to kiss Pedro Martinez', which seems to give such a desire undue influence on instrumental conditionals (Nissenbaum 2005; see also Huitink 2005).

[66] Reliability might be considered a secondary end because it can be traded off for other secondary ends. However, any such trade-off will involve reduction in the relative importance assigned to achieving the primary end itself (or success).

the relation of physiological facts on which the former is founded; but it is not merely this relation of facts that the word 'ought' imports... The "hypothetical imperative"... prescribes the fittest means to any end that we have determined to aim at. (1874: 39)

I'll ultimately agree in Chapter 5 that use of these sentences commonly does and communicates significantly more, and also (in Chapter 9) that this may influence the degree to which they are intuited as *normative*. The end-relational analysis applies equally to sentences not involving agents, actions, or desired ends, like 'If the tornado is going to destroy our house, it has to veer north', for example, which doesn't prescribe anything to anybody. But there is good reason to deny that anything is missing from our analysis of the *semantics* of these words. The grammatical and lexical features of the linguistic expression of instrumental conditionals can be exhaustively and compositionally explained by analyzing these sentences as end-relational applications of an ordinary, non-normative modal verb. So if 'ought' and other auxiliaries did have a distinct meaning in their normative sense, this would mean that instrumental conditionals are semantically ambiguous between two different meanings which coincidentally also happen to have coextensive truth-conditions. I don't perceive any such ambiguity, and it's simpler and more plausible to conclude that a single reading is both end-relational and normative.[67]

If some normative uses of 'ought' are end-relational, then the simplest and most unifying hypothesis is that they all are, and that apparently noninstrumental normative uses of 'ought' are elliptical, assuming an implicit 'in order that...' qualifier. This is highly plausible for *functional* uses: 'Jokes ought to be funny' and 'Ships' anchors ought to be heavy' can be naturally read as elliptical for '[In order to make people laugh,] jokes ought to be funny' and '[In order to stop ships from floating away,] their anchors ought to be heavy.' Generally, for any e_F-functional kind K that ought to φ, it will be true that in order that e_F, a K ought to φ, which unifies the functional uses of 'ought' with instrumental and non-normative uses.

The real question is whether this semantics also extends to moral and deliberative uses. One suggestive piece of evidence is that all normative senses of 'ought' and other modal verbs follow the same patterns of tense observed in the consequents of instrumental conditionals, and unlike those of epistemic sentences, which we exhaustively and transparently explained by the *Prior Modality* condition. These features need to be explained for other normative uses as well,

---

[67] A thorough defense of a unifying semantics would also need to address the various paradoxes of deontic logic; it's also sometimes argued that logical variations between different modal (or even normative) domains rules out any unifying account (e.g., Cosmides & Tooby 2008). While I can't show it here, I believe we have sufficient semantic and pragmatic resources to answer these challenges. For example, conditionalizing normative uses of 'ought' on ends, which needn't obtain, explains why normative logics distinctively exclude the axiom T: $\Box p \rightarrow p$.

and the most obvious solution is that the tense is a grammatical trace left by the omitted antecedent which triggers our sense for a normative verb.

Appendix: Ought-to-Do

I've assumed that 'ought' is always a "raising" verb that expresses a propositional operator $O(p)$, so that basic 'ought' sentences say that *it ought$_b$ to be the case that p*. Call this the *ought-to-be*. Although this assumption is common among philosophers and linguists, it is challenged at least for the uses of 'ought' that particularly concern moral philosophy. The practical 'ought' in sentences of the form '*s* ought to φ'—call it the *ought-to-do*—is claimed to be a "control" verb, expressing instead a normative relation $O(s, φ)$ between an agent and an action, akin to *having most reason to*. I'll now defend the rival view that *ought-to-do* is just a special case of *ought-to-be*,[68] and also explain the evidence motivating the rival view in a way parallel to Chapter 2's appendix's accommodation of the intuition that goodness is a property of objects.

The grammatical form, '*s* ought to φ', might naively be thought already to establish that 'ought' is a control verb expressing a relation between an agent and an action, given its subject-predicate form with an agent-noun in subject position, like '*s* wants to φ.' But recall the phenomenon of subject movement, where the subject of the prejacent sentence is raised to the subject position of the overall sentence to comply with the rule of English grammar that every sentence have a grammatical subject (hence a "raising" verb). Although 'might' expresses a propositional operator, for example, we don't say 'Might be today is Sunday', but instead 'Today might be Sunday.' Similarly, we don't say 'Ought to be Max mingles with the crowd', but rather 'Max ought to mingle with the crowd.' Alternatively and less efficiently, a dummy subject term can be used, as in '*It* ought to be that Max mingles with the crowd.' At least the grammatical form of '*s* ought to φ' is therefore fully compatible with a raising, *ought-to-be* interpretation.

'Ought' clearly seems to express a propositional operator in some uses, like other auxiliaries such as 'must', 'have to', and 'might'. This holds particularly for epistemic uses like 'It ought to rain today' or 'Today ought to be wet', but is also widely thought true of some normative (or "evaluative") uses of 'ought' that appear to evaluate a state of affairs as best. Consider the instrumental conditional 'If the dance is to be romantic, it ought to be slow', which surely doesn't mean that the *dance* is an agent who has most reason to be slow, but can be naturally interpreted as meaning that it ought to be the case that the dance is slow.

---

[68] The "*Meinong-Chisholm Thesis*"; see, e.g., Chisholm 1964, Williams 1981a, Horty 2001. Ambiguity is championed, e.g., by Harman 1973, Vermazen 1977, Price 2008, Schroeder 2011. This section summarizes the treatment in Finlay & Snedegar 2014.

Those who deny there is any raising 'ought' often dismiss the surface grammar, claiming that these sentences are used noncompositionally to talk about what some agent (e.g., the dancer) ought to do.[69] But some natural evaluative 'ought' sentences resist attempts at such translation. Consider 'Jenny ought to have better luck', or 'Everybody ought to be loved.' These sentences can seem true even if there is nothing that anybody relevantly has most reason to do; for example, Jenny *deserves* better luck, and everybody deserves to be loved, but there isn't anything that anybody can or ought to do to make it happen.[70]

Since the prospects for reducing *ought-to-be* to *ought-to-do* look dim, the best hope for a unifying semantics for 'ought' is as a raising verb. Being only one of a family of intersubstitutable auxiliary verbs, postulating a control meaning for 'ought' would presumably commit us to a systematic lexical ambiguity running through an entire class of words. Might the difference between personal and impersonal readings of '*s* ought to φ' sentences be a reason to accept such an ambiguity? Consider

(15) 'Lexy ought to kiss Lionel.'

This sentence can be read either impersonally (it would be in some way best if Lexy kissed Lionel) or as personally normative for Lexy (she herself has most reason to kiss Lionel). Lexical ambiguity between a raising and a control 'ought' would explain this, but other hypotheses are available which are compatible with a unifying raising (or propositional) semantics.[71] One is naturally suggested by our comparative probabilistic semantics for 'ought', as follows.

If 'ought' has an argument-place for a *contrast set R*, then 'ought' sentences will have distinct readings when relativized differently. A single proposition as expressed by a prejacent sentence like

(16) 'Lexy kisses Lionel'

allows for different dimensions of contrast, as ordinarily indicated by various forms of focus such as intonational stress or italics. For example, compare

(16a) '*Lexy* kisses Lionel.'

(16b) 'Lexy *kisses* Lionel.'

---

[69] E.g., Geach 1982, Thomson 2008. As Mike Ridge observes, these views can appeal to what some purely hypothetical agent (e.g., God) ought to do.

[70] Or consider 'Someone ought to tell the manager', which is naturally read as meaning *it ought to be that someone tells the manager*, not as meaning *there is some x such that x ought to tell the manager* (Wedgwood 2006).

[71] One proposal is that personal readings involve an implicit *agency operator*, 'sees to it that'; see Williams 1981a, Belnap & Horty 1995, Horty 2001, and objections in Price 2008, Schroeder 2011. Others propose ambiguity between raising senses of 'ought' that are indexed to agents and those that aren't; i.e., $O_s(p)$ and $O(p)$; e.g., Humberstone 1991, Broome 1999, Wedgwood 2006. This predicts the intelligibility of certain sentences that actually seem unintelligible, e.g., 'John ought that Lexy kisses Lionel'; see discussion in Schroeder 2004, 2011, Price 2008: 64–69.

(16c) 'Lexy kisses *Lionel*.'

(16d) 'Lexy *kisses Lionel*.'

In (16a) the focus on 'Lexy' naturally suggests contrast with a set of alternative propositions which each involve some person other than Lexy kissing Lionel; for example, {Jorja kisses Lionel, Ashleigh kisses Lionel, Sarah kisses Lionel...}. In (16b) the focus on 'kisses' rather suggests contrast with a set of alternatives which involve Lexy acting in some other way toward Lionel; for example, {Lexy hugs Lionel, Lexy says goodbye to Lionel, Lexy punches Lionel,...}. In (16c) the focus on 'Lionel' suggests contrast with a set of alternatives involving Lexy kissing somebody other than Lionel; for example, {Lexy kisses...}. In (16d) the focus on 'kisses Lionel' suggests contrast with a set of alternatives involving Lexy doing other things with other people.

These different contrasts are retained when a raising, propositional 'ought' operates on sentence (16) as its prejacent, yielding sentential ambiguities. Compare

(15a)   '*Lexy* ought to kiss Lionel.'

(15b) 'Lexy ought to *kiss* Lionel.'

(15c) 'Lexy ought to kiss *Lionel*.'

(15d) 'Lexy ought to *kiss Lionel*.'

The natural reading of (15a) is that it's better that *Lexy* is the person who kisses Lionel than somebody else. The natural reading of (15b) is that it's better that what Lexy does to Lionel is to *kiss* him than some other action. An 'ought' sentence is interpreted as personal for an agent s, I have suggested,[72] only if interpreted as relativized to a *deliberative set*: a contrast set of propositions that constitute deliberative options for s. The kind of contrast set suggested by (15a), that is, {Jorja kisses Lionel, Ashleigh kisses Lionel, Sarah kisses Lionel,...}, won't be a deliberative set for Lexy, for example, as these aren't her deliberative options. But (15b)–(15d) all may suggest a deliberative set for Lexy. Suppose she deliberates over whether to *kiss* Lionel, rather than hug him, say goodbye to him, or punch him; then (15b) will be at issue. A unifying raising semantics for 'ought' does therefore have resources to explain a personal/impersonal ambiguity in 'ought' sentences.

Champions of a control semantics for 'ought' have a final card to play: an argument based on how sentential grammar determines the availability of personal readings. Consider

(17a)   'Lionel ought to be kissed by Lexy.'

(17b)   'It ought to be that Lexy kisses Lionel.'

---

[72] With Justin Snedegar; also cf. Jackson 1985.

Both these sentences strongly suggest impersonal readings, resisting readings as personal for Lexy. This is predicted by the hypothesis that personal readings are generated by a control sense of 'ought', by which (15) on a personal reading expresses a proposition O(Lexy, kisses Lionel) that simply can't be expressed by (17a) or (17b), since neither has Lexy as the subject and thereby the agent of the *ought* relation. But a unifying raising semantics appears to lack an explanation of this, implying that the logical form of these three sentences is the same and that (17a) and (17b) are merely grammatical variants of (15). Sentence (17b) simply exchanges subject movement (of 'Lexy' from the subject position in the prejacent, 'Lexy kisses Lionel') for a dummy subject ('it'). Sentence (17a) is formed by subject movement from the prejacent 'Lionel is kissed by Lexy', which is simply the passive transformation of 'Lexy kisses Lionel', the prejacent of (15). So a unifying raising semantics seems to predict that these three sentences would allow all the same readings.

However, this argument falsely assumes that "merely" grammatical differences between sentences have no influence on their interpretation. Sentences (17a) and (17b) are less efficient than (15), so their use pragmatically signals that the speaker has some special reason for choosing them.[73] Consider first (17a), which has its prejacent in passive voice. Passive voice is known to differ from the active voice in how it places focus. A characteristic function of focus, as observed, is to influence the salience of contrast classes. It can therefore be hypothesized that passive 'ought' sentences like (17a) resist readings as personal for s because the passive voice places focus on the prejacent in a way that strongly raises the salience of nondeliberative contrast sets.

The *Oxford English Grammar* tells us that "a valid reason for resorting to the passive is that it is then possible to omit any mention of the agent...of the action"[74] But (17a) doesn't take advantage of this; compare 'Lionel ought to be kissed.' A speaker using (17a) therefore goes to the extra length of including a grammatically unnecessary complement clause ('by Lexy') referring to the agent, which naturally puts focus on the agent. We observed that putting focus on the agent suggests a contrast set where the agent is the dimension of contrast, such as {Jorja kisses Lionel, Ashleigh kisses Lionel, Sarah kisses Lionel,...}, which isn't a deliberative set for Lexy. This provides a simple pragmatic explanation for why an 'ought' sentence with a passive-voice prejacent resists interpretation as personal.

While this explanation doesn't extend to sentences like (17b), these are also significantly less efficient than sentences like (15), again indicating a special reason for their use. As suggested by the appeal of the supposed principle that

---

[73] By Grice's submaxim of manner to "avoid unnecessary prolixity" (1989); see Chapter 5.
[74] Greenbaum 1996: 57.

ought implies *can*, '*s* ought to φ' sentences apparently have a (highly defeasible) presumption of use with a deliberative set, so that the inefficient 'it ought to be that...' serves to indicate that a different reading is intended. This is also the only way of formulating 'ought' sentences that keeps the prejacent intact, which serves to place focus on the sentence as a whole; this suggests contrast sets where the dimension of contrast is the entire proposition, which would be nondeliberative sets. Although there isn't space for a fuller discussion here, we've seen that this ambiguity in 'ought' sentences is arguably compatible with a unifying raising semantics for 'ought' with the features of the end-relational theory, and therefore that the alleged control sense of 'ought' introduces unnecessary semantic disunity and complexity.[75]

---

[75] In Finlay & Snedegar 2014 we argue that personal readings are sometimes available for 'ought' sentences without an agent-noun in subject position, which is consistent with a pragmatic explanation but not with an appeal to lexical and logical ambiguity. Chrisman 2012 notes further evidence against the control hypothesis: like other raising verbs, 'ought' doesn't allow "er-nominalization" (compare 'the wanter' [okay], 'the oughter' [not okay]) or passive constructions (compare 'it was wanted' [okay], 'it was oughted' [not okay]). Shyam Nair points out to me that unlike control verbs, 'ought' requires "do-support" in interrogatives; e.g., 'Ought Lexy kiss Lionel?' models with 'Might Lexy kiss Lionel?' rather than with '*Does* Lexy *want* to kiss Lionel?'

{ 4 }

Explaining Reasons

Both 'good' and 'ought' are today often claimed to be definable by a more basic normative concept expressed by the word 'reason', perhaps our most general normative noun. That an action is "good" just in case there is some reason for doing it, and that it "ought" to be done just in case there is most reason to do it, are said to be platitudes, which according to popular "buck-passing" accounts provide analyses of the other concepts.[1] Reductive analysis of normativity is therefore often rejected by claiming that the concept of a normative reason is unanalyzable and that normative reasons are primitive.[2]

This claim needs care, however, since it's now generally agreed that normative reasons are just ordinary, "natural", facts. The fact that plaque decays teeth is a reason to brush your teeth daily, and the fact that the subsequent train isn't until 11:00 a.m. may be a reason for catching the 8:00 a.m. train. A fact that r qualifies as a reason because of some normative relation in which it stands to something else, commonly glossed as the relation *counting in favor of*, a contribution to justification or ought-making. Reasons for action generally don't justify actions individually, but supply degrees of normative "weight", so that what ought to be done is whatever has the "balance" of reasons in its favor. Strictly speaking it is the property of being a reason or the relation of favoring, and not reasons themselves, that is allegedly primitive.

Talk about normative reasons is only one of several ordinary uses of the word 'reason', but philosophers often dismiss other uses as irrelevant, holding that the word is ambiguous.[3] But I'll defend the simpler and more unifying hypothesis that these are different uses of the same word with a single meaning, offering a reductive analysis of normative reasons and the favoring relation as neither normatively basic nor irreducible. As before, I'll set aside moral cases until the following chapters, and focus on ordinary and basic 'reason' sentences.

---

[1] E.g., Scanlon 1998: 97 (on 'good').
[2] E.g., Scanlon 1998, Parfit 1997, 2011a.
[3] See e.g., Darwall 1983, Smith 1994.

Normative reasons for action are commonly addressed with sentences of the forms

NR1:   '*r* is a reason to φ.'

NR2:   '*r* is a reason for *s* to φ.'

As a grammatical class, NR sentences concern reasons for "action" only in a broad sense. Many important cases involve attitude-verbs for 'φ', and "reasons for action" proper can be distinguished from "reasons for attitudes" such as hope, fear, regret, anger, guilt, and belief. But we also speak about "motivating reasons for action" using sentences of the forms

MR1:   '*r* is the reason for which *s* φ-ed.'

MR2:   '*r* is *s*'s reason for φ-ing.'

Partly because these motivating reasons apparently needn't weigh in favor of the agent's acting to any degree, these sentences are commonly said to involve a different meaning of 'reason'.

We also talk about "explanatory reasons", which needn't concern agents or actions at all, with sentences of the form

ER: '*r* is the reason that *p*.'

Finally, noting differences in use between 'There is a reason for *s* to φ' (an existentially quantified version of NR2), and sentences of the forms

SR1:   '*s* has a reason to φ',

SR2:   '*s*'s reason to φ is that *r*',

some philosophers claim a further ambiguity in the meaning of 'reason', between an "objective" normative sense, as in NR sentences, and a "subjective" normative sense, as in SR sentences.[4]

These distinctions between normative and motivating reasons for action, normative and explanatory reasons, and objective and subjective normative reasons present a challenge for a unifying semantics. I'll argue that this can be met, though a *completely* unifying semantics for 'reason' is out of the question, as it's also used as a verb. I won't be concerned with what it means "to reason," although this is presumably related (polysemous).[5] There is also a derivative noun referring to the mental faculty that conducts this activity, which I'll also ignore: our concern is with what reasons are, not with what Reason is.

---

[4] Schroeder 2008c.

[5] An obvious hypothesis is that to reason is to engage in mental activity guided by what one takes to be reasons. A rival hypothesis discredited by this chapter is that reasons are rather to be defined in terms of Reason or rationality.

4.1. Reasons as Explanations Why

Consider sentences of the form ER, concerning (non-normative) reasons for ordinary facts, such as

(1)   'The reason the light isn't turning green is that the car didn't cross the sensor.'

(2)   'The reason this escape plan won't work is that the prison fence is electrified.'

Since this use of 'reason' is plausibly the most common, general, and easily analyzed, I propose to start the search for a unified meaning here and then examine how much of the other data this sense of 'reason' can be extended to cover.

Here a "reason" is a fact *that r* (e.g., that the car didn't cross the sensor) that stands in a relation R to another fact *that p* (e.g., that the light isn't turning green). The logical form of these sentences is thus approximately $R(r, p)$. Many writers have considered it obvious that 'reason' in these uses means *explanation why*. The relation R here is just the relation of explaining why, and for r to be the reason for p is simply for r to be the explanans to p's explanandum. Or as we may say, a reason is an answer to a 'why?' question, the content of a 'because…' reply.[6] The above sentences seem to be equivalent in meaning to

(1a)   'The explanation why the light isn't turning green is that the car didn't cross the sensor.'

(2a)   'The explanation why this escape plan won't work is that the prison fence is electrified.'

While not all explanations are of *why p*—there are also explanations of *how p*, at least—use of 'reason' is apparently limited to explanations why. We wouldn't use 'the reason one escaped from prison' for *the explanation of how one escaped from prison*, for example.[7] While the concept of explanation itself raises difficult issues, I'll simply assume that 'explanation' means roughly *information that reveals*,[8] and 'why' means *what makes it true that*. To assert a sentence of the form ER, '*r* is the reason that *p*', is therefore to say that *r* is information that reveals what makes it true that *p*. The fact that the car didn't cross the sensor, for example, is information that reveals what makes it true that the light isn't turning green.[9] If the various uses of 'reason' are to be given a unifying

---

[6] Cf. Hieronymi 2005, who proposes that "a reason is a consideration that bears on a question".

[7] Cf. Alvarez 2010.

[8] 'Explanation' is itself polysemous between (i) an explanans, and (ii) some communicative act or product which has a (putative) explanans as its content. Only the former is plausibly part of the meaning of 'reason'.

[9] Cases like this may suggest that 'reason' means simply *what makes it true that*. In German the relevant term is 'grund', which also has this more general meaning. I stick with *explanation*

semantics, speech about normative reasons must be analyzed as having this same logical form and meaning.

The hypothesis that normative reasons can be analyzed in terms of explanations why isn't novel or radical, and has been perennially popular among philosophers.[10] But it has proved difficult to implement and vindicate. One immediate challenge is to reconcile the grammar of normative reasons sentences with the logical form $R(r, p)$. A simple report of a normative reason may take the form NR1, 'r is a reason to φ', as in

(3)   'That plaque decays teeth is a reason to brush your teeth every day.'

(4)   'That the subsequent train isn't until 11:00 a.m. is a reason to catch the 8:00 a.m. train.'

Here 'reason' grammatically takes an infinitival verb-phrase complement, 'to φ', prompting a common view that normative reasons are logically distinct from explanatory reasons in being related to actions rather than to propositions. But as with 'good to φ', it can be asked "... a reason for *whom* to φ?", and these sentences can be explicated as elliptical for sentences of the form NR2, 'r is a reason for s to φ.' For example, (3) is naturally interpreted as 'That plaque decays teeth is a reason [for you] to brush your teeth every day.' While a distinction is often drawn between "agent-relative" and "agent-neutral" reasons, a natural thought is that a reason is agent-neutral just in case it is a reason *for anybody* (in a salient domain) to φ. Accordingly the property of being a normative reason is often claimed to have argument-places for both an action φ and an agent s rather than for a proposition, with approximately the logical form $R(r, s, φ)$ rather than $R(r, p)$.

This issue about logical form has a direct parallel in the case of 'good', and in Chapter 2 I analyzed 'good for s to φ' as equivalent to 'good that/if s φs', and thereby a case of 'good that p'. A unified logical form for ER and NR sentences could be identified if 'a reason for s to φ' can similarly be interpreted as 'a reason that s φs', and so a case of 'a reason that p'. While this mightn't seem any more promising than the parallel initially did for 'good', we apparently do ascribe normative reasons for the obtaining of states of affairs. Consider

(5)   'The brutality of war is a reason for hostilities to come to an end.'

This has the same grammatical form as NR2 sentences about agent-relative normative reasons, but it would be absurd to read it as ascribing a normative reason to the agent *hostilities* to perform the action of *coming to an end*. It's

---

because it fits better with our speech about "giving" and "having" reasons, but 'reason' could be held polysemous here.

[10] E.g., Toulmin 1950, Davidson 1963, Williams 1979, 1989, Audi 1986: 512, Searle 2001: 100, Broome 2004. Many more philosophers have endorsed the weaker claim that reasons are connected to explanation.

more naturally interpreted as saying that the fact that war is brutal is a normative reason favoring the state of affairs that hostilities come to an end, or as
equivalent to the sentence, 'That war is brutal is a reason for its being the case
that hostilities come to an end', with the logical form $R(r, p)$. Some will insist
that (5) is used to say roughly that the brutality of war is a reason *for somebody
to bring* hostilities to an end, but this is ad hoc and noncompositional: 'coming
to an end' can only describe an "action" of the hostilities, not of agents.[11]

Analyzing 'a reason for s to φ' as *an explanation why s φs* faces clear obstacles,
however. First a grammatical difficulty: 'explanation why' can't be substituted
for 'reason' in 'a reason for s to φ'. The sentence 'The brutality of war is an
explanation why for hostilities to cease' is ungrammatical and hard to interpret.
But more seriously, 'a reason for s to φ' seems to mean something quite different.
A reason for you to brush your teeth daily isn't the same thing as an explanation
why you brush your teeth daily, and a reason for hostilities to come to an end
isn't the same as an explanation why hostilities come to an end. One feature of
talk about normative reasons is that it seems in one way *nonfactive*: a normative
reason for s to φ doesn't entail that s actually φs.[12] Yet 'explanation why' seems
doubly factive: r can only be an explanation why p if both r and p are true. Being
explanatory of why s φs isn't necessary for being a normative reason for s to φ.
Nor is it sufficient: even if you do brush your teeth daily, your normative reason
for doing so (that plaque decays teeth) needn't explain it. Weighing in favor of
something can't be identified with explaining why it obtains.

Since the nonfactiveness of 'good for s to φ' was explained in Chapter 2 by
analyzing this as *good if s φs* rather than *good that s φs*, it might be speculated
here that 'a reason for s to φ' means rather *an explanation why, if s φs*. But here
this doesn't work, since it isn't true that if s φs then this is explained by her normative reasons for φ-ing.[13] Simply substituting 'explanation why' for 'reason' in
NR1 sentences seems natural, however: 'a reason to φ' is plausibly equivalent
to 'an explanation why *to φ*'. The fact that plaque decays teeth is an explanation why to brush your teeth daily, and the fact that the subsequent train
isn't until 11:00 a.m. could be an explanation why to catch the 8:00 a.m. train.
But although 'Why φ?' is a familiar kind of question, it requires interpretation,
since 'φ' (e.g., 'Catch the 8:00 a.m. train') isn't a real explanandum.[14] 'Why φ?'

---

[11] A common motivation is the idea that 'r is a reason for s to φ' implies that φ-ing is within
s's agential power. Our theory will explain this principle as pragmatic and therefore defeasible.

[12] The locus classicus here is Williams 1979.

[13] On the interpretation of Finlay 2009b, Williams 1979 analyzes normative reasons as explanations why *s would have acted under certain conditions*.

[14] This form may suggest that normative reasons are explanations for *imperatives*. But while
we can understand the idea of an explanation why someone *utters* an imperative, this is a different explanandum. People can also have reasons to do things that nobody does or should tell them
to do (e.g., pro tanto reasons). One view on the semantics of imperatives is that they are elliptical
for 'ought' claims, which converges with my analysis.

seems elliptical for a more complete question with propositional content. At least an implicit agent can be presumed for the action: Why: *I* catch the 8:30 train? Why: *you* brush your teeth daily? But we've seen that the question cannot be *Why does s* φ? or *Why is it the case that s* φ*s*?

While 'a reason for *s* to φ' always has an normative sense, explanations of action aren't in general normative. A unifying semantics for 'reason' as meaning *explanation why* therefore can't locate the normativity in the meaning of 'reason' itself. If normative reasons are answers to a particular kind of *Why?* question, then the normativity is presumably rather in the explanandum, as a question with normative content. A natural idea is that 'Why φ?' can be explicated as 'Why [ought *s* to] φ?', prompting some philosophers to suggest that 'a reason for *s* to φ' is analyzable as roughly *an explanation why s ought to* φ.[15] But this can't be exactly right, because normative reasons often have merely contributory ("pro tanto") rather than decisive normative "weight": a reason for *s* to φ doesn't entail *s* ought to φ, as there may also be weightier reasons for *s* not to φ. Since 'explanation' appears factive, there can only be an explanation why *s* ought to φ if in fact *s* ought to φ. A 'reason for *s* to φ' therefore cannot uniformly mean 'an explanation why *s* ought to φ'.[16]

Observe that if *r* is an outweighed or defeated normative reason to φ, then calling it "a reason *s* ought to φ" is no better than calling it "an explanation why *s* ought to φ". This implies that the problem here isn't a difference between the factiveness of 'explanation why' and 'reason', but simply that we're considering the wrong kind of normative explanandum. Since a normative reason claim usually only implies a degree of contributory normative weight, it implies a normative explanandum that is similarly pro tanto. We've already identified such a normative concept: what ought to be the case is whatever is best, or *most good*.

The word 'good' expresses the requisite kind of pro tanto concept, suggesting that 'a reason for *s* to φ' is used elliptically for 'a reason [it is good,] for *s* to φ', and means *an explanation why it is good (in some way and to some degree), if s* φ*s*.[17] The relation *R* of *counting in favor of* would then be the relation of *explaining the goodness of*. Analysis into explanations why *s* ought to φ needn't be abandoned altogether, however, as our semantics allows a distinction between *pro tanto* reasons why it's good for *s* to φ, and *strict* reasons why *s*

---

[15] Toulmin 1950: Ch. 11, Finlay 2001: 104, Broome 2004: 34. See discussion also in Schroeder 2007: 35.

[16] Broome (2004) proposes an ambiguity between this all-things-considered sense, and a pro tanto sense as *something playing a role in a weighting explanation of why s ought or ought not to* φ. This view is neither unifying nor compositional, and also faces significant philosophical problems; see Schroeder 2007: 36n, Brunero 2013.

[17] Also Finlay 2006. Similar views are suggested in Raz 1999: 23 ("reasons are facts *in virtue of which* those actions are good"), Searle 2001: 110. See also Darwall 1983: 38, who rejects, and Schroeder 2007, who advances an analysis of normative reasons in terms of "promotion" of desired ends.

ought to (or must) φ.[18] Both kinds of explanation can be expected to have a role in practical speech and thought; I suggest they are commonly discriminated by '*a* reason [why it would be good] to φ', and '*the* reason [why *s* ought] to φ'.

This analysis solves all the problems observed so far. Since the existence of a normative reason to φ is a sufficient condition for its being (in some way and to some degree) good to φ, the factiveness of 'explanation' is accommodated: normative reasons explain facts.[19] And while 'an explanation why for *s* to φ' is ungrammatical, 'an explanation why *it's good* for *s* to φ' is fine.[20] The analysis has other virtues. First, when combined with the end-relational semantics for 'good' it generates plausible analyses of our examples of normative reasons sentences. That plaque decays teeth is an explanation why it's *good for preserving your health* that you brush your teeth daily, because it explains why brushing your teeth daily increases the probability that you preserve your health. That the next train isn't until 11:00 a.m. may be an explanation why it's (e.g.) *good for getting to work on time* if you catch the 8:00 a.m. train, because it may explain why catching the 8:00 a.m. train increases the probability that you make it to work on time.

Second, straightforward accounts of the meaning of 'some reason', 'more reason', and 'most reason' (and thereby of the *weight* of reasons) can be derived, as follows. Observe that although 'reason' is a count noun (like 'pebble') rather than a mass noun (like 'sand'), we ordinarily talk about there being more/most "reason" for *s* to φ, rather than more/most "reasons". This anomaly reflects the fact that 'most reason' clearly doesn't mean *most reasons*. As reasons have varying degrees of weight, one strong reason to φ can outweigh many weak reasons not to φ. Notice also that talk about "some", "more", or "most" reason (or about the "weight" of reasons) is only intelligible for *normative* reasons: compare 'There is most reason why the light isn't turning green.' So the relevant gradability is presumably located in the normative part of the analysis.

As goodness comes in degrees, talk about what is "some good" (somewhat good, good to some degree), "more good", and "most good" is perfectly intelligible, which suggests:

Some Reason: 'There's some reason to φ' means *there's an explanation why it's good to some degree to φ*.[21]

---

[18] Cf. Gert 2003. *It's good for s to φ* is equivalent to *s ought ceteris paribus to φ*, where 'ceteris paribus' indicates a very sparse background *b*: all else being equal, if *p* is good to any degree it ought to be that *p*.

[19] 'A reason why *it would* be good if *p*' is slightly more natural than 'a reason why it *is* good if *p*', perhaps due to the practice of tensing modals to agree with their complements: i.e., the subjunctive is used because *p* is hypothetical, rather than its goodness. Compare saying, 'The title of my talk tomorrow *will be* 'N' even though the title already *is* 'N'.

[20] 'A reason for *s* to φ' is also okay. Observe grammar allows 'reason' to combine redundantly ("pleonastically") with 'why': i.e., we can say either 'a reason it's good for *s* to φ' or 'a reason why it's good for *s* to φ'.

[21] Or perhaps in this case (simply and compositionally) there is some explanation why it's good to φ.

More Reason: 'There's more reason to φ than to ψ' means *there's an explanation why it's more good (better) to φ than to ψ.*

Most Reason: 'There's most reason to φ' means *there's an explanation why it's most good (best) to φ.*

These analyses aren't fully compositional, but the expressions are evidently idiomatic,[22] which our account is well-placed to explain. The singular noun is explained as concerning a single (though possibly complex) explanation, and the need for an idiomatic construction is explained by the ellipsis of the normative element, which leaves the quantifier without a proper position in the grammar.

The normative weight of a reason to φ is therefore the degree of value it reveals φ-ing to have. By the end-relational semantics for 'good', the weight of reasons will be relative to particular ends *e*. This raises a challenge, as it's commonplace to compare and combine weights of reasons based on different ends. While this challenge will be addressed in Chapter 6, the following account can be derived of weight relative to a single end. A reason's weight toward φ-ing (or the degree to which *r* counts in favor of φ-ing), relative to an end *e* and background *b*, is just the degree to which φ-ing increases the probability of *e* relative to (b & r).[23]

This analysis accommodates widely accepted platitudes about the relationships between 'reason' and other normative terms like 'good', 'best', and 'ought', in combination with the end-relational semantics: something is *good* in some way and to some degree just in case it has *some reason* in its favor, and is *best* and therefore also what one *ought* to do just in case it has *most reason* in its favor.[24] It turns buck-passing analyses of 'good' and 'ought' on their heads, however, supporting the older view that 'good' and 'ought' express more fundamental normative concepts.[25]

This analysis also faces some objections. First, even appeal to the goodness of φ-ing may seem too strong to accommodate all pro tanto reasons, since (despite the platitude linking reasons and goodness) there can apparently be reasons to φ even when it wouldn't be good to φ. However, the analysis merely involves φ-ing's being good *in some way* and *to some degree*,[26] and

---

[22] They appear to be idiosyncratic to English; in some other languages (e.g., Swedish, as reported by Gunnar Björnsson) the expressions corresponding to 'more/most reason' translate literally as 'stronger/strongest reasons'.

[23] This is worked out in detail by Daan Evers (2010, 2013); e.g., "*More Reason*: a fact is stronger reason to φ than another fact is a reason to ψ (relative to *e*) iff (a) both are reasons for some act [in a set of relevant alternatives R] and (b) the first raises the probability of *e* given *b* & φ to a value higher than the last raises the probability of *e* given *b* & ψ."

[24] See Evers 2010, 2013 for more detailed discussion.

[25] If normative reasons are all constituted by "natural" or non-normative facts, then contrary to the arguments of primitivists like Scanlon and Parfit, the truth in these platitudes is actually that normative facts can always be explained by non-normative facts.

[26] See also Raz 1999: 23.

our semantics allows at least three ways of weakening the relevant value. (i) *End-Relativity*: φ-ing might be good for some salient (e.g., desired) end *e*, but not for ends that would justify a claim of goodness simpliciter (discussed in Chapter 6); (ii) *Contrast-Sensitivity*: As we analyzed claims about the goodness of *p* as assuming particular ways of its being that *not-p*, φ-ing might be good in contrast to certain salient ways of not φ-ing but not others. Any reason for φ-ing entails at least that φ-ing would be better in *some* respect than *some* alternative.[27] (iii) *Ceteris Paribus*: φ-ing might be good relative merely to a restricted background *b*, but not to all the facts or available information.[28]

Another objection suggests that normative reasons for *s* to φ rather or additionally consist in *evidence* that *s* ought to φ.[29] The fact *r* that a trusted adviser tells *s* that she ought to φ, for example, is plausibly a reason for her to φ. But it might seem that this fact *r* couldn't be an explanation why *s* ought to φ or why it's good if *s* φs: after all, the adviser surely doesn't believe that *s* ought to φ simply because he said it. This conclusion is too quick, however, because of the *subjective* senses of 'ought' and 'best', relativized to what she believes or her evidence rather than the facts. If no reason for or against *s*'s φ-ing is known other than *r*, then when *s* asks '*Why* ought I φ?' or '*Why* is it best if I φ?', it's appropriate to respond with the *explanation*, 'Because your trusted adviser says you ought to.'

Evidence that one ought to φ can be an explanation why one ought to φ. Our semantics explains this as involving an implicit shift in senses of 'ought' (or 'good'). Since *s*'s evidence that *p* is just information that increases the probability that *p* relative to *s*'s other information b_s, our theory predicts that *s*'s evidence that she ought to φ in a more objective sense (e.g., relative to her adviser's superior information) is information that increases her subjective probability (relative to b_s) that the more objective probability of the relevant end *e* is highest if she φs. Such evidence will therefore also be the right kind of thing to make her subjective probability of *e* if she φs greater than her subjective probability of *e* if she doesn't φ; that is, to make it *good* (for *e*) relative to b_s if *s* φs. Evidential reasons are therefore *explanations why it's good (for e) relative to b_s for s to φ.*

While evidence that *p* isn't generally an explanation why *p*, the end-relational semantics explains why evidence for (more objective) normative facts is

---

[27] Alternatively, these reasons claims might be elliptical for comparatives; e.g., an explanation why it's *better* for e, for *s* to φ [than to…]. For a case that normative reasons claims are always contrastive see Sinnott-Armstrong 2008, Snedegar 2013a, 2013b.

[28] Other theories are obliged to make the same conjecture; e.g., Kearns & Star 2008.

[29] Kearns & Star 2008, 2009 suggest normative reasons are evidence rather than explanations, partly on the grounds that reasons *for believing that p* consist in evidence that *p* rather than explanations why *p*. I applaud their scruple of parsimony, but their data is too narrow: to ask for an ordinary explanatory reason why *p* (e.g., the reason why the traffic light didn't change) isn't to ask for evidence that *p*.

sometimes an explanation of (more subjective) normative facts that are reported with the same sentence.[30] But it also avoids problems for the evidence theory of reasons, because it recognizes that (defeated) evidence that one ought to φ isn't always a reason to φ. Suppose s is certain that she ought not to φ; she could still concede that r is *evidence* she ought to φ, but to agree in this same context that r is a *reason* for her to φ would be peculiar. This is accommodated by observing that r doesn't explain why it's good relative to s's present information for her to φ.[31]

A further objection is that the fact *that φ-ing increases the probability of e* itself seems to be a reason for φ-ing, but cannot itself be an explanation why φ-ing increases the probability of e. Surely nothing can explain itself?[32] But this isn't quite right, because concepts can be opaque. The fact that a particular geometrical figure is a regular three-sided polygon, for example, is an explanation why it's a triangle. This is to explain something by its "formal cause" or essential nature. The fact that φ-ing increases the probability of e is similarly an explanation by essence, and thereby a reason why φ-ing is good for e.

The rest of this chapter examines other obstacles for our hypothesis about the unifying meaning of 'reason', concerning the *agent-relativity* of normative reasons, normative reasons for *attitudes*, and what it means to *have* and *act for* a reason. I'll argue that these problems are solved with the resources provided by the flexibility or vagueness in the concepts of *explanation* and of being *good in some way*.

4.2. The Agent-Relativity of Reasons

Our hypothesis is that 'a reason for s to φ' is used as elliptical for 'a reason [why it's good] for s to φ', and means *an explanation why it's good if s φs*. But this may seem to imply an implausible account of the "agent-relativity" of normative reasons: that r is a normative reason *for s* just in case it explains the goodness (in some way) of a state of affairs that p in which s features as the "agent". It can't be inferred from (5) that the brutality of war is a normative reason for the agent *hostilities*, for example. Or consider

---

[30] This makes sense of "Ewing's Principle" (that one ought to do whatever one believes one ought to do) as the principle that one ought (subjectively) to do whatever one believes one ought (objectively) to do; see Finlay 2010b.

[31] Kearns & Star point out that relative to b_s, r isn't evidence either, but this doesn't explain why s can naturally accept that r is "evidence" and deny it is a "reason" in the same breath. We avoid this problem because speech about evidence that p assumes that the truth value of p itself is excluded from the background b (or else the probability of p relative to b would be either 0 or 1).

[32] This objection is raised by Evers (2010: 412), and Mike Ridge (correspondence). The fact that φ-ing is good, and even that there is a reason to φ, can themselves plausibly be identified as reasons to φ. Some of these judgments may be explained by shifts in the salient senses of probability (as above), or ends.

(6)　'The need to deter others from killing is a reason for murderers to be punished.'

Accepting this sentence doesn't commit one to accepting that there is any reason that is normative for murderers, to be punished; it seems coherent to assert (6) and continue, '...but it isn't a reason for the murderers'.

A normative reason's being "for *s*" rather seems to require *s*'s having some kind of normative relationship to that reason. It might instead be said that the need to deter others from killing is a reason *for us* (or for society, judges, etc.), for murderers to be punished. Similarly, the brutality of war may be a reason *for politicians*, for hostilities to come to an end. Accommodating the agent-relativity of reasons therefore seems to require that 'a reason for *s* to φ' is logically incomplete, and used elliptically for 'a reason for s_1, for s_2 to φ.' This implies that 'a reason for *s* to φ' would be logically ambiguous between 'a reason [for s_1], for s_2 to φ' (e.g., 'a reason for hostilities to come to an end') and 'a reason for s_1, [for s_2] to φ' (e.g., 'a reason for you to catch the 8:00 a.m. train').

Chapter 2's treatment of a similar logical ambiguity in 'good for *s* to φ' suggests a second interpretation of agent-relativity: that 'a reason for s_1, for s_2 to φ', is elliptical for 'a reason [it is good] for s_1, for s_2 to φ'. On this view, *r* is a normative reason for an agent just in case it explains why it's *good for the agent* if she φs. This interpretation at least provides a normative kind of relationship to *s*, but it can't be correct.

While a few philosophers hold the controversial thesis of *ethical egoism* that all genuine reasons come from self-interest, this can't be what is ordinarily *meant* by 'a reason for *s*'. Reasons of self-interest are contrasted with reasons of altruism, and for self-sacrifice. Also, while we found that 'for *s*' functions in 'good for *s*' to identify a kind of end, and can be replaced by a 'for *e*' relativizer, this kind of substitution isn't possible for 'a reason for *s*'. While 'good for *s*' seems equivalent to 'good for promoting *s*'s interests', 'a reason for *s*' isn't equivalent to 'a reason for promoting *s*'s interests', which can only mean a reason (for an unspecified agent), to promote *s*'s interests. Finally, in 'good for *s*, if *p*', *s* can be any "patient" intelligibly ascribed an interest, including inanimate objects like trees and cars. But 'a reason for the car' isn't intelligible in the same way as 'good for the car' is. An "agent" *s* must apparently possess some cognitive abilities for there to be normative reasons for *s*.

Cognitive abilities aren't implied by 'good for s', but are implied by 'explanation for s', which therefore suggests a third interpretation of this agent-relativity. If 'reason' means *explanation why*, then 'a reason for *s*' might be expected to mean simply *an explanation for s*. Speech or thought about explanations is commonly relative to *subjects* in this way: a fact *r* that is an explanation why *p* for one person s_1 may fail to be an explanation why *p* for another person s_2, and so our hypothesis predicts that claims about normative reasons would be similarly relative. This avoids all three problems we observed for the previous interpretation in terms of 'good for s': (i) r can be an explanation for s of why it's good in some way if p, without being an explanation why it's good *for s*; (ii) 'an explanation for s' isn't plausibly understood as *an explanation for some end e*, as explanations are for subjects and not for propositions; therefore (iii) s must have cognitive abilities for there to be explanations for s.

This interpretation predicts an ambiguity in 'r is a reason for s to φ', between

NR2a: 'r is a reason/explanation for s_1, [why it's good, for s_2] to φ.'

NR2b: 'r is a reason/explanation [for s_1, why it's good,] for s_2 to φ.'

On the natural interpretation of NR2a, omitting 'for s_2' indicates that s_2 is identical to s_1 (as noted in Chapter 2). So 'a reason for you, to catch the 8:00 a.m. train' is naturally read as 'an explanation for you, [of why it's good, for *you*] to catch the 8:00 a.m. train.' On the natural interpretation of NR2b, omitting 'for s_1' suggests reference backwards to subjects already made salient. So (6), 'The need to deter others from killing is a reason for murderers to be punished', can be naturally read as 'The need to deter others from killing is an explanation [for us, of why it's good,] for murderers to be punished.'

To evaluate this hypothesis we need to investigate how explanations are relative to subjects. In ordinary explanatory sentences of the form ER, like (1) and (2), the explicit explanans doesn't explain why p by itself, but only in combination with or against a background of other facts or information. For (1), the car's not crossing the sensor doesn't by itself reveal what makes it true that the light isn't turning green, but only against assumptions about the design of traffic sensors, the construction of cars, etc. For (2), the fact that the prison fence is electrified doesn't by itself reveal what makes it true that the escape plan won't work, but only against background information such as that it requires scaling the fence with bare hands, the physiological effects of electricity, etc. Some philosophers would therefore say that the fact that the prison fence is electrified isn't really an explanation why the escape plan won't work, but merely part of an explanation.

The same issues are found in speech and thought about normative reasons, as our hypothesis predicts. The fact that the subsequent train isn't due until 11:00 a.m. doesn't weigh in favor of catching the 8:00 a.m. train by itself, but only against background information such as that it's the train that takes you to the office, and that you need to be there by 9:00 a.m. This is the "holism of reasons": what counts as a reason to φ in one context mightn't do so in other contexts (e.g., where the train doesn't take you to the office), just as what counts as an explanation of p in one context mightn't in other contexts.[33] Some philosophers therefore argue similarly that the fact that r (e.g., the subsequent train isn't due until 11:00 a.m.) isn't really the reason to φ (catch the 8:00 a.m. train), but merely part of the reason. Our theory needn't rule on this debate,

---

[33] E.g., Dancy 2004.

and can allow either that what are ordinarily called "explanations" or "reasons" are merely significant parts of the real explanations or reasons, or else that real explanations and reasons come in both sparser and more detailed forms.[34] Since we're taking our cues from ordinary language I'll continue in the second, ordinary way of speaking.

What are reported as reasons or explanations why *p* are facts which are decisive, against a background *b*, in revealing what makes *p* the case. In one clear sense, to be an explanation *for s* is to be an explanation *relative to the information s possesses, b_s*. The fact that the prison fence is electrified may be an explanation why the escape plan won't work for someone who knows the content of the plan, but not for someone who lacks that information. Similarly, the fact that the subsequent train isn't until 11:00 a.m. is an explanation for you why it's good (for your getting to work on time) for you to catch the 8:00 a.m. train, *if* you already know that the train takes you to the office, but not otherwise. So we might try analyzing 'a reason for *s*, to φ' as meaning *an explanation relative to s's information of why it's good, for s to φ*. This suggests a covert argument-place in the logical form of reasons sentences for a background *b*, yielding the form $R_b(r, p)$ and the relation *R* that *r* explains relative to *b* why *p*. The end-relational semantics for 'good' then implies that a fully explicit (pro tanto) normative reason sentence can take the grammatical form

R-ER: '*r* is a reason/explanation relative to b_1 why it is good for *e*, given b_2, for *s* to φ',

and that the full logical form of an NR sentence is $R_{b1}(r, G_{e,b2}(p))$.

An adequate account of agent-relativity is still lacking, however, because this interpretation provides only an epistemic and not a (practical) normative connection between agents and reasons. That the subsequent train isn't until 11:00 a.m. may also be an explanation *for me* (relative to my information) of why it's good for your getting to work on time, for you to catch the 8:00 a.m. train. But this doesn't necessarily make it a reason also for me, for you to catch the 8:00 a.m. train. There might be nothing that for me favors your getting to work on time. This difference can't be explained by observing that it's a reason why it's good if *you* φ, and not if *I* φ, as the following case shows. Suppose *r* is the fact that Terry has just stolen Victor's wallet: relative to both Terry's and Victor's information, *r* is a reason or explanation why it's good (for Victor's recovering his wallet), for Terry to be apprehended. But while *r* is apparently a reason for *Victor*, for Terry to be apprehended, it doesn't seem to be a reason

---

[34] Schroeder (2007) has to reject the *No Background Conditions* view to show that his Humean analysis of reasons as explained by agents' desires accommodates the intuition that facts about our desires aren't typically part of our moral reasons to act. This doesn't accommodate the related intuition that our moral reasons to act also can't be *explained* by our desires, however (cf. Johnson 2013: Ch. 4). On the end-relational theory, agents' desires aren't generally part of their reasons even given *No Background Conditions*.

for *Terry*, to be apprehended (though we can disambiguate and agree that *r* is a reason, for Terry to be apprehended). Therefore 'a reason for *s*, to φ' can't simply mean 'an explanation for *s*, [why it's good (in some way), for *s*] to φ'.

The distinctly normative character of the agent-relativity of reasons suggests looking more closely at the normative part of the analysis, the relativization of 'good'. Whereas we found obstacles to analyzing 'a reason for *s*' in terms of either 'good for *s*' or 'explanation for *s*', an analysis that appeals to both is more promising. Our semantics for 'good' being fundamentally end-rather than subject-relational, 'a reason to φ' should be ambiguous between *an explanation why it's good for e_1, for s to φ*, and *an explanation why it's good for e_2, for s to φ*, etc. If 'a reason for *s*, to φ' is used to mean roughly *an explanation for s of why it's good (for some end e) for s to φ*, this prompts the question, "Good for what end *e*?" If qualifying a normative reason or explanation as "for *s*" functions to make salient the intended kind of end, then a "reason for *s*" would be an explanation why something is good for an end *e* salient somehow in relation to *s*.

How might reference to an agent make a particular end *e* salient, if not by pointing toward the agent's welfare or what is good for *s*? Given that an explanation is an answer to a "Why?" question, 'an explanation for *s*' might be interpreted as meaning an answer to a "Why?" question salient in relation to *s*. A full pragmatic account must wait for later chapters, but an intuitive idea is that by "a reason for *s*" we mean an answer to a question, 'Why is it good to φ?' that *s* might himself ask in deliberating, and which *s* might himself therefore accept as relevant to the practical issue of what to do; that is, a question relative to ends *desired by s*. The fact that Terry has stolen Victor's wallet is naturally described as an explanation *for Victor* of why it's good, for Terry to be apprehended, but not as an explanation *for Terry* of why it's good, for him to be apprehended. This explains the agent-relativity of normative explanations not by sensitivity to explanatory backgrounds *b*, but by the different end-relativization of 'good' made salient by Victor's and Terry's different desires; that is,

(7)   '*r* is an explanation for Victor*$_i$*, of why it's good [for his*$_i$* ends], for Terry to be apprehended.'

(8)   '*r* is an explanation for Terry*$_i$*, of why it's good [for his*$_i$* ends], for Terry to be apprehended.'

This may seem to suggest a Humean theory of normative reasons for *s*, as considerations relevant to the satisfaction of *s*'s desires.[35] But our theory supports only a weaker pragmatic connection with agent's desires, suggesting that Humean theories are too narrow. While talking about reasons "for *s*" may often

---

[35] E.g., Foot 1972, Mackie 1977, Hubin 1999, Schroeder 2007, Goldman 2009. Williams 1979 is often but I think mistakenly considered a classic representative.

make s's desired ends salient, in some contexts it may make ends salient on the basis of some other relationship to s; for example, an end that the *speaker* wants the agent to pursue (see Chapter 7). Or it may simply signify an ordinary explanatory relativity to s's information b_s, the end being salient in another way. This flexibility is an advantage, as we'll see that speech and thought about normative reasons don't always respect Humean constraints. A virtue of this analysis is its ability to explain (pragmatically) the prevalence of both Humean and non-Humean intuitions here.

It's controversial whether the agent-relativity of the (objective) normative reasons described by NR sentences involves relativity to the agent's information, which may seem problematic for this analysis of 'a reason for s' as meaning *an explanation for s*. In addition to being doubly factive, entailing both that r and that p (it's good to some degree and in a salient way if s φs), these reasons sentences are said to be "objective" also in the sense of being true *whenever p* is the case because of r. Consider

(4a) 'That the subsequent train isn't until 11:00 a.m. is a reason for Jill to catch the 8:00 a.m. train.'

If Jill doesn't know that the train goes to the part of town where she works, then the fact that the next train isn't until 11:00 a.m. apparently can't be an explanation *for Jill* (i.e., relative to her information) of why it's good for her getting to work by 9:00 a.m., for her to catch the 8:00 a.m. train. While some philosophers agree that this would make (4a) false (as our analysis seems to predict), others maintain that NR sentences are true in such situations.

The beginning of an answer is provided by the logical ambiguity we've observed in 'a reason for s to φ'. One way to read (4a) is as elliptical for 'That the subsequent train isn't until 11:00 a.m. is a reason [why it's good,] for Jill to catch the 8:00 a.m. train.' When read like this, (4a) doesn't relativize the reason or explanation to Jill in the above way at all, and is easily interpreted as concerning an explanation for (e.g.) the audience, or relative to a fuller background which includes the train routes. Talk about explanations that isn't explicitly relativized to a subject can reasonably be presumed to assume a factual background, which is a step toward explaining why 'r is a reason, for s to φ' strongly prefers a more objective reading.

This logical ambiguity may go some way toward explaining the conflict in intuitions. But it may still be insisted that r is not merely a reason, for Jill to catch the 8:00 a.m. train, but is also a reason *for Jill*, to catch the 8:00 a.m. train, despite her ignorance. A second response accommodates this intuition. If 'for s' is functioning here to indicate a normative explanandum relevant to s (e.g., as relativized to an end she desires), then it is adequately explained without appeal to s's information. Some uses of (4a) might therefore be explicated as concerning a reason or explanation, relative to (e.g.) *our* fuller information or all the facts, of why it's good (in a Jill-relevant way) if she catches the 8:00

a.m. train. Put differently, 'a reason for Jill' can refer to something that Jill would recognize as an explanation why catching the 8:00 a.m. train is relevantly "good" were she to have fuller information. Since she would presumably be interested to know about any such explanation this would often be a useful thing to communicate. Conflicting intuitions about the information-relativity of 'a reason for s, to φ' can therefore be explained as resulting from different readings of the 'for s' relativizer.

4.3. Reasons for Attitudes

This analysis of normative reasons as explanations why faces a special objection for cases where the "action" is an attitude, that is, in accommodating speech and thought about normative reasons for attitudes, such as belief, intention, desire, hope, fear, and remorse. Consider

(9) 'Rosemary's performance tonight is a reason for her to be ashamed.'

(I'll assume that a noun phrase like 'Rosemary's performance' elliptically refers to a state of affairs such as *that Rosemary's performance was so sloppy*.) Is this sentence plausibly used elliptically for 'Rosemary's performance tonight is a reason/explanation [for why it's good,] for her to be ashamed'?

Having such attitudes can be beneficial: emotions are effective motivators and often dispose agents in desirable ways. Shame might motivate Rosemary not to inflict her talentless act on any future victims, or to practice harder. Remorse motivates people to make amends and to avoid repeating similar actions. Intentions dispose people to act, so if φ-ing would be good, then in general *intending* to φ would also be good; a reason to φ will therefore also usually be a reason to intend to φ.[36]

The analysis thus easily accommodates so-called state-given reasons for attitudes, based on consequences of having those attitudes. But ordinary speech about reasons for attitudes usually concerns "object-given" reasons, based not on the attitudes' consequences but on the nature of their objects.[37] Sentence (9) is naturally read as meaning that Rosemary's performance is a reason for her to be ashamed *of her performance*, for example, where this reason exists because shame is an appropriate or "fitting" attitude for Rosemary to have toward her performance because it was *shameful*.

The fittingness of an attitude is typically independent of actual or potential consequences: the nature of Rosemary's performance may give her a reason

---

[36] Philosophers often analyze reasons for actions (proper) as reasons for attitudes: i.e., 'a reason to φ' really means *a reason to intend to φ*. There isn't any linguistic support for this view, which is typically motivated by the mistaken idea that the notion of a *reason* has to be analyzed as something rationality ('Reason') directly responds to (see note 5).

[37] See Parfit 2001 for the state-given vs. object-given distinction.

to be ashamed of it even if this wouldn't promote any positive outcomes, only causing her to lose self-esteem, abandon her art and career, and eventually go insane, to the grief and burden of her family and friends. State-given reasons are therefore sometimes labeled the "wrong kind of reasons", in contrast to object-given reasons as the "right kind of reasons".[38] Some philosophers even claim that state-given reasons aren't genuinely reasons at all, because agents can't directly form the relevant attitudes in response to them. This presents a challenge to analyzing all normative reasons as explanations why something is *good* in some way.

Among the most important kinds of reasons for attitude are reasons for *belief*, which must also be accommodated by any unifying semantics for 'reason'. Reasons for belief are evidently normative; having reasons to believe that *p* doesn't entail believing that *p* (or vice versa), and having most reason to believe that *p* implies one ought to believe that *p*. So our analysis is committed to 'a reason to believe that *p*' being elliptical for 'a reason/explanation [why it's good (in some way), for *s*] to believe that *p*.' But instrumentalist theories in epistemology seem implausible.[39] Even if there are "pragmatic" reasons for belief (e.g., that believing that *p* will make you happy), this isn't how 'a reason to believe that *p*' is normally interpreted. *Epistemic* reasons for *s* to believe that *p* consist in *s*'s evidence for *p*, and are therefore object- rather than state-given. Evidence for *p* makes belief a fitting attitude toward *p*, but doesn't entail that believing *p* is good for any end *s* desires.

However, the end-relational semantics doesn't require giving 'a reason for *s* to φ' a narrowly instrumentalist interpretation, as meaning an explanation why *s*'s φ-ing is good for some end *desired by s*, but merely that there be some salient way of being good. There is an appropriate way of being good, referred to as "epistemic value", suggesting that 'a reason to believe that *p*' might mean an explanation why believing that *p* is *epistemically good*. Extending the analysis requires only that use of 'a reason to believe that *p*' makes salient some epistemic kind of end. The familiar platitude that *belief aims at truth* provides an obvious candidate. On a common implementation of this idea assumed below, belief is an attitude with its own subagential aim of truth (or knowledge), an end at which an attitude must ("constitutively") aim in order to be a belief at all. While these claims are controversial, all we need is the uncontroversial observation that referring to belief generally makes salient an end of truth. This can be developed into a sketch of epistemic reasons for belief in the following way.

Cognitive activity of forming and maintaining beliefs presumably doesn't aim at truth or knowledge per se, but only in relation to particular questions.

---

[38] Strictly this terminology concerns the right/wrong reasons for "fitting attitude" analyses of evaluative concepts; e.g., for *x* to be *shameful* is for there to be reasons *of the right kind* to be ashamed of *x*. Reasons to φ are sometimes analyzed as reasons of the right kind to *intend* to φ.

[39] See arguments in Kelly 2003, Shah 2006, Brunero 2013.

Forming a doxastic attitude toward the proposition p aims approximately at believing that p *if and only if p is true*. This is more precisely a general *kind* of epistemic end rather than a general epistemic end, and is also an end "in action" rather than "through action"; that is, believing that p doesn't aim at promoting future instances of true belief regarding p, but only at being itself an instance of true belief regarding p. (Otherwise a "wrong kind of reasons" problem arises for scenarios where the probability of correctly disbelieving that p at t_2 can be increased by incorrectly believing that p at t_1, although one wouldn't have any epistemic reason to believe that p.) I'll mark this by saying that the relevant end is "thereby" believing that p iff p is true.[40]

Our account then suggests that '*a reason for s to believe that p*' is used elliptically for 'a reason for s [why it's good for s's thereby believing that p iff p is true, for s] to believe that p', analyzed as meaning *an explanation for s of why it increases the probability that s thereby believes that p iff p is true, if s believes that p*. So to say, 'That the prison fence is electrified is a reason for Arthur to believe that the escape plan will fail' is to say that the fact of the fence's being electrified is an explanation for Arthur, relative to a background b, why his believing the plan will fail increases the probability that he thereby believes the plan will fail iff in fact the plan will fail. Since evidence for s that p is plausibly identified with information that increases s's subjective probability that p, this predicts correct truth-conditions for 'r is a reason to believe that p.' Our semantics for normative 'reason' sentences therefore extends systematically to speech and thought about epistemic reasons too.[41]

This case provides a template for analyzing speech about reasons for other kinds of attitudes. Plausibly, any kind of attitude which is made fitting by the nature of its object is one having a characteristic kind of constitutive aim. Just as belief aims at the true, shame aims (roughly) at the discreditable, fear aims at the dangerous, etc.[42] So Rosemary's reason to be ashamed might be analyzed, for example, as an explanation why it's good for Rosemary's thereby being ashamed of her performance iff it was to her discredit, for her to be ashamed of her performance. A reason "of the right kind" to be afraid of something would be an explanation why it's good for thereby being afraid of the thing iff it

---

[40] This is a general solution for accommodating deontological "side constraints" on the end-relational theory, and extends to moral rules like the alleged absolute prohibition on killing even in order to prevent more killings (e.g., Nozick 1974), which can be interpreted as relativized to a standing end-in-action *not thereby to kill*.

[41] See Chrisman 2008 for application of an end-relational semantics to '*ought* to believe'. A more nuanced analysis might be sensitive to degrees of probability (of p) and credence. Philosophers' tolerance for "pragmatic" reasons for belief varies, which we explain as variation in how strongly the "constitutive aim" of belief is taken to determine salience. Lay people generally seem more tolerant.

[42] Cf. Huemer 2005: 161.

is dangerous, to be afraid of it. These analyses also accommodate the intuitive truth conditions of claims about reasons for these attitudes.

Our unifying semantics for 'reason' as meaning *explanation why* therefore also extends systematically to reasons for emotional or conative attitudes, by taking the reference to the attitude to make some constitutive end salient. This also explains the intuition that something can only be a reason for an attitude if the attitude could be formed directly in response, given that the end is salient as its constitutive aim.

4.4. The Reasons We Have

While sentences of the form NR, '*r* is a reason to φ', are said to describe *objective normative* reasons, we have yet to accommodate two further kinds of 'reason' sentence, corresponding to two distinctions drawn between senses of "reason for action". First, SR sentences ascribe an agent *possession* of a reason, either by a verb of possession (as in SR1, '*s* has a reason to φ') or by the possessive case (as in SR2, '*s*'s reason to φ is that *r*'). Some philosophers posit an ambiguity between objective and subjective normative senses of 'reason', and a metaphysical distinction between different kinds of normative reason relations.

Second, MR sentences explain an agent's action by appeal to "reasons", as in MR1, 'the reason for which *s* φ-ed is that *r*', and MR2, '*s*'s reason for φ-ing was that *r*.' These are said to concern *motivating* reasons for action, and some philosophers posit an ambiguity between normative and motivating senses of 'reason', and a metaphysical distinction between normative and motivating reasons for action. I will argue that our unifying semantics explains both kinds of use in a common way. (Readers uninterested in this result may skip to the conclusion.) I begin with SR sentences.

Superficially, an SR sentence like '*s* has a reason to φ' mightn't appear to pose any special difficulties, and be thought analyzable as meaning simply that there is a reason for *s* to φ which (in some sense) *s* has. But this "factoring account" runs into trouble with the different entailments of NR and SR sentences, as Mark Schroeder observes, which prompts claims of a semantic ambiguity in 'reason' and a metaphysical distinction between kinds of normative reason relations.[43] In particular it sometimes seems appropriate to accept '*s* has a reason to φ' while rejecting 'There is a reason for *s* to φ', because the factiveness conditions for an objective normative reason aren't met; either because no relevant candidate for a reason *r* is true, or it isn't true that *s*'s φ-ing would be good.

---

[43] Schroeder 2008c, Skorupski 2010, Hornsby 2011.

Suppose Sarah knows that on Mondays she needs to collect her daughter from school late, and believes incorrectly that *r*: today is Monday. On this basis it's natural to say that Sarah has a reason to drive to her daughter's school late. If she does then drive to the school late, her action is justly described as "reasonable", although it's at least odd to say that it was reasonable for *s* to φ though she had no reason to φ.[44] But it also seems natural to say that there is no reason for Sarah to drive to her daughter's school late, which is evidently what somebody should tell Sarah if she asks! These claims about the differences between NR and SR sentences are controversial, however, and other philosophers maintain they are just different ways of saying the same things.[45] This conflict of intuitions poses a difficulty for philosophers, but our hypothesis will again offer an explanation for it.

These differences between the use of '*r* is a reason for *s* to φ' and '*s* has a reason to φ' present no problem at least for uniformly *translating* the word 'reason' with the words 'explanation why', because the same differences can be found between '*r* is an explanation why *p*' and '*s* has an explanation why *p*.' It seems natural to accept 'Sarah has an explanation why it's good, for her to drive to the school at 4:00 p.m.', while rejecting 'There is an explanation why it's good, for Sarah to drive to the school at 4:00 p.m.' But a uniform translation of a word isn't yet a unifying analysis, as the definiens may just share the ambiguity of the definiendum. We must examine what it means to "have" reasons or explanations, which suggests looking to linguistic evidence about the meaning of the possessive.

Verbs of "possession" and the "possessive" case turn out to be much vaguer or looser than their name implies. Compare 'my slave' (the one I possess) with 'my owner' (the one who possesses me), for example, 'my town' (the one where I live), and 'my teacher' (the one who teaches me). Semantically the possessive seems to signify only that there is some kind of relationship, where pragmatic cues indicate its nature. Use of 'my horse' can refer to the horse I own, for example, or the horse I ride, or the horse I bet on, etc.[46] Exactly the same vagueness can be found in speech about "having" an explanation/reason, or in something's being "*s*'s" explanation/reason why *p*. '*s* has an explanation why *p*' allows at least the following readings:

SE1:   *s* believes or offers something as an explanation why *p* (e.g., '*s* always has an explanation why she has to be late').

---

[44] See Gibbons 2010, who also finds it absurd to say that an action is reasonable though "there is" no reason for it. I agree at least that on some available readings of these sentences it would be absurd.

[45] E.g., Gibbons 2010. Others claim (mostly correctly, as I'll argue) that the different locutions merely *prefer* different readings; e.g., Williams 1979, Henning 2014.

[46] See discussion in Peters & Westerståhl 2006: 251f. I owe this example and the general point about the possessive to Gunnar Björnsson.

SE2: *s* believes something that is an explanation relative to her information, perhaps without realizing it's an explanation (e.g., '*s* already has the explanation, but she just hasn't put two and two together yet').

SE3: *s* has epistemic access to something that is an explanation relative to her information, perhaps without believing it (e.g., '*s* already has an explanation, because I gave her one. She just doesn't believe it').

The same three readings are available for '*s* has a reason to φ.'[47] Consider '*s* always has a reason to be late' (SE1), '*s* already has a reason to φ, but she just hasn't put two and two together yet' (SE2), and '*s* already has a reason to φ, because I gave her one; she just doesn't believe it' (SE3). Recall that we found at least one other way an agent can be related to a reason/explanation, which can be "for *s*" by virtue of having a (normative) explanandum relevant to *s*. This predicts that '*s* has a reason to φ' will also have a fourth permissible interpretation involving this relation, SE4. Consider '*s* has a reason to φ, but she has no way of discovering it', which seems a coherent thing to say, in accordance with denials that '*s* has a reason' always requires that *s* have some kind of epistemic or doxastic relationship to the reason. It's sensible to say, 'That Terry stole Victor's wallet is a reason that Victor has, for Terry to be apprehended, but not a reason that Terry has', for example, even if Victor unlike Terry has no evidence or clue that Terry is the thief.

While SE1 readings seem not to entail NR, 'there is a reason' sentences, at least some other readings (certainly SE2 and SE3) do, and therefore don't resist a factoring account or pose any threat to our unifying hypothesis. The controversy over whether NR and SR sentences differ in meaning is therefore easily explained, because while these do have a range of readings as equivalent, each also has at least one reading the other disallows. On one hand, SR sentences lack the logical ambiguity we identified in NR sentences: whereas 'There's a reason for *s* to φ' can be read as 'There's a reason, for *s* to φ' (which needn't concern a "reason for *s*" at all), the use of the possessive in '*s* has a reason' unambiguously connects *s* directly to the reason or explanans in some way, blocking this reading. 'Hostilities have a reason to come to an end' can't be used as an alternative for (5), for example, nor 'Murderers have a reason to be punished' for (6). On the other hand, only SR sentences invite the apparently nonfactive readings that motivate the notion of subjective normative reasons. Talk about the reasons that "*s* has" can also be predicted to lend itself more to shifting the salient background from the (default) perspective of the speaker or audience to the perspective of the agent *s* than speech about the reasons that "there are".[48]

---

[47] It's more difficult though not impossible to get SE2 and SE3 readings for the possessive *case* ('*s*'s explanation/reason'), perhaps because '*s* has a reason' more naturally allows an extensional reading as equivalent to '*s* has *x*, which is an explanation/reason . . .', while '*s*'s explanation/reason' prefers an intensional reading.

[48] See also Henning 2014.

So our analysis predicts that NR sentences will prefer more objective readings, while SR sentences will prefer more subjective readings. For pragmatic reasons these preferences will therefore be especially pronounced when the two kinds of sentence are directly juxtaposed, as when it is asked, '*s* has a reason to φ, but is there a reason for *s* to φ?' or 'There is a reason for *s* to φ, but does *s* have a reason to φ?' This explains the cacophony of philosopher's intuitions about SR and NR sentences as an artifact of logical incompleteness and vagueness, and the pragmatic influences on their interpretation.

We still need to address the obstacles to a unifying semantics posed by the nonfactive uses of SR sentences, but first I'll examine MR sentences and "motivating reasons", which present the same obstacles and will yield to the same solution.

4.5. The Reasons for Which We Act

Speech or thought about "motivating reasons" may initially seem of only tangential interest here. Although relevant to the case for having a maximally unifying semantics, they don't appear to be about *normative* reasons. But this appearance will prove illusory. The problem may also initially appear trivial, as our semantics superficially looks like it would extend to MR sentences easily. To state *s*'s reason for φ-ing is evidently to explain why *s* φ-ed, so it's natural to suppose that by a "motivating reason for action" is simply meant an explanation why *s* φ-ed. MR sentences would be merely a special case of ordinary ER sentences, where the explananda are facts that some agent acted in some way.

On an influential view, motivating reasons are explanations why an agent acted that cite the psychological attitudes (typically beliefs and desires) that caused *s* to φ,[49] as in

(9-ER)   'The reason why Jill caught the 8:00 a.m. train is that she wanted to get to work by 9:00, and believed the next train wasn't until 11:00.'

Actions are often explained by citing merely a belief or a desire alone. Although sometimes regarded as philosophically significant (e.g., as proof that desire isn't needed for motivation), this may just be an artifact of the information-relativity or holism of explanations. Reasons sometimes also seem to be identified with these attitudes themselves, or other kinds of objects, rather than with states of affairs concerning them (e.g., '*s*'s reason was his belief/desire that *r*'), but this can similarly be explained by the practice of identifying propositions elliptically by noun phrases.[50]

---

[49] E.g., Davidson 1963, Smith 1994. For the history of the distinction see Dancy 2000: 20–25.

[50] E.g., 'Jill's reason to catch the 8:00 a.m. train is the rail schedule'; see also Searle 2001: 100f, Schroeder 2008c. Davidson 1963 and Smith 1994 identify motivating reasons with attitudes rather than facts, which commits them to lexical ambiguity from the outset.

While many correct explanations of actions certainly take this form, this analysis encounters well-known problems and involves a significant confusion. First, it's in tension with the linguistic data. Contrast sentences of the form MR:

(9-MR1) 'The reason for which Jill caught the 8:00 a.m. train was that the next train wasn't until 11:00.'

(9-MR2) 'Jill's reason for catching the 8:00 a.m. train was that the next train wasn't until 11:00.'

These appear to identify Jill's motivating reason as the fact that the next train wasn't until 11:00, rather than any facts about her beliefs and desires.[51] Their grammar also differs from ordinary ER sentences. Consider MR2, '*s*'s reason for φ-ing'. We observed above that use of the possessive case in '*s*'s reason/explanation' indicates that *s* has some kind of relationship with the reason or explanans rather than with the explanandum, which means that '*s*'s reason for φ-ing' doesn't have a reading as *the reason/explanation, for s's φ-ing*: we wouldn't say, 'The escape plan's reason for not working is that the prison fence was electrified', for example. Something can only be *s*'s reason for φ-ing if *s* has some cognitive abilities, suggesting that *s*'s reason for φ-ing must be an *explanation for s*, in some sense.

Observe also the difference between (ER) 'the reason *why s* φ-ed', and (MR1) 'the reason *for which s* φ-ed'.[52] The MR1 construction isn't used in any other kind of non-normative 'reason' sentence; we wouldn't say, 'The fact that the prison fence was electrified was the reason for which the escape plan didn't work', for example. It also seems to indicate some kind of cognitive connection between agent and reason. In this scenario it would also be odd to say that the reason "for which" Jill caught the 8:00 a.m. train was that she wanted to get to work by 9:00 and believed that the next train wasn't until 11:00. The causal-psychological reasons why an agent acts apparently aren't what is meant by 'the reason for which *s* φs' or '*s*'s reason for φ-ing'.

However, the fact *r* that these MR sentences describe as *s*'s motivating reason is apparently a *normative* reason for *s* to φ. That the next train isn't until 11:00 is an explanation for Jill of why it's good for getting to work by 9:00 if she catches the 8:00 a.m. train, for example. This suggests a different way of applying our semantics: by 'the reason for which *s* φs' is meant *the reason to φ, for which s φs*. On this factoring account, the concept of a motivating reason is that of a normative reason that motivates, not a reason why the agent is motivated.[53] So (9-MR1) can be interpreted as elliptical for

---

[51] This needn't be a fatal problem, given holism; these facts may explain actions against the background that the agent is relevantly knowledgeable.

[52] Cf. Williams 1979.

[53] This view is widespread today; e.g., Darwall 1983, Williams 1989: 39, 2001: 93, Dancy 2000, Alvarez 2010.

(9-MR1a)   'The reason [it was good for her getting to work by 9:00, if she
            caught the 8:00 a.m. train,] for which Jill caught the 8:00 a.m.
            train, was that the next train wasn't until 11:00.'

This linguistic analysis is supported by some philosophical considerations.
Normative reasons are roughly things that agents are supposed to take into
consideration in deliberating. When all is going well, therefore, agents are motivated as a result of being aware of their normative reasons. This is plausibly
what is meant by describing r as the reason "for which" s φ-ed. By contrast,
identifying motivating reasons with facts about an agent's psychological attitudes introduces an incompatibility between normative and motivating reasons, since these aren't the kinds of facts to which an agent generally attends or
responds in deliberation.[54]

The principal objection to this identification is that motivating reasons
apparently don't entail normative reasons: (MR) 'The reason for which s φ-ed is
that r' doesn't entail (NR) 'There's a reason for s to φ.' At least most intentional
actions are done "for a reason", but agents often do things intentionally that
we wouldn't say there was a reason for them to do, and which we would deny
was in any way "good". These objections are directly parallel to those raised
in the previous section, against a unifying analysis of SR and NR sentences
and a "factoring account" of subjective reasons as objective reasons that s has.
Since MR sentences share the problematic features of SR sentences, (nonfactive) motivating reasons can be analyzed as *subjective* normative reasons that
motivate s to φ.[55] But our semantics allows that motivating reasons claims can
also concern objective normative reasons, and I see no grounds for denying that
an agent's motivation to φ is often attributed to an (objective normative) reason
which there is for her to φ, whenever such a reason exists.[56]

4.6. Nonfactive Reasons

As this interpretation predicts, MR sentences pose the same challenges to
semantic unification that we observed for apparently nonfactive uses of SR

---

[54] The incompatibility is more acute for Smith's account of motivating reasons as belief-desire
pairs that cause action (1994), which places motivating and normative reasons in different ontological categories; see Darwall 1983: 33, Dancy 2000.

[55] Especially MR2 sentences like (9-MR2), given that 's's reason/explanation' has a clear SE1
reading as (roughly) what s *believes* to be a reason. Plausibly (9-MR2) is logically ambiguous
between an MR reading ('Jill's reason why it was good, for her to catch the 8:00 a.m. train, for
which she caught the 8:00 a.m. train, was that the next train wasn't until 11:00') and a simple SR
reading ('Jill's reason why it was good, for her to catch the 8:00 a.m. train, was that the next train
wasn't until 11:00').

[56] These may be more natural readings of sentences of the form MR1 than of MR2, because
of the absence of a possessive verb or case. But the possessive might function to indicate yet
another kind of relation: being the reason that motivated s.

sentences. We observed that ordinary reason or explanation sentences of the form ER, '*r* is a/the reason why *p*', seem doubly factive in entailing both that *r* and that *p* (e.g., that it's indeed good if *s* φs).[57] But SR and MR sentences seem to lack these entailments on some readings. Consider first the condition that the explanandum *that p* be factual. Agents apparently "have" and "act for" reasons even when it isn't good if *s* φs.

The kind of example that has drawn the most attention involves *perverse* reasons, as when *s* has or acts on an evil motive. These cases of "desiring the bad" have prompted rejection of any conceptual link between goodness and the reasons we have or act for,[58] but they actually aren't problematic at all given the end-relational semantics for 'good'. Having or acting for perverse reasons simply involves having or being motivated to act by explanations why φ-ing is good for some perverse end *e* ("Evil, be thou my good!")

It's also easily explained why SR ('*s*'s reason', '*s* has a reason'), and MR ('The reason for which *s* φ-ed') sentences don't seem to entail NR ('There is a reason') sentences in these cases. The salient ends for NR sentences are typically associated with the speaker or audience, and so in cases of perversity it's natural to deny that there is any reason why it's good (i.e., for a salient end), for *s* to φ—as we'll discuss in later chapters. But since talking about the reasons that *s* "has" or "for which" *s* acts tends to make *s*'s perspective salient, SR and MR sentences are much more easily read as relativized to *s*'s perverse ends. This suggests an explanation for the controversy over whether agents *have reasons to* φ on the basis of desiring perverse ends, since we've found an ambiguity in 'has a reason' that generates readings supporting each side. In cases of perversity it is true that *s* has an explanation why it's good relative to *her ends* if she φs (i.e., on an SE4 reading of the possessive), but it's false that *s* has an explanation why it's good relative to *our* ends if she φs (i.e., on an SE1, SE2, or SE3 reading).

Other cases present a stiffer challenge, however. Suppose Jill is mistaken in believing that the train takes her to the office. Then catching the 8:00 a.m. train isn't good for her getting to work on time, so the fact that the next train isn't until 11:00 apparently can't be an explanation why doing so is good. Here φ-ing isn't good in the salient way, but Jill still seems to have and act for a reason, in some sense.

To see one natural way of accommodating these cases, consider this riddle: When is a "reason" not a reason? Answer: when it's a "reason". These nonfactive uses of 'reason' resemble SE1 uses of '*s*'s reason/explanation', as we observed, requiring only that *s* believes or professes *r* to be an (objective) reason or explanation. The simplest and most unifying way to understand these

---

[57] Their objectivity also consists in entailing that *p* is true *because r* is true. It's a further question how subjective or motivating reasons are reported when this condition is violated and the agent is wrong to view *r* as the kind of thing that could explain why *p*.

[58] E.g., Stocker 1979, Velleman 1992; see discussion in Raz 1999.

is as "inverted commas" uses, in which the speaker uses the term "advisedly", that is, applying it as another person would without endorsing that application. A compositional way of analyzing these is as elliptical for '*s* has [what she believes/claims is] "a reason"' and 'the [consideration that *s* believes is a] "reason" for which *s* φ-ed is that *r*', which also would explain why they involve *inverted commas*: they are genuinely disquotational. It can then be explained why a subjective or motivating "reason" that *r* doesn't entail that it's good if *s* φs, without violating the factiveness of *explanation why*: this is merely a *supposed* or *alleged* reason or explanation why it's good if *s* φs.[59]

This hypothesis accounts for all the problematic behavior we've observed in SR and MR sentences, but is it correct? One test for inverted commas is how the speaker would respond to the query 'But is it *really* a K?' The proposal passes this test easily, since as we've emphasized, in these cases it's natural to reply, 'No, that *r* isn't really a reason for *s* to φ.' However, I'll also suggest an alternative explanation below.

Different problems emerge when considering failures of the other condition, that the reason or explanation *that r* itself be factual. This is illustrated by Sarah's case: what she would identify as the reason she has to drive to school late and for which she does so (that it's Monday) isn't the case, and therefore apparently can't be an explanation why it's good if she φs.[60] But here too there's still an intuitive sense in which Sarah has and acts for a reason, which leads some philosophers to claim that while objective reasons are facts, subjective and/or motivating reasons are merely propositions.[61] The inverted commas solution predicts this: just as '*s*'s "explanation" why *p* is that *r*' isn't factive with regard to *p*, neither is it factive with regard to *r*. A merely supposed or alleged reason needn't be factual.[62] But this encounters a difficulty arising from the way subjective and motivating "reasons" are ordinarily described in these cases.

Our account seems to predict that the following sentences will be natural:

(10-SR1)   'The reason Sarah has to drive to school late is that it is Monday.'

(10-SR2)   'Sarah's reason to drive to school late is that it is Monday.'

---

[59] This doesn't prevent MR sentences from genuinely explaining why *s* φ-ed: it was *because s* believed herself to have this "reason".

[60] Reports of reasons generally select for *r* the information needed for an explanation why *p* relative to the *audience's* beliefs. For somebody who doesn't know that Sarah's daughter gets out of school late on Mondays, Sarah's reason wouldn't be identified as *that it's Monday*, but as (e.g.) *that her daughter gets out of school late that day*.

[61] E.g., Schroeder 2008c. On my view of propositions as "proposed" facts these differ in modal but not ontological status.

[62] Alternatively the apparent semantic factiveness of 'explanation' might be questioned. Factiveness in ER and NR sentences might be attributed to a default background *b* of what the speaker believes or knows, but relative to a different background (as suggested by '*s*'s reasons'), *r* is correctly identified as an explanation of *p* (relative to b_s) even if *r* or *p* is known to be false.

(10-MR1) 'The reason for which Sarah drove to school late was that it is Monday.'

(10-MR2) 'Sarah's reason for driving to school late was that it is Monday.'

However, most people find that use of these sentences implies that the speaker believes it is Monday, and is therefore inappropriate otherwise. Speakers usually prefer to say rather,

(11-SR1) 'The reason Sarah has to drive to school late is that she believes it is Monday.'

(11-SR2) 'Sarah's reason to drive to school late is that she believes it is Monday.'

(11-MR1) 'The reason for which Sarah drove to school late was that she believed it is Monday.'

(11-MR2) 'Sarah's reason for driving to school late was that she believed it is Monday.'

This seems to support the view I dismissed above, that an agent's motivating reasons consist in facts about her attitudes, while posing a difficulty for our unifying hypothesis, since the fact that the agent believes that r doesn't look like the right kind of thing to be an explanation of why it's good if s φs, even a supposed or alleged explanation, while it is potentially an explanation of why s φs (although this still doesn't account for the SR sentences, which don't imply that s φs at all).

The linguistic data here pose a genuine conundrum. Just as the first group of sentences seem unnatural if the speaker doesn't believe that r, the second group seem unnatural if the speaker does believe that r, although the agent's subjective or motivating reason might be expected to be the same kind of thing in each case.[63] This is a peculiar pattern of use that requires explanation.

Since speakers generally only prefer the psychologized (11) sentences over the (10) sentences if they don't themselves believe that r, it can be inferred that this preference is entirely explained by the apparent factiveness of the (10) sentences. The simplest hypothesis about the inclusion of 's believes' is therefore

---

Henning (2014) advances such a view, arguing that a subjective, nonfactive sense of 'reason' is required by the conceptual links to 'good' and 'ought', which have subjective senses. But on our theory these links are already accommodated by appeal to explanations of subjective goodness (see below), without invoking also subjective explanations of goodness.

[63] Williams 1979, Dancy 2000: 121. Another possibility is that because explanations are factive we can't explain with normative reasons when we don't believe that r, so we give an explanation why s φ-ed instead of an explanation citing the reason for which s φ-ed. I propose a similar view below which has the advantages of being compositional (by appealing to normative reasons) and accommodating also SR sentences.

that it functions in these sentences merely to cancel factiveness.[64] This kind of use of '*s* believes' can be observed elsewhere in ordinary speech; for example, 'If we fix the stalemate in Washington, then I believe the economy will rebound', where 'I believe' is inserted to hedge.[65] Sentence (11-MR1) might then be parsed as 'The reason for which Sarah drove to school late was that, she believed, it is Monday', for example, or as Jonathan Dancy suggests, 'The reason…was that, [as] she believed, it is Monday.' If so, then the (11) sentences don't actually differ from the (10) sentences in what they identify as the reasons *s* has and for which *s* acts, and so conform with our unifying hypothesis. Observe that the (10) sentences can sometimes be acceptable when *r* is false, especially if this is made explicit,[66] as in

(10-SR2a)   'Sarah's reason to drive to school late is that it is Monday, but of course she's wrong about that.'

(10-MR1a)   'The reason for which Sarah drove to school late was that it was Monday, but of course it was actually Tuesday.'

This seems to confirm that qualms about using the (10) sentences in these cases are entirely due to their suggestive factiveness, and also that the suggestion is pragmatic rather than semantic.

While this account extends our unifying semantics to the problematic SR and MR sentences, it may introduce an inconsistency. I proposed interpreting the SR and MR sentences that don't entail NR sentences as SE1 uses of '*s*'s reason', so as merely *supposed* or *alleged* reasons, and therefore nonfactive. But then it seems anomalous that the (10) sentences would naturally be interpreted as implying that *r* is a fact, making insertion of '*s* believes' necessary. These two proposals are in tension, but this anomaly can be explained in two different but compatible ways. First, recall that the possessive in '*s*'s reason' and '*s* has a reason' is ambiguous, having several readings (SE2, SE3, SE4) on which SR and MR sentences do entail NR sentences and that there is a reason to φ. On all these readings, to say that *s*'s reason is that *r* is indeed to commit to the truth of *r*, because of the factiveness of explanations.[67] This danger of being misinterpreted as implying that *r* is a strong pragmatic reason to opt for the (11)-variants whenever one doesn't believe that *r*.[68]

---

[64] As proposed in Collins 1997. Dancy (2000: 127) suggests that it additionally plays a role in the explanation of *s*'s φ-ing, but since we also insert '*s* believes' in SR sentences when we don't believe that *r*, and not in MR sentences when we do believe that *r*, Collins's simpler view seems superior.

[65] A rival interpretation is that 'I believe' really has wide scope over the conditional here.

[66] Dancy 2000: 132.

[67] These readings seem even more salient for MR1, 'The reason for which…' sentences.

[68] Consequently, since it is common practice to use the (11)-variants in these cases, the choice to use a (10)-variant instead will ipso facto suggest the speaker does believe that *r*, hence the appearance of factiveness.

Second, MR sentences actually do offer genuine explanations why *s* φ-ed (by reporting what she believed to be her reason or explanation why it's good to φ), even though 'the reason for which *s* φ-ed' doesn't mean *the explanation why s φ-ed*. It's understandable that speakers might become confused about this, and therefore balk at describing something nonfactual as a "reason" while explaining an action.[69] Understanding both that MR sentences are explanations of action, and that explanations are factive, it's a natural error to cite instead the reason that explains why *s* φ-ed which is most closely related to the reason for which *s* φ-ed, that *s believes* that *r*.

While the problematic data from SR and MR sentences has now been explained consistently with our unifying hypothesis, our semantics also suggests an alternative solution. Recall again the subjective use of 'good', as meaning to increase the probability of *e* relative to a subject *s*'s information. So far this section has assumed a more objective interpretation of its being "good" if *s* φs, but (as we noted in discussing evidence as reasons to φ) there are also explanations why it's good *relative to s's information* for *s* to φ, and our semantics predicts that this should be a possible reading of '*s*'s reason to φ'. This suggests a *fifth* way an agent might "have" a normative explanation, SE5: as an explanation of goodness relative to *s*-relevant information.

If the problematic SR and MR sentences are given an SE5 rather than an SE1 reading, then it isn't really true in cases like Jill's that *p* isn't a fact. Although the fact that the train doesn't take her to the office means that catching the 8:00 a.m. train isn't *objectively* good for her getting to the office by 9:00, if Jill is unaware of this fact, then catching the 8:00 a.m. train might still be *subjectively* good (relative to her information) for that end.

Rather than interpreting SR1, '*s* has a reason to φ', and SR2, '*s*'s reason for φ-ing is that *r*' as involving inverted commas and merely supposed reasons, we might therefore interpret them rather as describing (real, factive) explanations why it's good *relative to s's information* for *e*, if *s* φs. The fact that the next train isn't until 11:00 is indeed an explanation why it's good, relative to Jill's information, for her getting to work by 9:00, if she catches the 8:00 a.m. train. This solution is unifying, compositional, extensionally correct, and is also supported by philosophical considerations. An agent's subjective reasons are relevant for assessment of the reasonableness of her action, rather than its advisability, and her motivating reasons are relevant to its explanation, but these roles of assessment and explanation are better played by the subjective than by the objective

---

[69] It may be objected that agents can't be motivated by "facts" that don't exist, since motivation is a form of causation. But to be motivated by a supposed normative reason that *r* is just to be motivated as a result of believing that *r* is a normative reason to φ. Since this is an explanation of action in an intensional context it doesn't require that *r* actually obtains, just as we can be scared by Dracula and saddened by the death of Bambi's mother.

senses of 'good' and 'ought'. This solution may fare better in this respect than the SE1 reading.

What about the cases like Sarah's, where the subjective reason *r* is itself not factual? Here we could apply both our previous solutions, analyzing this as an inverted commas use (i.e., a mixed SE1/SE5 reading), and viewing the insertion of '*s* believes' as functioning to prevent factive misinterpretations. But another interpretation avoids SE1, nonfactive readings altogether. While the fact that *s believes that r* is neither the right kind of thing to explain why *s*'s φ-ing is objectively good, nor to explain why it is good relative to *s*'s information *de re*, it is the right kind of thing to explain why *s*'s φ-ing is good relative to *s*'s information, *de dicto*. The fact that Sarah believes it's Monday, for example, is an explanation why it's good relative to Sarah's information if Sarah drives to school late.

This solution entails that different kinds of "subjective reasons" and "motivating reasons" are reported depending on whether *s*'s belief is true, but given the different kinds of facts we cite as these "reasons" this shouldn't be surprising.[70] These psychologized "reasons" are of course not what *s* herself takes to be her normative reasons, which would explain why these sentences are sometimes viewed with suspicion. But they are directly relevant for explaining what point there is in φ-ing from *s*'s point of view. The difference between the two kinds of case might then be explained as follows: because talk about reasons or explanations is always factive, we can only felicitously explain what there is to be said for an action from an agent's point of view (SR), or why an action was performed (MR) by citing an agent's "*reason*" that *r*, provided that *r* actually is an explanation why *p*. When it's not the case that *r*, we therefore shift to the next best thing (relative to the end of understanding the action): citing a reason why *s*'s φ-ing was good from the agent's perspective (as opposed to a reason from the agent's perspective, why it was good).

As both solutions seem consistent with the linguistic evidence it's hard to know which to prefer. The important result here is that our unifying semantics for 'reason', when supplemented with the end-relational semantics for 'good', can accommodate the many different ways these words are used in SR and MR sentences—while also explaining the conflicts in intuition.

A unifying semantics for 'reason' as meaning *explanation why* can accommodate all the kinds of uses we surveyed, in talk about explanatory reasons, objective and subjective normative reasons for actions and attitudes, and motivating reasons. By a normative "reason to φ" we mean an explanation why it's good

---

[70] This can be extended to address reports of '*s*'s reason to φ/ for φ-ing' as either *that s desires that e, s's desire that e*, or *to make it the case that e* (e.g., Audi 1986: 512). Although not explanations why it's good *for e* if *s* φs (so arguably not normative or motivating reasons), these may explain why it's good *for s's ends (de dicto)* if *s* φs, as well as why *s* φs.

(or better, best) to φ. Combined with the end-relational semantics for 'good', this provides an end-relational semantics for normative reasons sentences that predicts the right truth conditions for a wide range of ordinary cases. This concludes our exploration of the semantics of normative language. Following the trail of linguistic evidence has led to unifying and compositional semantics for 'good', 'ought', 'reason', and related words, which connect to each other in ways that respect intuitive platitudes, extend to both normative and non-normative uses (of 'ought' and 'reason'), and generate intuitive truth-conditions for a wide range of claims. This constitutes a strong case for the end-relational theory, but the reader may now be justly impatient to address the numerous philosophical issues I've so far set aside, arising particularly for moral and deliberative speech and thought.

{ 5 }

Pragmatics and Practicality

My case for the end-relational semantics is that it's a maximally simple and unifying theory that accommodates the truth conditions of a wide variety of ordinary sentences. But so far I've ignored apparently inconvenient evidence from particularly the moral and deliberative uses of this language which primarily interest moral philosophy. These features consist in various forms of the practicality and objectivity of normative language, which have been thought incompatible with any theories that are variously descriptivist, reductionist, or relativistic—and therefore comprise much of the puzzles of metaethics.

The second half of this book addresses these challenges. This chapter examines the feature of *Practicality*—the especially close connection with motivation which seems to defy all descriptivist and especially reductive analysis. The following three chapters address a range of features together comprising the objectivity which seems to defy relational analyses: *All Things Considered*—claims weighing multiple ends against each other (Chapter 6), *Categoricity*—the distinctive characteristic of moral claims as "categorical imperatives" that apply to agents regardless of their ends (Chapter 7), *Finality*—claims about the "intrinsic value" of final ends (Chapter 7), *Disagreement*—the intuitive inconsistencies between normative claims (Chapter 8), and related difficulties with *Reports and Evaluations*—concerning the ways normative speech and thought is reported and evaluated as true or false (Chapter 8).

Our success at providing unifying explanations of other uses of these words counts for nothing if the end-relational theory can't also accommodate these special features of moral and deliberative use. But I'll argue that our semantics accommodates and explains them all by appeal to the *pragmatics* of how we use normative language in context, pursuing our desired ends, yielding what I'll call "quasi-expressivist" and "quasi-absolutist" solutions. Given only maximally simple and conservative principles of pragmatics, the end-relational theory predicts these features, which therefore can't present any real objections. If so, this is presumably the simplest and most conservative theory that accommodates all the data, and should therefore be embraced as the best explanation of our practices of normative speech and thought. I'll also suggest, more ambitiously, that it even accommodates and explains these allegedly problematic features better than rival theories like expressivism and primitivism can, which would make it the *only* adequate explanation of our practices. The first step, however, is to motivate and explain the conception and principles of pragmatics we'll employ.

5.1. From Semantics to Pragmatics

The need for a distinction between semantics and pragmatics is now widely recognized (though how to draw it is more controversial), but somebody might still resist it by appeal to the Wittgensteinian dictum that *meaning is use*: if in a context *C* a speaker uses a sentence to communicate that *p*, then in *C* that sentence *means* that *p*. Since normative sentences are often used to communicate information or do things that the end-relational semantics doesn't account for by themselves, our analyses would therefore be incomplete at best. But this dictum is now widely rejected, for good reason: it's in tension with ordinary intuitive judgments about what sentences mean, and with the common-sense observation that people don't always say what they mean or mean what they say (hence the distinction between *sentence meaning* and *speaker meaning*).[1] Consider sarcasm: we wouldn't say that in a sarcastic use, the sentence 'That was really smart' actually means *that was really stupid*, but rather that the speaker didn't mean what he said. Meaning and use of a sentence or word can come apart; more precisely, meaning is *conventional* use.

The rationale for the distinction is that there are two fundamentally distinct sources of information in linguistic communication. I shall take the essential difference to be (in Kent Bach's words) that whereas "semantic information is encoded in the sentence, pragmatic information is generated...by the act of uttering the sentence."[2] In other words, semantics concerns the information or signification associated by convention with words and sentences themselves, while pragmatics concerns the information or signification generated by the fact that a speaker utters a particular sentence in a particular context.

By "context" I'll understand any and all features of the world-state in which the utterance occurs, including the spatial and temporal locations of speaker and audience, their physical environment, the vocabulary at their disposal, the history of the world, and most importantly their beliefs and desires. One significant element of a context, which confusingly is itself sometimes labeled "context",[3]

---

[1] Grice 1968.

[2] Bach 2002: 284; note my treatment diverges from Bach's in other respects.

[3] E.g., Grice 1989, Stalnaker 1999, Bach 2002. Lewis/Kaplan-style "contexts" as *n*-tuples of world-state of utterance, time (etc.) indices are abstractions from contexts in my broader sense.

is the *common ground*, the background assumptions mutually understood by speaker and audience to be mutually understood.

Whereas semantic meaning arises from arbitrary social conventions of use (e.g., there's no intrinsic reason why 'good' couldn't have meant *bad* and 'bad' couldn't have meant *good*), pragmatic meaning is a form of natural signification, generated in a nonarbitrary and calculable way from the two factors of the semantic meaning of the words used and the particular features of the context of use.

A system of communication that can be factored into distinct semantic and pragmatic inputs is simpler than one that assigns all the variability to the semantics itself, and is therefore easier for people to learn, use, and interpret, just as representing squares on a chessboard by row and column is more practical than numbering them serially. Rather than learning a set of complicated, contextually variant rules for each word in our vocabulary,[4] we need only learn simpler, general rules for each word, and combine this semantic competence with our comprehension of the systematic ways in which meaning interacts with context.

Since particularly the pioneering work of Paul Grice from the 1960s, the distinction between semantics and pragmatics has proven highly useful for solving philosophical puzzles, and is heralded as one of the greatest advances in philosophical understanding of language in the last century. I will argue similarly that the supposedly problematic behavior of normative words in certain uses isn't a brute or arbitrary fact about those individual words, but is systematic and amenable to a principled pragmatic explanation.

By putting together an understanding of the conventional meaning of the sentence or words uttered with an understanding of the context, an audience or interpreter can draw a variety of inferences, consisting in propositions that are *pragmatically indicated* by the utterance. Pragmatic indication is therefore relative to interpreters or backgrounds, which I'll assume needn't generally be made explicit. So defined, pragmatics are ubiquitous, playing a role in any successful communication whatsoever. Even in a basic case where a speaker utters a completely explicit and unambiguous sentence that semantically determines a single proposition p, an audience relies (i) on the contextual assumption that he is speaking literally in inferring that he is asserting that p, (ii) on the assumption that he is speaking sincerely in inferring that he believes that p, and (iii) on the assumption that he is relevantly reliable in inferring that p is true (an assumption I'll also sometimes make in discussing pragmatic information).

In cases of ellipsis, where a speaker utters a logically incomplete sentence in order to assert some proposition p that is one of many possible logical completions of that sentence, an interpreter relies on pragmatic cues to identify which

---

[4] See Timmons 1999 for an example of this kind of contextually variant semantics in metaethics, not to be confused with our kind of context-sensitivity involving logical incompleteness.

proposition the speaker is asserting. By saying 'I can't get my shoes off', for example, my daughter both asserts and also pragmatically indicates that she can't get her shoes off *her feet* (whether by virtue of general contextual information about how shoes are usually worn, or particular contextual information about where her shoes happen to be).[5] Most of what an utterance pragmatically indicates, however, isn't anything the speaker also said or asserted. Much is information about the speaker's own psychological attitudes, as in the basic case where a speaker communicates that she *believes* that *p* by sincerely asserting that *p*. At other times the information pragmatically indicated by an utterance mightn't include any possible literal or asserted content, as in hyperbole, metaphor, and sarcasm; by saying 'That was really smart!', for example, you may indicate by virtue of your obvious disbelief in what you said that you believe to the contrary that the action was not smart. When a speaker indicates pragmatically that he has some attitude, I will say that he pragmatically *expresses* that attitude.[6]

We are all highly skilled at detecting these pragmatic features of language-use as part of the basic linguistic competence we acquire in childhood, and so we also expect each other to share these skills. Speakers exploit others' pragmatic competence in order to communicate much more than they say or assert. As this skill or know-how is tacit, like riding a bicycle or hitting a baseball, objections sometimes raised against the complexity of pragmatic solutions to philosophical puzzles are generally misguided. The mechanics of riding a bicycle, or of uttering words, are also surprisingly complex and beyond an ordinary person's capacity to grasp reflectively or articulate, yet almost everybody does it automatically; so too pragmatic inference.

This conception of pragmatics will be controversially broad in at least two ways. First, pragmatics is often restricted to what is communicated *without* being said or asserted (i.e., what is "implicated"), and it may therefore be worried that allowing pragmatic information to include what is asserted strips the claim to be offering "pragmatic" solutions of any interestingly controversial significance. However, my talk of "pragmatically indicating" that *p* can henceforth be read as assuming parenthetically *without saying or asserting it*. Second, while "pragmatics" is often restricted to what is communicated *intentionally*,

---

[5] This is consistent with the Gricean gloss that semantics concerns what is *said* while pragmatics concerns what is communicated *by the saying of it*, so long as 'what is said' is read as *the words uttered* (as in direct reports: 'He said, "..."'), and not as *the proposition asserted* (as in indirect reports: 'He said that *p*'). Recall from Chapter 1 that I'm not using 'semantics' for the (study of) *truth conditions* of sentences or utterances. On this view, pragmatics can contribute to the interpretation of what a speaker asserts though not directly to its determination, while semantics can contribute to both (as well as to any conventional implicatures), without necessarily determining what is asserted.

[6] Cf. Davis 2003: 59. Bar-On & Chrisman (2009) argue that normative speech expresses a speaker's attitude in a way distinct from either indicating that the speaker has the attitude or merely being caused by the attitude; I don't recognize any such sense.

I shall understand it as including unintentional communication.[7] An interpreter can often infer information from an utterance that the speaker never intended to communicate. One example is the inadvertent self-incrimination beloved by authors of crime and courtroom dramas. A: "I wasn't the killer, detective. I'd never shoot a man in the back"; B: "Aha, so you *do* know how the victim was murdered!"

The distinction between intentional and unintentional communication is orthogonal to the distinction between what can and can't be inferred from speech in context, so excluding the unintentional from "pragmatics" seems arbitrary and gerrymandered. The very same factors that permit unintended inferences would then be classified as "pragmatic" whenever a speaker exploits them intentionally, a difference that will be largely irrelevant for our purposes. A common reason given for excluding unintentional communication is that classifying an inference like *So he speaks English!* as pragmatic fails to respect an important difference between this and the paradigms of pragmatic communication. But there's a middle ground here; the inferences that will concern us are all *based on premises about the speaker's intentions* (hence the label 'pragmatics'), though they needn't be inferences *intended by the speaker*.[8]

Despite the breadth of this conception of pragmatics, some will object it's still too narrow to be the key to solving metaethical puzzles, because whereas the domain of pragmatics is speech or utterances, the challenges cataloged above arise also in normative *thought* or judgments. Pragmatic solutions are complained to be insufficiently general because they presuppose a conversation; for example, many of our results will turn on the significance of ellipsis.[9] But these objections overlook important connections and parallels between speech and thought.

On one hand, insofar as judgments are themselves linguistically formulated, they are plausibly internalizations of speech ("speaking to ourselves"), and therefore will resemble contributions to imagined conversations and inherit many pragmatically influenced features.[10] It's implausible that although when speaking aloud we may omit words the audience can easily recover, when saying things to ourselves we must mentally token only fully explicit sentences: introspection finds similar patterns of ellipsis in thought as in speech. Devices like

---

[7] Cf. Grice 1989, Bach 2002. Previously (e.g., Finlay 2001, 2004, 2005) my pragmatic solutions appealed to "conversational implicatures"; I avoid this terminology here partly because Grice defines implicatures as intentional.

[8] This also excludes the interpretation of indexicals like 'I' and 'today' from pragmatics, despite its contingency on context of use; here reference is determined and identified from the context by semantic rule regardless of the speaker's intentions. Cf. Bach's distinction (2002) between "broad" and "narrow" context.

[9] E.g., Joyce 2011, Olson 2011.

[10] More ambitiously we may argue (as Karen Lewis suggested in conversation) that as intentional thought has an ulterior motive, like speech, there is a direct mental analog to the instrumental principle of pragmatics proposed below.

sarcasm, metaphor, and hyperbole—though their standard explanations are pragmatic—are found as readily in thought (e.g., sarcastically thinking, 'You're a really smart guy!')

On the other hand, to whatever degree normative judgments aren't linguistically articulated, there will be a nontrivial step of interpretation in their linguistic representation, and it's therefore debatable whether corresponding challenges to the end-relational theory arise at all.[11] While I'll seek to be sensitive to relevant differences between normative speech and thought, the following chapters will largely focus on speech to avoid having to say everything in two different ways.

A different kind of objection to such philosophical appeals to pragmatics arises from a general methodological concern. Our data consist largely in linguistic intuitions of ordinary speakers about the appropriateness of using particular sentences in particular contexts, and it's complained that these intuitions are generally unable to discriminate between the influence of semantic and pragmatic factors. In this case, semantic and pragmatic theories must be selected together, holistically rather than individually. But then it may seem that whatever semantic theory is selected, a pragmatic story can be concocted to reconcile it with the data. Rescuing a semantic theory by appeal to pragmatics then proves too easy, with pragmatics effectively functioning as a "wastebasket"[12] into which philosophers can conveniently toss any data that don't fit neatly with their pet theories.

It seems to me that a fairly common reaction to this problem is to dismiss out of hand any philosophical appeal to pragmatics, as somehow not kosher. But this is surely an indefensible prejudice, since it isn't based on any reasons to think that there isn't a significant pragmatic dimension to use of language. To dismiss any appeal to pragmatics therefore may be to disqualify from the start every theory with any chance of being correct.

The real worry here is that the project of analytic metaethics is hopeless, because accommodating the data by appeal to pragmatics is so easy that there's no such thing as a "best explanation", and so no basis for choosing between theories. If a theory requires vindication by resources that indiscriminately vindicate the rival theories too, then this surely counts against it. But the situation isn't so dire. The objection assumes that pragmatic stories are all basically ad hoc, so each is as good or bad as the next. It is disarmed by first identifying a minimal set of independently motivated and compelling fundamental principles of pragmatics, and then deriving all our solutions directly and systematically by applying these to our semantic theory. This is what I propose to do.

---

[11] Some problematic features of normative speech have no direct mental analog, like its interpersonal effects.

[12] A metaphor due to Bar-Hillel 1971.

5.2. A Principled Pragmatics

How is it possible to infer anything from the fact that a speaker utters a particular sentence in a particular context? My answer is guided by one simple and conservative observation: that speaking is an instance of motivated behavior. We're not mere information-exchanging machines, but use language in pursuit of our intended ends. As Donald Davidson writes, "each use of language has an ulterior purpose."[13] Every pragmatic solution offered in this book is an application of this observation that speech is a means.

I therefore propose the following as a universal norm of language-use (or "conversation"):

Instrumental Principle of Conversation: In order to achieve your
conversational ends you ought
to speak in a way that is best for
those ends.

By a "conversational end" I mean in particular the end(s) that an utterance is most saliently (e.g., in the speaker's mind) aimed to promote.[14] Speakers will often have a number of more derivative ends, and sometimes also more basic or ultimate ends. In a normal use of 'Pass the salt', for example, the speaker may aim (e_1) to express to the addressee her wish to have the salt, in order (e_2) to have the salt passed to her, in order (e_3) to shake salt on her meal, in order ultimately (e_4) to enjoy the taste of seasoned food. In this case the most relevant conversational end for our purposes seems to be e_4, her enjoying the taste of seasoned food: if she is mistaken in believing that her utterance is (one of) the best available means to e_4 (e.g., if the diner she addresses can't actually reach the salt) then her utterance violates the principle even if it's the best means to some of her derivative ends like e_1. However, since more basic ends are often difficult to identify confidently and precisely, it's often convenient to indicate them loosely by reference to some derivative end, and I'll attempt only to characterize conversational ends as accurately as needed.

This principle may seem trivial, and our analyses suggest it is analytically true, with the caveat that we haven't yet accounted for cases of multiple ends. Since (trivially) speakers are always trying to achieve their conversational ends, this is a "hypothetical imperative" with universal application. It can further be taken as a constitutive norm of conversation, one with which necessarily any

---

[13] Davidson 1984: 272. For application of the idea to metaethics see also Price 2008.

[14] This use diverges from a distinction drawn between "conversational goals" and "domain goals" (Grosz & Sidner 1986), where the former is an end to be realized in the conversation rather than merely promoted by its means. Conversational ends in my sense include "domain goals".

speaker aims to conform.[15] Successful conformity isn't necessary, of course, as speakers frequently fail to alight on a best option. (However, as conversational ends will typically include economy of time and effort, all else equal the best sentence will come easily to one's tongue.) We can therefore make the following generalization:

Instrumental Law of Pragmatics (ILP):   Speakers always speak in the way they believe best for their conversational ends.

I suggest that a tacit understanding of this law (perhaps subject to some further refinement and qualification) can safely be presumed to be partly constitutive of competence as a speaker and interpreter. This grasp of ILP will be the only foundational principle of pragmatics to which I appeal.

The basic character of pragmatic reasoning is then this: what can be inferred from the fact that the speaker believed that uttering *that* particular sentence was best for promoting her conversational ends in the context? To really understand another person's utterance it isn't enough to recognize which propositions (if any) are semantically expressed by the sentences she utters. One must also have some comprehension of her conversational ends, or her intentions in uttering those sentences or asserting those propositions.[16]

Suppose a stranger sitting on the bus turns abruptly and says to you, 'Five is a bigger number than three.' This is a perfectly clear sentence, yet you would naturally be bewildered. In response you might naturally say, 'What do you mean?', 'What's your point?', 'So?', or 'What do you want from me?' You come to understand her utterance as a human action only by identifying some possible kind of intention that makes sense of it, given also attribution of certain beliefs, by explaining how she could have thought that uttering that sentence would be best for promoting those ends. Does she want to draw you into a friendly chat, and oddly believes that people find simple mathematical facts interesting? Might she be a psychologist gathering data on how people react to incongruous utterances? Perhaps she's a spy with a ridiculous recognition signal, who has mistaken you for her contact? Without any such interpretation we wouldn't say that you understand her utterance, despite your knowledge of what her sentence means.

By contrast, Grice posits as the basic principle of pragmatics instead the "Cooperative Principle": "make your conversational contribution such as is required, at the stage at which it occurs, by the accepted direction of the

---

[15] Strictly, speakers don't aim at conformity with the principle *de re*, but at acting in ways best for their conversational ends. It's been suggested that the qualification *insofar as they are rational* is needed; while I've argued elsewhere that such supposedly "irrational" behavior is impossible (Finlay 2008a, 2009c), our pragmatic solutions will require only that interpreters ordinarily presume conformity.

[16] This is central to Grice's conception of communication as the recognition of intentions.

talk exchange in which you are engaged."[17] Taking some liberties we might reformulate this in a way that draws a clear contrast with the instrumental principle above:

Cooperation Principle of Conversation: In order to achieve the ends accepted in the conversation in which you are engaged, you ought to speak in a way that is best for those ends.

I take the "accepted direction" of a conversation to be the shared conversational ends, and Grice's notion of what is "required" by this to be essentially instrumental. (An important departure here is that while Grice's principle is [literally] "categorically imperative", this principle is only "hypothetical"—a distinction we'll discuss in Chapter 7.)

This cooperation principle also comes out on the end-relational theory as analytically true (with the same caveat). But this isn't plausibly a constitutive norm of conversation, and doesn't support any universal law or generalization analogous to ILP. Not every speaker or utterance aims at cooperation, or shared conversational ends.[18] Neither does Grice consider his Cooperative Principle a constitutive norm; he rather postulates a defeasible presumption that speakers aim to be cooperative. But cooperation therefore seems not to be fundamental for pragmatics. An aim of cooperation isn't even possible in many cases: sometimes there's no preexisting conversation for a speaker to already be "engaged" in, as when the utterance begins or constitutes a conversation, and at other times there are no "accepted" or shared ends, the participants engaging in conversation for transparently different ends (e.g., A: 'Do as I say!'; B: 'You're not the boss of me!'). Since even utterances in these circumstances often have significant pragmatic dimensions we should conclude that the cooperation principle applies too narrowly to be fundamental.

My point isn't to dismiss the relevance of cooperation to pragmatics; on the contrary, the arguments of this and the next chapter focus exclusively on the pragmatics of cooperative use of normative language. But in order to address all the challenges we'll also need to appeal to the more fundamental law ILP; we'll begin addressing the pragmatics of *noncooperative* use of normative language in Chapter 7. The pragmatic significance of cooperation can be directly derived as a specific application of the more fundamental instrumental principle to the contingency that the speaker's conversational ends are shared by the audience. The cooperation principle is therefore a constitutive norm

---

[17] Grice 1989: 27.
[18] There's arguably a very thin notion of a "shared conversational end" on which this is true (e.g., *successfully communicating*), but it's too thin to account for the richness of pragmatics.

of conversations conducted under such circumstances, yielding a restricted generalization:

Cooperation Law of Pragmatics (CLP): If speakers know their conversational ends to be shared, then they always speak in ways they believe best for the shared conversational ends.

The default presumption of cooperation in Gricean pragmatics then derives from a recognition that speakers most commonly participate in conversations with shared conversational ends.

We can follow Grice in identifying this as a default expectation: conversational ends can normally be assumed to be shared at some level. Somebody's choosing (even reluctantly) to engage in a conversation requires some motive for doing so, and a speaker's assumption of his audience's consent to being addressed indicates he expects them to have some such motive. While this doesn't yet require shared motives, there are reasons to expect this as the norm. First, individual conversations are fitted by design to promote particular ends rather than others, like most instruments, which constrains the range of likely motives for participating in a particular conversation—though without ruling out all possibility of "ulterior motives". Second, humans have a natural impulse toward cooperation that is reinforced by socialization. Psychologically normal (i.e., empathetic) people are predisposed to become spontaneously concerned with the ends they perceive others being concerned with. These dispositions operate also in communication, inclining us to adopt reflexively others' conversational ends as we encounter them.

A contrast can be drawn between ends being of *native* concern and of *borrowed* concern, and thereby between two kinds of cooperative conversation: on one hand, where ends are shared as being of native concern to all participants (e.g., exchanges between teammates in sport, colleagues or comrades in business or war, or at an academic conference), and on the other, where ends are of native concern only to some participants and of borrowed concern to others (e.g., asking strangers for directions). Interpreters will commonly assume that the context is of one of these kinds, and therefore that the speaker is cooperatively acting as he believes best for these shared ends. This chapter and the next explore how this pragmatics of cooperation interacts with the end-relational semantics.

5.3. Practicality: The Challenge

The special practicality of normative language is often alleged by expressivists to be the downfall of all purely descriptivist semantics. Primitivists respond by offering a different conception of practicality, but agree at least that no reductive account like the end-relational theory could accommodate it. To assess this challenge we'll need to clarify the nature of this "special practicality", which takes a variety of forms and is interpreted in various ways. I'll show that our theory meets this challenge with the aid of our pragmatic principles,[19] and ultimately argue that it even provides a better account of practicality than either expressivism or primitivism can.

Discussions of practicality focus variously on at least three interrelated features. The first concerns what normative speech or thought implies about the speaker's motivational attitudes. According to the popular doctrine of *Motivational Internalism*, there's a special connection between normative judgment and having some kind of corresponding motivation or motivational attitude, like a desire or intention.[20] It's often claimed that any agent who judges himself to have a reason to φ must have some motivation to φ, for example.

The second feature concerns the effects of normative speech on an audience (*Interpersonal Influence*). Normative utterances characteristically have motivational effects on others, functioning to "put pressure on choice and action", which the early expressivist Charles Stevenson even called the "dynamic meaning" of normative language. This is a corollary of motivational internalism, which implies that getting others to share one's own normative judgments will cause them to be similarly motivated.

The final feature concerns what a speaker is doing when uttering a normative sentence or word (*Practical Illocutionary Force*). Expressivists observe that normative sentences are used to perform speech acts of distinctly practical kinds, in contrast to ordinary declarative speech acts of communicating information. To call something "good" is to *endorse* it, to tell an agent that she "ought" to φ is to *recommend* or *prescribe* it, or to perform a directive or imperatival speech act. This practical illocutionary force might be treated as a corollary of one of the previous features, by identifying it with either the "expression" of the speaker's motivational attitudes ("emotivism"), or with the attempt to influence an audience ("prescriptivism"). An expressivist may say that to endorse something is to express one's approval of it, for example, while it's been suggested that to recommend φ-ing is roughly to express the intention to φ if in similar circumstances.[21]

The problem is therefore that on descriptivism, the only semantic function of normative words like 'good', 'ought', and 'reason' is to contribute to the descriptive or informational content of sentences. Sincere assertion of a

---

[19] This develops accounts in my previous papers beginning with Finlay 2001, 2004, 2005. Others suggesting pragmatic treatments of practicality include MacIntyre 1984, Copp 1997, 2001, Harman 1996, Phillips 1998, Strandberg 2012.

[20] For a survey of the various forms of motivational internalism see Finlay & Schroeder 2008.

[21] E.g., Gibbard 2003.

normative sentence would therefore seem to require only a *belief* that the world contains certain facts, and not any particular motivation, desire, or intention. It would have declarative force, but apparently not the practical force of endorsement, recommendation, etc. So Simon Blackburn writes,

> The reason expressivism in ethics has to be correct is that if we suppose that belief, denial, and so on were simply discussion of the way the world is, we would still face the open question. Even if that belief were settled, there would still be issues of what importance to give it, what to do, and all the rest. For we have no conception of a "truth condition" or fact of which mere apprehension by itself determines practical issues. For any fact, there is a question about what to do about it. But evaluative discussion just is discussion of what to do about things. (1998: 70)

Allan Gibbard writes,

> I the chooser don't face two clear, distinct questions, the question what to do and the question what I ought to do. *Descriptivism*, in contrast, is the doctrine that *ought* claims describe rather than prescribe, that an *ought* claim describes an act as having a certain special property. This gives the wrong picture, we expressivists say: *ought* claims instead are claims about what to do. (2003: 9–10)

However, it would be too hasty to conclude that if a theory is descriptivist it can't provide any account of the practical features of normative language, because this neglects the factor of pragmatics. Illocutionary force, for example, is first a matter of use or what speakers are doing with language on particular occasions. While language has semantic devices for signaling particular kinds of use or force, like the interrogative, imperative, and declarative moods,[22] to infer directly from what a speaker does with a word or sentence to the meaning of that word or sentence is to commit the pragmatic fallacy and confuse use with meaning.[23] Before any descriptivist theory is rejected on account of the practicality of normative speech and thought, its pragmatic implications must be examined.

Even expressivists often concede that ordinary descriptive utterances can be pragmatically practical. Charles Stevenson noted that asserting the descriptive sentence 'I want you to close the door' typically has imperatival force—and we might add that it both implies speaker motivation and has characteristic interpersonal influence.[24] Here this is simply a pragmatic effect of assuming the

---

[22] Just as words can be used nonliterally, so too (e.g.) the declarative mood can be used to ask questions, and the interrogative mood to make assertions, as in rhetorical questions and on *Jeopardy*.

[23] Geach 1960, Searle 1962; see Kalderon 2005 for a case against contemporary expressivists.

[24] Stevenson 1937: 21.

speaker to be sincere and to mean what she says. But speakers can also pragmatically mean things other than what they say.

Blackburn notes that an ordinary descriptive predicate like 'has south-facing windows' can be used in the right contexts to endorse. Suppose Matilda is known to be a sun-loving homebuyer in Scotland; if she asserts that a particular house has south-facing windows, she can be taken to indicate that she approves of the house, at least in that respect, and so to pragmatically express approval. Or consider the force of recommendation, which we might loosely define as follows:

Recommendation: To recommend to *s* that she φ is to draw *s*'s attention
to the possibility of φ-ing ostensibly with the intention
to motivate *s* toward φ-ing in pursuit of her own
desired ends.

Suppose Matilda's realtor tells her that a particular house has south-facing windows. By ILP we immediately look for his motive, and in the context it is transparent that his utterance is aimed at motivating Matilda toward buying the house in pursuit of her desired ends, by informing her of a fact that would be motivating for her. By virtue of her tacit grasp of ILP Matilda easily recognizes the realtor's purpose, as he himself expects her to do. Here the illocutionary force of recommendation is secured pragmatically.

While descriptivist theories can in this way easily capture various practical features and uses of normative language, the real challenge arises from the way the practicality of normative language is allegedly "special", or in the closeness of the relationship. Gibbard writes,

> The special element that makes normative thought and language
> normative...involves a kind of endorsement—an endorsement that any
> descriptivistic analysis treats inadequately. The problem is...that a single
> loophole remains unpluggable by descriptivistic analysis. In a community
> of stable, widely accepted norms, this element of endorsement might be
> carried by properties—the properties that, in everyone's mind, qualify a
> thing for this kind of endorsement....No one, though, has found such a
> property, and so we still need a language fit for fundamental normative
> inquiry. (1990: 32)

The connection between the use of normative language and the features of practicality is allegedly too close to be accommodated by a purely descriptivist semantics. "Too close" is vague, however, and how to spell it out is controversial. Classically it is construed strongly in terms of *necessity*. According to what I'll call the *strong practicality requirement*, sincere normative utterance entails some degree of speaker motivation, and necessarily involves some practical kind of force such as endorsement or recommendation. (Claiming necessary interpersonal influence would obviously overreach.) Such a view is implied, for example, by expressivist theories on which calling something "good" is just to express approval of it, or saying that an agent "ought" to do something is just to recommend or prescribe it.

This strong practicality requirement would indeed pose a serious, perhaps fatal difficulty for purely descriptivist semantics, if it were correct. The simple and conservative Humean psychological model of motivation draws a fundamental distinction between beliefs, as attitudes that aim at reflecting the world, and desires, as attitudes that aim at shaping it. All beliefs and desires are contingent rather than necessary, and are also "separate existences", no belief entailing any particular desire or motivation. So if normative sentences have purely descriptive content, then their sincere assertion only necessarily expresses beliefs, and can express desires or motivation only contingently.[25] 'Has south-facing windows' connects with Matilda's motivations only because of her contingent desire for sunshine, for example, and has no such connection for those who are indifferent or averse. If the realtor knew her to be indifferent to sunshine, then all else equal he wouldn't be able to perform a recommendation by his utterance. This difficulty extends to the end-relational theory: saying or thinking that φ-ing increases the probability of a particular end has no necessary connection with being motivated in any particular way, or expressing any particular motivational attitude. Rather, a motivational connection seems to depend roughly on a contingent desire for that particular end.

Expressivists conclude that any kind of pure descriptivism must be false. As pragmatic connections are merely contingent, this necessary connection with motivation can only be explained by *semantic* conventions associating correct use of normative language with the speaker's motivations or purposes. To accommodate the strong practicality requirement, purely descriptive theories must apparently reject the Humean psychological model for more radical views, such as that normative language refers to special facts or properties that necessarily motivate any agent who perceives them. This could be attributed either to a magnetic power of the normative facts themselves, as proposed by early primitivists like Plato,[26] or to desires necessarily possessed by any agent, perhaps in virtue of being constitutive of agency itself.[27]

Primitivists sometimes advance their own account of the special practicality of normative language, as referring to necessarily action- or attitude-guiding facts and properties, conceding to expressivists only that no facts *reducible to the non-normative* have the requisite practicality. I won't pursue these psychological solutions here, as I find them too fantastic, and agree with Gibbard that (to paraphrase) "no-one has found a property that in *everybody's* mind qualifies

---

[25] Cf. Smith 1994.

[26] See, e.g., Wittgenstein 1930/1996, Mackie 1977: 40, and Joyce 2001, who reject the possibility. Contemporary primitivists generally repudiate the idea, though see Huemer 2005: 192.

[27] E.g., Korsgaard 1996, Velleman 1996.

a thing for endorsement." A sober survey of human life reveals too much variety, contingency, perversity, and freedom. By contrast, the end-relational theory will need nothing more than the common-sense Humean model to explain the special practicality of normative language.

Our theory doesn't satisfy the strong practicality requirement, but this isn't really a problem, as it's almost universally agreed today that this requirement is too strong. Even most expressivists and primitivists concede that competent and nondeceptive use of normative language without corresponding motivation is both possible and common. Expressivists often characterize the attitudes expressed by normative language as merely *normally* motivating,[28] while contemporary primitivists argue that construing the practicality of normative language in psychological rather than normative terms was a fundamental confusion: normative facts are simply those that necessarily *ought* to motivate us, regardless of whether they actually do.[29] The strong practicality requirement is generally motivated by narrow focus on particular uses of words like 'good', 'ought', and 'reason', which overlooked or ignored a wide range of other ordinary uses, which I'll now survey.

First, we've observed that at least 'ought' and 'reason' have entirely non-normative uses, which clearly lack the features of practicality. Champions of a strong practicality requirement for these words therefore have to posit lexical ambiguities, though we've seen that a good case can be made for a simpler, unifying semantics identifying a common meaning across these uses, in which case these words can't themselves be tied by semantic conventions to motivation or practical force.[30] While lexical ambiguities between normative and non-normative meanings mightn't seem too hard to swallow, the features of practicality are also only generally evident for the use of *unrelativized* normative sentences, and generally disappear when words like 'good', 'ought', and 'reason' are explicitly relativized. If a speaker says, 'Adultery is good for destroying marriages', for example, she wouldn't necessarily be taken to have expressed approval of adultery, as she arguably would if she said simply 'Adultery is good.' Similarly, calling a person a "good liar" or a "good thief" doesn't appear to express approval of them, or of their lying and thieving abilities. If somebody says, 'In order to become a famous mass murderer you ought to kill as many people as you can', he wouldn't seem to have recommended that anybody kill as many people as they can, or to have indicated any corresponding desire or motivation.

---

[28] E.g., Blackburn 1998: 61, Timmons 1999, Gibbard 2003: 154; see discussion in Strandberg 2012.

[29] See especially Parfit 2006, 2011b, Enoch 2011.

[30] This is compatible with those words sometimes being *qualified* or *relativized* in ways that are essentially practical, which is to locate the expressive conventions elsewhere in language (e.g., in the adverb 'morally').

It might be replied that relativization qualifies the attitude or force somehow; that 'good for destroying marriages' expresses approval *conditional on desiring to destroy marriages*, for example, and that 'ought... in order to become a famous mass murderer' recommends *conditional on intending to become a famous mass murderer*. But even if this is granted,[31] the more attenuated the "necessary practicality" becomes, the more easily it can be pragmatically accommodated by purely descriptivist theories. It could similarly be claimed that 'has south-facing windows' is necessarily practical since it pragmatically expresses approval *conditional on desiring to buy a sunny home in the northern hemisphere*.

Not every champion of motivational internalism is willing to claim, as Philippa Foot reports one expressivist claiming, that to say that a tree has "good roots" is to express the intention to have roots like that for the hypothetical circumstance of being a tree.[32] Motivational internalism is sometimes advanced as a doctrine specifically about moral and deliberative speech (or thought), rather than normative speech more generally, since the relativized uses of normative words are (in Wittgenstein's words) "not how Ethics uses them".

Maintaining the strong practicality requirement therefore requires further lexical ambiguities between the unrelativized uses of 'good', 'ought', and 'reason' found in moral speech, and the relativized uses found in the various ordinary cases analyzed in previous chapters. This motivates a central objection to our end-relational theory: even if it's correct about the ordinary kinds of use we've examined, this would only be of marginal metaethical interest, since this language is systematically semantically ambiguous between (philosophically unimportant) relative meanings and (philosophically important) nonrelative or absolute meanings. This objection will be answered below, but many philosophers are justifiably reluctant to embrace such a radically disunified semantics, which would require duplicating a large section of the lexicon—and not only the English lexicon.

Even such a radically disunified semantics wouldn't rescue the strong practicality requirement from a third kind of counterexample, however: the *embedded* or nonassertoric use of normative sentences that prompts the original charge of pragmatic fallacy against expressivism. Logically simple normative sentences generally express motivation and have practical illocutionary force only when directly asserted, and lack these features in almost every other kind of use, as when embedded in negations, disjunctions, conditionals, attitude reports, and questions. Whereas saying, 'You ought to φ' is plausibly to perform a speech act of recommendation and implies some kind of corresponding

---

[31] It is questionable whether these involve actual expression of an attitude, or merely indicate that a speaker would have a motivational attitude under certain circumstances, as I argue in Chapter 8.

[32] Foot 2001. The expressivist is identified as R. M. Hare by his son John, though see also Gibbard 2003.

speaker motivation, for example, this isn't plausibly claimed of saying, 'It's not the case that you ought to φ', 'If you ought to φ, then. ..', '*s* believes she ought to φ', or 'Ought you to φ?' Since these differences surely aren't due to different meanings of the same normative words, this is a serious difficulty for the view that normative words have their illocutionary force or practicality by semantic convention. While some of these uses may have other, nonrecommendatory kinds of practical force, this provides no support for the view that normative language has its force by convention, which entails a conventional force.

Contrast this behavior of 'ought', for example, with the embedded behavior of words that less controversially express attitudes by semantic convention, such as slurs like 'faggot' or interjections like 'alas'. A speaker expresses contempt for homosexuals not merely in asserting '*s* is a faggot', but also in saying '*s* is not a faggot', 'If *s* is a faggot, then. ..', 'Is *s* a faggot?', etc.[33] This difference between embedded and unembedded uses of normative sentences is, however, directly predicted by a pragmatic account. If practicality derives from the significance attributed to the *state of affairs* described by the sentence (e.g., that the house has south-facing windows), then we would expect to find it only in assertions, being the uses pragmatically indicating that the speaker believes it to be a fact. While it's beyond the scope of this book to evaluate the various complex solutions to this problem proposed by contemporary expressivists, the lesson here is that even expressivists have to concede and accommodate the fact that embedded, nonassertoric uses of normative sentences appear to be counterexamples to a strong practicality requirement.

Further counterexamples to at least some intuitively appealing claims about the conventional force of normative language are provided by differences in *tense* and *person*. While it seems natural to describe assertoric uses of 'ought' which are prospective (present or future tense) and second-personal (e.g., 'You ought to φ') as acts of recommending or prescribing, it's at least strained to describe retrospective, past-tense, or third-personal uses (e.g., 'You ought to have φ-ed'; 'He ought to φ') this way, as *Recommendation* predicts since they don't ostensibly aim at motivating the agent to φ. In general, the only uses of 'ought' naturally described as recommendations are those which are normative, unrelativized, assertoric, unembedded, prospective, and second-personal. In response to this problem, contemporary expressivists often offer more complex and attenuated proposals about the conventional force or conceptual role of particular words rather than of sentences. While these may be less vulnerable to counterexample, they sacrifice much of the intuitively compelling character

---

[33] See Schroeder 2009b, Finlay 2001: 230–31. Ryan Hay (2013) suggests that for this reason normative terms should rather be modeled on "general pejoratives" like 'jerk', which are expressive only in assertoric use (see also Copp 2009), but the embedded behavior of these can rather be taken as evidence of a purely descriptive semantics; e.g., 'jerk' means *person who shows disregard for others' feelings*.

of naive expressivist claims, such as that 'ought' is used to recommend or prescribe.[34]

Despite all these counterexamples to strong practicality, descriptivism may still be in trouble even if only morally normative, unrelativized, assertoric, unembedded, prospective, and first- or second-personal uses of these words were necessarily practical, given the contingency of the connection between belief and motivation. But even this extremely restricted version of strong practicality is reasonably and widely doubted, as motivational internalism is a highly controversial thesis. Its denial, motivational externalism, has many champions who insist that people can and sometimes do make sincere normative or moral assertions (or judgments) unaccompanied by the allegedly requisite motivations, as perhaps from depression or perversity. This dispute often turns on whether there are or could be *amoralists* who make judgments about what agents morally ought to do without caring a whit, as is said to be the case with psychopaths. Many people find nothing incoherent about somebody saying, 'You *ought* to φ, of course. But don't do that! Come ψ with me instead—it's much more fun!', and such an utterance wouldn't naturally be interpreted as incorporating a recommendation to φ.

The dispute between motivational internalism and externalism is one of the most entrenched and intractable in metaethics.[35] Internalists adopt various strategies for explaining away these apparent counterexamples, arguing for example that amoralists are really misusing normative language, using it in a derivative and non-normative sense (e.g., in inverted commas to mean approximately *what other people call "good"*), or trying but failing to make normative claims as arguably people born blind might try but fail to make color judgments.[36] But I know of no argument for accepting an internalist rather than an externalist interpretation of these utterances that doesn't beg the question by relying on an assumption of expressivism or internalism.[37]

Descriptivist theories therefore have no obligation to satisfy the strong practicality requirement. Does this mean they face no viable practicality objection, as externalists sometimes claim? Perhaps goodness is merely something humans contingently but reliably happen to like a lot, like the sensations of pleasure. This misses something importantly right in internalist intuitions,

---

[34] E.g., Gibbard's (2003) claim that 'ought' expresses contingency plans, Boisvert's (2008) claim that 'wrong' expresses disapproval of wrongness, Schroeder's (2008b) toy hypothesis that 'wrong' expresses an attitude of being for blaming for, and Ridge's (2014) claim that 'ought' expresses acceptance of a norm that recommends while 'must' expresses acceptance of a norm that requires (which he acknowledges needn't be transparent to competent speakers).

[35] A 2009 survey by Philpapers.org finds 35% of philosophers accepting internalism and 30% accepting externalism (about specifically moral judgments).

[36] See respectively Copp 2001 & 2009 (though he rejects an internal connection between moral *judgment* and motivational attitude), Hare 1952, Smith 1994.

[37] A point made by Svavarsdóttir 1999; see also Wallace 2001, Enoch 2011.

however, and versions of a practicality requirement can be formulated that are weak enough to be plausible while still strong enough to pose a challenge to purely descriptivist semantics. One claims a necessary *normal* connection between moral assertions and judgments and corresponding motivation, for example: although some individuals may fail to be motivated in accordance with their moral judgments, necessarily this isn't the case for normal or para-digmatic individuals in any society.[38] While Chapter 7 will provide resources for an explanation for this, here I'll bypass it for some stronger principles that don't focus narrowly on moral speech or thought.

One plausible principle of weak practicality is

Indispensability: Any agent, whatever her desires and intentions,
                     necessarily employs concepts that actually can be
                     expressed by the words 'good', 'ought', and 'reason' in
                     her practical thought aimed at decision and action.

In other words, while use of normative concepts doesn't plausibly entail practi-cality, practicality plausibly entails the use of normative concepts. Such a claim is commonly made by expressivists and primitivists,[39] and is sufficiently strong to pose a challenge. Whereas human desires seem to vary dramatically and there is extensive divergence from psychological normality, no matter how unusual or perverted a person's desires or intentions may be, at least some uses of 'good', 'ought', and 'reason' will still have the features of practicality for him: he'll be able to conduct his practical speech or thought (endorsing, recommending, deliberating) in these terms, and others will still potentially be able to use these words to guide and influence him. Consider how Milton in *Paradise Lost* has Satan express his perversity, for example: "Evil, be thou my *good!*" Even when agents are motivationally alienated from particular species of normative judg-ment (as amoralists are alienated from moral judgments and the self-destructive are alienated from their prudential judgments), they still apparently act for what they conceive as some kind of value or reason, and so it's often observed that seeking and responding to reasons, or acting as one thinks in some sense best (i.e., under the "guise of the good") seems to be constitutive of agency.

This presents a problem for descriptivism, because given the contingency and variability of human desires, presumably no facts or properties could have such an indispensable connection to agential motivation. Primitivists may again object that this is only true of facts or properties that aren't *irreducibly nor-mative*, but the conservative and common-sense view here is that reasoning to

---

[38] E.g., Dreier 1990, Wedgwood 2007, van Roojen 2010.

[39] Among primitivists, Enoch (2011) argues that normative concepts are "deliberatively indis-pensable", while Wedgwood (2007) identifies these practical functions as their essential concep-tual role. Among expressivists, Gibbard (2003) and Timmons (1999) identify roughly this same conceptual role as evidence against a descriptivist semantics.

decisions under the influence of one's desires is sufficient for deliberating. But the end-relational theory accommodates *Indispensability* easily, without any radical psychological hypotheses. Although no end-relational facts or properties have a guiding or motivating role for any agent whatever their desires, if we merely grant that necessarily any agent desires some end or other, it follows that for every agent there will be *some* end-relational facts or properties that have a guiding or motivating role for that agent. For anybody who desires that *e*, facts and properties involving what increases the probability of *e* will have a practical role. Arguably this is the only kind of facts and properties that has a practical role for any possible agent. Joseph Butler famously wrote in 1726 that "probability is the very guide of life", which can of course also be claimed of value (oughts, reasons); our probabilistic semantics for normative language resolves this apparent tension.

While the end-relational semantics is therefore (perhaps uniquely) a descriptivist theory that accommodates *Indispensability* (so far without any assistance from pragmatics), a second principle of weak practicality can be formulated which poses a greater challenge, as follows:

Evidentiality: Assertion of an unrelativized normative sentence is sufficient though defeasible evidence of corresponding motivation, independently of any information about the speaker's desires.

As observed, the paradigms for a strong practicality requirement involve assertoric normative use of 'good', 'ought', and 'reason' without explicit relativization to ends. Consider the sentences 'This is good, and it hurts' and 'This hurts, and it's good', for example. Despite the strong and almost universal human disposition to dislike pain intensely, these sentences are instinctively interpreted as expressing an overall favorable rather than unfavorable attitude, and even as suggesting a perverse and unusual liking of pain rather than a disliking of goodness. This is testimony to a remarkably close connection between the unrelativized use of 'good' and positive motivation, which may seem to demand a semantic explanation. But I'll show that the end-relational semantics meets this challenge with the assistance of our pragmatic principles.[40]

5.4. Conversational Practicality

According to our semantics, a logically complete normative use of 'good', 'ought', or 'reason' must always be relativized to an end. The use of these words

---

[40] It remains possible that some other requirement is both sufficiently weak to be plausible, and strong enough to be irreconcilable with our semantics; any proposal must be considered on its individual merits.

in sentences without relativization is sometimes treated as an objection to such a unifying semantics—and evidence for lexical ambiguity and the existence of nonrelational (or "absolutist") meanings, properties, and facts—but the mere use of unrelativized normative sentences is poor evidence of an absolutist semantics, in view of the ubiquity of ellipsis. The distinctive practicality of unrelativized sentences may seem to pose a stronger objection by providing evidence of special semantic features found only in these unrelativized sentences. For any agent, the vast majority of end-relational facts and properties will be of no practical significance whatsoever. The fact that φ-ing would increase the probability of e has no guiding or motivational role for an agent who is indifferent toward e. So we may seem poorly placed to explain why assertions or judgments that something is "good", or "ought" to be done, or is a "reason" could be sufficient evidence of corresponding motivation.

By our theory, use of an unrelativized sentence involving 'good', 'ought', or 'reason' only expresses a complete normative proposition if elliptical for another sentence that is relativized to an end, and only successfully communicates a normative proposition if interpreted as such. But we've seen that making an end explicit tends to remove the features of practicality like the indication of corresponding motivation and the practical illocutionary force, as between 'Adultery is good' and 'Adultery is good for destroying marriages.' This might be thought to show that the unrelativized sentences couldn't be elliptical for relativized sentences, but it's compatible with an alternative diagnosis: that the ellipsis is itself the evidence of corresponding motivation, which pragmatically generates the special practicality of unrelativized sentences. The challenge of explaining *Evidentiality* and accommodating the weak practicality requirement is for the end-relational theory therefore just the challenge of explaining why leaving ends implicit would generate practicality. This challenge can be met.

By the default presumption of the Cooperation Law of Pragmatics, CLP, speakers are ordinarily expected to speak cooperatively, making the utterances they believe best for promoting the shared conversational ends. One of the basic requirements of cooperation is *to make oneself clear*, part of Grice's maxim of manner.[41] This implies a constraint on permissible ellipsis: generally a speaker can omit articulating a logical constituent of the proposition he is asserting only if it is sufficiently salient that his audience can easily identify it in the context.

Ends can of course be salient in a conversation in many different ways. Often the cue is in what is explicitly said: we've observed how ends are made salient indirectly by reference to particular "patients" whose interests are thereby highlighted (e.g., 'good for Mary'), to functional objects (e.g., 'Anchors ought to be

---

[41] This follows directly from ILP whenever the speaker's ends are best promoted by communicating asserted information. In Finlay 2004 I appealed instead to the maxim of quantity, which was confused.

heavy'), or to attitudes with constitutive aims (e.g., 'a reason to believe that *p*'). At other times a sentence can omit an end because it was explicitly introduced earlier in the conversation; for example,

(1) 'In planning the gruesome work of genocide, the SS studied various means of mass murder. They discovered that using the gas Zyklon B was best.'

(2) 'Seeking to inflict the greatest possible blow to the United States, the terrorists chose to attack the World Trade Center and Pentagon. They ought to have attacked the Mall of America instead.'

These unrelativized uses I've just listed are all among the exceptions to practicality, however, where the evidence is defeated. It shouldn't be inferred from utterance of (1) or (2), for example, that the speakers are expressing approval of the SS's use of Zyklon B, or recommending that terrorists attack the Mall of America (unless in a highly attenuated and easily accommodated sense). The cases featuring practicality are those where no such cues are present, so we need to ask what kinds of ends are salient by default.

Ends (or potential future states of affairs) are the kinds of things creatures like us desire and pursue, so will most commonly be of conversational interest as the objects of desire or pursuit—especially when thinking about what increases or decreases their probability.[42] Generally and by default, an end will therefore be salient as desired or intended by salient *persons*. One way of making persons salient is of course to refer to them, so 'a reason for *s*' or '*s* ought to φ' will tend to encourage a reading as relativized to an end saliently desired or intended by *s*, which would explain the appeal of narrowly Humean theories of normativity. So interpreted, these third-personal utterances don't generally have (unattenuated) practicality. But for any communicative act there are always two other obvious candidates for salient persons without any explicit reference or cue: the speaker and the audience.

This can be observed in the interpretation of unrelativized use of other logically incomplete terms, such as 'nearby' (which I assume concerns a relation to a location). Suppose Jenny is in a hotel talking on the phone with her husband at home, and says, 'There's a Laundromat nearby.' It's natural to assume she means either *nearby the hotel* (preferred if the prior conversation concerned the clothes she's wearing, for example), or *nearby our home* (preferred if the

---

[42] Ends so defined are also the kinds of things creatures are averse to and try to avert, which presents a problem (thanks to Mike Ridge and Brian Coffey for pressing this concern). To explain the valences of 'good' and 'bad' I need to suppose that the salient end for normative speech is always the object of desire rather than the object of aversion (assuming that to desire *e* is to be averse to *not-e* and vice versa). This may appear ad hoc, but a semantic link seems too inflexible since 'good' and 'bad' can be explicitly relativized to any end, and is unnecessary as this coordination problem can be solved by a general social convention of presupposing the object of desire.

conversation concerned the broken dryer in their house). So by default and in the absence of other cues, an end will be salient similarly as being desired or intended by the speaker and/or audience.[43]

Whereas it might be thought that somebody can only be in one location at once, we often desire or intend more than one end at once, and a person's motivations are also often less evident than their location. So an underdetermination issue arises, as the salience of a person mightn't always or automatically make a particular end salient. But even the case of 'nearby' involves considerable indeterminacy, which is resolved by a variety of contextual clues: is the location to be identified with the building, or the street, or the town, etc? An end might be made determinately salient by the person's known attitudes, for example, or by charitable interpretation of what they said (e.g., a fan of a particular team tells another, 'Don't bother to watch today's game. It was *bad*'). But we've also observed that to understand any communicative act, an interpreter must be able to identify in some way the speaker's *conversational end*, or what she's actively trying to accomplish or promote. By default (context and charity permitting), the most salient end will therefore presumably be the speaker's conversational end. I'll call this a context of *direct interest*.

Given also the default presumption of cooperation, it can be further inferred that the most salient end will by default be the *shared* conversational end of speaker and audience. In a conversation between teammates during a game of football, for example, unrelativized normative language is naturally interpreted as assuming an end like *our winning the game*. In a philosophical conversation, such as the one you and I are currently engaged in, it's naturally interpreted as assuming something like *settling the truth about our topic*.

Many cases will diverge from this paradigm, of course, involving contexts of *indirect interest*; sometimes an audience will lack sufficient cues for any particular end to be salient (Chapter 6), sometimes context or charity rules against the intended end being the conversational end (as in retrospective claims, which don't aim at changing the past), and some conversations aren't cooperative (Chapter 7). But identifying this default association of unrelativized normative language with the shared conversational end enables us to accommodate and explain *Evidentiality* and the defeasible practicality of normative speech and thought.

Consider first an assertion of a sentence like 'Adultery is good', interpreted as implicitly relativized to an end salient as being an object of the *speaker's* desires or intentions. On our theory, this is to interpret the speaker as expressing a belief that adultery increases the probability of some end she desires. Since desire for an end is or provides motivation toward both it and the means to it,[44] the speaker therefore pragmatically indicates that she has favorable

---

[43] Cf. Harman 1996: 15–16.
[44] I argue this is a necessary connection in Finlay 2008a.

motivation also toward adultery. In this way she *expresses approval*. Since her utterance is apt to indicate her attitudes in this way, an audience will often also be justified in understanding her to have spoken with the communicative intent of expressing this approval, in which case her utterance will have the practical illocutionary force of *endorsement*. We can also explain the close connection between (assertoric, unembedded, unrelativized, prospective) *first-personal* use of 'ought' (i.e., 'I ought to φ') and speaker intention, as emphasized by Gibbard. If this is implicitly relativized to the speaker's desired end (as also suggested by the explicit self-reference), it expresses a belief that the speaker's own desired or intended end is most reliably promoted by φ-ing, which will characteristically produce an intention to φ.

Consider next an assertion of a normative sentence interpreted as implicitly relativized to an end salient as being the object of the *audience's* desires or intentions. These cases will evidently accommodate *Psychological Influence*: discovering information about what increases or decreases the probability of their desired ends is apt to influence the audience's motivations. The characteristic recommendatory force of (normative, unrelativized, asserted, unembedded, prospective) second-personal uses of 'ought', as in 'You ought to φ', is also easily explained.

In a cooperative context of direct interest, a speaker is aiming at a shared conversational end e, which is therefore by default the most salient end. So when she says to an agent s, 'You ought to φ', she will be understood to be asserting that in order that e, s ought to φ; i.e., that φ-ing is the surest means to e. By CLP, an interpreter looks to see why the speaker might have thought she could best promote the shared conversational ends by such an assertion. Communicating this information to s is an optimal way of motivating s to φ, as a means to their shared end e. So this is naturally inferred to be what the speaker is trying to do. This satisfies *Recommendation*, accounting for the intuition that the speaker performs a speech act of recommendation. If the speaker were to say in the same context, 'We're most likely to achieve our ends if you φ', this would naturally be interpreted as having the same purpose and recommendatory force. By performing an ordinary declarative act of asserting a purely descriptive sentence with end-relational content, a speaker in a cooperative context of direct interest thereby also pragmatically performs a practical speech act of recommendation.

Although our semantics for 'good', 'ought', and 'reason' strictly supports motivational externalism, a pragmatic explanation can now be given of the intuitions supporting internalism. The philosophical case is usually launched with an invitation to consider assertion of an unrelativized normative sentence, as I did above with 'Adultery is good' and 'This is good, and it hurts', in the abstract without any contextual information. Ostensibly this is to highlight only *general* features of normative language. Such a datum is intuitively interpreted as expressing speaker motivation, so unless we opt for radical psychological hypotheses it appears as if semantic competence must be responsible.

But our theory suggests that these intuitions are really due to our *pragmatic* competence responding to the paucity of contextual information.

By CLP we naturally assume that a speaker reporting an utterance to us has provided sufficient information for us to be able to understand roughly what was being said or done. Since it's necessarily true of anything whatsoever that it's good *for some end or other*, a reported use of an unrelativized normative sentence only has significant informational value if the implicit end can be identified under some description. Because we haven't been given any other clue, we naturally assume that the implicit end is of the kind salient by default: an end desired by the speaker of the utterance. Under these assumptions the features of practicality straightforwardly follow by our pragmatic principles. If an assertion of (2) were reported simply by saying, 'She said that terrorists ought to have attacked the Mall of America', for example, then the speaker can justly complain that she's been misrepresented and her utterance taken out of context: 'I merely said that *in order to inflict the greatest possible blow on the United States*, they ought to have attacked the Mall of America.' The internalism debate would therefore be another metaethical controversy due to confusion over the rich pragmatics of normative language.

The end-relational theory accommodates many of expressivism's central claims, despite being a purely descriptive semantics. By asserting unrelativized normative sentences, speakers do typically express their motivational attitudes without describing them, and perform practical speech acts like endorsements and recommendations. The theory achieves these results while rejecting expressivism's essential claim that this is an element of the semantic conventions for this language, attributing it rather to the pragmatics of omitting the relevant end. I'll call solutions of this kind "quasi-expressivist", as they explain the seemingly expressivist features of normative speech and thought with purely descriptivist resources.[45]

5.5. Bearding the Lion

We've found that the end-relational theory is (perhaps uniquely) a descriptivist semantics that meets the challenge from practicality. I'll conclude this chapter by suggesting additionally that whereas expressivists and primitivists have each claimed that this practicality is fatal for any reductive account, our theory actually accommodates and explains it better than either can, enjoying the virtues of each (and some others besides) while avoiding their vices.

---

[45] This contrasts with "quasi-realism", Simon Blackburn's label (1993) for the project of explaining the "realist" (or descriptivist) appearances of normative speech and thought with purely "antirealist" (or expressivist) resources.

First, our theory uniquely preserves a unified semantics based on other, ordinary uses of these words, while expressivists and primitivists must choose between either extensive lexical ambiguities or analyses that become increasingly bizarre the further we depart from the moral uses they take as focal. Second, unlike primitivism (but like expressivism), our theory accounts for practicality with just conservative, Humean psychological resources, without requiring any radical psychological claims about human motivation or agency. It also *explains* the special action-guiding character of normative facts and properties, which remains mysterious on primitivist theories.

My remaining two points are aimed at expressivism. The third point is that (pure) expressivism has some counterintuitively radical implications about the practical role of normative speech and thought, as a result of its unequivocal rejection of normative facts and properties. This commits it to an uncompromising rejection of the most popular horn of the *Euthyphro* dilemma: that we desire or are motivated toward things because we judge them to be good, rather than vice versa. I'll look first at the practical role of first-personal, deliberative normative speech or thought, and then at the interpersonal role of second-personal, advisory normative speech.

To fix a determinate target I focus on Gibbard's recent view that normative sentences conventionally express *plans* (intentions, decisions) about what to do. To form a normative judgment is therefore essentially to decide what to do in some (possibly remote) circumstance; we judge that we *ought* to φ, for example, just because we decide to φ. But as primitivists object, this intuitively puts the cart before the horse. Parfit writes,

> When we conclude that we ought to do something, we are not deciding to do this thing, but coming to have a normative belief. Though our decisions to act are often based on such beliefs, these decisions are not the same thing as coming to have these beliefs. (2011b: 386)

Normative judgments are supposed to function as *guides* for our decisions, not their consequences or epiphenomena. As Gibbard himself describes the issue, "Do we discover how best to live, or is it a matter of arbitrary choice—or what?"[46] If we reject normative facts and properties, then we seem to be left

---

[46] Gibbard 2003: x. Gibbard seems not to offer any third option. While he allows that 'ought' judgments are typically based on weighing *reasons*, as he is also an expressivist about what it is to judge *r* to be a reason (it's to intend to give *r* a certain weight in deliberation) the problem reappears at this level. *Why* give *r* a certain weight in deliberation, if not because that is its actual weight? Wherever this analysis ends, normative judgment is identified with brute, arbitrary choice. (A dilemma now looms: does 'ought' express an agent's decision about what to do, or does it signify what she has most reason to do, i.e.. the aggregation of all the agent's decisions about how to weigh considerations in deciding what to do?) While this decisionism is avoided by accounts appealing to nonvoluntary attitudes like desire and preference (which in conversation Gibbard recently endorsed instead), these are less plausible as accounts of the authority of 'ought' in our deliberations, and also may implausibly psychologize the content of deliberation.

with the implausibly radical idea that normative thought is simply a matter of arbitrary choice.

In those cases which clearly do involve simply an arbitrary choice or decision (as when in the predicament of Buridan's ass) normative language doesn't seem appropriate.[47] A person who decides between one of two equally attractive options does so without judging it to be the option she "ought" to choose. Gibbard claims that the constitutive aim of deliberation is reaching a decision, or settling on what to do, but this seems curiously incomplete. Deliberation is sometimes painstaking, difficult, costly, even agonizing, but if its goal were merely to make a decision this would be pointless and perverse; one could simply flip a coin. We might say 'Make a choice, already!', as to someone dithering over which flavor of toothpaste to buy. Rather than an epistemic virtue, the disposition to deliberate carefully would look instead like the vice of prevarication.

Gibbard's claim here is analogous to saying that the aim of a criminal trial is to reach a verdict. If this were the whole truth then the burdens of a trial would be gratuitous. These burdens are explained by the aim of reaching the *best* verdict, which isn't a projection of being the result reached but a factual matter requiring discovery. The burdens of deliberation are explained similarly by the aim of reaching the *best* decision, the likelihood of which is increased by taking the trouble to deliberate.

By contrast, although our theory agrees that deliberation is ultimately grounded in or motivated by contingent desires, it identifies the content of normative thought with facts and properties, which justify the burdens of deliberation and function to *guide* our decisions and *cause* corresponding motivation. Contra the objections raised by some primitivists against reductive theories, it doesn't psychologize normative facts and properties: end-relational facts aren't psychological at all.[48] It respects the dictum that we generally choose and are motivated toward things *because* we believe them to be good or what we ought to choose; as Butler observed, probability is the very guide of life. It also recognizes that an arbitrary choice between equal options doesn't involve a judgment that this is what *ought* to be done. The end-relational theory therefore enjoys the intuitive advantages claimed by primitivists with regard to the deliberative role of normative concepts.

Despite expressivists' common claim that the characteristic interpersonal influence and role of normative language strongly support their views over descriptivists', their accounts of this influence and role in advice are similarly radical and implausible. The expressivist model of normative force is that the speaker merely expresses her own motivational attitudes. But it's hard to see why this would have much recommendatory force at all. Suppose we're standing at the dairy counter buying milkshakes, and I say to you, 'I like creaming

---

[47] Cf. Wedgwood 2007, Parfit 2011b.
[48] E.g., Parfit 2006: 332.

soda', or perhaps, 'I want you to have creaming soda.' I would have expressed my attitudes, but intuitively wouldn't have performed the same act of recommendation as if I'd said, 'You ought to get creaming soda.'

Gibbard's analysis of normative advice as expressing the speaker's own decision about what to do in the advisee's situation may initially seem more promising, since 'If I were you, I'd get the creaming soda' is a familiar way of conveying a recommendation. But this is plausibly only insofar as it (pragmatically) indicates the existence of unmentioned *reasons* for that choice, justifying the plan. If normative claims are merely expressions of our own contingency plans for what we'd do in the other's situation, and not based on any supposed facts that make these the *best* plans for those situations, then it isn't clear what point or license we'd have for pressing them on others, especially against their own plans. Rather than a social virtue, the disposition to dispute normative issues with others would look instead like the vice of meddlesomeness.

Expressivists characteristically explain the interpersonal influence of normative speech as a kind of psychological contagion, manipulation, or "osmosis",[49] appealing to a contingent human disposition to be motivationally influenced by others' evident motivations. To advise you about what you "ought" to do is to try to manipulate you psychologically into having the motivations I want you to have; to ask for normative advice about what I ought to do is just to invite psychological manipulation. Gibbard describes such a process as "normative discussion".[50] While I've already acknowledged we're susceptible to these kinds of psychological influence (and in Chapter 7 I'll offer a related analysis of the illocutionary force of *prescription* as found in moral speech), as a general account of normative discourse and recommendatory force this verges on the scandalous.

By contrast, our theory conservatively respects the common-sense view that our practice of giving normative advice (in circumstances of cooperation) generally treats others as autonomous, "rational" agents, seeking to influence them by sharing information they can recognize for themselves as justifying action, without any psychological manipulation. So the end-relational theory provides a more conservative, plausible, and charitable account of both the intrapersonal and interpersonal practical roles of normative speech and thought than expressivism.[51]

---

[49] E.g., Stevenson 1937, Gibbard 1990, see also Slote 2010, and Anscombe 1958 on "mesmeric force".

[50] Gibbard 1990.

[51] Two reviewers point out in response that expressivism can tell the same psychological story as the end-relational theory: both can recognize a factual basis for recommendation, and both explain practicality in terms of contingent desires (etc.) This is correct, but it misses my point, which is that expressivism assigns normative concepts the wrong *role* in this story.

The fourth and final point is that because our account of practicality is *pragmatic* rather than semantic, unlike expressivism it is able to explain why the use of normative language is practical "to just the extent that it is".[52] Just as the case for expressivism is often made on the assumption of the *strong* practicality requirement, our finding that this requirement is *too* strong poses a serious difficulty for any account that ties normative language to motivation and practicality directly by semantic convention—and therefore not only for pure expressivism, but also for hybrid theories that posit both descriptive and expressive meaning.[53] Since semantic conventions determine the boundaries of fully intelligible competent use of words, use of normative language without the allegedly required motivation or force wouldn't be fully intelligible to an audience ("Why would he say that, rather than...?"), unless they supposed the speaker to be less than fully competent.[54]

By contrast, since pragmatic explanations turn on contingent features of the context of use, they have no difficulty accommodating the defeasibility of practicality; Grice appeals precisely to this "cancelability" as distinguishing conversational from conventional cues. The end-relational theory explains not only why use of normative language is practical when it is, but unlike expressivism also why it's not practical when it isn't. It easily explains why it's only (normative, asserted, unembedded) unrelativized uses of normative words that generally have the features of special practicality—and even then only defeasibly. All these exceptions are difficult if not impossible for the expressivist to explain. Additionally, we've seen that the particular illocutionary force of a normative word can vary according to context of use; for example, that only prospective, second-personal, cooperative uses of 'ought' are naturally described as acts of *recommendation*. While our theory predicts and explains these variations in force by appeal to our pragmatic principles, they are problematic for any theory associating normative words with particular forces by semantic convention.

Despite often being identified as the Achilles heel of any descriptivist or reductivist theory, the special practicality of normative language is easily accommodated and explained by the end-relational semantics in light of our simple and conservative pragmatic principles. The resulting quasi-expressivist solution even seems better placed than its rivals to explain why normative language is practical to just the extent and in exactly the ways it is. Rather than an objection, the features of practicality therefore strengthen our case. We'll see that solutions to other challenges can be derived from the pragmatic principles and results of this chapter.

---

[52] Smith 1994: 136.

[53] The end-relational theory makes these additional conventions redundant and superfluous. Hybrid theories have been claimed superior because the pragmatic account rests on a particular semantic theory (Boisvert 2008, Copp 2009, Bar-On & Chrisman 2009), but this is no objection in the present context of evaluating that semantic theory.

[54] David Copp's response (2009, to Finlay 2005) is to insist such uses do betray a lack of full linguistic competence. Here we have a basic clash of intuitions.

6

Multiple Ends

The end-relational semantics analyzes normative uses of 'good', 'ought', and 'reason' as asserting propositions relativized to single ends, and in the previous chapter I suggested that a speaker can omit reference to ends just in case one is sufficiently salient in the context. Many uses of normative language resist this treatment, however. This chapter addresses challenges concerning normative speech and thought where multiple ends are relevant, and *all things considered* claims and judgments. We'll examine contexts of obscure ends where no single end is uniquely salient, contexts of competing ends, balancing ends under uncertainty, and how to understand normative weight or gradability in these cases. These challenges are more specific to our end-relational semantics than the challenges addressed in other chapters, because most rival relational semantics (like Kratzer's) build in sensitivity to multiple ends. But I'll argue that when combined with the basic pragmatic principles identified in the previous chapter, our simpler semantics accommodates and predicts these uses too, even providing a better treatment than more complex semantics.

6.1. Obscure Ends

We saw in Chapter 5 that the end-relational theory predicts that use of normative sentences not explicitly relativized to ends will be interpreted by default as implicitly relativized to ends saliently desired by the speaker and/or audience. Audiences can identify which particular end the speaker has in mind by various cues, such as the shared conversational end in contexts of direct interest. But speakers often utter unrelativized normative sentences in contexts where no end is uniquely salient. Suppose Jethro says to his daughter, 'You ought to brush your teeth every day.' While there may be no lack of candidates for a relevant end yielding the right truth conditions, the problem is that an interpreter has no decisive reason to prefer any one of the possibilities. Does he mean "in order to avoid tooth decay", "in order to avoid toothache", "in order to avoid a painful visit to the dentist", "in order to form a beneficial habit of dental hygiene", etc.?

Ends can be obscure due to a variety of factors: multiple ends might be equally salient, the conversational end might only be vaguely recognized, or charitable interpretation may rule it out, and so on. The theory seems to imply that such an utterance would fail to communicate any asserted proposition, although it appears sufficiently clear. The problem seems even more pressing for normative thought: surely it is possible to have coherent normative beliefs without having any particular end in mind, and to disambiguate one's own thought (or speech). It also arises for normative *questions*, like asking or wondering "What ought I to do?" While some such enquiries plausibly presuppose a particular salient end, others seem "open-ended" (excuse the pun), as in paradigmatic contexts of deliberation.

While no particular ends may be uniquely salient, in these cases there are still salient *persons*, and thereby salient sets of ends, being those desired or intended by the speaker and/or audience. (Since persons are both temporally and modally extended, salient desires needn't always be their present or actual attitudes, but may be dispositional or counterfactual. In contexts of giving and asking for recommendations, for example, the salient ends may more plausibly be what the agent *would desire if relevantly informed*.) We saw previously that it isn't necessary to identify a particular end in order to infer significant information from a use of normative language. To infer that a speaker has motivation toward p, for example, it's enough to know she believes p is good for some end she desires. By our quasi-expressivist account of practicality, any utterance expressing such a belief is apt to express endorsement or approval of p even if the end remains unidentified.

Similarly for the interpersonal influence and recommendatory force of 'You ought to φ': provided an agent cares that her desires are satisfied (as is normal), learning that she desires some end that is most likely to obtain if she φs will provide her with some motivation to φ.[1] Expressing such a belief is therefore apt to have recommendatory force even if the end isn't identified. So if a speaker's primary intention is to express her attitudes or recommend an action, then uttering an unrelativized normative sentence may serve her purposes despite her audience's inability to identify any particular end as most salient.

The pragmatic reasoning from Chapter 5 can also be reversed. When a speaker says 'You ought to φ', it will often be evident he means to recommend φ-ing although no particular end is salient. Other possible cues for recommendatory force include the explicit reference to the addressee, a context where the addressee is deliberating or has asked for advice, the speaker's subsequently expectant behavior, and the simple fact that the conversational relevance of

---

[1] This suggests an explanation why young children, having yet to develop second-order desires, are often unmoved by abstract normative claims.

end-relational information is generally due to this kind of reason.[2] If someone said to you completely out of the blue, 'You are more likely to become a great guitarist if you practice every day', it would be natural to infer that she is trying to motivate you to practice guitar every day. On our semantics an 'ought' sentence is generally an effective instrument of recommendation just in case it is interpreted as relativized to an end the agent desires. By CLP, the speaker is therefore talking *as if* the agent desires the end she has in mind. This is a case of *pragmatic presupposition*, where an utterance is only felicitous or advances the conversational ends on the assumption of some further information.[3]

When presupposed information isn't already part of the common ground, an audience tries to *accommodate* it. To preserve the assumption that the speaker is acting cooperatively (CLP), or at least consistently with her own aims and beliefs (ILP), the audience interprets her as communicating that information, adding it to the common ground. Suppose Mrs. Benson declares, 'I'm looking for whoever drove over my flowers!' and Kirk responds, 'Russell already left.' This response is only cooperative on the assumption that *Russell drove over the flowers*, so Mrs. Benson will naturally understand Kirk to be expressing that belief. Our semantics therefore predicts that a speaker saying, 'You ought to φ' with evident recommendatory force thereby pragmatically expresses the belief that an end desired by the agent is most likely to obtain if she φs (and that a speaker saying 'It's good that *p*' who is evidently expressing approval thereby pragmatically expresses the belief that *p* increases the probability of an end he desires, etc.).

While this explains the conversational utility of using sentences with obscure ends, it leaves open what these utterances actually assert. There are several possibilities here. Where the speaker has a particular end *e* in mind she might simply use the sentence opaquely as elliptically relativized to *e*, since it doesn't matter for conversational purposes if the audience can't identify the asserted proposition. Speakers can communicate propositions and express approval or recommend pragmatically, without communicating any *asserted* proposition. So if she aims merely to express approval or recommend, for example, there may be no need for the audience to recognize what she asserts. An interpreter may still naturally consider himself to understand such uses perfectly well. If somebody listening to CB radio hears a speaker at an unknown location say, 'There's been an accident here', he will generally take himself to understand what was said, despite being ignorant of which of indefinitely many propositions was asserted courtesy of the indexical 'here'. Understanding that the speaker has asserted of wherever she is that an accident has occurred there is

---

[2] Copp 2001 and Strandberg 2012a argue for a generalized conversational implicature of attitude due to this customary use. Our theory attributes this implicature (and custom) a more basic source in the nature of the facts the language refers to.

[3] E.g., Stalnaker 1972, Lewis 1979: 339–40.

sufficient for many contexts. Similarly, normative claims or judgments are often understood sufficiently well if it is known that the speaker asserted of some end she has in mind that p is good for that end.[4]

Alternatively, if a speaker has no intention to communicate a particular proposition, then we might reasonably doubt he asserts it. These utterances may also simply be vague, not asserting logically complete or determinate propositions, which fits better when the speaker (or judge) doesn't even have a determinate end in mind. Vagueness is an ordinary feature of speech and thought, which are often only as determinate as needed for our purposes. In these cases a speaker may be disposed to accept a range of different, incompatible completions of the sentence if suggested to her.

However, a speaker should arguably be interpreted by default as asserting the proposition she intends to communicate whenever it's a potential content of her utterance. First, consider cases where a speaker asserts 's ought to φ' having in mind a particular end that isn't identifiable by the audience. We predicted that these utterances pragmatically express at least the speaker's belief that *the end she has in mind is most likely to obtain if s φs*. The content of this belief is itself an end-relational proposition with roughly the logical form

(the x: x is the end the speaker has in mind)($ought_{x,R}(p)$).

Being relational rather than indexical, our semantics provides an argument-place for an end (strictly, the background b) in the logical form of normative language, which can therefore be bound by a description. So on the assumption that the speaker is obeying Grice's submaxim to be clear (easily derived from CLP/ILP), it can be inferred that when the end is salient only under a definite description, like *the mutually desired end the speaker has in mind*, then the end-argument of the asserted proposition is implicitly bound by that salient description. To avoid implausibly subjective truth-conditions, this end can be taken to be rigidly designated (by *dthat*):[5] *in order that dthat(the mutually desired end I have in mind), s ought to φ.*

Next consider cases where the speaker doesn't have a particular end in mind. Since these claims can't be completely open-ended (i.e., *ought in order that something or other*), presumably she must have an *indefinite* description in mind, such as *an end desired by s*. She may thereby assert an existentially quantified proposition, such as *there is some end(s) x desired by s, such that in order that x, s ought to φ*:

($\exists x$: s desires x)($ought_{x,R}(p)$).

---

[4] This is to grasp the "diagonal proposition" (Stalnaker 1999), the set of different propositions the speaker would assert depending on which context obtains.

[5] Kaplan 1989: 521–22.

If the end is salient only under an indefinite description then the audience might reasonably interpret the speaker as asserting such a proposition, which can be sufficient for expressing motivation when interpreted as bound by the speaker's desires, and sufficient for recommendatory force when interpreted as bound by the audience's desires.[6]

This provides a general solution for obscure ends:

Variable End: Where an end is salient only under a definite or indefinite description, the proposition asserted by an unrelativized normative sentence is interpreted as relativized to a end-variable bound by that description.

This solution extends also to open-ended normative questions, like 'What ought I to do?' These enquiries couldn't be completely open-ended, and the speaker presumably has in mind some general description of a relevant end; for example, *What ought I to do [in order to achieve an end I would desire if I was aware of the possible outcomes]?* Pragmatically this would be interpreted as having the illocutionary force of inviting direction.

The end-relational theory can therefore accommodate these obscure uses of unrelativized normative language and explain their communicative function. But our pragmatic principles require us also to show that speakers might reasonably believe these utterances to be optimal ways of promoting their conversational ends. These practices are justified and predicted because, in J. L. Mackie's words, "there are advantages in not specifying them precisely."[7] First, the unrelativized sentences are less wordy and more efficient, and therefore comply with Grice's submaxim of manner to *be brief*. (Speakers and audiences generally prefer not to waste their time uttering or listening to unnecessary verbosity; on our pragmatic principles the shorter sentence is therefore better, all else being equal.)[8]

One consequence is that the permissibility of ellipsis generally implies an *expectation* or requirement of ellipsis. If somebody says, 'I want you to take your shoes off your feet', her failure to omit reference to the already salient feet of the audience strongly suggests some special reason, perhaps such as that she doesn't want the shoes taken off something else. This is significant for some metaethical puzzles: since omitting the end is generally permissible when saliently desired, making the end explicit will generally be infelicitous and impermissible in these cases, and therefore will tend to pragmatically indicate

---

[6] Various cues can help an audience distinguish between these two alternatives, e.g., if the speaker says, 'I'm not sure what will happen, but you ought not do that!', but this seems a real ambiguity in unrelativized normative claims, prompting the inquiry, 'Do you have a particular consequence in mind?'

[7] Mackie 1977: 44.

[8] Things often aren't equal: a speaker may have reasons for stalling, or simply like the sound of her own voice, etc.

that the end is *not* saliently desired. This will strengthen the pragmatic separation between unrelativized use of normative words as typically having practicality, and relativized use as lacking it.

Failing to make an end explicit when one isn't uniquely salient can also have other advantages. Sometimes an end is difficult to describe even when the speaker has something determinate in mind, because it is complicated or defies description by its nature. This seems characteristic of *aesthetic* ends, involving kinds of emotional, intellectual, and spiritual experiences, for example, making it difficult to adequately articulate the way in which paintings, sculptures, musical compositions, or sunsets are good. Sometimes an audience may be incapable of easily comprehending the end, so the speaker's purposes are better served by communicating merely that it's an end that is or would be desired. Parents often seem to speak this way; for example, 'Eating too much candy isn't good' (explaining dental or pancreatic health to young children isn't easy), or 'There are reasons for our rules.' At other times specifying the end may be too traumatizing for the audience: 'You ought not talk to strangers'... in order *not to be abducted, molested, or murdered!*

A speaker may just be confident that some relevantly desired ends are at stake, without having any particularly in mind. Perhaps she has no particular reason for selecting one out of a cluster of ends she has in mind. Jethro's case may fit this model; if his daughter asks, 'Do you mean I ought to brush every day in order to avoid tooth decay? Or to avoid toothache? Or to avoid the dentist?' he might reply, 'Yes, any and all of those things.' Or perhaps the speaker is unaware of the potential outcomes, but expects they would be saliently desired. Leaving ends obscure can also serve more deceitful purposes by enabling a speaker to bluff or pretend such an end exists in order to manipulate her audience; we'll discuss these cases further in Chapter 7. The end-relational theory therefore predicts that speakers can have a variety of sufficient reasons for asserting unrelativized normative sentences with obscure ends.

6.2. All Things Considered

While the Variable End solution still relativizes normative language to single ends, normative judgments and enquiries are often sensitive to multiple ends at once. Appeal to existentially quantified propositions is too weak to solve the problem of obscure ends in many cases, for example. When Jethro says, 'You ought to brush your teeth every day', he can't be saying or communicating merely that there is *some* saliently desired end that is best promoted thereby. For this is consistent with there being another desired end (perhaps desired much more strongly) relative to which his daughter's brushing her teeth every day would be a very bad course of action. Jethro's utterance is naturally interpreted as ruling this possibility out, and would be perversely uncooperative and deceptive if he believed it to be the case.

For example, suppose Alan tells Paul that he ought to fish on Lake Rotoiti rather than on Lake Rotorua, and cites the reason that the fish are more plentiful on Rotoiti, which explains why fishing on Rotoiti would be better for getting a larger catch. But Alan also knows that fishing on Rotoiti (but not Rotorua) is illegal, and therefore likely to result in a steep fine, and also that Paul greatly prefers avoiding a steep fine than getting a larger catch. Alan's statement would then be uncooperative, deceptive, and plausibly false.

Typically when a speaker says without relativization that an agent "ought" to φ, or that φ-ing is "best", or that the agent has "most reason" to φ, he communicates that φ-ing is best not merely in relation to *some* desired end, but "all things considered". Relativistic semantic theories are therefore claimed to be unable to account for these centrally important cases, requiring instead an *absolutist* (or nonrelational) semantics.[9] Allegedly, if 'ought', 'good', and 'reason' were always relativized to single ends, they would be unable to fulfill their essential functions in practical speech and thought, as in recommendation and deliberation. Knowing what I ought to do in order to please my children, and what I ought to do in order to please my wife, and what I ought to do in order to please myself, etc., doesn't resolve the practical issue of what to do. Practical problems call for decisions, which aren't relative to ends but are "simpliciter". Normative speech and thought can apparently only play their decisive practical role if there is a question of what an agent just plain ought to do, simpliciter.

The end-relational theory may seem absurdly to deny the coherence of such questions. But linguistic evidence suggests an alternative analysis. Common variants of 'simpliciter' are 'period', 'full stop', and 'sans phrase'. These qualifiers are all explicitly linguistic, which suggests that the concept of (e.g.) *ought-simpliciter* may simply be that of a normative proposition assertable with an unrelativized 'ought' sentence:

Simpliciter: s ought to φ "simpliciter" just in case it would be correct and felicitous in the absence of any special context to assert simply '*s* ought to φ.'

Our theory has already predicted that such cases exist, being those relativized to ends that needn't be made explicit because salient by default. We've also seen that ends are salient by default on account of being desired by salient persons. To accommodate speech or thought about 'good', 'ought', and 'reason' simpliciter we therefore need only account for "all things considered" uses.

---

[9] E.g., Piller 2001, Thomson 2008, Kiesewetter 2011. Thomson insists on absolutism for 'ought' while rejecting it for 'good', which is unstable given that parallel considerations apply and the platitude that one ought to do whatever is best; cf. Piller 2001, Shanklin 2011.

Looking at its general use, 'all things considered' seems to function as a kind of universal quantifier. Some uses in normative sentences can therefore be accommodated as identifying the background b with everything in some salient domain (e.g., given *everything we know*, or *all the facts at t*), allowing us to make sense of 'In order that e, all things considered s ought to φ.' Here it contrasts with 'ceteris paribus' or 'other things being equal', which indicate a restricted or stereotypical background. But this isn't the 'ought'-simpliciter we're seeking.

An obvious hypothesis is that 'all things considered' sometimes quantifies instead over ends in some domain E; for example, what an agent ought to do *taking all her desired ends into consideration*. (Many claims about what an agent ought to do "all things considered" won't be restricted by her desires, of course, as when the domain E includes moral ideals. These cases are addressed in Chapter 7, but for now I'll focus only on the challenges posed by the agent's desiring multiple ends.) But this move isn't as obviously available for our semantics as for some rival relational theories, like Kratzer's, since it relativizes normative terms to single ends e rather than to sets of ends E. Appealing to a universally quantified proposition doesn't work—for example, $(\forall x{:}\ x$ is desired by $s)(ought_{x,R}(p))$—as typically no action is best for every desired end.

I'll build a complete solution incrementally, by starting with artificially simple cases and adding complications one at a time. At the very least, we need a basis for distinguishing some desired ends as more salient than others. A simple and conservative extension of the Humean psychological model is that desires aren't all equal: they vary in strength, generating *preferences* for some ends over others. Given a simple situation where an agent must choose between incompatible desired ends that are each completely within her power, she can be expected to pursue whichever end she prefers.

Our pragmatic principles therefore imply that speakers will be concerned not merely with *some* saliently desired end, but with the saliently *preferred* end in the context:

Preferential Selection: Where multiple incompatible ends are salient in
                            a context, the most saliently preferred end is the
                            most salient.

In cooperative contexts of direct interest where the salient end is the conversational end the speaker borrows from her audience, for example, this will be the end the speaker believes the audience prefers. When Alan says to Paul, 'You ought to fish on Lake Rotoiti', he is understood as addressing the end he believes Paul prefers, and therefore pragmatically expresses the belief that Paul is most likely to achieve his preferred end if he fishes on Rotoiti.

This fixes the problem observed for our account of recommendatory force. To be told that φ-ing is the most reliable way to promote your preferred end is to be provided with reliably action-guiding information. Alan's statement is deceptive because it communicates something he knows to be false: relative to

Paul's preferred end of avoiding a large fine, fishing on Rotoiti is not a good choice.

This suggests that what an agent ought to do simpliciter is just whatever ought to be done relative to the relevantly preferred end. Here it may be objected that if Alan were to say without ellipsis, 'In order to get a large catch you ought to fish on Rotoiti', he wouldn't seem to communicate the same information or the same recommendatory force as saying simply, 'You ought to fish on Rotoiti.' He wouldn't necessarily be taken to have lied or spoken deceptively, and Paul might reply, 'Okay, but what ought I to do *period*?' This may seem to indicate that we haven't captured the force of 'ought'-simpliciter. But recall that it's precisely the omission of the end that pragmatically communicates the essential information that the speaker believes the end to be relevantly preferred, and thereby generates the recommendatory force.[10] Since permissible ellipses are generally pragmatically required, using the explicit sentence would therefore not only fail to pragmatically indicate the essential information, but would also indicate that the speaker doesn't believe the end is relevantly preferred, blocking recommendatory force.

The objection can also be addressed by combining the Preferential Selection solution with the Variable End solution. Omitting the end makes salient a description such as *the end you most prefer*, especially if the identity of this end is obscure. Alan can therefore be interpreted as not merely indicating but asserting the essential information that some end Paul most prefers is best promoted by fishing on Rotoiti.[11]

Preferential Selection also provides a solution to another difficulty concerning *scalar ends*. Whereas I defined ends as potential states of affairs, ordinary talk about "ends" which admit varying degrees of realization resists this definition. Consider the "ends" of wealth, longevity, fame, or a large catch. The "desire to be rich" typically isn't directed at any particular state of affairs consisting in one's having a certain sum of money, for example. It may be satisfied to some degree by having five million dollars, but to a greater degree by having ten million, and an even greater degree by having fifty million. At least in principle the aspirations of such desires needn't have any limit. So consider the question: relative to the end of "being rich", which amount of money ought one to choose? Given the options of five, ten, or fifty million dollars, one ought to choose the fifty million, which is best. But a person doesn't seem any more *likely* to be rich by having fifty rather than five million dollars, just *more* rich: an apparent problem for the end-relational theory.

---

[10] Since 'relevantly preferred' is often to be interpreted dispositionally, if the speaker has information that the audience lacks then the audience may not be aware of what it relevantly prefers.

[11] Explicitly saying, 'The end you most prefer' is also predicted to raise questions if this description is already salient; e.g., it might suggest the speaker doesn't herself prefer it, which may undermine recommendatory force.

By our definition, these cases don't really involve individual ends, but rather *preference scales* of ends. Somebody who "desires to be rich" desires the end of having five million dollars, and the end of having fifty million dollars, and also all ends in between and beyond—and for any two of these ends he prefers the greater amount over the lesser.[12] Our theory therefore accounts for these uses of 'ought' and 'best' by application of Preferential Selection. (Comparatives like 'better' present a greater challenge, discussed below). If choosing between A: having five million dollars, B: having ten million dollars, and C: having fifty million dollars, then C is the preferred end. By uttering 'I ought to choose C' or 'C is best' one therefore asserts something true, and by 'I ought to choose A' something false, because the most preferred end is more likely on the choice of C than of A.

6.3. Balancing Ends

Commonly an agent's ends aren't all mutually incompatible, as in the simple cases above, so what all things considered ought to be done (is best, etc.) doesn't require choosing one desired end over all others but finding the best *balance* between multiple ends. In these cases the best action (choice, state of affairs, etc.) often isn't best for any one desired end individually, so Preferential Selection alone doesn't help.

This is where the extra complexity of rival theories like Kratzer's semantics is supposed to prove superior. I argued in Chapter 3 that all else being equal, the end-relational theory is superior because it provides a simpler and more intuitive account of basic cases involving single ends. But if the more complex semantics fare better with these cases of multiple ends, then all is not equal, and perhaps our theory should be rejected as too simple. However, we'll see that this extra complexity of rival theories also struggles to accommodate basic cases of multiple ends, despite being specially designed for this purpose, and that the end-relational theory yields a pragmatic solution that fares at least as well with this challenge.

The most obvious and simple way of extending our semantics to cases where multiple ends are mutually compatible is just by conjoining them. Suppose Letty is deciding between equivalent job offers in three different cities, with just three desiderata: (e_1) affordable housing, (e_2) a moderate climate, and (e_3) close proximity to family. There is then a further end or outcome e_4 which is the conjunction of these, and a question about what she ought to do in order

---

[12] Evers (2011: Ch. 8) objects that actual agents don't have all these desires, but this solution only requires *dispositional* desires and preferences.

that e_4. When an agent believes all her desired ends can be achieved together she won't pursue only the individually desired end she most prefers, but rather all her desired ends. Or assuming that the strengths of desires are additive (as on a simple Humean model), the end she will most prefer is the conjunctive end.

Our pragmatic principles therefore imply

Conjunctive End: Where multiple ends are desired the most salient end is the conjunction of those ends, all else being equal.

This correctly predicts that if there is just one city that has affordable housing, a moderate climate, and is close to family then that's the job offer Letty ought to accept. Often the conjunction of all one's individually desired ends is unattainable, however. Suppose no cities satisfy all three desiderata, but a different city uniquely satisfies each pair: which offer ought she then to accept? If the salient end here were e_4, the answer would be that there isn't any offer she ought to accept, or even any offer she *could* accept (i.e., in order to achieve that end). Yet it's perfectly possible in this scenario that there is a job offer that Letty ought to accept, all things considered.

Although this case is still very simple it also poses a problem for Kratzer's semantics. Recall that this posits an additional argument-place in the logical form of modals, for an ordering source, o (e.g., $must_{b,o}(p)$), which selects a set of propositions (ends) that orders the possibilities roughly by how closely they conform to that set. Unlike our Conjunctive End strategy this semantics can return a positive result even when no possibilities are consistent with all the relevant ends, by selecting the possibility that is highest in the ordering. But this extra machinery fails to achieve its purpose, because it only works for artificially simple cases.

The immediate problem concerns *incomplete* orderings. Any two possible world-states w_1 and w_2 are ordered according to the following rule: w_1 ranks higher than w_2 if and only if the part o_2 of the ordering source o with which w_2 is consistent is a proper subset of the part o_1 of the ordering source with which w_1 is consistent. In plainer language, w_1 is better than w_2 if and only if it satisfies all the same desiderata plus at least one more. But if neither o_1 nor o_2 is a proper subset of the other (i.e., if each has at least one unique member) then there is no ordering of w_1 and w_2. Since that's true of Letty's scenario, this semantics also seems unable to generate the result that there is some job offer Letty ought to accept.

The reason why Letty may have a job offer she ought to accept is that certain of her ends may have more weight or (on our assumptions) be *preferred* over others. Suppose she prefers e_1 to e_2, and e_2 to e_3; then she ought to accept the offer that would satisfy both e_1 and e_2 but not e_3. So the problem is that Kratzer's semantics, like ours, doesn't provide a way of weighting ends; the ordering source treats every end as on a par.

Chapter 3 observed one modification introduced to address this shortcoming: positing multiple, nested ordering sources in the logical form of 'ought': in effect an ordering of ordering sources.[13] This gives each rank of ends its own argument-place in the logical form. In Letty's case there are three ranks of ends, for example, so the logical form of the relevant use of 'ought' can be represented as $ought_{b,o1,o2,o3}(p)$. The highest-ranked ordering source o_1 operates first, selecting from the domain defined by the base b all the possibilities it ranks highest, then o_2 selects from that set the possibilities it ranks highest, and finally o_3 does the same from the remainder. 'It ought to be that p' is therefore true just in case p is true in all possibilities that remain after these successive filtrations.

This modification clearly introduces considerably more complexity into the semantics: people's preference structures can involve indefinitely many different tiers, requiring indefinitely many argument-places in the logical form (potentially as many as an agent has desired ends). It is also ad hoc, as there is no grammatical evidence for these additional argument places in the logical form of modals. But it does generate the right results for Letty's case.

A simple alteration of the scenario quickly stymies this strategy too, however. Suppose Letty's only choices are a city satisfying e_1 and a city satisfying both e_2 and e_3. The revised semantics predicts that Letty ought to choose the city that satisfies e_1, since the first ordering source ranks it uniquely highest. But it doesn't follow from e_1's being preferable to each of e_2 and e_3 individually that it's preferable to both e_2 and e_3 together. This reveals a fundamental flaw in the idea of an ordering source. What ought to be done with respect to a set of desired ends depends not on the ranks of the ends but on their weights, or (on our present assumptions) the *degree* to which each end is desired. For a semantics to generate the right output algorithmically for any situation, it would need to build in a sensitivity to weight or degrees of preference. While this would require a cardinal scale, ordering sources provide only ordinal scales and for that reason cannot yield the correct results systematically. An ordering of worlds is not enough.[14]

---

[13] von Fintel & Iatridou 2005, developing a suggestion of Kratzer's; see also Price 2008.

[14] This might be resisted on the grounds that ordinal semantics have the flexibility to generate any desired ordering of outcomes, and can therefore reproduce any output of a weighting semantics or utility calculus. Suppose the only ends or outcomes are $\{e_1, e_2\}$ and e_1 is preferred to e_2. The right results can then be generated with the ordering source $\{e_1\&e_2, (e_1\&e_2)\lor(e_1\&{\sim}e_2), (e_1\&e_2)\lor(e_1\&{\sim}e_2)\lor(e_2\&{\sim}e_1)\}$ (thanks to Mark Schroeder for discussion). The complexity increases exponentially as more ends are added. An ordinal semantics can also formally give the right results with a separate ordering source for every combination of ends; three ends would require seven ordering sources, perhaps as follows: $o_1 = \{e_1\&e_2\&e_3\}$; $o_2 = \{e_1\&e_2\}$; $o_3 = \{e_1\&e_3\}$; $o_4 = \{e_2\&e_3\}$; $o_5 = \{e_1\}$; $o_6 = \{e_2\}$; $o_7 = \{e_3\}$. This also obviously increases semantic and logical complexity exponentially; only ten desiderata are needed to exceed 1,000 ordering sources. These are just formal solutions for generating the desired outputs in individual cases, which don't generate them in a systematic or psychologically realistic way from anything recognizably representing cardinal weights, and they sacrifice much of the intuitive appeal of the ordering source idea.

More complex semantics can be designed, of course, which can handle cardinal weights for indefinitely many different ends.[15] But the more complex a semantics gets, the less plausible it becomes (all else being equal) that it accurately reflects the conceptual competence with which ordinary speakers use and interpret those words. I find it implausible that the ordinary concepts associated with 'ought', 'best', and 'most reason' could have argument-places for complex weight assignments to indefinitely many different ends (as well as for probability assignments, as we'll see below), from which they algorithmically generate the right truth-conditions. We also don't seem to have any ordinary linguistic means of making such arguments explicit. Less ambitious semantic theories don't face this problem: primitivism and expressivism can assign the work respectively to normative metaphysics and to psychology, for example. I'll now argue that the end-relational theory generates the right predictions pragmatically in a more psychologically realistic way, making this extra semantic complexity otiose.

In cases like Letty's, what is salient is evidently neither the conjunction nor simply the set of all desired ends. Compare:

(1)   'If you want/in order to live in a city that has affordable housing, a moderate climate, and is close to family, you ought to accept the job in Vancouver.'

(2)   'All things considered, you ought to accept the job in Vancouver.'

Saying (1) would be interpreted as expressing the belief that living in Vancouver satisfies all three ends, and would be deceptive if the speaker believes Vancouver doesn't have affordable housing, for example. Our theory predicts this, although it seems anomalous for Kratzer's semantics: if the antecedent of (1) functions to specify the contents of an *ordering source* then we shouldn't expect the speaker to believe the recommended action to be compatible with *all* the listed desiderata. By contrast, uttering (2) or simply 'You ought to accept the job in Vancouver' wouldn't express the same belief or be deceptive. 'All things considered, you ought...' therefore can't be equivalent to 'In order to achieve all your ends, you ought...'

By virtue of invoking "consideration" it may reasonably be taken rather as a metalinguistic quantifier, like 'Having taken everything into consideration'. "Everything" here presumably includes at least all relevant preferences, so we should ask whether an all-things-considered perspective makes salient any kind of single end by default. The conjunction of all desired ends usually won't be a candidate due to the obvious fact that agents generally don't pursue ends they believe impossible to attain, no matter how strongly they may desire them. Particularly in contexts of direct interest, as in deliberation and

---

[15] See Wedgwood 2007, for example.

recommendation, speakers' purposes are therefore only served by addressing ends that are believed attainable (or at least not believed unattainable). "All things considered" can also be expected to include information about what is possible, providing a pragmatic basis for the intuitive principle that *ought* implies *can*.[16] Whenever the conjunction of all saliently desired ends is believed unattainable, it therefore won't be the most salient end. Since ordinary agents know it's often impossible to attain all one's desired ends, practical speech and thought also won't presuppose such conjunctive ends by default.

However, since agents prefer to attain multiple desired ends over any one of those desired ends by itself, smaller conjunctions of desired ends will be preferred if believed attainable. This suggests simply combining the Conjunctive End and Preferential Selection solutions: agents can be expected to pursue whichever *attainable conjunction of individually desired ends they most prefer*— or in simpler language, their most preferred overall outcome. By default, the most salient end will therefore be *the saliently preferred attainable conjunctive end* (whether *de dicto* or *de re*).[17] So if (2) is asserted to Letty in a cooperative context of direct interest, the salient end will be *the attainable conjunction of Letty's desired ends that she most prefers*, which is to live in a city with a moderate climate that is close to family. The speaker will be understood to be saying that this preferred outcome is most likely if she accepts the job in Vancouver. This provides the right truth-conditions and recommendatory force.

The end-relational semantics therefore makes the correct predictions for all-things-considered claims in simple scenarios like Letty's where some but not all desired ends are co-attainable, on the basis of our pragmatic principles.

6.4. Uncertainty

While we've accommodated cases where the attainability of ends is believed or known with certainty, often the probability of attaining a particular outcome is *uncertain*, falling between 0 and 1.[18] This might be supposed congenial to a probabilistic semantics, but the influence of uncertainty on agents' choice of ends raises difficulties for our account of salient ends, as illustrated by the following scenario.[19]

---

[16] The agent's ability to φ is also relevant; see Stocker 1971, Sinnott-Armstrong 1984.

[17] In *de re* cases this has to be qualified as the *believed* attainable conjunctive end. Whose beliefs are relevant will depend on context; we'll return to this in Chapter 8.

[18] Following bad linguistic analysis in Knight 1921, decision theory assigns technical meanings to 'uncertainty' and 'risk' which unfortunately diverge from their ordinary meanings in English: *p* is under "risk" if uncertain, and "uncertain" if its *probability* is uncertain. I shall use the words with their ordinary senses, preferring the risk of confusing decision theorists to the risk of confusing everyone else.

[19] The scenario is adapted from Ross 2006, a variant of a problem in Regan 1980, Jackson 1991.

You are to choose one out of three envelopes labeled 'A', 'B', and 'C'. You know that C contains $1,000, and that one of A and B contains $1,500 while the other is empty. Assuming a linear preference for more money over less, the most preferred attainable outcome is therefore getting $1,500. If this amount is in fact in A, then in one clear (objective) sense you ought to choose A; our semantics interprets this as relativized to your preferred end and roughly all the facts. But since you aren't in a position to know this, it isn't the sense you would employ in your deliberations or that a similarly informed adviser would employ in giving you advice. Given your information it's intuitive to say that the best choice, which you ought and have most reason to make, is C—even though you're fully aware it isn't objectively best.

None of the pragmatic solutions so far explain how our semantics could generate these results. Choosing C isn't the option on which the subjective probability of attaining the preferred end of $1,500 is greatest; indeed by this measure it's the single worst choice, being the only option that guarantees you don't attain that end. Because you also know this, it can't simply be said (as some are tempted to say) that judging that you ought to choose C is false though justified.

Scenarios of this kind are the province of decision theory, which standardly holds that the action an agent ought (simpliciter) to choose under conditions of uncertainty is that which *maximizes expected utility* by balancing her preference-satisfaction ("utility") against her estimations of probability ("credences"). The expected utility (EU) of an option is the sum of the products of (i) the degree of preference for, and (ii) credence in, each possible total outcome. You ought to choose C in the three-option scenario because the EU of doing so (= $1.0 \times \$1,000 = \$1,000$) is greater than the EU of your other options of choosing A or choosing B (=$.5 \times \$1,500 + .5 \times \$0 = \$750$).[20]

Standard decision theory is controversial, but provides at least a good approximation of intuitive truth-conditions for normative claims balancing ends under uncertainty because it recognizes that normative weight is sensitive both to the degree the ends are desired and to their degree of probability. While our theory is sensitive to both these factors individually—the end-relational semantics is sensitive to degrees of probability,[21] and our pragmatic solutions introduce sensitivity to degrees of preference in the selection of ends—the challenge is to accommodate their systematic interaction.

Our pragmatic principles suggest examining how a speaker will be motivated in contexts of multiple ends under uncertainty. We've observed that an agent's

---

[20] Here I'll follow the convenient convention of representing utility with dollars.

[21] As in Chapter 2, I assume a difference between *credence*, as estimation or belief of probability, and *subjective probability* proper, as probability relative to *s*'s information (i.e., what is expect*able*, rather than expected). This predicts two different subjective *ought*s, (i) what ought to be done relative to *s*'s information (in order to…?—see below), and (ii) what ought to be done in order to maximize expected utility.

overall motivation isn't always toward the potentially attainable total outcome she most prefers, because she may believe it to be sufficiently less likely to be attained than another desired end as not to be worth the risk. Perhaps the most obvious hypothesis here, given the plausibility of decision theory, is that the relevant end in these contexts is to maximize expected utility:

Expected Utility: When multiple ends must be balanced under
                      uncertainty, by default the most salient end is
                      maximization of expected utility.

This solution generates the right results for many normative claims, because the alternative that (uniquely) maximizes expected utility is also the alternative on which maximizing expected utility is most likely, so long as a single set of probabilities is involved. It correctly predicts that the *best* option in the three-option scenario, the one you *ought* and have *most reason* to choose, is C.

But this simple solution is problematic in a number of ways. First, decision theory focuses only on simple contexts of direct interest (i.e., of subjective decision-making) involving a single set of known credences or probabilities and a single set of known preferences; while I'll assume these simplifications in this section, ultimately we'll need to account for more complex contexts where the speaker, agent, and/or audience don't all transparently share the same credences and preferences, or the credences don't match the subjective probabilities.

More pressingly, maximization of expected utility seems an overly abstract and psychologized end to be the concern of ordinary agents and speakers. The issue isn't that agents don't ordinarily have the vocabulary to represent such an end (since an inability to describe an end doesn't seem an obstacle to having it in mind), but rather that we don't intentionally aim at such higher-order ends, especially as explicitly psychological as *my expected preference-satisfaction*. Suppose you have to weigh a slight risk of losing a person you love dearly against an immediate peril facing five mere acquaintances. Whatever you decide to do, it seems perversely narcissistic for your concern in deliberation to be maximizing your own expected preference-satisfaction. Agents don't generally deliberate about their own desires and preferences; rather these operate in the background by motivating us to seek out and respond to various external facts (i.e., reasons) in deliberation.[22]

How does an agent come to maximize expected utility, if not by aiming at it as his end? A natural answer is that agents' overall motivation tracks this outcome as an unintended product of the various motivational influences of their

---

[22] Pettit & Smith 1990. See Evers 2010, 2011 for discussion of problems this raises for the Expected Utility solution, especially given my other commitments.

different desires and credences.[23] This may seem to imply that in these contexts of multiple ends under uncertainty agents don't have any single end in mind, but these different motivational factors don't simply move agents about like forces on an inanimate object; rather they contribute to determining a particular object of intention, the end the agent has in mind in acting.

This suggests a refinement of Preferential Selection. Since ordinary agents' preferential selection of ends is sensitive to two different factors—their credences, as well as their intrinsic preferences—these interact psychologically to yield what can be called *contextual preference*:

> *Contextual Preference*:   Agents have contextual preference for the ends they are most motivated toward after intrinsic desire is balanced against credence.

While you intrinsically prefer getting $1,500 over getting $1,000 in the three-option scenario, your contextual preference is therefore to get the $1,000 because of your greater expectation of success. If this sounds counterintuitive, bear in mind that 'contextual preference' is here a term of art, and this means merely that you'd be more motivated in the context to pursue the $1,000 than to pursue the $1,500.

The most salient end in these contexts therefore won't be maximization of expected utility per se, but rather a first-order end equivalent to it, the contextually preferred conjunctive end (or in simpler language, the total outcome the agent is most motivated to pursue). This end will often only be vague, or salient to an audience under a description such as *the most preferred balance of possible outcomes*, as above.[24] This solution achieves the desired results of the Expected Utility solution for our three-option scenario but without the unrealistic psychological claim; it is therefore how I shall understand Expected Utility below.

This Contextual Preference solution may still appear to diverge unacceptably from the Expected Utility solution. The problem isn't immediately obvious when focusing only on the simple three-option scenario, where maximizing expected utility requires choosing a single, particular end or outcome that is certain (e.g., choosing A guarantees the contextually preferred end of getting $1,000). But in other cases, maximizing expected utility requires acting in a way

---

[23] Decision theorists also sometimes explain this behavior as an unintended side-effect; cf. Harsanyi 1977: 381–82: "he simply cannot help acting…*as if* he then tried to maximize his expected utility.…The basic claim of Bayesian theory does not lie in the suggestion that we *should* make a conscious effort to maximize our expected utility, rather, it lies in the mathematical theorem telling us that *if* we act in accordance with a few very important rationality axioms then we *shall* inevitably maximize our expected utility."

[24] This might also seem to imply an objectionable psychologism, but the audience's relying on psychological cues to identify the end doesn't require the speaker to be thinking about or referring to his own attitudes, which can still be backgrounded; i.e., the communicated proposition is that *in order that dthat(the most preferred balance of possible outcomes), s ought to φ.*

that apparently doesn't guarantee any contextually preferred end, even a conjunctive end, and rather balances expectations of different possible outcomes.

Consider a *five*-option scenario: you're to choose between five envelopes A–E. Your information is that of envelopes A and B, one holds $1,000 and the other $0, while of envelopes C, D, and E, one holds $1,000 and the other two hold $700. To maximize expected utility you clearly ought to choose one of C, D, or E (EU = $800), rather than one of A or B (EU = $500). But what is the contextually preferred end in this scenario? Suppose we say it is getting $1,000, being the highest-utility outcome you can hope to attain by performing the action that maximizes expected utility. But choosing one of C, D, and E is neither the only way nor the most reliable way of getting $1,000; this end is more likely to be attained by choosing one of A and B (*pr* = .5 versus *pr* = .33), so we seem to predict, incorrectly, that you ought to choose one of A or B rather than one of C, D, or E.[25]

This problem arises because expected utility is based on credences for and utility of *all* possible outcomes of an option, not only the most desired outcome. So it's incorrect to identify contextual preference with any simple preferred outcome in such cases. The contextual preference is rather for a particular *probabilized balance* of possible outcomes.[26] In the three-option scenario, the contextually preferred end isn't strictly *getting $1,000*, but rather *being guaranteed to get $1,000*. In the five-option scenario, the contextually preferred conjunctive end is *having a 1 in 3 chance of getting $1,000 and a 2 in 3 chance of getting $700*. With this as the salient end our semantics predicts correctly that you ought to choose an envelope out of C, D, or E.

It may be objected that such a probabilized conjunctive end is no more plausibly what a speaker making an all-things-considered claim could have in mind than maximizing expected utility. My characterization of it may indeed involve some artificial idealization, as people's credences presumably aren't ordinarily numerical. (A geometrical representation may be more plausible, consistent with the classical model of probability).[27] So speakers needn't have a *linguistic* representation or description of such ends in mind; these can be counted among the cases where the difficulty of describing the end is one of the "advantages of not specifying it precisely". But surely when judging that you ought to choose one of C, D, or E, such an end must be being represented in some way, as these

---

[25] See Evers 2011; thanks also to Mike Ridge for this worry. We might try saying that the contextually preferred end is to get *the $1,000 that is concealed in C, D, or E*, but this isn't a general solution, as scenarios can be devised where multiple options have the same possible outcome. The end also can't be to get (at least) an amount equal to the maximal expected utility of $800, which is also more likely on the choice of A or B.

[26] As suggested in Evers 2011: Ch. 8.

[27] Some biases apparently "resemble visual illusions more than computational errors" (Tversky & Kahneman 1986: 260).

all-things-considered judgments are made after weighing the possible outcomes against our credences, apparently by arriving at a net preference for a particular probability-weighted combination of possible outcomes. This implies that the hypothesis is psychologically realistic.[28]

A further worry about any version of the Expected Utility solution is that it commits the psychologistic fallacy of mistaking normative laws for psychological laws, or norms for factual generalizations. Decision theory is commonly taken to concern how agents *ought* to be motivated (or how "rational" agents are motivated) rather than how agents are actually motivated, and the judgments and behavior of actual agents apparently diverge from this ideal in well-documented ways. So it might be denied that either maximization of expected utility or an equivalent could be the saliently preferred end for ordinary normative speech or thought in these contexts.[29]

On the other hand, decision theory can and has been argued to accurately describe our motivational structure.[30] On a simple psychological model, net motivation is a direct product of the strengths of preferences and credences. Alleged "irrational" departures from decision-theoretic axioms are argued to result merely from misestimating probabilities relative to information (a kind of error to which human beings are prone)[31] and therefore are consistent with agents' motivation always tracking maximization of expected utility. If ordinary normative judgments weren't attuned to maximizing expected utility then we couldn't expect to find the normative claims of decision theory as intuitively plausible as we commonly do.

The end-relational theory can afford to be neutral on this issue. If the axioms of decision theory accurately describe the actual structure of agential motivation, actual normative speech and thought can be interpreted accordingly, as above. If they don't, they can reasonably be taken to represent merely one optional normative perspective among many. The normative claims of decision theory are controversial, and there are many competing versions. A prominent example involves risk-aversion: standard decision theory holds that agents

---

[28] This may seem to surrender an advantage claimed over expressivism in Chapter 5, as all-things-considered judgments are now just expressing motivation rather than guiding it. But they are summative judgments guided by multiple probability judgments, i.e., cognitive judgments of the goodness of or weight of reasons for action relative to various ends, so contextual preference is guided by normative belief. Also as we'll see below, where the relevant "expected utility" isn't the speaker's they needn't express the speaker's preferences at all.

[29] Denying that agents ought to maximize expected utility doesn't seem absurd, as might be expected if this implicitly assumed 'in order to maximize expected utility'. In response we can appeal at least to Contextual Preference, and our pragmatic objection to the OQA in Chapter 2 (regarding interpretation of logically incomplete utterances).

[30] E.g., Cohen 1982: 251. I argue against alleged forms of instrumental "irrationality" in Finlay 2008a, 2009c.

[31] E.g., Kahneman & Tversky 1988: 205–6.

ought to pursue at great expense even an incredibly improbable outcome if it is
desired sufficiently strongly. But many people don't only seem psychologically
risk-averse, but also reject the claim that they ought not be—a normative view
that contemporary decision theory often tries to accommodate.

Ultimately these normative disputes about how ends ought to be balanced
under uncertainty seem to ground out in conflicting subjective intuitions.[32]
Plausibly there are no objective or perspective-independent facts about the
right way to balance desire against credence, or how risk-averse one ought
to be, so all-things-considered normative speech and thought may therefore
express contingent and optional stances. The objects of contextual preference
may then only roughly approximate maximization of expected utility, but this
wouldn't be a problem for our semantics. The ability to predict this result may
even be an advantage over any rival theory that inflexibly builds a utility calculus into the semantics itself.

6.5. Gradability in Two Dimensions

While the Expected Utility solution predicts the correct truth conditions for the
use (in simple contexts) of sentences concerning what is normatively *optimal*—
involving 'best', 'ought', and 'most reason'—it introduces problems for the
gradability of normative language, in use of sentences concerning the potentially suboptimal (involving 'good', 'may', and 'a/some reason'), and in use of
comparatives ('better', 'more reason'). To explain this problem I'll summarize
the thread of this chapter so far.

Whereas the end-relational semantics provides a one-dimensional scale for
degrees of probability, we observed that normative speech and thought in cases
of multiple ends are also sensitive to utility, or degrees of intrinsic preference
for ends. This second dimension of intrinsic preference was accommodated
with the Preferential End and Conjunctive End solutions, delegating it to the
pragmatics of how salient ends are determined. But we then observed that in
cases of uncertainty, probability is balanced against intrinsic preference, so that
judgments of 'ought', 'best', and 'most reason' track maximization of expected
utility, requiring a properly two-dimensional scale identifying normative weight
or degrees of goodness with degrees of expected utility. We achieved this with
the Expected Utility and Contextual Preference solutions, delegating the probability scale also to the pragmatics of how salient ends are determined. This

---

[32] Decision theorists often argue by appeal to "money pumps" or "Dutch books" that agents
ought to conform to their axioms. Our theory easily accommodates these claims: *if you want not
to be susceptible to being a money pump*, you ought to conform to the axioms of decision theory.
Since most of us share this desire, this may provide some reason to conform, though only a weak
reason as the risk of actually being turned into a money pump seems negligible.

provided a properly two-dimensional scale, but located in the pragmatics and psychology rather than the semantics of normative speech and thought.

The difficulty we therefore now encounter is that normative language is *semantically* gradable. Indeed, it was supposed to be one of the central advantages of our semantics that it accommodates and explains this gradability, by being probabilistic. But now this probabilistic semantics may seem worse than useless, turning the supposed advantage into a liability. Not only does a probabilistic semantics appear redundant once probability is assigned this pragmatic role of selecting ends, but it may interfere with its proper functioning.

Our semantics identifies the gradability of goodness or normative weight with degrees of probability-increasing, so that *p* is *better* than *q*, relative to an end *e*, if and only if *p* increases the probability of *e* more than *q* does. But as decision theory teaches, all-things-considered goodness or normative weight is measured on a two-dimensional scale of expected utility that balances probability or credence against intrinsic preference or utility. Just as *most* good is maximal expected utility, *degrees* of goodness are degrees of expected utility. So *p* might be good to some degree even though guaranteed not to maximize expected utility, and it may also be better than *q* even though it doesn't make maximization of expected utility any more likely than *q* does.

Consider the six-option scenario constructed by adding to the five-option scenario the option to choose no envelope. Even though choosing one of A or B isn't the best option, intuitively it's still better than choosing no envelope, and may still be a good option. But by the Expected Utility solution, our semantics seems to imply rather that choosing one of A or B (EU = $500) is neither better than choosing no envelope at all (EU = $0), nor even good to any degree, since it's incompatible with the preferred end of maximizing expected utility (EU = $800). It implies that choosing one of A or B can only be good to any degree if it increases the probability of maximizing expected utility, and that it can only be better than choosing no envelope at all if it increases the probability of maximizing expected utility more than choosing no envelope would. These results are clearly unacceptable.

While the Expected Utility solution may enable us to accommodate optimality and necessity judgments, it doesn't enable us to accommodate judgments involving suboptimal points in normative space. A guarantee of getting $1,000 is better than a guarantee of getting $500, which is in turn better than a guarantee of getting nothing, and probability doesn't appear to have anything to do with that. Relatedly, we seem to have lost the important distinction between 'ought' and 'must', or optimality and necessity, since in these contexts anything that makes it *most likely* that expected utility is maximized will also be *necessary* for maximizing expected utility.

So it may seem that our simple end-relational semantics has finally met its comeuppance, and should be rejected for a properly two-dimensional semantics taking probabilities and preferences as inputs. But we've so far assumed a narrow range of still quite simple contexts. Our pragmatic principles actually imply that in these contexts speakers would never be motivated to address what is normatively suboptimal, and so would have no use for these words. (Indeed, decision theory is generally interested only in what agents "ought" to do—and in a very narrow sense—and doesn't employ these other terms at all. There is also plausibly no space between what is optimal or *ought* to be done and what is necessary or *must* be done in order to act "rationally", as this seems an essentially optimizing notion. Philosophers have therefore often assumed that 'ought' expresses normative necessity.)

According to our pragmatic principles, speakers always act in ways they believe *best* for their conversational ends—and this has now been clarified, for contexts of multiple ends under uncertainty, as equivalent to doing what is best *for maximizing the speaker's expected utility* (hence the default salience of this kind of end). But then why would speakers ever be motivated to address what they believe to be normatively suboptimal, and to make claims about what is merely "good" or what there is only "some reason" to do—on any semantics?

Consider cooperative contexts of direct interest where the salient end is the speaker's conversational end borrowed from the audience. Here telling an agent what she has "most reason" or "ought" to do, or what is "best", is an optimal way of promoting this end (as observed in Chapter 5), and is therefore interpreted as having recommendatory force. But this doesn't explain the point or felicity of telling her what she has "some reason" or "a reason" to do, or what is merely "good" or "better". Making sense of these utterances requires identifying the point they serve in their contexts.

One relevant kind of context involves an inability to identify what is best or maximizes the (relevant) expected utility. Sometimes this is just because no *unique* option is best.[33] But speakers are often uncertain or ignorant about what is best in the relevant sense. Previously we assumed that the speaker's credences coincide with salient probabilities, but often this isn't so and there is a second order of uncertainty or probability. This can be uncertainty about either the relevant probabilities, or the relevant preferences, or both.[34]

---

[33] In these cases expected utility can often be maximized by reporting just one of the equally best options; here we predict that terms like 'good', 'could', and 'a reason' can be correctly used, but not 'best', 'ought', or 'most reason', which would communicate falsely that the options are uniquely best. If the salient end is maximizing expected utility (e.g., the speaker is responding to the query, 'All things considered, what ought I to do now?'), then saying 'φ-ing would be good' or 'You could φ' pragmatically indicates that the speaker is unable to identify any better option, and so has the force of a weak (defeasible) recommendation. But a speaker would often be expected to identify all the best options if he can (e.g., 'You ought to choose A *or* B'), so even here there's a suggestion that the speaker is ignorant of what is best.

[34] "Uncertainty" in the decision theorist's sense may be analyzable as probabilities of probabilities (or of "risk"); cf. Skyrms 1980.

In cooperative contexts of advising an agent *s* who has lesser information, for example, the relevant preferences (though not the relevant probabilities) may be the advisee's, and the speaker might not know exactly what they are. Or in contexts of evaluating a third party's choices given her information and preferences, a speaker may be uncertain about both the relevant probabilities and preferences. Even in first-person practical thought about what "*I*" ought to do, relevant probabilities and preferences may be uncertain. Sometimes we're interested in the objective value of our options (i.e., relative to a circumstantial background). At other times we may have in mind counterfactual or future probabilities and preferences; for example, plausibly in deliberation we don't always know exactly what we relevantly prefer, because we have in mind preferences that we're disposed to have on being (e.g.) fully informed, or subjective probabilities relative to the information we'll be able to acquire by the time we must decide.[35] Indeed, we often can't estimate with accuracy or confidence even our own, present subjective probabilities, relative to our present information (i.e., as distinct from our credences). In any of these contexts, confident and warranted claims or judgments about what maximizes the relevant kind of "expected" (or probability-weighted) utility won't be possible.[36]

Even if a speaker isn't in a position to communicate any useful information about what maximizes the relevant probability-weighted utility, it doesn't follow that he will have nothing to say or contribute. In many contexts he'd act best (i.e., maximize his own conversational expected utility) by communicating information about options realizing lower degrees of the relevant weighted utility, and what is judged to be merely "good", "better", or "a reason". If Ken doesn't know the degree to which Letty prefers each of her three ends then he can't sincerely tell her what job offer she ought to choose, for example, but he can tell her what is good about particular options or what reasons she might have to choose them. This may aid her decision, and in the context would be a weak or defeasible recommendation.

There can be other reasons besides second-order uncertainty for addressing the normatively suboptimal. Sometimes a speaker in a cooperative context of direct interest believes her advisee is psychologically disposed not to choose the option the speaker believes is relevantly best, and so will try instead to

---

[35] This "news-sensitivity" of deliberation is discussed in Björnsson & Finlay 2010.

[36] The double role our theory suggests for probability (in both the semantics and the pragmatics) might here be supposed an advantage over rival theories rather than a liability, as accommodating second-order uncertainty. Perhaps we commonly advise agents about what they "ought" to do rather than what they "must" do to indicate we merely consider it *most likely* (relative to our information) that φ-ing is maximizing. Talk about what is "good", "better", and "best" would then differentiate between being somewhat, more, and most likely to maximize. I won't pursue this idea; it doesn't account for all-things-considered claims about options believed to correspond to nonmaximal "expected utility", and a separate probability operator seems more natural in many contexts (e.g., 'You probably ought to φ').

direct him toward the better of the remaining options ('You *ought* to φ, but since I know you're not going to do that, you *could* ψ instead', or 'φ-ing would be best, but ψ-ing is good'). The salience of a suboptimal option can also be forced, as by asking, 'What if I ψ?'; in a retrospective context (of evaluating past action) options are salient as being what the agent actually chose, even if not relevantly maximizing.

In all these contexts the speaker clearly doesn't have in mind the end of maximizing the salient probability-weighted utility, which therefore couldn't be the implicit end for these uses of 'good' (etc.), as the objection assumed. The speaker will rather have in mind some other, less preferred but still saliently desired end. An agent's *preferring* an end e_1 to another end e_2 doesn't entail he is *indifferent* to e_2. Bear in mind also that maximizing expected utility (or its probability-weighted conjunctive equivalent) isn't itself an intrinsically desired end, but merely the net motivational result of various desires and credences. In these contexts a speaker will therefore often be content to address what *satisfices* (or is good enough), rather than what maximizes; that is, he maximizes his own expected utility (acts best) by talking about what satisfices relative to the relevant kind of probability-weighted utility.

With this understanding of speaker motivation, our semantics can also accommodate claims about what is "good", "better", "some reason", etc. Attention to particular options generally makes salient the possible outcomes of those options. So an explicitly comparative judgment of "better than" narrows the salient ends to those potentially attainable by the options being compared. By Preferential Selection, the most salient end will be whichever of these is contextually more preferred. Therefore, when comparing two options, a speaker correctly judges as "better" or supported by "more reason" whichever makes this more preferred end more likely. 'Choosing A is better than choosing no envelope' is true in the six-option scenario, for example, because the more preferred of the relevant outcomes (having a 1 in 2 chance of $1,000) is more likely on the choice of A than of no envelope.

Use of 'good', 'some reason', or 'could' raises the salience of ends that might thereby be attained (provided they're sufficiently desired). Being asked about choosing envelope A makes salient the end of *having a 1 in 2 chance at $1,000*, for example, which is sufficiently desired to motivate consideration. Relative to this end it's true on the end-relational semantics that you have "some reason" for choosing A, and that it's a "good" option, which you "could" choose.

This analysis may appear to imply, incoherently, that two different ends can be "most salient" at once. Consider 'You ought to choose one of C, D, or E, but choosing A would still be good'; if the most salient end is maximization, as needed to accommodate the 'ought' claim, then the 'good' claim is false. But if the most salient end is either *getting $1,000* or *having a 1 in 2 chance at $1,000*, as needed to accommodate the 'good' claim, then the 'ought' claim is false.

This objection underestimates the fluidity of pragmatics. Conversational salience can shift rapidly in conversation under the pressure of accommodation, changing between sentences, clauses, and sometimes even from word to word, with sufficient cues. Consider 'He criticized John, saying he was the worst friend Jim could have, because he had left him for dead.' A competent interpreter immediately assumes that the first occurrence of 'he' refers to some other (unidentified) speaker, the second and third refer to John, while 'him' refers to Jim. Hence,

> *Dynamic Context*: When attention is directed to a less but still sufficiently preferred end, this momentarily becomes the most salient end for that fragment of the conversation.

This predicts the truth of serial comparisons, like 'Choosing C is better than choosing A, which is better than choosing no envelope.' Comparing C and A momentarily raises the salience of the end that is contextually preferred relative to that choice (having a 1 in 3 chance of $1,000 and a 2 in 3 chance of $700), for which C is indeed better than A, whereas comparing A and choosing no envelope momentarily raises the salience of the end contextually preferred relative to that choice (having a 1 in 2 chance of $1,000), for which envelope A is indeed better than none. Our pragmatic principles predict that the implicit end shifts from comparison to comparison, yielding the right truth-conditions.

6.6. Logical and Illocutionary Strength

These solutions leave us with two puzzles. First, the solution for all-things-considered use of nonoptimizing words introduces a new problem about the use of optimizing words like 'best' and 'ought'. Dynamic Context seems to predict incorrectly that optimizing language would be used even when a less preferred end is most salient. Given that asking about the value of choosing envelope A in the six-option scenario narrows the salient ends to those that can thereby be promoted, for example, we seem to predict that it can felicitously be judged not merely "good", or "better than choosing no envelope", but also the "best" or even the "only" choice (i.e., for the salient end of having a 1 in 2 chance of $1,000). But clearly it's incorrect to say, 'Choosing A is best', or 'You ought to choose A', simpliciter.

This problem is sharpened by Grice's pragmatic principle that "one should not make a weaker statement rather than a stronger one unless there is a good reason for doing so."[37] Since 'φ-ing is best for e' is stronger than 'φ-ing is good

---

[37] Grice 1961: 132.

for e',[38] it might be expected to be preferred whenever both are true. Using 'good' would then tend pragmatically to express the belief that φ-ing isn't best for e, which the Dynamic Context solution seems to predict would be misleading. This problem also arises for the ordinary practice of using 'ought' rather than 'must' even when φ-ing is the only way of maximizing probability-weighted utility, since *necessary* is stronger than *most likely*.

The second puzzle concerns the salience of ends to an audience. While we've considered what ends a speaker would be motivated to address, this leaves a question about how an audience can distinguish a default context from a special one when it isn't made explicit, as there would often seem to be insufficient cues. If somebody asks about the option of φ-ing, for example, how can she tell whether the response assumes a maximizing end or some lesser end made salient by the option under discussion?

However, these two puzzles provide solutions to each other. The short answer is that an audience indeed can't always reliably tell the difference, which is the "good reason" for making the weaker statement, as I'll now explain.

A requirement to say the strongest thing one can only follows from our pragmatic principles given the premise that the speaker best promotes conversational ends by doing so. A weaker utterance will be pragmatically permissible if it can be expected to promote the conversational ends just as well, and required in case it can be expected to promote those ends more effectively than the stronger utterance. These conditions are frequently met; for example it can be more felicitous to answer 'Where is Obama today?' with 'He's in California' than with 'He's in Costa Mesa', for various reasons. The speaker may be unsure whether the audience knows where Costa Mesa is, the audience might have less trust in the speaker's knowledge of the stronger claim, or the state might be more relevant than the city (e.g., if the enquirer is wondering which senator Obama is campaigning for), etc. Weaker normative claims would be similarly required whenever they would better serve the speaker's purposes for some such reason.

The opacity of speakers' intentions provides just such a reason. Since the default assumption is that an end left implicit is contextually most preferred, whenever the speaker has in mind a less preferred end there will often be a considerable risk of the audience's mistakenly assuming it is most preferred. This is liable to have unfortunate practical consequences. We've seen that communicating that the contextually most preferred end is most likely if s φs will pragmatically indicate that the speaker prefers that s φs, for example, and in basic cooperative contexts has a reliable influence in motivating s to φ and the

---

[38] I.e., the former implies the latter but not vice versa. Strictly 'best' isn't stronger, because sometimes p is merely the best of only bad options (which I interpret as involving comparison with only a subset of the salient alternatives, e.g., the *available* options), but it is commonly interpreted that way, by contrast with 'least bad'.

illocutionary force of a strong recommendation. These are all pragmatic effects a speaker will usually seek to avoid when the end isn't most preferred.[39] One way to achieve this is by making the end explicit, of course, but whenever the exact identity of the end doesn't matter for practical purposes a more efficient and easier solution is simply to use words that have appropriate pragmatic force and effects even if interpreted as relativized to the most preferred end.

Use of 'good', 'could', and 'some reason' differs from use of 'ought' and 'best' by suggesting that there may be other options the speaker does or would prefer, or would recommend instead, even when relativized to the most preferred end. So it pragmatically expresses only a favorable attitude rather than a preference, with the illocutionary force of mere commendation or sometimes weak recommendation. These are also the appropriate effects and force for normative claims relative to less preferred ends, giving speakers a strong pragmatic reason to use a logically weaker term like 'good' instead of 'best' in these contexts.

By our pragmatic principles, the end-relational semantics therefore predicts that unrelativized use of optimizing language would be pragmatically reserved for claims relative to the most preferred end, and that nonoptimizing language would be used in relation to other ends. It also follows that use of nonoptimizing words will often function as the missing cue that the speaker may have a less preferred end in mind, allowing omission of the end and solving our second puzzle.

To these pragmatic solutions it may be objected that saying (e.g.) 'Choosing either envelope A or B is best' isn't only to say something pragmatically infelicitous, but actually to say something clearly *false*. By the Dynamic Context solution, our semantics may rather seem to suggest it would be true. But this objection underestimates the influence of pragmatic accommodation on available interpretation, which provides an explanation for why this claim would not only be infelicitous but also strictly false.

Given the default interpretation of unrelativized use of 'best' and 'ought' as relativized to the contextually most preferred end, it follows from our pragmatic principles that no competent speaker would use that sentence in such contexts to communicate a normative proposition relativized to any other kind of end. So any speaker uttering the sentence in that context intending *not* to assert the false proposition must either be incompetent or actually trying to deceive. It's unproblematic to allow that he may assert something true under those particular assumptions (granted that asserting *p* is even possible without an attempt to communicate that *p*). If competent and cooperative, he wouldn't utter that sentence to assert anything except the false proposition.

---

[39] Many other kinds of contexts will involve different but analogous effects; here I'll focus on direct interest and cooperation.

Analogously, suppose I say, 'I took my shoes off', when I am obviously still wearing my shoes. Although this sentence can be used literally to assert many different propositions, typically the only salient reading is the false one that I took my shoes off *my feet*. I can therefore only use this sentence to assert a true proposition without a special context if I were either an incompetent speaker or perversely trying to deceive my audience about my meaning.

A similar explanation is available for why 'ought' is more appropriate than 'must' in all-things-considered claims balancing multiple ends under uncertainty, even when the speaker is confident that φ-ing is the only maximizing option. Whereas using 'ought' relativized to the most preferred end expresses all-things-considered preference and thereby a strong recommendation, it also suggests there may be other "good" options, and is therefore consistent with recognizing satisfactory alternatives. By contrast, using 'must' implies that no other option is any good at all, and therefore suggests that φ-ing isn't merely preferred by some (possibly marginal) degree, but is the only tolerable option. It therefore expresses even stronger, *strict* recommendation; that the speaker dismisses the possibility of any satisfactory alternative.

But when a speaker has in mind a maximizing end, the relatively weaker pragmatic effects and force expressed by 'ought' are the appropriate ones. Since maximizing probability-weighted utility isn't itself an intrinsically desired end, it is usually preferred only marginally over other satisfactory alternatives. This means that 'ought' is pragmatically more appropriate than 'must' even in many cases where only one option is compatible with a maximizing end.

A virtue of this pragmatic account is that it explains a peculiar difference observed between ordinary uses of 'ought' and 'must', which has so far defied adequate explanation. Whereas saying 'You ought to φ, but you won't' is perfectly natural, saying 'You must φ, but you won't' is odd somehow, even when a normative rather than epistemic reading is clearly intended.[40] This oddity evidently doesn't arise from the sentence being *false*, since abstaining from doing something you've been told you must do isn't a way of proving that the speaker said something false: clearly it's possible to fail to comply with an obligation.[41] It also disappears in many embedded uses of 'must', as in '*s* knows he must φ, but he won't.'

Dilip Ninan points out that understanding 'must' as having imperatival or practical force, involving an attempt to bring it about that the agent φs, suggests a speech act solution.[42] People don't generally attempt to achieve goals they believe to be impossible, so if the speaker genuinely believes that the agent

---

[40] E.g., Palmer 1986: 100, Condoravdi 2002, Ninan 2005, Copley 2006.

[41] Another suggestion (Condoravdi 2002) is that 'must' requires an epistemic modal base that incorporates all available information, so that if the speaker is warranted in asserting that *s* won't φ, then *s* doesn't φ in any of the possibilities in the domain. But as an explanation why 'must' differs from 'ought' this seems ad hoc.

[42] Ninan 2005.

won't φ, then she wouldn't try to get the agent to φ by telling him he must. This solution is insufficient, however. First, it's not clear why this account of oddity wouldn't extend also to the use of 'ought'. Ninan claims that saying 'You ought to φ' doesn't have the practical force of trying to get the agent to φ, but this seems mistaken. It might be replied, however, that whereas 'ought' has merely pragmatic and therefore contingent practical force, 'must' has its practical force by semantic convention.

Second, however, this seems ad hoc: given a unifying semantics for 'must' as a necessity operator, why would its (unrelativized, unembedded) normative use have this unique conventional feature not shared by 'ought'? Ninan offers no explanation for this, or why it can be "stripped off" in embedded contexts. Third, this solution isn't sufficiently general, because many *third person* uses are also odd. While there's nothing odd about saying, 'Obama must end drone strikes', it is similarly odd to say, 'Obama must end drone strikes, but he won't'—although (contra Ninan) such claims aren't necessarily interpreted as having the practical force of attempting to make it so.

Observe that this oddity is only found in *unrelativized* uses: there's nothing similarly strange about saying, 'In order that *e*, you must φ—but you won't.' By our theory, this ellipsis indicates relativization to the contextually most preferred end. By saying '*s* won't φ', the speaker thereby expresses the belief that a necessary condition for this contextually most preferred end won't obtain, and thereby that the end is impossible to attain. By our results above, the use of 'must' rather than 'ought' also pragmatically indicates that this end is *strongly* preferred over any others, such that the speaker isn't interested in any other outcome. But it's highly odd that a speaker would so strongly contextually prefer an end she considers impossible, which explains the pragmatic oddity of '*s* must φ, but won't.'

Since this oddity turns on the preference for the implicit end, rather than on an intention to bring it about that *s* φs, it extends directly to third-person cases. But it doesn't extend to the use of 'ought', which pragmatically indicates that there are either other paths to the contextually preferred end or other acceptable ends. It also doesn't always extend to 'must' when embedded (e.g.) in knowledge ascriptions, since these contexts often make salient preferred ends other than the speaker's. We therefore have a pragmatic solution to this puzzle.

These pragmatic results support one further prediction. When certain kinds of use of particular words or sentences pragmatically indicate a particular kind of information or force in paradigmatic contexts, then a default association can be expected to develop between use and information/force. Audiences will then be disposed to infer directly from such utterances to the usual information/force, without engaging in pragmatic reasoning or attending to what the speaker may have asserted. Speakers can then exploit this disposition to communicate the usual information/force directly by the associated kind of use, perhaps without intending to assert anything in particular by them. This corresponds roughly to what Grice calls "generalized conversational implicature":

Pragmatic Generalization: When use of a word or sentence pragmatically indicates a particular kind of information or force in paradigmatic contexts, it can then be used directly for that purpose, without regard for asserted content.

Illustrations include the common use of 'Good morning' and 'How are you?' to greet others without regard for their literal meaning: observe the infelicity of many direct and literal responses. Or at the lexical level, consider the common but incorrect use of 'literally' in nonliteral claims (e.g., 'I literally fell out of my chair') for its usual exclamatory force. Finally, as a result of these normal associations, we can expect a presumption against these kinds of use when the usual information or force isn't intended.[43]

Since the end-relational semantics predicts that the unrelativized use of particular normative words paradigmatically indicates particular kinds of information or force, such associations can be expected. A speaker who says that s "ought", "has most reason", or "does best" to φ will be directly interpreted by default as indicating that φ-ing is the most (saliently) preferable of multiple satisfactory options, and thereby as strongly recommending that s φ, in second-person prospective contexts. Saying that s "must" φ will be directly interpreted as indicating that φ-ing is the only satisfactory option, and thereby as strictly recommending in such contexts. Saying that s "could", "has some reason", or "does well" to φ will be directly interpreted as indicating that φ-ing is merely one of multiple satisfactory options, thereby commending or weakly recommending in relevant contexts. These associations can also be expected to influence the linguistic formulation of judgments. While this suggests that normative language is sometimes used and interpreted as if expressivism were true, it is rather a quasi-expressivist solution since these are merely defeasible generalizations derived pragmatically from the basic descriptive meanings of these words.[44]

Although the end-relational semantics relativizes normative language to individual ends, on the basis of our pragmatic principles it accommodates the various ways that normative speech and thought are sensitive to multiple ends. These pragmatic solutions may be unexpectedly complex, but they follow

---

[43] Consider also the infelicity of applying virtue terms (e.g., 'courageous', 'generous') to morally bad agents. This inspires Plato and others to deny that the immoral can possess any virtues, but may just be due to the presumptive force of commendation from typical use.

[44] See Copp 2001, Strandberg 2012a for other metaethical appeals to generalized implicatures.

directly from the simplest and most unifying semantics together with our basic pragmatic principles and conservative observations about agent motivation. The extra semantic complexity of rival theories that build in a utility calculus plays no role in either non-normative or simpler normative uses, and is ad hoc from a linguistic standpoint as there is no grammatical evidence for their additional argument-places. The end-relational theory may even accommodate more data than rival theories, as it offers pragmatic solutions to several general puzzles.

7

Categorical and Final

Some uses of normative language have features of objectivity that appear incompatible with relativization to ends altogether, either single or multiple, and are widely thought to demand an absolutist or nonrelational semantics. These features are characteristic of peculiarly *moral* speech and thought, though found at least also in prudential and aesthetic uses. Philosophers sometimes go so far as to claim that if we "give up on absolute moral facts," we'll be left "without any normative vocabulary whatsoever,"[1] and even many who have given up on absolute moral facts agree at least that moral speech and thought are committed to their existence (J. L. Mackie writes, "I do not think it is going too far to say that this assumption has been incorporated in the basic, conventional, meanings of moral terms"),[2] endorsing an error theory claiming moral speech and thought are systematically untrue.

Three main absolutist challenges to relational theories can be distinguished: from *Categoricity, Finality*, and *Disagreement*. This chapter addresses the first two, arguing that the end-relational theory accommodates and explains these allegedly absolutist features of moral speech and thought too, providing pragmatic, "quasi-absolutist" solutions.[3]

7.1. Categoricity: The Challenge

Since Kant it has been dogma in metaethics that moral speech and thought involves "categorical imperatives" like 'You ought not tell lies' and not mere "hypothetical imperatives" like 'If you want people to trust you, then you ought not tell lies.' While this feature of categoricity is found across our normative vocabulary, I'll follow the custom of focusing on 'ought'. The semantics

---

[1] Boghossian 2011; see also Enoch 2011, Parfit 2011b.
[2] Mackie 1977: 35; see also Joyce 2001.
[3] Cf. Harman 1996: 34.

developed in Chapter 3 was largely driven by the need to analyze "hypothetical imperatives", so its extendability to the categorical uses of primary philosophical interest may reasonably be doubted: Kant writes that "the categorical
imperative would be one which represented an action as objectively necessary
in itself, without reference to another end" (*Grundwerk* 414). However, it isn't
entirely clear what the relevant notion of categoricity is.

A superficial glance at the sentences used to illustrate the difference might
suggest a *grammatical* definition of a categorical use as one without explicit relativization to an end. This poses no challenge to our theory because of ordinary
ellipsis: sometimes relativization is left implicit. But it is obviously inadequate.
The essential characteristic of categoricity rather involves a form of *inescapability*, as illustrated by a kind of story used to persuade generations of students that
moral language can't be relativized to ends or anything similar. For example,

1. *The Case of Ernest Hacker.* Dora encounters Ernest hacking
    ineffectually at a tree with a hatchet. Observing the futility of his
    efforts, she says to him, 'You ought to use a chainsaw.' He replies, 'But
    I don't care whether I fell the tree. I just enjoy hacking at it like this.'
    It would then be natural for Dora to say, 'Oh, I see. Never mind then,
    go ahead.' She couldn't appropriately insist, 'Still, you ought to use a
    chainsaw.'

2. *The Case of Frank Feller.* Dora encounters Frank busy felling a tree
    with a chainsaw. Observing that he is felling it toward his neighbor's
    house, she says to him, 'You ought to stop doing that.' He replies, 'But
    I don't care whether I crush his damned house—in fact, I hope I do!'—
    and goes on to add that he doesn't care what consequences he suffers.
    In this case Dora certainly wouldn't say, 'Oh, I see. Never mind then, go
    ahead.' Rather she can appropriately insist, 'Still, you ought to stop.'

This latter kind of prospective, second-person context is the paradigm of categorical use of normative language; we'll start our investigation here before
considering other contexts.

Dora addresses Ernest with a normative claim that is escapable in not
"applying" to him unless he desires or intends certain ends. She addresses Frank
rather with a claim that is inescapable, applying to him whatever his desires and
intentions may be. This inescapability is an essential feature of moral speech
and thought that must be accommodated by any semantics for moral language.
To be compatible with the end-relational theory, these categorical uses must
all be relativized to ends implicitly, but is this plausible? Paradigmatic cases
like *Frank Feller* always provide an obvious candidate: the end identified by
the agent's declaration of indifference.[4] The story assumes Frank can instantly

---

[4] Strictly, Frank isn't *indifferent* as he has a contrary preference, but I'll ignore this difference
where it isn't relevant.

recognize preservation of the neighbor's house as the end Dora has in mind, suggesting that Dora's claim can be interpreted as about what Frank ought to do *in order to preserve his neighbor's house*. This hypothesis is allegedly ruled out by inescapability, but how? We need to clarify what it means to "apply inescapably" to an agent.

Consider a truth-conditional account of categoricity: a normative claim applies inescapably to an agent just in case it is *true of* the agent regardless of his desires and intentions. Frank's declaration of indifference might be thought to reveal that Dora's claim would be false if it were implicitly end-relational, for example, so her justification in continuing to insist is evidence that it isn't. It might be reasoned as follows:

SC1.   If the end-relational theory is correct then all normative 'ought' claims are hypothetical imperatives, elliptical for sentences of the form IC1: 'If *s* wants to ψ, then *s* ought to φ.'

SC2.   In hypothetical imperatives of the form IC1 the truth of the 'ought' claim is conditional on the agent *s* desiring a particular end to which φ-ing is a means.

SC3.   If a normative 'ought' claim is moral then its truth isn't conditional on *s* desiring a particular end to which φ-ing is a means.

SC4.   Therefore the end-relational theory isn't correct.

This objection confuses the end-relational theory with a straightforwardly Humean view. Our semantics relativizes normative sentences merely to ends, or potential states of affairs, not to the desiring or intending of them, and we analyzed 'If *s* wants…' as here having a relevance- rather than a truth-conditional function. The truth conditions of end-relational claims are therefore generally independent of such psychological facts; whatever Frank wants or intends, it remains true that in order to preserve his neighbor's house he ought to stop. Agents cannot escape having these sentences be true about them simply by failing to care about the end, so the truth-conditional account of categoricity presents no challenge.

A different problem emerges from this story, however, which can be observed from a contrast with *Ernest Hacker*. Whatever Ernest desires or intends, it also remains true that in order to fell the tree he ought to use a chainsaw; in this respect Ernest's case is just like Frank's. But then why is it natural for Dora to retract her claim in response to Ernest's declaration of indifference?[5] An explanation is needed for why she wouldn't similarly insist on her 'ought' claim to

---

[5] If the asserted proposition were, *In order to attain Ernest's preferred end he ought to use a chainsaw*, then his disavowal would reveal it to be false, but this isn't a general solution since Ernest can appropriately respond similarly even to 'In order to fell that tree you ought to use a chainsaw.'

him, given that his response doesn't provide any more reason than Frank's for thinking she asserted something false.

Our theory easily explains this escapability in *Ernest Hacker*. Observe that exactly the same kind of disavowal and retraction would be appropriate if Dora had instead said, 'The easiest way to fell that tree is with a chainsaw', or 'You are more likely to fell that tree if you used a chainsaw.' Even if these statements are clearly true, Ernest can still naturally reply the same way, 'But I'm not trying to fell it', and Dora can naturally respond, 'Oh, I see. Never mind then, go ahead.' At this point in the story we characteristically find vocabulary about relevance rather than truth, that is, pragmatic assessment: 'it would be *appropriate* to insist...', '*never mind* what I said.'[6]

The inappropriateness of the utterance to Ernest is also straightforwardly predicted and explained by our cooperation law, CLP. Dora's utterance is motivated by her mistaken supposition that Ernest is trying to fell the tree, which leads her to borrow this cooperatively as her conversational end. The relevance of her 'ought' claim then presupposes that this end is shared, since the significance of end-relational information to an agent is generally contingent on desire for the end. Ernest's declaration of indifference reveals that her utterance failed to make a cooperative contribution as she intended, and thereby that it is pragmatically inappropriate regardless of its truth. Dora therefore retracts her utterance as uncooperative and irrelevant, but not necessarily as false.

Now a more serious objection can be identified concerning the exchange with Frank Feller. Contrasting the cases suggests a *pragmatic* account of categoricity: a normative claim "applies inescapably" to an agent in the sense that it is *appropriately addressed* to that agent regardless of his desires and intentions. The claim Dora addresses to Frank is categorical in this sense: his declaration of indifference doesn't make her utterance inappropriate like Ernest's does. It might seem that if moral 'ought' claims were really end-relational then they couldn't be pragmatically categorical, so that continuing to press them despite the agent's declared indifference would be inappropriate, as in Ernest's case. Call this the objection from pragmatic categoricity:

PC1. If an 'ought' claim is relativized to an end *e*, then addressing it to an agent *s* who lacks a preference for *e* doesn't promote conversational ends (as shown by *Ernest Hacker*).

PC2. Any utterance that doesn't promote conversational ends is pragmatically inappropriate.

---

[6] Sometimes we may offer apparently semantic rather than pragmatic retractions, however; i.e., 'I was mistaken'/ 'what I said was false', rather than 'never mind what I said'; see the previous note, and discussion in Chapter 8.

PC3.   If an 'ought' claim is moral then no end e is such that if s lacks
       a preference for e then addressing the claim to s is pragmatically
       inappropriate (as shown by *Frank Feller*).[7]

PC4.   Therefore if an 'ought' claim is moral, it isn't relativized to an end.

This more plausibly captures the reasoning that makes the stories illustrating inescapability so persuasive against relational theories, so I'll provisionally assume that pragmatic categoricity is the relevant notion. This objection fails because premise PC1 is false: not all contexts are relevantly like *Ernest Hacker*.

7.2. Pragmatic Categoricity

On our theory the difference in pragmatic escapability between the two cases doesn't lie in the relevance of the asserted proposition to the agent's preferences: Frank's declaration of indifference about the preservation of his neighbor's house implies that information about what increases its probability is of no greater interest to him than information about how best to fell his tree is of interest to Ernest. Pragmatically categorical use of end-relational language would clearly not be *cooperative*.

But not all speech aims at cooperation, as we observed in Chapter 5. Sometimes people speak in the service of their own individual ends which conflict with ends preferred by their audience, which is why we found the instrumental law ILP to be more fundamental to pragmatics than the cooperation law, CLP: speakers always attempt to promote their own conversational ends, whether or not those ends are shared. Even though Dora's categorical use of 'ought' doesn't promote any of Frank's ends, it might still be pragmatically appropriate by promoting her own preferred ends.

Paradigmatically categorical uses of normative language indeed appear not to be intended to promote shared ends. Dora's normative utterance to Frank is naturally interpreted as motivated by her preferred end *that the neighbor's house is preserved*. Like her cooperative address to Ernest, it clearly has a practical kind of illocutionary force, aiming to influence Frank's motivation and direct his behavior. But categorical uses intuitively have a distinct kind of practical force. Whereas the 'ought' addressed to Ernest has the force of advice or recommendation, the categorical 'ought' addressed to Frank rather has the force of a *demand* or *prescription*, as in paradigmatic uses of imperatives like 'Stop doing that!'

The essential difference is apparently that prescription isn't intended to be cooperative or helpful. Recall our definition in Chapter 5:

---

[7] This needs qualification to allow for moral claims conditioned on agent's desires, like 'If Henry wants to be a famous mass murderer then he ought to seek psychological help.'

Recommendation: To recommend to *s* that she φ is to draw *s*'s attention to the possibility of φ-ing ostensibly with the intention to motivate her toward φ-ing in pursuit of her own desired ends.

The contrast is captured by the following loose definition:

Prescription: To prescribe to *s* that he φ is to draw *s*'s attention to the possibility of φ-ing ostensibly with the intention to motivate him toward φ-ing regardless of his own desired ends.

While recommendation aims at helping agents achieve their own desired ends (i.e., those they saliently do or would desire), prescription aims rather at coercing agents to act in ways desired by somebody else, typically the speaker.[8]

This contrast sheds light on the difference in escapability. In contexts of advice like *Ernest Hacker*, the speaker's preference for the end is borrowed from the agent and therefore evaporates upon his declaration of indifference. But in cases of prescription like *Frank Feller*, the speaker's preference isn't borrowed from the agent, whose declaration of indifference therefore doesn't cause her to lose interest in the end. Dora's preference for the preservation of the neighbor's house isn't borrowed from Frank, and if she is a normal, decent person she will strongly prefer this end over any she could borrow from Frank out of mere helpfulness, as she will empathize much more strongly with relevant desires of the neighbor than with whatever vindictive desires are motivating Frank. So she obviously wouldn't respond to Frank as to Ernest, by saying 'Never mind, then. Go ahead.'

However, the challenge here is to explain how pragmatically categorical uses of end-relational language would serve speaker's purposes and function prescriptively at all. While end-relational information generally has a directing or motivating influence on an agent's behavior in case he has some desire for that end, categorical uses don't meet this condition by definition. So how could a speaker reasonably believe that persistently asserting an end-relational proposition to an agent indifferent to the relevant end (or even with a contrary preference, like Frank) would be an effective way to promote her conversational end (let alone be best, as required by ILP)? If the normative language in moral and other categorical claims were semantically end-relational then they might seem utterly useless for promoting the conversational ends for which they are actually used. They would then lack prescriptive force and motivating influence, and be pragmatically inappropriate: call this the *Indifference* problem.

---

[8] This contrast might be thought incoherent, especially on a Humean psychological model: if motivation requires desire, then how could an agent be motivated regardless of what he does or would desire? We can either invoke different counterfactual desires (e.g., if fully informed vs. if browbeaten), or identify desire narrowly as *intrinsic* motivation (see Finlay 2008a). The key difference is that prescription assumes only the agent's potential susceptibility to influence.

Additionally, the agent will often already believe the relevant end-relational proposition: Frank is already aware that his neighbor's house is more likely to be preserved if he stops, but this doesn't deter Dora from insistently pressing her 'ought' claim. It's hard to see how telling somebody what he already knows could be an effective way to promote your ends, underscoring the apparent futility of pragmatically categorical use of end-relational language: call this the *Information* problem. These two problems may seem to indicate that moral language has a different, absolutist meaning, whether referring to absolute normative facts (primitivism) or expressing absolute demands (expressivism).

Characteristically, categorical uses of normative language aren't explicitly relativized to any end.[9] While often treated as evidence for absolutist semantics, by our theory this indicates instead that the speaker has in mind an end she believes is salient enough for the audience to identify it (sufficiently for her purposes) from the context, which by default will be a saliently preferred end. In a paradigmatic context of second-personal address like *Frank Feller*, the most salient preferences are those of the speaker, and/or the agent who is also the audience. Since this is a categorical use (as established by the declaration of indifference) the agent's preferences are ruled out, leaving the speaker's preferences.

It might be worried that preferences that aren't shared may not be salient to the audience, but audiences often have enough contextual cues to identify what the speaker has in mind: in paradigms like *Frank Feller* the target of a categorical address immediately knows which end to disavow in order to reject the utterance as not cooperative, and in any case the end need only be salient under a description such as *the speaker's preferred end*, as we saw in Chapter 6. Dora is naturally interpreted as speaking in a context of direct interest, for example, expressing her preference that the neighbor's house is preserved and thereby also her derivative preference that Frank stops.

These categorical uses of end-relational language would therefore express the speaker's own preferences for the agent's behavior. Dora's utterance to Frank pragmatically expresses what she could also assert by saying, 'I prefer that you stop, and preserve your neighbor's house', which would also be naturally interpreted as a prescription. Early expressivists like Carnap, Hare, and Stevenson similarly analyze the prescriptivity of the moral 'ought' as nonassertoric expression of the speaker's attitudes; here we have another quasi-expressivist result. But why would expressing preferences have prescriptive force?

Our pragmatic principles provide an answer. When a speaker expresses her preferences in a context like Dora's, she is evidently trying to promote the very end for which she is expressing preference (e.g., preserving the house). The most obvious explanation of how she might think this end best promoted by

---

[9] Though they *can* be; e.g., we can interpret 'You ought not fell the tree that way, in order to preserve your neighbor's house' as categorical.

expressing her preference to the agent is that she thinks she might thereby be able to motivate him to conform with her preference—either to share it or at least to respect it (e.g., Dora thinks she may be able to influence Frank to stop). This belief is justified by the strong disposition in psychologically normal people for cooperation and to be empathetically influenced toward others' ends.

In a context like *Frank Feller*, the speaker is therefore also behaving uncooperatively by trying to motivate the agent to comply with her preferences despite his declared indifference or contrary preference. (By virtue of the strong disposition for cooperation, this violation of ordinary social etiquette also pragmatically indicates that the speaker prefers her end over the agent's quite strongly and not just to some marginal degree. By continuing to express her preference in the face of Frank's declarations, Dora expresses a strong preference, pressuring Frank to comply.)

Our definition of prescription is thereby met pragmatically: the speaker is ostensibly trying to motivate the agent to comply with her preferences regardless of his own. The Indifference and Information problems are also solved: although the asserted proposition isn't itself either motivating or informative for the agent, by asserting it in that context and manner the speaker expresses her preferences with prescriptive force, which may be both motivating and informative, or motivating without being informative. Our theory therefore predicts and explains the pragmatic categoricity distinguishing *Frank Feller* from *Ernest Hacker*.

To explain not merely why end-relational language could be used this way but also why it would be, our pragmatic principles require also that speakers may consider it best for their purposes. But if the primary purpose is prescriptive, it may be wondered why a speaker would use such indirect means (especially if the agent already believes the asserted proposition) rather than simply and directly asserting that she has the preference ('I prefer that you stop'), or using an imperative ('Stop!').

A first, partial answer is that this indirect means can efficiently convey additional information. If Dora says merely, 'I prefer that you stop' or 'Stop!' she doesn't indicate that she has any reason or basis for this preference, which therefore could just be an arbitrary whim. By saying instead, 'You ought to stop' she also expresses preference for the implicit end and indicates that her preference concerning Frank's behavior is factually guided by a relation to that end; that is, she expresses her belief that Frank ought to φ *in order that her preferred end obtains*.[10]

This answer isn't sufficient for specifically *moral* speech, however. Referring to one's own preferences (*de dicto*), as in 'In order that my preferred end obtains, you ought to stop', isn't only unnecessary for but also incompatible

---

[10] Alternatively, by Pragmatic Generalization this needn't be indirect at all.

with making a categorical claim with intuitively moral force. To explain this we might try invoking our principle that pragmatically permissible ellipsis is generally also pragmatically required, as illustrated by the infelicity of the All Blacks captain explicitly qualifying his mid-game advice to his rugby teammates with '…if you want us to win the game'. But this is inadequate; as Richard Joyce objects,

> It would be a very different kind of weirdness if the judge at the Nuremberg trials kept relativizing his condemnation of the war criminals with the suffix '…by our moral standards.' This would not just be weird and irritating; it would be *scandalous*; there would be protests. The All Black captain would be committing the infelicity of redundancy; he would be saying too much. The relativist Nuremberg judge, by contrast, will be interpreted not as adding something unnecessary, but as revealing himself, in adding the suffix, to be saying too little. The displeased audience will want the judge not merely to suppress that suffix in conversation; they will want him to *eliminate* it.[11]

Observe also that directly prescribing ('Stop!') or describing one's own preferences ('I prefer that you stop') similarly lacks moral force, without being unnecessarily verbose. Moral use of normative language seems incompatible with explicit reference to the speaker's attitudes. But our account of pragmatic categoricity above seems to predict the opposite. If expressing preferences is essential for prescriptive force, then speakers might be expected to make the relativization to those preferences explicit whenever it isn't completely clear— as when the agent or audience saliently has different preferences or declares indifference. This feature of moral discourse prompts widespread skepticism about expressivist theories as failing to capture the objectivity of moral prescriptions, which appears to involve a practical force independent of speakers' own contingent preferences. It is equally a challenge for quasi-expressivism, but one I'll argue our theory accommodates and explains as a special rhetorical kind of pragmatic categoricity.

7.3. Rhetorical Objectivity

On the end-relational theory, the objectivity of moral prescription means that these utterances involve speaking as if the relevant end isn't merely the object of the speaker's preferences. They are rather made as if (i.e., pragmatically presuppose that) the preference is also *shared by the audience*—even if this presupposition is transparently false. Leaving the intended end implicit suggests there

---

[11] Joyce 2011. He assumes a different kind of relativization ('by *our standards*'); see discussion in Finlay 2011.

is one uniquely salient end in the context which the audience can immediately identify under some description or other, whereas if the agent's/audience's preferences diverge from the speaker's (and especially if they are declared) then typically there will be competition for salience and therefore pressure to be explicit. Additionally, these are transparently contexts of direct interest where the speaker aims to direct or influence the agent, and end-relational information is generally only motivating for agents who care about the end.

In paradigmatic contexts of morally categorical use this presupposition of shared preference is false, of course. So what is the point and effect of speaking with a false presupposition?

To be thorough we can begin by observing a range of cases that don't strictly involve categorical or prescriptive uses, though are easily mistaken for them. If the speaker is unaware that the presupposition is false then the utterance may just be a failed recommendation. She may alternatively be *hoping* the agent prefers the end, despite his declarations of indifference or other contrary evidence. Others' psychological attitudes can be murky to us, and their testimony unreliable. One also often encounters a rosy view of human nature that even the most reprobate monster deep down has a hidden core of "humanity", and some utterances that appear categorical may rather be optimistic attempts to appeal to this supposed inner humanity. Or a speaker may be bluffing, or deceitfully *pretending* there is some end the agent would relevantly prefer, which might successfully engage the agent's second-order desires;[12] for example, Dora may try to persuade Frank that some unspecified but nasty consequence may befall him if he doesn't stop. Relatedly, some claims may be intended "proleptically", making themselves true by promising or threatening some kind of reward or sanction.[13]

In all these cases utterances that superficially appear categorical really aren't. But I don't deny that pragmatic categoricity is a genuine feature of at least some moral speech and thought, so I'll stipulate that we're now only considering contexts where a presupposition of shared ends is *transparently* false, and it is common ground that the agent addressed doesn't or wouldn't prefer the end.

When a speaker pragmatically presupposes something not already in the common ground, an audience tries to accommodate her, taking her to be indicating that information. So an agent addressed with such a categorical use of end-relational language will interpret it as pragmatically communicating that the relevant end is shared—even though this is transparently false. This might be thought a fatal problem: the point of communicating a proposition, one might reason, is to get the audience to believe it, which isn't possible if the speaker transparently doesn't herself justifiedly believe it—hence the idea that knowledge is the norm of assertion.[14] But our pragmatic principles and

---

[12] Cf. Williams 1979.
[13] Williams 1989.
[14] E.g., Williamson 2000: 243.

a survey of linguistic practices suggest this is overly simplistic: communicating things that are transparently false or unjustified often has relevantly useful applications.

Consider how assertions of the following declarative sentences are naturally interpreted when the speaker transparently lacks epistemic justification:

(1)   'Nobody in our family belches at the dinner table.'

(2)   'You will come here.'

These are naturally interpreted not as expressing belief that the asserted proposition is true, but rather as demanding or prescribing it be true.[15] The same force can be observed for direct assertion of the presuppositional content we've predicted for categorical utterances; for example, if Dora were instead to say either of

(3)   'We both prefer that your neighbor's house is preserved.'

(4)   'You prefer that your neighbor's house is preserved.'

Or suppose she replies to Frank's declaration by saying, 'Yes, you care', or tells him, 'You don't want to do that.' These transparently false claims are naturally interpreted as prescribing that Frank have this preference or acts accordingly.[16]

Our pragmatic principles explain these interpretations. Since the agent can see that the speaker clearly doesn't expect him to come to believe the asserted proposition, by ILP he can infer this isn't what the speaker intends, and therefore that she must be advancing the proposition with some nonassertoric or nondeclarative force. When this proposition is also something the speaker evidently prefers and the agent has the power to make true (or closer to the truth), then the natural conjecture is that she is advancing the proposition rather as an imperative, with prescriptive force.

While the above examples all involve direct assertion, the same phenomenon is easily observed when the proposition is only pragmatically expressed. If somebody carelessly drops litter in the park, one might say to him, 'The rubbish bin is over there.' This feigns helpfulness, by speaking as if he preferred to dispose of his rubbish in a considerate way—that is, saying something that would be cooperative under that condition. Since this presupposition is transparently unjustified, the speaker is automatically interpreted rather as demanding it be true. Similarly therefore, when Dora pragmatically presupposes that Frank shares her preferences despite transparently lacking justification for believing it, she thereby prescribes it.

By speaking as if something were true of the audience though transparently lacking any justification for believing it is, a speaker effectively expresses

---

[15] Cf. Stevenson 1937: 24–25.

[16] Relevantly, there is a familiar use of the definite article (e.g., 'It's not *a* classic movie, it's *the* classic movie'), which illustrates this rhetorical device of expressing preferences and prescriptions.

a prescription, demanding they make it true.[17] This is illustrated by ambiguity in the word 'expect': by pretending to express the doxastic expectation that an agent will φ, a speaker rhetorically expresses the *moral* expectation that the agent will φ; consider 'England expects that every man will do his duty.' I suggest this is the rhetorical device we know as "moralism", and that it can be set beside sarcasm, hyperbolism, and irony as immediately recognizable gambits of conversation. Our theory predicts that paradigmatically categorical uses of normative language would have this moralistic kind of prescriptive force.

Why would a speaker choose to use *this* device, rather than some other, more direct way of prescribing, like an imperative ('Stop!') or a direct assertion ('I want you to stop!')? She may have many reasons for supposing this the best available way to motivate an indifferent agent. First, indirect speech acts and pragmatic presuppositions are much more difficult to express disagreement with. Consider sarcasm, for example; A: 'You're a really smart guy!'; B: 'No / that's false / you're wrong'[?], or the classic loaded question, 'Have you stopped beating your wife?' Here the Information problem (that the proposition asserted may be transparently true) actually becomes a virtue. We can infer that by making her prescription indirect through the device of moralism, the speaker also pragmatically expresses her intolerance of refusal,[18] making this a much more forceful way of prescribing than merely saying, 'I'd prefer that you don't do that', which may just invite the retort, 'I don't care what you prefer.'

Second, by speaking as if the prescribed proposition were factual, the speaker ostensibly puts her epistemic authority on the line, in effect challenging the agent not to prove her a liar. Some psychological efficacy may derive from our social impulse not to antagonize others in this way. Third, this device leaves the door open for some benefits of the merely pseudo-categorical uses canvassed above, like bluff or optimistic appeal to the agent's "humanity". Finally, this is an especially efficient way of communicating a strong prescription, and for this reason alone can be expected whenever all else is equal.[19]

Our theory therefore predicts that pragmatically categorical use of normative language would be a particularly effective way of exerting strong prescriptive force on an agent. We also have an answer to Joyce's objection. Since it's precisely the speaker's failure to identify the relevant end as being merely *her own* preferred end that pragmatically generates the strong prescriptive or moralistic force, we agree that Joyce's relativistic judge has "said too little". By explicitly relativizing his utterance to his own or his community's preferences

---

[17] See also Barker 1999 on the "rhetorical objectivity effect" of speaking as if preferences were shared.

[18] Dennett (1995: 506) and Joyce (2006: 111f) argue that morality's basic function is as a "conversation-stopper".

[19] The speaker may also mistakenly believe, or think her audience believes, that moral language refers to absolute moral properties. See discussion in Chapter 8.

he fails to express the strength of preference and the intolerance of indiffer-ence that are essential elements of the condemnation we want (and "expect"!) him to express. By failing to employ the available communicative device for the strongest kind of prescription, and instead making explicit and more verbose reference to his own attitudes, our pragmatic principles imply he actually indi-cates that his prescription and preference are not so strong. So of course we would be scandalized.[20]

7.4. Categoricity and Morality in Other Contexts

The end-relational theory pragmatically accommodates categorical uses of normative language in paradigmatic contexts like *Frank Feller*, but moral and categorical uses also occur in various contexts of indirect interest where the speaker isn't trying to promote the relevant end. This might be thought a problem, since our account of pragmatic categoricity and rhetorical objectivity above depended crucially on special features of contexts of direct interest. But discussions of categoricity have focused on these contexts largely because the challenge also depends on some of these features, and categoricity in other con-texts poses no great difficulties. I'll examine several kinds of departure from the paradigm: *retrospective* contexts involving an agent's past actions, *third person* contexts where the audience being addressed isn't the agent, *alienation* contexts where the speaker isn't expressing her own preferences, then *first person* con-texts, *judgments*, and *questions*.

Retrospective Contexts. Suppose Dora addresses Frank after he has felled the tree onto his neighbor's house, and says, 'You ought not to have done that.' This is pragmatically categorical, as it is appropriate regardless of his prefer-ences. But the previous explanation of this appropriateness doesn't apply here. The salient end is presumably *in order to have preserved your neighbor's house*, but since the deed is already done and the end has already become counterfac-tual, this transparently isn't Dora's conversational end, and she can't be trying to motivate Frank to comply with it. This use therefore doesn't satisfy our prin-ciple of *Prescription*—which isn't itself a problem, since we wouldn't say Dora here "prescribes" that Frank not have felled the tree.

The illocutionary force of retrospective claims is naturally described with different words, like 'admonish' or 'rebuke'. Plausibly, this can be loosely defined as follows:

---

[20] I also agree with Joyce that many people would be scandalized by any suggestion that moral properties are relativized to ends or standards, but this kind of reflective or metaethical view is fully compatible with first-order practice being end-relational and quasi-expressivist. See further discussion in Chapter 9.

Admonition: To admonish *s* for having φ-ed is to draw *s*'s attention to his having φ-ed ostensibly with the intention to motivate him to regret it.

This helps us identify Dora's purpose, and explains how her utterance serves it. She aims to motivate Frank to regret his action (for which she may have various ulterior motives, such as influencing him to make reparation, imposing a psychological sanction, or improving his character). Plausibly an agent regrets φ-ing in case he prefers some end he believes was demoted by his φ-ing. The pragmatic derivation then proceeds as before. By speaking as if the preservation of the house were the only salient end, Dora speaks as if Frank shared her preference for it despite that being transparently false, and thereby puts rhetorical and psychological pressure on him to share that preference, which would cause him to regret his action. This is a quasi-expressivist explanation for why retrospective normative claims are an effective way of admonishing agents.

Third-Person Contexts. Suppose Dora is watching Frank fell the tree from a distance, and says to her companion Gladys, 'Frank ought to stop.' Assume again that the implicit end is *in order that the neighbor's house is preserved*, and that Frank transparently lacks any preference for it. While this utterance is also naturally classified as moral or categorical, here our definition of pragmatic categoricity seems inadequate, as unlike the paradigmatic second-person cases it isn't addressed to the agent at all.

Our definition needs to be relaxed: the essential feature is that the claim can appropriately be *asserted of* the agent regardless of his preferences, whether or not it is also addressed to him. By our theory this is also implied by the platitude that a (normative) 'ought' is categorical just in case it isn't hypothetical. Given our analysis of "hypothetical imperatives" of the form IC1 as conditioning the *relevance* or conversational appropriateness of the 'ought' claim on the agent's attitudes toward the end, an 'ought' claim will be non-hypothetical and hence categorical just in case its relevance isn't conditional on the agent's attitudes toward the end.

How does our theory explain the appropriateness of third-person categorical uses? Suppose this isn't a context of direct interest, and Dora isn't trying to prevent the destruction of the house (e.g., by motivating Gladys to intervene somehow). Her utterance therefore doesn't have prescriptive or recommendatory force. But third-person categorical claims may serve various other purposes. A further distinction can be drawn between third-person contexts where the audience is assumed to share the speaker's preference for the salient end, and *doubly* categorical contexts where they transparently don't (e.g., if Gladys is an accessory to Frank's act). In the former, the pragmatic presupposition of shared preference isn't false, and so the rhetorical analysis doesn't apply, though the speaker still expresses her own preferences in the ordinary way described in Chapter 5 (which can serve various motives). Categorical and moral use of normative language therefore doesn't entail moralistic force, as between people who share a moral perspective.

In the doubly categorical contexts, by contrast, the rhetorical analysis still applies, mutatis mutandis. By speaking as if the end were of shared preference although it transparently isn't, Dora puts moralistic pressure on Gladys to share her preference and thereby her disapproval of Frank's action. Normative utterances in these contexts are naturally described not as prescriptions nor admonitions, but as *condemnations* or criticism, which might loosely be defined as expressing disapproval of an action.

Alienation Contexts. In other uses of normative language naturally classified as categorical or moral, the speaker herself transparently doesn't have any preference for the salient end. A mundane illustration: a schoolboy emerges from the principal's office after some escapade and says to his friend, 'We have to do a week's detention.' Here the implicit end might be roughly *in order to receive our punishment*. Since this utterance is appropriately addressed to and asserted of the agents regardless of their preferences it is pragmatically categorical.[21] But since the speaker doesn't ostensibly have any preference for the end, the previous explanations of pragmatic appropriateness don't apply here.

With regard to moral speech and thought, this alienation is exemplified in amoralism, where a person makes claims or judgments about what somebody (morally) ought to do, without having any corresponding preference. Accordingly, the amoralist's categorical uses of normative language don't have moralistic or prescriptive force as defined above: he doesn't make rhetorical demands or express any preference about what other agents prefer or how they act. While it is controversial whether the amoralist's practice is genuinely *moral*, clearly it is a kind of categorical use we have yet to accommodate.

Because these are categorical uses, no relevant end is salient from the agent's preferences, and by stipulation these are contexts where the speaker's preferences also don't identify the end. But a solution is obvious for the schoolboy's claim: here a *third person's* demands and preferences are most salient, and this 'ought' is presumably relativized to an end saliently preferred by the principal. Here the speaker isn't naturally described as *prescribing*, but rather as merely conveying another person's prescription.

This analysis extends naturally to amoralism, where also there is a salient third party with relevant preferences and prescriptions. The amoralist's practice is commonly observed to be parasitic upon the normal moral practice of his society. He is therefore plausibly interpreted as making claims implicitly relativized to ends saliently preferred by normal or paradigmatic members of his society, perhaps only under that description. He too makes no prescriptions

---

[21] It isn't absurd to suppose this to be the schoolboy's *contextually preferred* end, e.g., because he'd rather not get expelled. But his utterance can be appropriate even if he has no intention of obeying; I stipulate such a case here.

and expresses no preferences of his own, but does convey prescriptions and preferences from a moral point of view. This needn't merely mimic (in "inverted commas")[22] what others say, or merely communicate others' prescriptions; our analysis recognizes that he can factually disagree with the moral claims of other people in his society, because he can have differing beliefs about what increases or decreases the probability of those ends.

While there seem to be many real-life examples of amoralism, most famously in psychopaths, philosophers often profess an intuition that no such claim or judgment can be genuinely moral, and some metaethical theories (like many forms of expressivism) seem to entail that they aren't. The issue here is what it means for speech or thought to be "moral". While the end-relational theory needn't commit either to any particular theory about what distinguishes peculiarly moral speech and thought from other kinds of normative speech and thought, or to any position in the dispute over whether the amoralist makes genuinely moral claims, the analysis in this chapter suggests some natural conjectures.[23]

A "moral" claim might be defined in a first, *formal* sense as a normative claim made about an agent s in the moralistic way as defined above; as expressing a preference that trumps any motivation to cooperatively defer to s's preferences.[24] This sense accommodates the intuition that the amoralist fails to make a genuinely moral claim. It's also content-neutral: conceivably any end-relational proposition could be the content of a moral claim in this sense, or of a nonmoral claim.

But a second, *substantive* sense of 'moral' can be derived as follows. In a society, people converge upon common mores or customs, including practices of "expecting" concern or respect for certain (usually prosocial) kinds of ends from each other. So the practice of moralizing in a society will converge around a largely stable set of preferences, forming a moral *institution* or "morality". (A characteristic function of moralities is also to solve coordination problems, as contractualists argue). Accordingly, we speak about the moralities of different peoples, times, and places. Claims that are "moral" in this second sense needn't be "moral" in the former, formal sense (or vice versa), since speakers needn't either express or share preferences for the ends expected in their society.

Philosophers have long insisted, against the claims of anthropologists, that moral speech and thought isn't about what is merely customary or normal

---

[22] Alternatively, two senses of "inverted commas" use might be distinguished, as involving the words others use and the words others *would* use (e.g., if correctly informed).

[23] Previously explored in Finlay 2001, 2004, 2007b.

[24] Cf. Tresan 2006. Arguably not all categorical or moralistic use of normative language constitutes *moral* use; claims of etiquette seem to be one exception, for example. While the 'ought' of etiquette is applied to agents whether or not they care about etiquette, it isn't applied *regardless* of agents' contextual preferences, e.g., even when it puts them in risk of some harm, for example; otherwise etiquette would be morality.

(or customarily expected) in a society. But finally, we can distinguish between morality and Morality. Although there are many moralities of many different societies, and important divergences also within societies, to speak about Morality (unrelativized and in the singular) is to speak as if there were only one salient—and so uncontroversial—morality or set of preferences. This can now be recognized as itself employing the rhetorical device of moralism, pragmatically expressing endorsement of that morality and the moral expectation that one's audience shares these attitudes. Consider for example the usual (prescriptive) rhetorical force of telling someone, 'In your position it is Customary to φ', or 'That's not the Way it's done.' Suggestive linguistic evidence here is that the very words for morality are etymologically derived from words meaning *ways*—'mores' becomes 'morals', 'ethos' becomes 'ethics'—and the same distinction can be observed between descriptive and normative senses or use of 'ways', 'customary', 'norms', and 'manners'.

As members of a moral community we ourselves "expect" others to respect a particular hierarchy of ends (which may be vague, amorphous, and contested), which is what we treat as determining the content of Morality. Since alienation from this morality doesn't prevent a speaker from using normative language in a way that defers to those preferences, this substantive sense of 'moral' accommodates the intuition that the amoralist succeeds in making moral claims. A virtue of our analysis is therefore that it accommodates the intuitions motivating each side in the long-standing dispute over the conceptual possibility of amoralism, not only adjudicating it but also explaining why it arose in the first place. While this is only a brief speculative sketch, it shows that the end-relational theory is consistent with a defensible account of what it is to make a specifically moral claim or judgment.

Three other kinds of context might seem to present special difficulties for our account: moral and categorical uses that are *first-personal*, in *thought* rather than speech, and in *questions* rather than assertions. Our account of pragmatic categoricity turned on the pragmatics of noncooperation, but these may seem to be contexts where no such pragmatics could be operative. But the account extends to these contexts in straightforward ways. Consider first-personal moral judgments, such as thinking, 'I ought to φ', which are characteristically made without regard for what one does or would desire. While there is no question here of such thoughts being "conversationally appropriate", there is a direct mental analog, in *relevance* to one's cognitive aims. We can classify these judgments as pragmatically categorical by extension, as they can be relevant regardless of whether one saliently does or would desire the relevant end.

These can also be divided into alienated and nonalienated contexts. Categorical judgments in alienated contexts, whether first-personal or otherwise, are simply the analogs in thought of the amoralist's utterances—of which alienated first-personal utterances are simply special cases. These present no difficulties: one is just judging disinterestedly what is best, etc., relative to ends salient on grounds other than one's own preferences; for example, those ends designated as "moral". (Genuinely akratic judgments on this account are those where the saliently preferred ends in judgment diverge from the operative preferences at the moment of action.)

By contrast, in the nonalienated contexts one is actually concerned for those ends; what makes these categorical is that one judges without regard for what one does or saliently would prefer. Suppose I judge, 'Even if I didn't care about my children's health, still I ought to take them to the dentist'; this is a context where the implicit end is the one I actually prefer, such as *that my children stay healthy*. The categorical relevance of such a judgment can be explained by an intrapersonal analog of noncooperation and interpersonal influence. My actual preference for certain ends, like my children's well-being, is sufficiently strong that it trumps my empathy or concern for any conflicting preferences I will or would have under other conditions. We can prescribe to ourselves (e.g., resolutions), admonish ourselves, etc., just as we can others, and for similar purposes.

What about interrogative categorical uses, as in asking or wondering, 'Morally, what ought I to do?' The previous analyses of questions and of categorical use extend systematically to these contexts too. Categorical normative questions can be alienated, asking indifferently about what is best for the salient (e.g., morally sanctioned) ends, or they can be nonalienated, asking about what is best for moral ends the speaker actually cares about. Either kind can be either closed or open-ended; the enquirer may have a particular end in mind, or only a general description—in which case the uncertainty partly concerns which ends those are. An illustration of an alienated open-ended question is asking an authority whom one defies, 'So what ought I to do, then?', that is, *in order that the end you have in mind obtains*. This has the force of inviting a prescription (which one intends to flout). A nonalienated open-ended question, by contrast, would have the force of inviting effective influence, as when one lacks the confidence to make one's own decisions and so seeks to defer to another's will, or (as in private judgments) of expressing one's desire to settle on a preference for ends.[25]

Many different kinds of speech acts can be performed using the same normative words: we can recommend, warn, prescribe, proscribe, admonish, praise, condemn, commend, invite any of the above, and much more.[26] While we've only touched on a few of these kinds, we've seen how our semantics explains different illocutionary forces for the same words by appeal to the varying pragmatic significance of end-relational information given the conversational ends of speakers in different contexts. This flexibility of the quasi-expressivist

---

[25] Compare open-ended interrogative uses of other relational words; e.g., 'Is he tall?', 'Is this a lot?'

[26] The same word used to *prescribe* is used to *proscribe* when combined with 'not'; e.g., 'must φ', 'must not φ'.

account is a significant advantage over true expressivist accounts assigning practical forces to normative words by semantic convention.

7.5. The Wrong Kind of Categoricity?

The end-relational theory predicts that in a pragmatically categorical use, normative language would have a rhetorically objective kind of prescriptivity. This quasi-expressivist account of categoricity invites objections from opposite directions.

First, I might be accused of employing a double standard, since in Chapter 5 I argued that the end-relational theory provided a superior account of recommendatory force than expressivism because it accommodates the intuition that this force involves factual guidance rather than mere psychological pressure. However, this seems much more plausible an analysis of prescriptive force than of recommendatory force, and I consider it a virtue that the theory accommodates intuitions of both primitivists and expressivists here: some (recommendatory) uses of normative language offer factual guidance, while other (prescriptive) uses merely exert psychological influence.

Primitivists (and other absolutist descriptivists) will object instead that our account misses the real categoricity challenge, and mistakes the nature of morality's "objective prescriptivity", which isn't properly construed as pragmatic or rhetorical at all, but rather as *metaphysical*. It's said to be the moral properties and facts themselves that are prescriptive. In Mackie's words, "to-be-pursuedness" is built into the "fabric of the world"; or as Wittgenstein puts the idea, a moral state of affairs would "have in itself . . . the coercive power of an absolute judge". Mackie writes,

> Any analysis of the meanings of moral terms which omits this claim to objective, intrinsic, prescriptivity is to that extent incomplete; and this is true of any non-cognitive analysis, any naturalist one, and any combination of the two. (1977: 35)

This claim that moral properties and facts are themselves "prescriptive" seems to mean that in some sense they themselves *guide* agents regardless of desires. But what sense of guidance is this?

One idea is that objective prescriptivity or guidance consists in *motivational efficacy*: moral facts have a "magnetic" power to move agents regardless of their desires or preferences. Call this *motivational* categoricity. Mackie attributes a strong version of this idea to Plato:

> The Form of the Good is such that knowledge of it provides the knower with both a direction and an overriding motive; something's being good both tells the person who knows this to pursue it and makes him pursue

it. An objective good would be sought by anyone who was acquainted with it, not because of any contingent fact that this person, or every person, is so constituted that he desires this end, but just because the end has to-be-pursuedness somehow built into it. (1977: 40)

However, moral speech and thought don't plausibly presuppose that knowledge of moral facts necessarily motivates agents regardless of their desires and preferences: the idea of self-conscious evil (or Satan) isn't popularly viewed as incoherent. They may more plausibly be claimed to presuppose just that moral facts have a defeasible power to motivate agents regardless of their preferences.[27] But the evidence for this just seems to be that speakers can appropriately and sometimes successfully use moral claims to influence agents regardless of those agents' preferences—which our quasi-absolutist account of pragmatic categoricity has already explained, in a metaphysically and psychologically conservative way.

Today this motivational interpretation of categoricity is almost universally dismissed, as conflating normative force with motivational force.[28] Objective prescriptivity is now usually interpreted as involving a *normative* kind of categoricity. Moral claims "apply inescapably" to agents not in being either motivating or (merely) pragmatically appropriate regardless of their preferences, but in describing facts or properties that are in some way *normative* regardless of their preferences. Many champions of this interpretation, including Wittgenstein, Mackie, and Joyce, themselves find the notion of normatively categorical facts too metaphysically radical, and therefore accept an (ethically radical) error theory holding that all positive moral claims are untrue.

But to treat this normative categoricity as an objection to the end-relational theory is question-begging. Any reductive theory that rejects Humean instrumentalism and so accommodates what we called truth-conditional categoricity will also accommodate this normative categoricity on its own terms. The most common formulation, for example, is that categorical uses of 'ought' and 'good' (etc.) imply that the agent has a *reason* to act regardless of his preferences.[29] But our end-relational analysis of 'reason' predicts this as trivially true on one clear reading, since the distinction between motivationally internal and external use extends throughout the normative vocabulary we've investigated.[30]

---

[27] At best it isn't moral knowledge but rather moral belief that motivates (true or false), which is a problem for the idea that moral facts themselves exert this power. It might be attributed to moral properties instead, but as abstract universals these don't seem likely causes of psychological events.

[28] Motivational interpretations of categoricity can be found in Plato, Wittgenstein 1930/1996, Mackie 1977 (describing Plato's view), and Joyce 2001 (noncommittally), and are rejected in Parfit 1997, 2011, Joyce 2001, Enoch 2011.

[29] E.g., Foot 1972, Mackie 1977, Williams 1979, Joyce 2001.

[30] The right reading, since categorical claims only plausibly imply motivationally external or categorical reasons.

Other popular doctrines are that moral claims imply that the agent would necessarily be motivated if he were *virtuous*, or *rational*. But 'virtuous' can plausibly be defined as meaning roughly *disposed to act as one morally ought*, so this connection is easily accommodated. And 'rational' seems conceptually linked to reasons: it's a platitude that an agent acts rationally just in case he does what he *has most (subjective) reason to do*. While the possibility of rational immorality is one of the most controversial issues in moral philosophy, our theory easily accommodates both sides of the debate (thereby even explaining why it arises). Those who accept the possibility of rational immorality, as in the person of Hume's Sensible Knave, do so on the basis of a narrow ("procedural") conception of rationality, which our theory analyzes in terms of the subjective reasons relative to the agent's desired ends. Those who deny the possibility have a broader ("substantive") conception of rationality implying responsiveness to categorical moral reasons, which our account analyzes as relative to moral ends. In either case there is no challenge for the end-relational theory here.

Normative categoricity could therefore only be viewed as problematic by first assuming that the relevant normative concepts aren't themselves end-relational. As we haven't analyzed every normative word, it might be replied that the problematic kind of categoricity can be articulated in other normative terms that require an absolutist rather than a relational semantics: perhaps that moral facts "matter" or are "important" for agents regardless of their preferences, for example. We'll discuss these further terms in the final chapter.

Is there evidence of any other kind of categoricity in normative language not yet considered? We've seen that the standard kind of story used to argue for the special categoricity of moral language actually only demonstrates pragmatic categoricity, which our theory accommodates, and that the evidence in moral practice of a more objective prescriptivity allows a rhetorical explanation. The only other evidence offered is the intuitions and protestations of some people that they mean something different by their moral claims, which Richard Joyce vaguely calls "practical oomph". But they decline to analyze or explain what this is: primitivists like Derek Parfit maintain it is ineffable, while error theorists like Joyce and Wittgenstein hold the concept to be inchoate and nonsensical. Such a "fugitive thought", which makes no testable predictions about moral practice, poses no genuine challenge.

In fact, our theory suggests that confused metaphysical interpretations of one's own practice of moral prescription would be commonplace. Lacking a sophisticated theoretical understanding of our implicit pragmatic competence, our own quasi-absolutist moral practice is most naturally interpreted upon reflection as genuinely absolutist, making reference to objectively prescriptive facts.[31] Our simple, unifying semantics therefore accommodates and explains

---

[31] Contrast Harman 1996: 3–4, who argues for relational truth-conditions without relational meaning, locating the error in the first-order practice rather than the theory of the practice.

this characteristic feature of moral speech and thought, perhaps even better than either primitivism or expressivism can; without postulating any lexical ambiguities or special moral meanings, countenancing mysteriously prescriptive facts or properties, or ascribing systematic errors to ordinary moral practices. I conclude that this categoricity can only support and not undermine the end-relational theory. However, it isn't the only alleged evidence for an absolutist semantics.

7.6. Final Good and Final Ends

Although our theory relativizes normative language to ends, it isn't instrumentalist in the narrowly Humean sense of making the truth of normative claims depend on the agent's desires and preferences. But it may still seem instrumentalist in a broader sense that invites a second kind of absolutist challenge: what about the normative status of *ends*?

If we want to say that Frank Feller ought to stop felling the tree because it's necessary for preserving his neighbor's house, for example, then we'd naturally say also that he ought to preserve his neighbor's house. Is this further normative claim itself relativized to an end? Possibly we can identify another more basic end to make sense of this claim; Frank ought to preserve his neighbor's house in order that other people not be harmed at his hands, for example. But this regress of ends surely doesn't stretch backwards forever. At some point we must reach a fundamental end that is preferred but not because it promotes any further end. As David Hume writes,

> Ask a man *why he uses exercise*; he will answer, *because he desires to keep his health*. If you then enquire, *why he desires health*, he will readily reply, *because sickness is painful*. If you push your enquiries farther, and desire a reason *why he hates pain*, it is impossible he can ever give any. This is an ultimate end, and is never referred to any other object. (*Enquiry*, Appendix 1)

These ultimate or *final* ends are also naturally judged to be "good", and what "ought" to obtain.[32] It would be peculiar to call an object "good" because it promotes an end *e* while denying that *e* is also "good". These are judgments of *final value*, concerning what is good or ought to be done "for its own sake".

The end-relational theory faces the challenge that it cannot accommodate these uses of normative language. The very idea of final value is of a kind of value that is *noninstrumental*, and doesn't consist in promotion of some further

---

[32] Whether there are *reasons* for final ends is more controversial. One might maintain against Hume that their goodness is a reason for them to obtain (e.g., Nagel 1970), or that they're good because there are reasons for them—though the analysis in Chapter 4 suggests this is backwards.

end. Additionally, final value is said to be *intrinsic*, a property things possess solely by virtue of their own nature—but end-relational value consists in a relation to an end, and so might seem necessarily extrinsic. Facts about what has final value are also said to be *necessary* and knowable *a priori*—but probabilistic relations between states of affairs are apparently contingent and discovered empirically. These uses of normative language are therefore alleged to require an absolutist semantics, making reference to normative facts and properties that are nonrelational.

If speech and thought about final value are also uses of end-relational language, they too must be explicable with some kind of 'for e' relativizer. Observe that the primary linguistic device for making a final use explicit is indeed a 'for' complementizer: 'good *for its own sake*'. Whereas this is commonly assumed to indicate the absence of any relativization, compositionally it's rather a reflexive relativizer, equivalent to 'for itself'. Saying 'He did it for his own sake' can only mean that he did it *for himself*, for example, and not that he didn't do it for anybody.[33] This suggests the hypothesis that for p to be good "for its own sake" is simply for p to be good *for p*.[34]

This immediately accommodates the platitude that to have final value isn't to be good for any *further* end. It also accommodates the truth of paradigmatic sentences like 'Pleasure is good for its own sake', since it's obviously true that having pleasure is *more likely* given that one has pleasure than otherwise. But there is an obvious problem here: necessarily and trivially, *everything* is more likely given that it obtains than that it doesn't! So this hypothesis implies that everything is good and ought to be for its own sake, including pain, torture, hatred, slavery, etc. While I believe there is such a reading of "good for its own sake" which trivially applies to everything, this isn't the usual sense that interests moral philosophers, which applies only to a few things, nontrivially.

One important piece of the puzzle is still missing, however. Observe that our theory also trivially entails that everything is good for some end or other. (A simple proof by reductio: if anything were not good for some end or other, then it would be good for proving this claim false.)[35] So it might seem also to entail that everything has *instrumental* value, trivially. This shows that the normal philosophical concept of "instrumental value" with which final value is contrasted isn't simply the concept of end-relational value. By orthodoxy, an

---

[33] Notice that 'good for nothing' only means *not good in any way*. We may however say, 'I didn't mean to say it was good *for* anything'; our theory must interpret this as '...good for anything [else]'.

[34] See also Ziff 1960. This section assumes Chapter 2's analysis of '*n* is good' sentences like 'pleasure is good' as elliptical for '*n* is good [for *s* to φ]' sentences, and as meaning that it's good (for *e*) for *s* to φ *n*; i.e., that propositional complements are often grammatically represented by nouns (e.g., 'desire' and 'want' can also take simple noun complements; I analyze 'We desire pleasure' as 'We desire [that we experience] pleasure').

[35] See also Finlay 2001, Thomson 2008, Coffey 2014.

object is "instrumentally good" only if (roughly) it promotes something of final value.[36] (This prompts a further objection: since instrumental value is derived from final value, our theory can't even account for speech or thought about what is instrumentally good.) While money and medicine are paradigms of the instrumentally valuable, for example, it's naturally denied that a Doomsday Device is instrumentally good, despite its being good for destroying the universe.

This reveals that claims about what is instrumentally or finally good are all instances of 'good' simpliciter, lacking explicit relativization to an end (which I indicate below with capitalization). A distinction can be drawn between *p*'s being good for its own sake, and its being Good, for its own sake. The revised hypothesis focuses only on the second sense of 'good for its own sake', which isn't trivially predicated of everything. This revision may seem incompatible with the hypothesis that 'for its own sake' is itself a reflexive qualifier, but consider how it is used. Speakers don't ordinarily declare, spontaneously, '*p* is good for its own sake'; the qualifier is rather employed (usually by philosophers)[37] only after a question is raised about the basis for a claim that *p* is Good: "What is it Good *for*?" Philosophers have generally been interested only in judgments of the Good, Ought, etc., and not in other ways the words 'good' and 'ought' are ordinarily used.

In Chapter 6 we predicted that simpliciter uses of end-relational language would by default be implicitly relativized to ends that are saliently (contextually) preferred, so by this hypothesis we can also predict that *p* will be judged to have final value just in case it is itself saliently preferred as a *final end*. Of the things that we judge to be Good, some are judged Good because they promote some further desired end, while others are judged Good because they are desired ends in themselves. The usual function of the qualifier 'for its own sake' would then be to distinguish between these different grounds for judging something Good.

This is a promising result, because this view of the distinction has had many philosophical champions. We can even enlist the support of Plato and Aristotle: although widely regarded as the originators of the distinction between *good for its own sake* and *instrumentally good*, neither philosopher ever uses (as translated) 'for its own sake' as a qualifier for the adjective 'good', writing instead:

> Are there not some [goods] which we welcome for their own sakes, and independently of their consequences, as, for example, harmless pleasures and enjoyments, which delight us at the time, although nothing follows from them? (*Republic* Bk II)

---

[36] See, e.g., Moore 1903, Korsgaard 1983, Bradley 1998.

[37] The first thirteen hits from my Google search on 'good for its own sake', for example, were philosophical texts.

If, then, there is some end of the things we do, which we desire for its own sake (everything else being desired for the sake of this), and if we do not choose everything for the sake of something else (for at that rate the process would go on to infinity, so that our desire would be empty and vain), clearly this must be the good and the chief good. (*Nicomachean Ethics* I.2)

The only concept of "good for its own sake" to be found in Plato or Aristotle is the concept of a Good thing which we *desire* for its own sake, which is exactly the account our theory suggests.[38]

The hypothesis also accommodates and explains both the noninstrumentality and intrinsicality of final value, as follows. *Noninstrumental*: Normative language as such concerns only differences in probabilities of ends. (Causal) promotion of an end is only one relation by virtue of which something can be Good or increase the probability of the end; another is *self-identity*. As this isn't an instrumental relation, it follows that final value is noninstrumental. The end-relational theory therefore isn't instrumentalist per se, even in the broader sense.[39] *Intrinsic*: Being good for itself is a reflexive relational property that something possesses solely by virtue of its own nature (i.e., its self-identity), independent of anything else in the world, and so is indeed a metaphysically intrinsic property.[40]

Here it might be objected that while being *good for its own sake* in the *trivial* sense is intrinsic, being *Good for its own sake* isn't, because it depends upon a relation to some agent's desires or preferences. But this objection overlooks the merely background role that these psychological attitudes play in normative thought. To judge that *p* is Good isn't to judge that *p is good for a saliently desired end* (*de dicto*), but rather to judge, of a saliently desired end *e*, that *p is good for e*. Normative speech or thought about final value is therefore speech or thought about intrinsic properties.

While these are desirable results, this account of final value also faces some further objections: (i) that it fails to accommodate final uses of 'bad' (or final *dis*value) and the gradability of normative language, (ii) that it fails to account for the pragmatic appropriateness of speech or thought about final value, and (iii) that it fails to account for final uses of normative language in questions rather than assertions. I'll address these in turn.

---

[38] Neither would agree with my analysis of what it means to be Good, however.

[39] Recall also the case of *signatory* value discussed in Chapter 2, which is classifiable as noninstrumental.

[40] Other kinds of intrinsic (and noninstrumental) value are also accommodated, such as *constitutive* value (the relation by virtue of which playing tennis is good for getting exercise) or *mereological* value (the relation by virtue of which having all the spades is good for having a full deck of cards).

(i) If there is final value or goodness, then presumably there is also final *dis*value or badness. But since everything is good for its own sake in the trivial sense, it follows that nothing can be bad for its own sake in this trivial sense. Nothing is *less* likely given that it obtains than otherwise! So it also follows that nothing can be Bad for its own sake. Similarly, nothing can be better, best, worse, or worst for its own sake, in the trivial sense, than anything else. But things can intuitively be Better, Best, Worse, or Worst as final ends, or intrinsically.

While this may seem a serious problem for our hypothesis, it is actually another serendipitous result, because most people apparently find 'bad for its own sake' to be an intuitively peculiar construction, while having no such qualms about 'intrinsically bad'—an apparent anomaly our hypothesis predicts and explains. All these other normative terms except for 'good' present the same pattern, as usage data strikingly shows (Table 7.1).[41]

TABLE 7.1 Google search results

	'It is —— for its own sake'	'It is intrinsically ——'
'Good'	4,600,000	990,000
'Bad'	1	480,000
'Better'	1	420,000
'Best'	0	5
'Worse'	0	27,000
'Worst'	0	2

Note: The results are from a search on April 20, 2013.

But while our theory correctly predicts the oddity of 'bad for its own sake' (etc.), it also accommodates the existence of final, intrinsic badness. If the finally and intrinsically Good is that which is saliently desired for its own sake, then the finally and intrinsically Bad will be that which is saliently an object of aversion for its own sake. To be averse to something is to prefer its negation. Therefore, in a context of basic aversion to *p*, the saliently preferred end will be *not-p*. Trivially, *p* is bad for *not-p*, and this is based on a noninstrumental and intrinsic relation: *p* doesn't causally demote *not-p*, but *negates* or contradicts it, and solely in virtue of *p*'s being *p*, independently of anything else in the world. From the perspective of somebody with a basic aversion to pain, to be in pain is therefore intrinsically Bad.

---

[41] Searching on the shorter string 'bad for its own sake' (etc.) does yield more results, but a high proportion are variations on '*desiring* the bad, for its own sake' (i.e., 'for its own sake' is qualifying 'desiring', and 'bad' occurs as a noun); the remainder are almost entirely philosophical, and most are variations on '*good*/bad for its own sake', where 'bad' is included as an afterthought.

The gradability of final value or disvalue might seem to pose a difficulty: some final ends are intrinsically Better/Worse than others which are still Good/Bad to some degree, although there are no degrees of self-identity or negation. But this is a problem about *weighing* ends, which are already addressed by the pragmatic solutions in Chapter 6.

(ii) On our hypothesis, what would be the point of using normative language in these contexts? If the value is final, then the asserted proposition would apparently be just that p is good for p, which is trivially and analytically true, guaranteed by the meaning of 'good'. Why would a speaker bother to assert such a proposition?

We've observed that asserting trivial or uncontroversial propositions can serve a purpose by virtue of what is thereby expressed pragmatically. As these are simpliciter uses of 'good', they pragmatically express the speaker's belief that p increases the probability of an end that is saliently preferred. So asserting the trivial proposition will express that p itself is saliently preferred, which is non-trivial information that we already know is apt to support practical illocutionary force such as recommendation or prescription. Speaking this way therefore wouldn't be *utterly* pointless, but it might still be doubted that a speaker would have any reason to prefer it over alternatives. If this is the important information communicated or speech act performed by these utterances then why not speak directly, rather than indirectly by asserting this trivial proposition?

Speakers have a variety of possible reasons for using normative language in these contexts. First, even if the relevant value is actually final and the relevant preference is intrinsic, the speaker might not realize this and therefore not intend to assert a trivial proposition. In Chapter 6 we observed that in normal contexts of deliberation, advice, or evaluation, it needn't be transparent or important exactly what the relevantly preferred end is. Human motivation is often opaque, and identifying the ultimate object of desire or the final end can be difficult even introspectively. After thousands of years of philosophical debate it remains controversial, for example, whether anything other than pleasure or happiness is desired or good for its own sake.

Speakers also typically have little reason to figure it out. What matters for deliberation or advice concerning p is typically just whether p increases the probability of a saliently desired or preferred end, and not also whether this end is a further potential consequence of p, or is simply p itself. In either case somebody can truthfully and felicitously say or judge that p is Good or Ought to be, without having to determine whether the value in question or the relevant motivation toward p is instrumental or final. The distinction therefore comes into use only in those rare (usually philosophical) contexts where there is a reason to differentiate, as with the qualifier 'for its own sake' itself.[42]

---

[42] Presumably the great majority of cases don't involve final value, adding further reason to use normative language by default.

What end-relational proposition is asserted in a normal context? Here all the possibilities cataloged in Chapter 6 are again available: it might be vague, indeterminate, or bound by a salient description. In the latter case, the asserted proposition needn't be trivial after all; for example, if it's that *p is good for the end I contextually prefer*. However, (for the reasons given in Chapter 6) the most promising analysis is that the asserted proposition simply involves the end itself, as ostensively determined by the salient person's attitudes—even if its identity is only vaguely recognized. That is, *p is good for dthat(the end the speaker prefers)*. This respects the intuition that thought about value isn't about our attitudes, which are rather backgrounded, and it accommodates the falsity of claims like '*p* is good for its own sake because I desire it', and 'If I didn't desire it, it wouldn't be good.'[43] On this interpretation, if the value is final then the sentence will assert a necessary truth without being analytic or trivial, like 'Hesperus is Phosphorus', accommodating other common claims about final and intrinsic value.

A second reason for final uses of normative language is *moralism*. I argued above that expressing preferences by simpliciter use of normative language when the relevant preferences aren't shared is a rhetorical device that generates the strongly categorical force of moral prescription, admonition, or condemnation, etc. Asserting a trivial proposition does nothing to diminish the appropriateness of this kind of use; on the contrary, it's advantageous in these cases to be able to assert an uncontroversially true proposition. People often have little to say in support of a claim that something is good for its own sake except to insist that it's *self-evident*; while this self-evidence remains mysterious on primitivism, our theory both accommodates and provides an explanation for it.

A third reason may be theoretical confusion, again. This is predictable both on the grounds of (a) the opacity of linguistic competence and (b) the psychology of practical thought. (a) As with categorical and other unrelativized uses, in the absence of a sophisticated theoretical grasp of pragmatics these uses are naively interpreted in an absolutist way as ascribing a common intrinsic property that prompts desire. Clearly many people believe this is what they're doing; witness the prevalence of primitivism in metaethics. We can agree with

---

[43] Jon Tresan (conversation) suggests the theory is committed to the truth of some problematic *indicative* (rather than counterfactual) conditionals, like 'If I do desire to boil babies for fun, then boiling babies for fun is good.' Besides appealing to the possible salience of *counterfactually* desired ends (which I don't think totally blocks the objection), my reply is as follows. The relativization of simpliciter uses of 'good' (etc.) is generally *rigidified* and takes *widest scope*. So if the antecedent is false, so is the conditional; i.e. (*the x: x is my actually preferred end*)(*I desire to boil babies for fun → boiling babies for fun is good for x*). There's potentially a problem here only for the circumstance where the antecedent happens to be true, and I do desire to boil babies for fun, in which case our theory predicts the conditional is true; this problem is addressed in the next chapter.

error theorists this far, without also convicting ordinary first-order practice of being infected by the error.

(b) Given that in first-personal normative thought we're not thinking *about* our attitudes but *with* them, the projective fallacy can be expected to be common (due to naive misinterpretations of our use of normative language and lack of reflective understanding of our own sensitivity to pragmatics), leading many people to believe that their preferring *e* for its own sake is really a matter of being motivated by a perception or cognition of *e* as having a property of absolute value.[44] So in some cases the disposition to use normative language to express these basic preferences rather than simply describing our attitudes may indeed be partly due to an assumption that such a property is perceived.

(iii) So far we've only examined contexts of assertion or belief. Another objection concerns the practice of asking or wondering about what is Good or Ought to be done for its own sake, which apparently doesn't involve having any particular end in mind. But there are a number of things we can say about these practices.

First, notice that this is an unusual, philosopher's question: ordinary people might ask themselves about what is Good, but don't ordinarily ask themselves specifically about what is Good for its own sake. So there is again a possibility of theoretical confusion. If we mistakenly infer from our ordinary use of language, or by virtue of the projective fallacy, that there is such a (single) property as being Good for its own sake, then we may well wonder (confusedly) what has it.

But second, since the ultimate objects of our desires are typically unclear to us, there often is a serious question about what it is that we actually desire for its own sake. Since the relevant proposition needn't be analytic or trivial even when the value is final (e.g., if the end is ostended in a nontransparent way), these questions may sometimes be interpreted as asking, *What is noninstrumentally good for some end x such that x is a member of dthat (the set of ends I desire for their own sake)?*

Third, recall that the salient desires or preferences needn't be the *speaker's present* desires or preferences. In third-person contexts (e.g., considering what *s* ought to do for its own sake), the salient preferences may be *s*'s. But even in first-person contexts like deliberation, the salient preferences might be (e.g.) *those I would have if I were fully informed*. Plausibly, to answer such a question one tries to identify what one would prefer for its own sake under such idealized conditions. This is largely a matter of trying to get a full appreciation of the nature of the object, rather than of introspecting.

---

[44] Many philosophers make such claims, e.g., Hume, Nietzsche, Santayana, Mackie, Blackburn.

I conclude that the challenge from finality also fails: our theory accommodates and explains these uses of normative language. It predicts the intuitive features on which primitivists and error theorists insist: that speech and thought about what is "good for its own sake" is indeed about a property of value that is noninstrumental, intrinsic, and necessary, and that these judgments aren't reached by empirical methods but nonetheless convey substantive information (i.e., are apparently "synthetic" rather than trivially analytic). It also provides an explanation for why this kind of use would dispose many people toward absolutist and primitivist theories upon reflection: unlike expressivism it interprets these claims as having descriptive content, and unlike error theory it doesn't interpret them as all being untrue. (It may, however, appear to commit the opposite sin of implying that they're all true; this challenge is addressed in Chapter 8.) But it finds that we judge something to be Good for its own sake because it is saliently desired for its own sake, not vice versa, and therefore also accommodates expressivists' claims that speech about final value expresses intrinsic desires.

This quasi-absolutist account of final value is even superior to its absolutist rivals in several ways. It accommodates all these features with our maximally unifying semantics (by appeal only to pragmatic results we'd already derived from our basic principles), whereas absolutist theories seem committed to lexical ambiguities, as between merely end-relative, instrumental, and final senses of normative words. It accommodates more of the linguistic evidence, being compositional and accounting for the otherwise anomalous peculiarity of 'bad for its own sake', etc. It also *explains* the features of final value, rather than simply postulating them (like primitivism), without appeal to any mysterious properties or faculties. And it explains the practicality of judgments of final value in a psychologically conservative way without appeal to mysterious motivational forces or necessities—thereby providing natural solutions to some puzzles about the psychology of final value, as follows.

According to absolutist theories, we desire things of final value because we judge them to have this property. But then it may seem, contrary to what Plato and Aristotle say, that we don't really desire these things *for their own sake*, but *for the sake of their goodness*.

Absolutists will here reply that desiring p because it has a certain property doesn't entail desiring it for a further *end*. But at least by our definitions this move looks questionable. If s desires that p because she believes that p is pleasing to God, or embarrassing to her parents, then it's natural to suppose she must have a desire that God is pleased, or her parents are embarrassed. It's natural to say that p is a means to this more basic end, and that she desires that p for the sake of pleasing God/embarrassing her parents. If she desires that she takes a long walk because it's a way of exercising, then she views it as a constitutive means to exercising, and it's natural to say that she doesn't desire to take a long walk for its own sake, but for the sake of getting exercise. Finally (an example of an intrinsic property), suppose she desires to eat broccoli, because it has high iron content. Then it's natural to say that she doesn't desire to eat broccoli for its own sake, but for the sake of getting iron in her diet. So analogously, it seems that if s desires that p because she believes that p has a property of final goodness, then p is just a constitutive means to her more basic end of there being more goodness in the world, and she desires p not for its own sake, but for the sake of goodness.

So it's not clear that absolutist semantics can accommodate Plato's and Aristotle's intuitive claim.[45] But even if they can, it also seems both psychologically bizarre that people might have just one basic concern, for the promotion of a single objective property, and normatively bizarre that they should. Plausibly, a perfectly virtuous person reliably prefers whatever ends she judges best, so that whenever her judgments of final Goodness change so do her preferences. But if final value is simply an objective property to which desire responds, this seems to imply that the only thing the perfectly virtuous person nonderivatively cares about is this property, or *doing what is best* (*de dicto*), and her other motivations are all derived from this basic desire to maximize Goodness. As Michael Smith objects, this single-minded devotion to Goodness seems like a moral *fetish* or vice, rather than virtue.[46] (Don't desire it for goodness' sake; just desire it, for goodness' sake!) A virtuous parent is expected to have a basic or underived desire for his child's happiness, and a prudentially virtuous agent is expected to have a basic or underived desire for her own happiness.

Our account of final value conservatively accommodates these intuitive claims, whereas primitivism (and other forms of absolutist descriptivism) rather seem committed to radically implausible psychological and moral claims. I conclude that the apparently absolutist feature of finality, like the feature of categoricity, is not merely compatible with the end-relational theory, but if anything lends it further support.

---

[45] Absolutists may counter with narrower theories of desire, arguing that these beliefs directly cause desires without implying more basic desires (e.g., Darwall 1983). In Finlay 2007a I argue that this makes response to normativity too involuntary.

[46] Smith 1994: 71–76; see also Williams 1981b. The oddity of this fetish is nicely illustrated in the movie *Curse of the Pink Panther*: "Do you know why I am smoking on ze wrong end?" "No darling, but I'm sure you have a very good reason." "Right! I'm smoking on ze wrong end because I have a very good reason!"

8

A Disagreeable Problem

Our final challenge concerns normative *disagreement*, which poses a general problem for any "contextualist" semantics on which simple normative sentences like '*n* is good', '*s* ought to φ', or '*r* is a reason to φ' are used to assert different propositions in different contexts: this includes relational theories like ours, as well as indexical views. While this is equally a problem about agreement, we'll focus on disagreement, as is customary. Given the natural idea that disagreement involves logical inconsistency, these theories seem to imply that many uses of superficially incompatible sentences like '*n* is good' and '*n* isn't good' wouldn't really disagree, though they clearly do.

A first, naive formulation of this natural idea is

Inconsistent Belief: B's assertion/belief that *p* disagrees (agrees) with A's assertion/belief that *q* iff *p* and *q* are logically inconsistent (equivalent).

If an assertion or belief of B's disagrees with one of A's, then by extension B himself can be said to disagree with A herself in that respect. This can be said in a familiar sense even where there isn't any interaction between them, though talk about "disagreement" may sometimes suggest it.

Two classic targets of the disagreement problem are subjectivism ('*n* is good' means roughly that *n meets the standards I the speaker accept*) and cultural relativism ('*n* is good' means roughly *n meets the standards accepted in my society*).[1] These imply that assertions of '*n* is good' and '*n* isn't good' are only logically inconsistent if made by the same speaker or within the same society, respectively, and by *Inconsistent Belief* entail that speakers don't ever disagree or agree with the normative claims made by other speakers or in other societies (respectively) by uttering normative sentences. These consequences seem absurd; fortunately, the end-relational theory easily accommodates both interpersonal and intercultural disagreements, so long as the speakers have in mind a common

---

[1] E.g. Moore 1903, Stevenson 1937.

end. But it may still seem unable to account for the extent of normative disagreement, especially between moral claims; arguably any moral assertion of
'*n* is good' expresses disagreement with any moral assertion of '*n* isn't good.'

This feature of moral objectivity may seem to require an absolutist semantics, though a relational semantics can be reconciled with objectivism about a
particular normative domain if all claims in that domain are plausibly relativized to the same thing:[2] moral objectivity would be accommodated, for example, if all moral claims could be interpreted as relativized to a common moral
end. But this strategy strikes me as implausible, as discussed below, and in any
case is particularly ill-suited to the end-relational theory, which relativizes normative claims to individual ends rather than (e.g.) sets of ends or standards.

Moral and other normative disagreements evidently occur between people
who aren't united by preference for any common end. These *fundamental disagreements* pose difficulties for our previous solutions. Consider categoricity: if
Frank Feller embraces a morality of revenge and believes his neighbor poisoned
his dog, then when Dora tells him 'You ought to stop', he may respond 'No, this
is what I ought to do!' Here he expresses moral disagreement, though he may
accept whatever end-relational proposition we interpret Dora as having asserted.[3]

Or suppose Saddam Hussein declares to his generals, 'We ought to use our
chemical weapons on the Kurds'; surely we disagree morally with this claim if
with any at all, yet our theory suggests that he may have asserted only a true,
perhaps even obviously true proposition; similarly with many other appalling
claims. Or suppose he continues, 'If the Kurds suffer agony as they die, this
would be good ... for its own sake!' Our analysis of final value suggests that the
asserted proposition is roughly that *the Kurds' suffering agony would be good
for the Kurds' suffering agony*, which is trivially true.[4] We appropriately disagree
with many such claims about final value, though Chapter 7's analysis seems to
imply otherwise. Similar problems arise for our account of weighing multiple
ends under uncertainty, which had to appeal to rapid shifts in relativization
between speakers, sentences, and even from word to word.

To address this problem I'll first explore a different source of disagreement problems. Our semantics relativizes normative propositions not only
to ends but also to informational backgrounds, which generates structurally
identical puzzles about disagreement. But information-relativity is much less
controversial than end-relativity, and I'll argue that on careful reflection it
can't be sensibly denied. This shows that the problem of disagreement isn't

---

[2] Firth 1952.

[3] Rhetorical objectivity suggests a solution: if the end is picked out by the description *the
end we both prefer*, then Frank may correctly reject the asserted proposition (though it might
be lacking truth value rather than false). But this doesn't work for moral disagreements from a
conversational distance, like the Hussein case below.

[4] In both cases all the pragmatically communicated information may also be transparently true.

an especially embarrassing difficulty for our theory and its closest relatives, but rather a general philosophical puzzle confronting every metaethical theory (and in fact also the semantics for many other kinds of words, which pose similar difficulties). I'll argue that any adequate account of disagreement must appeal to pragmatics, and show that the end-relational theory supports a quasi-expressivist and quasi-absolutist solution that extends straightforwardly from information-relative disagreement to end-relative disagreement.[5] This solution accommodates and explains our ordinary practice and sense of normative disagreement, including some features that are anomalous for rival theories. I'll end by discussed related problems about how normative speech and thought is reported and evaluated.

8.1. The Problem of Disagreement from Information-Relativity

Consider the following scenario:

> *Two-Gun Roulette.*   Angie has been kidnapped by Sadie, a member of the Society of Honest Sadists, who tells her the following. Sadie will torture Angie to death unless she plays a special game of Russian roulette. She must choose between two six-chambered revolvers, L to her left, and R to her right. L has been loaded randomly with one round, R with three rounds. Angie must aim her chosen revolver at her head and pull the trigger once. If she survives she will be released with no further harm. She has no other realistic options like trying to shoot Sadie.

Evidently, Angie could appropriately conclude her deliberations by saying (or judging),

> A: 'I ought to use L, not R.' (*Deliberation*)

Our semantics accommodates this as assertion of the true proposition that she is more likely relative to her information to survive unharmed if she uses L than if she uses R.[6]

Now let's supplement the scenario:

> *Advice*:   Bertie is a fellow captive who has all Angie's information plus the following: since the revolvers were loaded, five captives have already played Sadie's game. All five chose L and survived. Bertie has one opportunity between Angie's concluding her deliberation and pulling the trigger

---

[5] This develops ideas advanced in Björnsson & Finlay 2010.
[6] Strictly this should be *more likely to use L, given that she survives unharmed*, but I'll put it this way for simplicity's sake.

to whisper briefly in her ear. He doesn't have enough time to share his additional information.

The implication of Bertie's information is that the next use of L will be lethal.[7] Evidently he would speak appropriately by saying,

B: 'You ought to use R, not L.' (*Advice*)

Our semantics accommodates this as assertion of the true proposition that Angie is more likely relative to Bertie's information to survive unharmed if she uses R than if she uses L.

To accommodate these claims, the end-relational semantics apparently must interpret them as relativized to different information. Consequently, Angie and Bertie assert logically consistent propositions. It further seems they needn't have any inconsistent beliefs. Bertie accepts the proposition assigned as the content of Angie's claim, and Angie doesn't believe anything inconsistent with the content assigned to Bertie's claim. By *Inconsistent Belief* they therefore don't disagree, yet intuitively Bertie does disagree with Angie's statement. (It isn't so intuitive that Angie disagrees with Bertie; we'll return to this puzzling asymmetry below). He seems able to say appropriately, '*No*, you ought to use R, not L', and while our theory suggests that Angie asserted a proposition that Bertie may know to be true, for him to say, 'Yes, that's right. You ought to use L, not R' would clearly be perverse and deceptive.

Here we confront a puzzle: Angie and Bertie seem to assert propositions whose truth-conditions are determined wholly by their own differing information, and are therefore logically consistent; but Bertie seems thereby to disagree with Angie, so by *Inconsistent Belief* must have asserted a proposition inconsistent with her assertion.

This puzzle arises equally for any theory that relativizes normative propositions to different information. One response simply denies that these normative claims really are information-relative, or (equivalently) interprets both as relativized to something like *all the facts*.[8] On this view, Angie asserts a proposition concerning what she *objectively* ought to do, which is simply false though she may be justified in believing it, and Bertie is therefore correct to reject it. But this analysis can't be correct, because Angie may know it's quite likely she objectively ought to use R. She can appropriately say, 'I ought to use L, although it's quite likely that given all the facts I ought to use R', but she can't

---

[7] In this version of the game the revolvers' cylinders are spun once upon being loaded but not between each use.

[8] Judy Thomson holds that all 'ought' claims are sensitive to the ("objective") probability of an outcome relative to the *information that is available to human beings at the time* (2008: 195). *Two-Gun Roulette* is inspired by one of her scenarios.

say, 'Given all the facts I ought to use L, although it's quite likely that given all the facts I ought to use R', since accepting that p is likely to be false is incompatible with warranted assertion of it. Angie thereby can't be using 'ought' in an objective sense.[9] Similar reasoning shows that Bertie also can't be using 'ought' objectively: he knows that using R is quite likely also to be fatal, which would also make it false that Angie objectively ought to use R. Making sense of these claims requires recognizing their relativity to the speakers' incomplete information.

A second response is that Angie's and Bertie's statements are actually relative to the same incomplete information. Deliberating agents presumably don't aim to make decisions on the basis of merely the information in their possession when they begin deliberating, but on roughly *the fullest information they can utilize at the time of decision*, which will include information others are in a position to make available to them. Whereas we stipulated that Bertie is unable to share his information with Angie, information can be "available" for use in the relevant sense without being possessed by the agent, as when others communicate the probability of p relative to that information. By our pragmatic principles, Angie's use of 'ought' can therefore be expected to be relativized to information selected this way rather than merely to her own information: call this solution *news-sensitivity*.[10] Her statement would then be false because sensitive to Bertie's additional information, although perhaps still justified since she lacks reason to suspect this information exists. Bertie's statement would directly contradict hers, accounting for disagreement by *Inconsistent Belief*.

But while news-sensitivity seems plausible for cases of advice like Bertie's, it isn't a sufficiently general solution. If Bertie were rather a long-distance eavesdropper (via CCTV), intuitively he could still disagree with Angie though his information couldn't be available to her.[11] To simplify discussion I'll proceed under the assumption that news-sensitivity doesn't account for the disagreement in the original case either.

A third response rejects these ordinary intuitions as mistaken: Bertie doesn't genuinely disagree with Angie, because their claims are consistent. The intuitions result from failing to appreciate that the claims are implicitly relativized to different information, as Bertie does himself.[12] If intuitions of normative disagreement are systematically unreliable in this way then the entire problem

---

[9] This point is clearer for three-option scenarios where the speaker knows one of the other options is objectively best, but not which (e.g., the miner case in Regan 1980, Jackson 1991, Kolodny & MacFarlane ms, the three-envelope case in Ross 2006 and Chapter 6.) I employ *Two-Gun Roulette* so as to address the problem relative to a single end, which is simpler.

[10] Proposed in Björnsson & Finlay 2010. Dowell 2013 argues it's an adequate solution.

[11] See also other cases of disagreement below, and particularly the point that Connie can appropriately either agree postmortem with Angie or disagree in hindsight.

[12] Cf. Bach 2009 on disagreement with epistemic 'might'. I endorse a related but weaker hypothesis below.

could be dismissed as based on faulty data. But while I'll ultimately recognize some truth in this idea, it fails to account for the *subtlety* of ordinary intuitions of normative disagreement. Not just any two speakers asserting superficially incompatible normative sentences are taken to be disagreeing—in many cases such claims are recognized as talking past each other—and we'll see below that intuitions of disagreement exhibit a high level of sensitivity to information-relativity.[13] Our semantics will account for the intuition that Bertie disagrees with Angie more charitably. (Note that I take no stand on what should be classified as "genuine" disagreement; the challenge here is rather to explain the *intuitive sense* of normative disagreement.)

These cases of disagreement from diverging backgrounds thus pose a general puzzle for metaethics—or rather for philosophy and linguistics in general, since analogous problems are now commonly observed for many kinds of words that encourage relativistic treatments, such as language about possibility ('might'), knowledge ('knows that'), taste ('tasty', 'disgusting'), and for use of gradable adjectives ('tall', 'rich', 'old'). Normative language inherits its disagreement problem with information-relativity directly from language about modality and probability, which is the same problem given that we've analyzed normative modals as different uses of the same words.[14] The same issues can therefore be observed for the following exchanges (suppose Sadie knows the next use of either revolver will be lethal):

(1) ANGIE: 'I might survive if I use L.'
    BERTIE: 'No, you can't survive if you use L. But you might survive if you use R.'
    SADIE: 'No, you're both wrong. Angie can't survive no matter which she uses.'

(2) ANGIE: 'The probability of my surviving if I use L is five in six.'
    BERTIE: 'No, the probability of your surviving if you use L is zero. The probability of survival if you use R is greater.'
    SADIE: 'No, you're both wrong. Angie has no chance of survival whichever she uses.'

A fourth response to these problems is *relativism about truth*.[15] The idea is that claims made relative to some parameter k don't assert propositions about relations to k, but nonrelational or absolutist propositions that only have truth values relative to various perspectives of assessment characterized by indices of k's kind. So on a truth-relativist interpretation, normative claims aren't

---

[13] See particularly the asymmetry discussed below.

[14] Lennertz 2014 advances a pragmatic solution to the problem of disagreement for epistemic modals broadly similar to the solution for normative disagreement proposed in Bjornsson & Finlay 2010 and developed here.

[15] E.g., Kölbel 2002, MacFarlane 2007, Richard 2011. Truth-relativism is applied to the normative disagreement problem from information-relativity in Kolodny & MacFarlane ms.

information-relative in their content, but instead are true or false only relative to particular information-perspectives. Angie and Bertie would then both address the same simple proposition that *Angie ought to use L and not R*, which isn't true or false simpliciter but only relative to different perspectives. Angie correctly asserts this proposition, as it's true relative to her information $i_{(-)}$. Bertie correctly rejects it, as it's false relative to his information $i_{(+)}$. Because the proposition Bertie rejects is the same proposition Angie asserts, truth-relativism generates the result that they satisfy *Inconsistent Belief*.

The end-relational theory could easily be translated into a truth-relativist framework, if it were superior. But whereas the primary case for preferring truth-relativism over contextualism is its supposed ability to solve the disagreement problem,[16] this solution isn't as straightforward as advertised. We'll see that truth-relativism needs to appeal to pragmatic resources which are also sufficient for solving the problem on our contextualist semantics. Contextualism then has the advantage of being the more conservative view, since relativizing truth is a radical proposal which also requires rejecting the attractive view of propositions as the informational content of speech and thought: the relativist's simple unrelativized propositions aren't units of information about the world, but at best information-schemata.[17]

8.2. Disagreement as Pragmatic

Truth-relativism's claim to account for the sense that Bertie disagrees with Angie is based on its satisfying *Inconsistent Belief*: Bertie denies as false the same proposition Angie asserts as true. But this is only sufficient for disagreement given a traditional, nonrelativist view of truth.

Consider

Postmortem: Connie is a detective investigating the crime after the fact. As it happened Angie didn't hear Bertie's urgent whisper and played the game using L, shooting herself in the head. By an incredible fluke, the bullet passed through her skull nonfatally, leaving Angie with a severe but survivable head injury. Connie has interviewed Bertie and learned all his information. She visits Angie in the hospital weeks later.

On truth-relativism, the proposition Angie asserted by saying, 'I ought to use L, not R' is false relative to Connie's information, which is relevantly similar

---

[16] E.g. MacFarlane 2007, Richard 2011.

[17] Cases against truth-relativism are proliferating; see, e.g., Cappelen & Hawthorne 2009. Contextualism and truth-relativism may turn out just to be notational variants, given their different definitions of 'truth', 'proposition', 'believes', 'asserts', etc.

to Bertie's. Connie knows this, but intuitively she can agree with Angie's claim, unlike Bertie, making what I'll call a (figuratively) *postmortem* claim:

>   C: 'You were right. You ought to have used L, not R. In light of what you knew it was the only sensible action.' (*Postmortem*)

This case behaves as would naively be expected if contextualism rather than truth-relativism were correct. As contextualism also predicts, Connie wouldn't seem to have disagreed with Bertie. (She could alternatively say, 'Bertie was right, you ought to have used R.')

Consider also

>   *Less Informed*:   Debbie is Angie's friend, captured with her. Debbie has even less information than Angie, not knowing how many rounds were loaded into L or R, though she knows that Angie knows.

On truth-relativism, Angie's claim that she ought to use L is false relative to Debbie's inferior information. Debbie knows this, but she doesn't intuitively disagree with Angie's claim.[18] It would obviously be inappropriate for her to say, 'No, you're wrong. Neither option is any better than the other.' She can rather say,

>   D: 'I don't know whether you ought to use L or R.' (*Less Informed*)

This identifies a general problem for truth-relativism. In its least ambitious forms, truth-relativism holds that truth is relative to a *world-state* and a *time* of assessment, which it therefore excludes from the propositions themselves. But consider:

>   *Alternate Reality*:   Bertie$_2$ is Bertie in an alternate world-state where Sadie sets up her game in reverse so that R holds the single round and L holds three. Bertie$_2$ has the correspondingly altered information that the next use of R will be lethal, so he asserts, 'You ought to use L, not R.'

>   (*A Really Bad Case of*) *Déjà Vu*: One week after surviving Sadie's game, Angie has the terribly bad luck to be kidnapped by Sadie again, who compels her to play the same game with the same revolvers, but reversed as above. Eddie is a fellow captive who knows that the next use of R will be lethal, so he asserts, 'You ought to use L, not R.'

---

[18] Perhaps D can infer from A's claim that A is more likely to survive if she uses L, which would make A's claim true relative to D's information too. But suppose D also hears B speak without knowing who is better informed: then it would certainly be false relative to D's information that A ought to use L, but still D intuitively wouldn't disagree with A.

According to this basic version of truth-relativism, Bertie$_2$ and Eddie each accept as true (relative to his own world-state and time of assessment, respectively) the same proposition Angie originally asserted in *Deliberation*, and reject as false (similarly relativized) the proposition Bertie originally asserted at the world-state and time of *Advice*. Each thereby satisfies the *Inconsistent Belief* criterion for agreeing with Angie's original claim and disagreeing with Bertie's. But intuitively they don't seem to be talking about the same thing, as a contextualist treatment would predict.

These cases illustrate that asserting superficially inconsistent normative sentences, like '*s* ought to φ' and '*s* ought not to φ', isn't sufficient to trigger intuitions of disagreement. Contextualist theories provide a simple and conservative explanation: the same normative sentence is used to express different propositions. But truth-relativists are obliged to conclude that satisfying *Inconsistent Belief* isn't sufficient for intuitively disagreeing, and therefore they concede the story to be more complex and to involve further conditions.[19] Contextualist theories are still in trouble so long as inconsistent beliefs are necessary for disagreement, but I'll now argue that the missing conditions are sufficient by themselves, without inconsistent belief.

These intuitions of normative disagreement are evidently responding to differences between the contexts of *Advice, Postmortem*, and *Less Informed*, rather than simply the sentences used. Two kinds of variability can be ruled out. First, while the speaker's *information* may vary between these contexts, Bertie and Connie possess relevantly identical information yet Connie but not Bertie can appropriately agree with Angie. Second, while the speaker's *temporal relation* to the original claim may also vary (Bertie speaks prospectively, Connie retrospectively), notice that *Sadie* can felicitously agree prospectively with Angie, though occupying the same temporal and informational perspective as Bertie:

S: 'Yes, you're right. You ought to use L, not R.' (*Pseudo-Advice*)

Since Sadie doesn't want Angie to survive unharmed, she isn't (like Bertie) interested in making her fuller information $i_{(+)}$ available for Angie by telling her what she ought given $i_{(+)}$ to do. But she can still sincerely express agreement with Angie or Connie about what ought to be done relative to Angie's inferior information.

The relevant factor is evidently the *conversational ends* of the speakers, as truth-relativists themselves acknowledge: Mark Richard argues that whether an assertion that *p* disagrees with an assertion that not-*p* depends on its point,[20] and Niko Kolodny and John MacFarlane have claimed that a speaker like Bertie must be genuinely disagreeing with the original claim because he is

---

[19] E.g., MacFarlane & Kolodny ms, Richard 2011.
[20] Richard 2011.

offering *advice*, which by its nature aims to help the agent solve the practical problem she deliberates over.[21] In other words, the sense of disagreement here depends on recognizing that Bertie speaks *cooperatively*, making it sensitive to pragmatic and not merely semantic cues. The problem of disagreement is another central puzzle of metaethics generated by pragmatics.

This role of pragmatics in generating disagreement intuitions can also be demonstrated by observing a flaw in the naive formulation of *Inconsistent Belief*. Speakers can evidently disagree without asserting contradictory propositions. Suppose A says, 'We ought to go stargazing at 8:00 p.m.', and B replies, 'Daylight savings started today.' B is naturally interpreted as disagreeing with A, though the propositions asserted aren't inconsistent. The disagreement lies not in what is said but in what is pragmatically expressed. Roughly, in saying that *p*, B disagrees with A by pragmatically expressing the belief that *not-q*, by virtue of what is entailed by *p* together with other propositions in the common ground. In this example, *p* (daylight savings started today) implies *not-q* (it's not true that they ought to go stargazing at 8:00 p.m.) on the assumptions that they ought to go stargazing only after dark, and that the sky isn't dark at 8:00 p.m. during daylight savings. This suggests a modified principle:

> *Inconsistent Belief**:   B's assertion that *p* disagrees (agrees) with A's assertion that *q* iff B thereby expresses the belief that *not-q* (*q*).

Since disagreements in judgment don't raise similar complications, they are adequately handled by the original principle.

As pressed by Kolodny and MacFarlane, the objection is that contextualist semantics can't accommodate normative disagreements between advisers and agents, because the cooperative nature of advice means that a claim like Bertie's must be intended to help the agent reach the right answer to the question she is asking in her deliberations about what she ought to do. This can't be a question about what the agent ought to do relative to her own information, for which she neither needs nor receives any help from the adviser, but it also can't be a question about what she ought to do relative to the adviser's information, since this wasn't her concern in deliberating. We'll see that this objection fails, and that the end-relational theory accommodates and explains the practice and sense of normative disagreement.

8.3. Information-Relativity in Contexts of Direct Interest

Let's begin with the pragmatics of agents' claims, like Angie's. This is a context of deliberation, so by our pragmatic principles we need to identify the motivations of deliberating agents. The objection assumes this to be the end of discovering which

---

[21] Kolodny & MacFarlane ms.

proposition of the form *I ought to φ* is true, but the end-relational theory supports a simpler and more natural answer: that agents deliberate with the aim of achieving their particular motivating ends. Angie's ultimate goal in deliberating is simply *that she survives unharmed.*

This may seem to conflict with the role of normative belief, but the end-relational theory dissolves any tension.[22] It is a matter of long-standing controversy whether deliberation or first-personal practical reasoning is just a special case of theoretical reasoning aimed at reaching true belief, concerning a distinctively practical subject, or an irreducibly practical kind of reasoning aimed at reaching an intention directly rather than a belief. On a simple and conservative psychological model, reasoning with the aim of achieving some end or ends is sufficient for deliberating, prompting the charge that the former view introduces too large a gap between deliberation and action. If reasoning were practical merely by virtue of its content, agents could presumably deliberate without any intention of acting on the results—but reasoning so detached from action doesn't seem to merit the label "deliberation". On the other hand, the latter view is charged with ignoring either the obvious role of 'ought' judgments in deliberation or the obvious difference between believing one ought to act and intending to act.

The end-relational theory resolves this dilemma: deliberation is ordinary theoretical reasoning aimed at knowledge about a subject of special practical significance to the deliberator, and thereby forming an intention. Knowing the truth of an 'ought'-proposition relativized to an end is of special instrumental interest to an agent in a context of direct interest, derived from her interest in the end itself. Knowledge of what is most likely to achieve an end is an ideal basis for making a decision aimed at achieving that end. But this depends on the quality of the informational background for this probability. An 'ought'-proposition relativized to the fullest available information (excepting symmetry of choice) will provide the instrumentally best available basis for a decision; that is, it most increases the probability of the end relative to the available information. On our theory, an agent therefore has no better means from her own point of view for promoting her end through deliberation than by identifying what she ought to do relative to the fullest information available. So Angie would conclude her deliberation by judging what she ought to do relative to the information available to her, in order to survive unharmed.

Now consider the pragmatics of Bertie's utterance. This is a context of advice, where (at least in this case)[23] the speaker is expected to cooperatively

---

[22] Isn't deliberation "of ends" (Kolnai 1961–62), rather than "of means" as Aristotle claimed? Not in cases like Angie's, at least; it would be peculiar for anybody in *Two-Gun Roulette* to deliberate about whether to seek to survive unharmed. More open-ended deliberations may be motivated by a higher-order end like *making a decision I won't later regret*.

[23] As observed in Chapter 5, advice sometimes guides agents toward ends they *would* prefer if better informed.

borrow the agent's motivating end with the aim of guiding the agent toward it. Bertie also therefore speaks in a context of direct interest in the end of Angie's surviving unharmed. Because he is better informed than her, he knows what she ought to do (in order to survive unharmed) relative to fuller information. This truth is of greater instrumental value relative to their shared end than the truth she asserts, and so Bertie best promotes their shared conversational end by communicating the proposition relativized to his information. Since Angie's fundamental interest is in surviving unharmed, and not in knowing the truth of the proposition she asserted, this is the most cooperative thing he can do. He thereby makes his information available for her to act on; because it provides a better basis for a decision aimed at Angie's surviving unharmed,[24] she would prefer to act on the basis of this proposition rather than the one she asserted. So our theory accommodates the intuition that Bertie's advice is cooperative even though he addresses a different proposition. Our pragmatic principles therefore predict (i) that this is the proposition he would assert; (ii) that he wouldn't waste his or Angie's time by addressing the proposition she asserted (which his information makes moot), and also (iii) that this is what Angie would expect him to do.

It is also now easy to explain why Connie, Debbie, and Sadie aren't similarly expected to deny that Angie ought to use L, although it's false that she ought to use L relative to their respective information. Unlike Bertie they wouldn't thereby promote their conversational ends, though for very different reasons. While less-informed Debbie has direct interest in Angie's end of surviving unharmed, denying the proposition relativized to her lesser information wouldn't promote it in any way. On the contrary, because of the expectation of cooperation in such contexts, Debbie would thereby pragmatically indicate that she has more information than Angie, which is likely to cause Angie to make a (subjectively) worse decision.

By contrast, Connie and Sadie each speak in contexts of indirect interest, addressing a proposition relativized to a salient end toward which they have no active motivation. Connie speaks in a postmortem context where achieving Angie's end is no longer at issue, while Sadie speaks in a noncooperative context of pseudo-advice, hoping that Angie's end doesn't obtain. They therefore aren't pragmatically obliged to address the proposition relative to the fullest available information, unlike Bertie and Debbie.

This explains the appropriateness of the 'ought' claims in the various scenarios, but doesn't yet explain intuitions of disagreement (e.g., that Bertie disagrees with Angie, or that he can appropriately say, 'No, you ought to use R').

---

[24] The proposition that *relative to fuller information* $i_{(+)}$ *e is most likely given p* itself makes it the case that *e* is most likely given *p* relative to the lesser information $i_{(-)}$. A subjectively better basis for decision doesn't necessarily result in an objectively better decision, of course; better information can lead to a worse outcome.

But it provides the resources for a solution. We saw in Chapter 5 that in contexts of direct interest, asserting that *in order that e it ought to be that p* (relative to the fullest available information, as we must now add) pragmatically expresses a preference that *p*. Angie's utterance therefore expresses her preference that she uses L and not R, while Bertie's utterance expresses his preference that Angie uses R and not L. By asserting consistent propositions they pragmatically express a common attitude toward inconsistent propositions.

Could an expressed conflict of preferences be sufficient to trigger intuitions of normative disagreement? This isn't a radical proposal, as expressivists since Charles Stevenson have labeled this kind of conflict a "disagreement in attitude", in contrast to a "disagreement in belief", and have used it to explain normative disagreement accordingly.[25] It accommodates the natural idea that disagreement involves inconsistency in attitudes, but without satisfying *Inconsistent Belief*, the principle motivating the objection. Whereas purely descriptivist semantics are generally assumed to be committed to explaining disagreement through some version of *Inconsistent Belief*,[26] our semantics suggests rather that normative disagreement can occur through pragmatic expression of inconsistent attitudes of a different kind, a quasi-expressivist solution.[27]

8.4. Information-Relativity in Contexts of Indirect Interest

So far we only have an account of normative disagreement in one particular kind of context. A complete solution requires a general theory accommodating disagreement intuitions across a full range of contexts. If some normative disagreements consist in pragmatically expressed disagreement in preference, then the simplest remaining theory is that all are:

> *Inconsistent Preference*:   B's assertion that *p* normatively disagrees (agrees) with A's assertion that *q* iff B thereby expresses a preference inconsistent with (equivalent to) the preference A thereby expresses.

As our semantics maintains that normative utterances express beliefs in addition to any preferences, it may seem strange if no normative disagreements consisted solely in inconsistent beliefs; expressivists might then justly complain that the descriptive semantics is a boondoggle doing no significant work. Another possibility is that disagreement intuitions are sensitive to inconsistency

---

[25] Not all kinds of attitudes toward inconsistent contents intuitively disagree; e.g., wondering, hypothesizing. A hypothesis: attitudes with inconsistent contents intuitively disagree in case they are attitudes that can't ("rationally", if you prefer) coexist occurrently in the same mind at once: one might simultaneously wonder whether *p* and whether *not-p*, but one can't believe or prefer *p* and *not-p* (under the same guise).

[26] E.g., Horgan & Timmons 1992.

[27] See also Robinson 2009, who calls this "quasi-disagreement".

either in belief or preference—which threatens to be messy, and might seem unnecessarily complex in comparison to pure expressivism. To avoid objections of being ad hoc, a mixed account must take the form of a general principle with testable predictions. While the theoretical space here is large, we won't need to look far beyond the simplest, disjunctive version:

Inconsistent Belief or Preference: B's assertion that *p* normatively disagrees (agrees) with A's assertion that *q* iff B thereby expresses *either* (i) an end-relational belief inconsistent with an end-relational belief A thereby expresses, *or* (ii) a preference inconsistent with (equivalent to) the preference A thereby expresses.

I'll ultimately argue that a version of the disjunctive principle best accommodates the data—and that our theory even explains normative disagreement in attitude better than expressivism itself can.

On first glance, contexts of indirect interest favor a mixed account. Our quasi-expressivist account of the disagreement in preference between Angie (*Deliberation*) and Bertie (*Advice*) appealed to two contingent features of contexts of direct interest: the speaker's aiming at the salient end, and relativizing to the fullest information available. Normative speech and thought in which either of these features is absent, like Connie's (*Postmortem*) and Sadie's (*Pseudo-Advice*), won't in the same way express preferences on the end-relational theory, or thereby disagreement in preference. But Connie and Sadie both seem to agree with Angie when they say, 'You ought to use / have used L, not R', which may seem to rule out *Inconsistent Preference*. These results are independently plausible: in her postmortem context, Connie presumably prefers rather that Angie *didn't* use L, since she'd prefer Angie had been released unharmed.[28] Because Sadie shares Bertie's information, she may as a matter of fact prefer that Angie uses L, but her utterance won't express this since her audience has no reason to interpret it as relativized to her full information, given that she is offering uncooperative pseudo-advice.[29] Their expressed agreement with Angie therefore couldn't consist in indicating that they share Angie's preference for her using L and not R.

By contrast, *Inconsistent Belief or Preference* accommodates these cases as agreements in belief. Connie and Sadie both know that Angie asserted a true proposition relativized to her own information, and our pragmatic principles straightforwardly explain the appropriateness of agreeing with it in

---

[28] If Connie doesn't know for sure that Angie would have survived using R, she arguably might prefer that Angie used L since she miraculously survived; assume she does know.

[29] Since Sadie's and Connie's actual preferences aren't pragmatically indicated we don't predict that their *utterances* disagree with Angie's, but might predict that they disagree in *judgment*. We'll address this below.

their contexts of indirect interest. Since Angie's surviving unharmed isn't their conversational end, our pragmatic principles don't require them to address a proposition relativized to the fullest information available. These speakers are interested instead in what deliberative conclusion Angie should reach in her epistemic situation. Connie's end might be to comfort Angie, by reassuring her that she couldn't reasonably be expected to have done anything differently. Sadie might find perverse amusement in "helping" Angie make a good decision within her epistemic limitations, or perhaps she just wants Angie to hurry up and choose. In these contexts evaluating the information-relative proposition Angie asserted is directly relevant to the speakers' goals, so Connie and Sadie are each naturally interpreted as expressing agreement in belief.

Other disagreements in contexts of indirect interest are problematic for *Inconsistent Belief or Preference* as well as for *Inconsistent Preference*, however. So far we've found speakers in contexts of direct interest disagreeing in preference, and speakers in contexts of indirect interest disagreeing in belief. But sometimes a speaker in a context of indirect interest intuitively disagrees with a normative claim when our semantics predicts that no inconsistency in belief is expressed.

One illustration is what I'll call a *hindsight* context, where a speaker addresses retrospectively what ought to have been done, in light of her present information. Consider Connie again, who can not only appropriately agree post-mortem with Angie's earlier claim, but in the very same circumstances could appropriately say instead,

C: 'It turns out you were mistaken. You ought to have used R, not L.'
     (*Hindsight*)

Indeed, Angie herself may appropriately say at this later time, 'In hindsight I was mistaken. As I now know, I ought to have used R and not L.' Intuitively, she thereby expresses disagreement with her earlier deliberative statement. But according to our theory, Connie and Angie know that the belief Angie earlier expressed (that *she ought relative to her information to use L rather than R*) was true, so these hindsight claims don't express disagreement in belief. Given that the theory also doesn't predict that these claims express any preference, as we're assuming, these disagreement intuitions are unaccommodated.

The problem can also be observed for agreement, from a variation on the retrospective context:

Hindsight Agreement: Freddie is a detective who investigates the revolvers after Angie has miraculously survived her injury from using L, discovering that use of R would have been fatal. Freddie is misinformed on two counts: he was told that L was loaded with a blank so that Angie survived her ordeal unharmed, and also that Sadie lied to Angie that L held the three rounds and R only held one. He therefore believes that Angie was badly confused about her own information when she said that she ought to use L and not R.

In this context, Freddie can appropriately say in hindsight,

F: 'Angie was right; she ought to have used L, not R. Though not for the reason she thought!' (*Hindsight Agreement*)

Here Freddie seems to have agreed with Angie's statement. But according to our theory he must believe that the proposition she asserted (*she ought relative to her information to use L and not R*) is false, so this can't be agreement in belief. If our theory predicts that he also fails to express any preference, then this agreement intuition is also unaccommodated.

The assumption that normative speech doesn't express preferences in contexts of indirect interest should be reconsidered. Preferences might be expressed in some such contexts even if our previous explanation doesn't apply. Indeed, the hindsight claims made by Connie, Angie, and Freddie do plausibly express preferences. Regardless of their conversational ends, all three can be presumed to prefer that Angie survived unharmed. Since these hindsight claims are relativized to the fullest information available to the speaker, they concern what was optimal from the speaker's present point of view for achieving an end she prefers. Connie's and Angie's hindsight claims will therefore express the preference that Angie used R rather than L, just like Bertie's advice, which is inconsistent with the preference expressed by Angie's original claim, while Freddie will express the same preference as Angie.

This solution isn't sufficiently general, however, because preference for the salient end is contingent; for example, Sadie can also appropriately disagree in hindsight with Angie. As she is dragged off in handcuffs she might say, 'You were wrong. You ought to have used R, not L', perhaps gloating over how she manipulated Angie into harming herself. On our theory this can't be disagreement in belief (as for the previous cases of hindsight), but since Sadie transparently prefers that Angie didn't survive unharmed, her statement also doesn't indicate she prefers that Angie used R (if anything, it indicates the contrary preference). This case of alienated hindsight therefore still resists both *Inconsistent Preference* and the disjunctive principle. Additionally, Connie's and Sadie's hindsight claims seem to express the same kind of disagreement with Angie's deliberative claim, which suggests this isn't the right solution also for the cases where the speaker is known to prefer the salient end.

In general terms, pragmatic expression of preferences seems to depend on end-relational claims being relativized both to an end the speaker prefers and to the fullest information available to the speaker, but intuitively normative disagreements and agreements arise between speakers with different preferences and information.

8.5. Attitudes with Conditional Content

If some intuitive cases of normative disagreement can't be explained as disagreements in either belief or attitude this poses a problem for any theory. The prospects for a solution appealing entirely to inconsistent beliefs look hopeless, as we've seen. But expressivists offer a way to account for these problematic cases as disagreements in attitude.

Allan Gibbard proposes that the relevant attitudes aren't directed toward options simpliciter (e.g., that Angie uses R and not L) but toward *conditionals*, or options under particular conditions.[30] A normative utterance of '*s* ought to φ' expresses the speaker's attitude toward φ-ing *on the condition of being in s's situation* (somehow), or *of being s herself*; that is, toward the proposition expressed by 'I φ if I am *s*.' Sadie's disagreement with Angie might then be accounted for in the following way: Sadie's hindsight statement that Angie ought to have used R and not L expresses her attitude toward using R and not L if she herself were Angie/in Angie's situation *C*. Angie's deliberative statement that she ought to use L and not R expresses the same attitude toward using L and not R if in *C*.

This approach derives some intuitive appeal from its similarity to the following kind of exchange, which is naturally interpreted as a case of disagreement:

A: 'If *I* were *s*, I'd φ.'

B: 'Well if *I* were *s*, I'd ψ.'

It might also seem easily extended to identify disagreements or agreements in attitude expressed in the contexts *Advice, Postmortem,* and *Hindsight,* which would support some version of the simpler principle *Inconsistent Preference* and suggest that expressivism offers a simpler, better account of normative disagreement than any descriptivist semantics. But this expressivist strategy encounters some serious problems, and we'll see that the quasi-expressivist solution suggested by the end-relational theory is superior.

This strategy requires a different kind of attitude, as *preferences* toward conditionals generate the wrong results. Connie's postmortem claim that Angie ought to have used L can't express the preference that if she were in Angie's situation she uses L, for example, since she knows that using L is worst relative to her preferred end of surviving unharmed.[31] Gibbard therefore appeals instead to attitudes of *planning* or intention, which seems to evade this problem. Connie's utterance more plausibly expresses her plan to use L and not R if in Angie's situation. Since plans are designed to be efficacious and implementable

---

[30] Gibbard 2003: 69.

[31] It doesn't help to say that the relevant preference is that if she were in a situation *subjectively like* Angie's then she uses L rather than R, since Angie is in just such a situation and Connie prefers that she would use R in it.

in the salient situation, Connie can only make plans for what to do if in Angie's situation that would make sense to her if she was indeed in Angie's situation—including being limited to Angie's lesser information. I'll temporarily switch to talking about plans, though we'll see that this introduces new problems.

Another question concerns how to understand the idea of the speaker's "*being s*". Taken literally, worries arise about the coherence of this condition. Isn't (e.g.) Sadie's being Angie a metaphysical impossibility? In such a counterfactual why wouldn't Sadie do exactly the same thing as Angie—since she would now simply be Angie? These problems can be avoided by understanding the strategy in terms of *being in s's situation*: there is nothing absurd about Sadie's contemplating herself being "in Angie's shoes". But this move problematizes the claim of inconsistency in speakers' attitudes. One perhaps minor problem is that different speakers' uses of 'I' refer to different people. The propositional content of Sadie's thought, *I use R and not L, if I am in C*, would therefore seem to be that *Sadie* uses L and not R if *Sadie* is in C. But Angie expresses no attitude toward that proposition, and so we are some distance from *Inconsistent Preference*.

Accordingly, Gibbard doesn't analyze disagreement in attitude by appeal to logically inconsistent contents, and rather tries to motivate an intuition that some other kind of incompatibility can arise between different subjects' plans. While it is unclear whether there is any such intuitive notion, I won't place weight on these controversial issues here. One way of trying to identify inconsistent contents is by appeal to *de se* propositions, such that every person who thinks, 'If I am in C, I φ' entertains the same proposition. While *de se* propositions are controversial, I'll assume them here for the sake of argument.

A different issue about inconsistency is fatal for this strategy, however. Being "in *s*'s situation" needs clarification in two particular respects. Does it imply *having s's preference for ends*? I'll assume it does, as necessary for accommodating Sadie's disagreement in plan with Angie.[32] More importantly, does being in *s*'s situation imply *having only s's information*? To be able to account for all cases of normative disagreement as consisting in an expressed disagreement in plan, being "in *s*'s situation" must sometimes involve being in *s*'s epistemic or subjective situation, and sometimes involve being in *s*'s objective situation but with different information. Connie's postmortem statement that Angie ought to have used L and not R, for example, must express the plan to use L and not R if in *C with the same information as Angie*. But Bertie's advice that Angie ought to use R and not L must instead express the plan to use R and not L if in *C but with his own fuller information*; similarly with hindsight claims.

This scuttles any hope of explaining problematic cases of disagreement by appeal to attitudes toward inconsistent conditionals, since what I do *if I have*

---

[32] This poses a problem for fundamental disagreement; see note 34 below.

information i₁ isn't logically related to what I do *if I have information i₂*. While this may have some welcome implications (e.g., that Connie's hindsight judgment that Angie ought to have used R doesn't disagree with Connie's postmortem judgment that Angie ought to have used L), it also yields results incompatible with intuitions about some basic cases of normative disagreement.

In particular, it implies that better informed advisers don't disagree with the agents they advise; for example, Bertie doesn't disagree with Angie. Bertie must express the plan to use R, *if in Angie's situation but with his own fuller information i₍₊₎*. But Angie can't have expressed the conflicting plan to use L in that very situation. Rather she must have expressed the plan to use L *in her own actual epistemic situation with information i₍₋₎*. The contents of these plans are logically consistent. Indeed, these plans couldn't be incompatible in any plausible sense, since a prudentially virtuous agent could and arguably should have both plans simultaneously. (This same problem afflicts cases of hindsight disagreement, as between Connie and Angie.) But Bertie's disagreement with Angie was the basic case that motivated abandoning *Inconsistent Belief* for some version of *Inconsistent Preference* in the first place. So even on its own terms, the appeal to attitudes with conditional content fails to accommodate intuitions of disagreement.[33,34]

8.6. Conditionals with Attitudinal Content

The cases still lacking any viable solution involve hindsight, or better-informed disagreement in a context of indirect interest, especially when the speaker doesn't prefer the end (e.g., if Sadie says 'Angie ought to have used R'). Normative claims in these contexts don't plausibly express actual preferences or similar attitudes, either toward simple or conditional contents. The end-relational theory predicts this, but it also predicts a subtly different kind of conditional attitude solution: that these normative claims pragmatically indicate *conditionals with attitudinal content*.

Since our theory predicts that somebody who in a context of direct interest asserts *ought(p)*—relativized to her preferred end *e* and present information—will express the preference that *p*, it therefore also predicts that anybody who

---

[33] Gibbard indeed maintains (in conversation) that there is no genuine normative disagreement from unequal information, dismissing these intuitions as mistaken. He distinguishes between the 'ought' of rationality and the 'ought' of advisability (see also Ridge 2014); however, we've also observed the need for multiple 'oughts' of advisability.

[34] "Hypothetical imperatives" present a similar problem. Suppose Sadie says, 'In order to survive you ought to use R.' Gibbard's analysis (confirmed in conversation) appeals to a plan conditional on having the goal of surviving; i.e., *I use R if I am in Angie's situation with the goal of survival*. But this isn't compatible with a Gibbardian analysis of categorical claims. Suppose Sadie continues, 'But morally, you ought to use L…and die!', which must express the plan *I use L (and die) if I am in Angie's situation*. These plans are incompatible, but Sadie wouldn't seem to have contradicted herself.

asserts *ought(p)* relativized just to her present information will pragmatically indicate the following conditional: *if her preferred end were e then she would prefer that p*. This is a counterfactual anchored in the normative belief she expressed, concerning only world-states where she still has that same belief and information.[35] So Sadie's hindsight statement will pragmatically indicate that if she were to share the preference that Angie survived unharmed then she would prefer that Angie used R. The same will be true of hindsight statements where the end is preferred, like Connie's, Angie's, and Freddie's (although strictly these aren't "counterfactual"). I'll call these *hypothetical preferences*, in respect of their kinship to "hypothetical imperatives", and to distinguish them from the kind of "conditional attitudes" discussed above.

Might some intuitions about normative disagreement be responsive to pragmatic expression of hypothetical preferences? A first test for this hypothesis is to see whether directly asserting the suggested information has the same effect. Suppose the conversation had gone like this:

> ANGIE: 'I prefer to use L.'
>
> SADIE: 'If I were to prefer your ends, I would prefer that you use R.'

It seems natural to say that Sadie would thereby have expressed some kind of disagreement with Angie. This is also very close to the colloquial vehicle for normative disagreement, 'If I were you I'd φ.' Since 'I would φ' is tantamount to a description of a counterfactual preference, these utterances draw very close given that 'If I were you...' can be read as *if I were in your objective situation with your ends*. Whereas expressivists invoke this turn of speech to support their appeal to attitudes with conditional content, strictly here the conditional takes wide scope over the attitude.[36]

Appeal to hypothetical preferences avoids the problems observed for the expressivist's appeal to attitudes with conditional contents. First, since these conditional preferences have simple and unconditionalized contents, disagreeing claims relativized to different information (like Angie's and Sadie's, but also Bertie's advice, Connie's hindsight, etc.) thereby express hypothetical attitudes toward logically inconsistent contents (e.g., that *A uses L and not R*, and that *A uses R and not L*), so no unexplained kind of inconsistency is required. Second,

---

[35] Familiar worries about counterfactuals might be raised, e.g., that in the closest possibilities the speaker might be "irrational", so her preference for *e* isn't transmitted to *p*. The qualification 'if rational' is therefore suggested, though I believe unnecessary; for discussion see Finlay 2008a, 2009c.

[36] This expression may seem to suggest plans rather than preferences, but these "plans" can be identified with preferences *for what I do*. This isn't to propose a general analysis of plans: arguably not every plan entails a preference, but plans without preferences don't plausibly ground normative judgments. Having a general plan to call heads on coin tosses doesn't entail believing one *ought* to call heads; some plans exist to help us make decisions when reasons weigh equally. (Gibbard tells me he now favors analysis by preferences, for such reasons.)

the relevant attitudes can be identified simply as *preferences* about the same proposition rather than as plans or intentions, so we don't have to countenance *de se* propositions or make sense of (e.g.) Sadie's being Angie.

This also avoids a number of baroque consequences of Gibbard's approach that I didn't canvas above. Sense can be made of claims that *s ought to φ* involving remote circumstances (e.g., 'Caesar ought not to have crossed the Rubicon') without saying bizarrely that the speaker must actually have contingency plans for being in those circumstances (e.g., deliberating whether to cross the Rubicon with your legions to seize Rome). Similarly, sense can be made of a nonagential 'ought' claim like 'Trees ought to have deep roots' without saying either that it expresses the speaker's plan about what kind of roots to have if she were a tree, or (noncompositionally) that it expresses the plan of some unmentioned agent like a gardener or designer of trees. There isn't anything similarly bizarre about indicating that if you were to prefer the salient end (e.g., that the Roman Republic was preserved, that trees grow healthy and strong) then you would prefer that *p* (e.g., that Caesar didn't cross the Rubicon, that trees have strong roots).

It may seem counterintuitive that an actual disagreement could be explained by merely hypothetical attitudes. This may also seem to predict an absurd proliferation of normative disagreements. Since there are indefinitely many true counterfactuals about what somebody would prefer under some condition or other, if hypothetically preferring *p* under one set of conditions C_1 were sufficient for disagreeing with somebody who hypothetically prefers *not-p* under different conditions C_2, wouldn't everybody at every moment both agree and disagree with every possible normative claim?

A first response is that these hypothetical preferences and disagreements are grounded in expressed actual beliefs, although those beliefs may be logically consistent. They might rather be described as disagreements in actual dispositions, grounded in beliefs. But another necessary condition for disagreement can be adduced. Intuitively, disagreement with an attitude requires some kind of robustness, such that a disagreeing attitude *resists* the other in some way.[37] These preferences differ in robustness, according to the completeness of the information on which they're based. Angie's preference to use L is provisional on no fuller information being available, for example, so it yields without resistance to Bertie's preference based on fuller information, which "trumps" hers and makes it moot.

Our pragmatic principles therefore predict that disagreement in hypothetical preference will be asymmetrical on this basis, *or Robust Inconsistent Hypothetical Preference*:

---

[37] Stevenson suggests a similar (but not identical) condition: "at least one of [the disagreeing parties] has a motive for altering or calling into question the attitude of the other" (1944: 3–4).

RIHP: B's assertion that p normatively disagrees (agrees) with A's
assertion that q if B thereby indicates that if he were to prefer
e he would on the basis of his information i_B have a preference
inconsistent with (equivalent to) the preference A thereby
indicates she would have on the basis of her information i_A if she
were to prefer e, and $i_B \geq i_A$.

Although this may seem an untidy complication, it's actually a serendipitous
result that accommodates ordinary intuitions. I've been describing normative
disagreements asymmetrically, because many are intuitively asymmetrical: Bertie
intuitively disagrees with Angie, for example, but Angie doesn't intuitively disagree with Bertie. This has been observed but not explained by other writers,[38]
and it poses a significant difficulty for any theory proposing to explain normative disagreement by *Inconsistent Belief*, which implies symmetry.[39]

A satisfactory theory must also predict the *correct* asymmetries, of course,
but the end-relational theory seems to do well here: Bertie's advice disagrees
with Angie's deliberative claim, but not vice versa; Connie's hindsight claim disagrees with Angie's claim but not vice versa, and agrees with Bertie's advice and
vice versa. Freddie's hindsight claim agrees with Angie's claim and disagrees
with Connie's (hindsight) and Bertie's (advice) claims, but not vice versa.[40]
These results support our pragmatic account of normative disagreement, and
also undermine the rival, uncharitable hypothesis that intuitions of disagreement are systematically blind to the information-relativity of normative claims.

RIHP is only formulated as a sufficient condition for normative disagreement,
however, and at least two obstacles prevent it from being also a necessary condition and thereby providing a general theory: *postmortem claims* and *negations*
(not to mention fundamental disagreements just yet). The former consists in normative claims in contexts of indirect interest that are relativized to information
that the speaker considers inferior to her own (whether incomplete or false); for
example Connie's postmortem claim that Angie ought to have used L, and Sadie's
pseudo-advisory claim that Angie ought to use L. These won't express hypothetical preferences as defined, since in the nearest possibilities where the speaker prefers the end they still won't be relativized to the speaker's full information.

Our theory easily accommodates the agreement expressed by these claims as
agreement in belief, however, since these cases concern the same end-relational
proposition Angie asserted. This suggests a disjunctive view that generates

---

[38] Dietz 2008, Ross & Schroeder 2013.

[39] An alternative hypothesis is that disagreement requires *responding* to the other claim. So
Bertie disagrees with Angie because Bertie is responding to Angie's claim, but not vice versa.
But cases are easily found where an earlier claim intuitively disagrees with a later one; see also
Cappelen & Hawthorne 2009, Richard 2011.

[40] It seems less obvious that Angie doesn't agree with Freddie, but this may be explained by
the lesser divergence from truth in this case (i.e., between *A agrees with F, A would agree with F*)
than in others (i.e., between *A disagrees with B, A would agree with B*).

some intuitive predictions; for example, that Connie's postmortem claim that Angie ought to have used L doesn't disagree with Bertie's advice or with her own hindsight claim that Angie ought to have used R, and vice versa.

Rather than simply giving a disjunctive theory, we can here distinguish different kinds of normative disagreement. *Instrumental* disagreement consists in a conflict of hypothetical preferences; it is disagreement over what to do to achieve a particular end. *Rational* disagreement consists rather in inconsistency in end-relational belief. But this rational disagreement also implies inconsistency in a different kind of counterfactual preferences, which we can call disagreement in *doubly-hypothetical preferences*: if the speaker were to prefer that *e and only had information i*, then on the basis of her belief she would prefer that *p*. For example, Connie's postmortem claim that Angie ought to have used L pragmatically indicates that if Connie were to prefer that Angie survived unharmed and only had Angie's information, then she would prefer that Angie had used L. Rational disagreements can therefore also be glossed as concerning what to do to achieve a certain end with certain information.

Asserting a normative sentence can therefore express multiple attitudes. In saying 'I ought to use L', Angie expresses (i) an end-relational belief, (ii) an actual preference to use L, (iii) a hypothetical preference to use L on the (as it happens, actual) condition that she prefers to survive unharmed, and (iv) a doubly-hypothetical preference to use L on the (actual) conditions that she prefers to survive unharmed and only has information *i*. This implies that two people may also stand in multiple relations of normative agreement or disagreement at the same time, which seems another serendipitous result: intuitively, while Bertie instrumentally disagrees with Angie (in hypothetical preference), they rationally agree (in belief and doubly-hypothetical preference). He only *expresses* his instrumental disagreement, since this is the felicitous thing to do in his context of direct interest. With relevantly the same information in a context of *indirect* interest, Connie can rather felicitously express either her rational agreement (postmortem) or her instrumental disagreement (hindsight). Intuitions of disagreement *simpliciter* will be sensitive to whatever is the most salient kind of disagreement expressed in the context.

The second recalcitrant piece of data concerns negations, which pose a well-known problem for expressivism. Recall Freddie, whose forensic investigations revealed that the next use of R would have been fatal, and suppose now that he is informed that the round in L wasn't a blank, causing him to believe that Angie couldn't possibly have survived. He may then say, in hindsight:

F: 'It was not the case that Angie ought to have used L. But not because she ought to have used R; she simply had no good options.' (*Hindsight Negation*)

Freddie seems to disagree with Angie, but we don't yet have an explanation for this. It can't be a rational disagreement (in belief), because Freddie is concerned with different information. But neither does he express an inconsistent hypothetical preference, as if he said instead, 'Angie ought not to have used L', since *not ought(p)* doesn't entail *ought(not-p)*. Negative claims don't seem to express preferences at all, in which case they couldn't express disagreement in preference.

However, our theory does predict that Freddie's utterance indicates something about his preferences: that he *doesn't* hypothetically prefer that Angie used L and not R.[41] He pragmatically indicates that on the basis of his belief if he were to prefer that Angie survived unharmed, he wouldn't prefer that she used L.[42] While this doesn't identify attitudes toward inconsistent contents, it does provide a different kind of inconsistency of attitudes: preferring *p* and not preferring *p* are logically inconsistent states of mind (in a broad sense which also subsumes preferences toward inconsistent contents).

Might negations of normative claims express disagreement by virtue of this attenuated kind of "inconsistent preferences"? This proposal runs straight into the expressivist's problem with negation. If Freddie's saying, 'It wasn't the case that Angie ought to have used L' expresses merely his lack of preference for Angie's using L, how can we explain the difference with Debbie's saying, 'I don't know whether you ought to use L', for example? Or if believing *not ought(p)* is merely lacking the preference that *p*, what distinguishes it from not believing *ought(p)*?[43] As we predict, Debbie also indicates she has no preference about Angie's using L rather than R, but unlike Freddie she doesn't intuitively disagree with Angie. Lacking an attitude doesn't in general seem to be a way of disagreeing with the attitude.

But unlike expressivism, our theory identifies a significant difference between Debbie and Freddie. Whereas Debbie's lack of preference is due to lacking any relevant belief about whether Angie ought to use L, Freddie's lack

---

[41] Something stronger can be said in Freddie's case: that he is (hypothetically) *indifferent* about whether Angie uses L rather than R. Since indifference is arguably an actual preference state, it may seem a more promising basis for disagreement than mere lack of preference. This isn't sufficiently general as an account of believing *not ought(p)*, however, since one may also do so on the basis of believing *ought(not-p)*, which rather involves hypothetically preferring *not-p*.

[42] What prevents Freddie from having a further desire that would cause him to prefer that A used L in the nearest possibilities? (Suppose the evidence links Sadie to L, but not to R; Freddie's desire for justice may then lead him to prefer that A used L.) By Chapter 6, the counterfactual condition must specify a *contextually preferred conjunctive end*, so if his claim is relativized entirely to A's ends his own desires will be irrelevant (though he could instead talk about what A ought to have done relative to his own preferences).

[43] E.g., Unwin 1999, 2001, Dreier 2006. Some expressivists suggest that believing *ought(p)* and believing *not ought(p)* involve two different kinds of attitude, which begs an explanation for their inconsistency. Schroeder (2008a, 2008b) argues that pure expressivism can only solve the problem with a "biforcated attitude semantics", on which all normative claims express one kind of attitude ("being for") toward having some other attitude—which he demonstrates requires radical revisions to naive theories of many different concepts and words.

of preference is grounded in his belief that it isn't the case that Angie ought to have used L.[44] The difference between *believing not ought(p)* and *not believing ought(p)* is therefore that whereas in one case the lack of preference results from *having* a relevant normative belief, in the other it results from *lacking* a relevant normative belief.

An explanation why expressing a lack of attitude by negation can intuitively express normative disagreement then follows from our previous explanation of why inconsistency in merely hypothetical preferences can be sufficient for actual disagreement. As with those hypothetical preferences, Freddie's hypothetical lack of preference is grounded in and expressed by an actual normative belief, unlike Debbie's. (Perhaps these could even be labeled "disagreements in belief" in an attenuated sense.) The end-relational theory therefore provides a quasi-expressivist solution to the negation problem that isn't available to (pure) expressivism itself.

The end-relational theory supports a pragmatic, quasi-expressivist account of normative disagreement that accommodates intuitions across a wide range of different contexts involving differing information. Whereas these disagreements are alleged to be incompatible with relational semantics, this account actually solves general puzzles about normative disagreement that confound other theories. This leaves two remaining tasks: to examine contexts of fundamental disagreement involving different ends, and to address a challenge about how we report and evaluate normative claims.

8.7. The Pragmatics of Disagreement from Different Ends

Some of the most important normative disagreements are apparently fundamental (particularly in moral speech or thought), involving a conflict in basic ends. Relational theories are accused of making such disagreements impossible, but as this objection has assumed some version of *Inconsistent Belief* it no longer looks so formidable. Can our quasi-expressivist solution to the disagreement problem from information-relativity be extended to the more famous problem from end-relativity? The prospects for explaining fundamental disagreement in terms of inconsistent preferences look promising, since it's just this kind of disagreement that originally inspires the idea of disagreement in attitude, and we've already seen how categorical and final uses of end-relational language pragmatically express preferences.

Many disagreements that appear fundamental may not be so at all. Attempts have been made to accommodate the absolutist character of moral

---

[44] Although Debbie believes it isn't the case that A ought *relative to D's information* to use L, in her context of lesser information this isn't relevant, and the robustness condition explains why it doesn't intuitively disagree with A's claim.

disagreement in a way compatible with *Inconsistent Belief* by analyzing moral claims as all relativized to the same thing, a common end (standard, set of norms, etc.). If two speakers both have in mind a description such as *the end anyone would prefer in C if fully informed*, then they may disagree in normative belief despite having entirely different ideas about the identity of this end, in which case at least one of them must be factually mistaken.

Some philosophers maintain that moral speech and thought as such presupposes that agents' attitudes would converge under some such ideal conditions.[45] Others propose that moral claims might be unified as a class by relativization to a description involving a more basic normative property; for example, the "moral", "rational", or "most important" end.[46] In this case no moral disagreements would really be "fundamental" by our definition, but would be a case of rational disagreement in belief. This strategy is broadly compatible with our semantics, and offers a simple solution to the problem of moral disagreement.

However, it has radical commitments that are widely found implausible: psychologically, that there is a single property of ends which is of shared, basic concern to every unalienated moral agent (counterintuitively equating the illocutionary force of moral prescription with recommendation). While moral disagreements may indeed be naturally described as concerning what is "moral" or "most important" ("rational" is more controversial), this strategy requires an absolutist analysis of these as referring to a common property, rather than simply (e.g.) a way of expressing attitudes. I find these metaphysical claims also implausibly radical, though others disagree and we'll discuss these other normative notions further in the final chapter.

Even setting these worries aside, moral absolutism may still fail to account for all apparently fundamental disagreement: if morality is unified by concern for a common property then it is surely possible to debate whether to act morally, which is naturally identified as normative disagreement over whether one ought (all things considered) to do what one morally ought to do. Here I'll demonstrate that our theory explains (genuine) fundamental disagreements, with only conservative metaphysical and psychological resources.

The previous section identified two different kinds of normative disagreement predicted by our theory: rational disagreement in belief (and in doubly-hypothetical preference), and instrumental disagreement in hypothetical preference. Evidently, fundamental disagreements can't be subsumed under either category on the end-relational theory, but this isn't a problem since they apparently involve a distinct kind of disagreement. The question isn't how to apply the preceding pragmatic account to these cases, but how to extend it.

---

[45] E.g., Smith 1994.
[46] E.g., FitzPatrick 2008, Olson 2011: 75.

As before I'll begin with contexts of direct interest where each speaker is actively aiming at the salient end; the case of *Frank Feller* provides a handy illustration. Unlike contexts of advice, here these will be two different, incompatible ends. By our theory, when Dora says, 'You ought to stop', she expresses her preference both for the omitted end (that the neighbor's house is preserved), and also thereby that Frank stops. When Frank responds, 'I ought to continue', he likewise expresses his preference both for the omitted end (that he takes revenge) and also thereby that he continues. So by their categorical uses of end-relational language, Dora expresses the preference that Frank stops while Frank expresses the preference that he continues; here we have attitudes toward inconsistent contents, and a disagreement in preference.[47]

This is an expressed disagreement in *actual* rather than hypothetical preferences, which might be called *outright* normative disagreement, by contrast with instrumental disagreement.[48] I'll defend the simplest hypothesis that all fundamental disagreements are outright, giving us three basic kinds of normative disagreement. Not all outright disagreements are fundamental, however: Angie (*Deliberation*) and Bertie (*Advice*) express not only hypothetical preferences but also actual preferences, for example, so Bertie disagrees with Angie not only instrumentally (about what to do to survive), but also outright (about what to do). This disagreement isn't fundamental, since these conflicting preferences are derived from a shared intrinsic preference for the same end.

Contexts of indirect interest may seem to pose a greater challenge, since here the use of normative language doesn't always express actual preferences. But this isn't really a problem, because neither do normative claims relativized to different ends always intuitively agree or disagree with each other. Suppose A says disinterestedly, 'In order to preserve his neighbor's house, Frank ought to stop', while B says disinterestedly (perhaps in a separate conversation), 'In order to take his revenge, Frank ought to continue'; here there's no disagreement. Given the definition of fundamental disagreements as involving a basic conflict in preferred ends, only contexts where actual preferences are expressed will be relevant.

The moral disagreements expressed by an amoralist might be thought a counterexample. But by our theory, either he speaks insincerely and expresses preferences he doesn't actually have, in which case he expresses only feigned outright disagreement—or else his amoralism is transparent, in which case he

---

[47] As categorical utterances can also express *prescriptions*, we might also appeal to a "disagreement in prescription". Ridge (2014) gives this the central role in his expressivist account, whereas our theory gives it a pragmatic basis as applying only to a narrow class of disagreements (e.g., strictly speaking only Dora prescribes in this exchange).

[48] To express an "actual preference" as intended here is to indicate one actually has it. One may therefore express an "actual preference" one doesn't actually have, in cases of insincerity.

expresses only a hypothetical preference (that *if he shared the intrinsic preferences of the salient moral community, then* he'd prefer that *p*), and thereby expresses instrumental but not fundamental disagreement with others' moral claims. A virtue of this result is that it accounts for the ambiguity of the question about whether amoralists can morally disagree.

Our theory doesn't only accommodate the existence of fundamental disagreement, but is also able to explain otherwise puzzling facts about its extension, by virtue of the natural asymmetry of disagreements in preference. We've already observed one case of outright disagreement that is asymmetrical: Bertie (*Advice*) disagrees outright with Angie (*Deliberation*), but because Angie's preference is disposed to evaporate in the face of Bertie's claim based on fuller information, it fails the robustness condition, so Angie doesn't disagree outright with Bertie. In the case of fundamental disagreements, the analogous asymmetry is that speakers prefer some *ends* over others.[49] But unlike the asymmetry of information, here the "quality" of an end will differ from speaker to speaker, so our theory predicts less asymmetry in fundamental disagreements than in instrumental disagreements: Dora and Frank each prefers her or his own end, for example, so their disagreement in preference is symmetrical. But other cases will be asymmetrical, where the second speaker makes salient an end that the first speaker is also disposed to prefer.

This provides a solution to a difficult puzzle for any theory of moral disagreement, which I'll call *Thomson's Observation*. Judy Thomson holds the radically anticontextualist view that 'ought' has only one, absolutist normative meaning, and therefore that every claim about what an agent ought to do is a moral claim.[50] So if Alfred is playing chess and Smith says, 'Alfred ought to move his queen', then Smith implies that if Alfred does anything else his action is morally wrong. This rejects the orthodox view that the moral sense of 'ought' is only one of many, including prudential and instrumental senses, and those of institutions like legal systems, etiquette, and games.

In support of this bold view, she makes a point philosophers have widely overlooked: that *any* normative statement about what an agent ought to do can become an appropriate target of moral disagreement. Suppose Jones knows that a villain will blow up Chicago unless Alfred moves his bishop rather than his queen; then it seems Jones can appropriately disagree with Smith's claim: 'No, you're wrong. Alfred ought to move his bishop.' This point holds even for explicit "hypothetical imperatives", as Thomson insists: even if Smith had said, 'If Alfred wants to win the game, he ought to move his queen', Jones can disagree,

---

[49] Some cases will involve both kinds of asymmetry, of course; I won't explore this complication here.

[50] Thomson 2008.

'No, even if he wants to win the game he still ought to move his bishop.'[51] Jones thereby seems to express moral disagreement with Smith's claim, but what they assert is only inconsistent if Smith's claim itself has moral content. Thomson concludes that every statement about what an agent ought to do is moral.

Thomson's Observation seems importantly right, but it backfires here as an argument for absolutism. On one hand, her absolutist diagnosis of these disagreements is untenable. Let's grant for the sake of argument the surprising claim that ordinary 'ought' claims about chess moves and etiquette are moral. But consider an instrumental claim where the speaker disprefers the salient end; for example, 'The terrorists ought to have attacked the Mall of America', which we interpret as implicitly relativized to the end (e.g.) of inflicting maximum damage on the United States. Thomson is correct that somebody can respond by saying 'No, that's false! They ought not to have attacked the United States at all!', thereby expressing moral disagreement.[52] But the explanation of this can't be that the first speaker was making a moral claim, which would entail he was assuming that the terrorists were morally obliged to inflict damage on the United States. (This problem similarly stymies any attempt by contextualists to explain away all apparently moral or fundamental disagreement as involving common relativization to [e.g.] the "most important" end, as it would require interpreting *every* normative claim in this way, implausibly.)

On the other hand, the objection against the end-relational theory fails, because it tacitly depends on *Inconsistent Belief*, which we've already rejected. Thomson's Observation is plausibly explained instead by our quasi-expressivist account of disagreement in preference. Jones expresses a (moral) preference that is inconsistent with the preference that Smith expresses, and thereby an outright, moral disagreement. But Smith's claim needn't be taken to have any moral content, as this disagreement seems asymmetrical: Smith doesn't express outright, moral disagreement with Jones's claim (assuming he's a decent fellow who prefers the welfare of Chicagoans to Arthur's winning at chess). Jones's preference trumps his, because normative claims about chess strategy aren't generally intended to express moral stances, and Smith will immediately adopt Jones's preference when that end is made salient.

While it might be objected that this misdescribes the fact that Smith *wouldn't* disagree if he knew what Jones knows, consider the terrorist case. Our theory predicts that the speaker doesn't express an actual preference that the terrorists

---

[51] It seems not to apply to 'In order that...' claims, however, which suggests that this response turns on willfully misinterpreting 'If *s* wants...' as an ordinary rather than an instrumental conditional.

[52] The appropriateness may be disputed, as the first speaker may reasonably resist by making the qualifier explicit (as discussed in Chapter 5). But appropriate or not, the second speaker might stick to her guns like Thomson: 'No, even if they *want* to harm the United States, still they oughtn't attack innocent people!', and would still intuitively be expressing normative disagreement with the first speaker's statement.

attacked the Mall of America, but only the hypothetical preference that *if* he preferred the terrorists' ends, then he'd prefer that they did. To express fundamental moral disagreement with this is to express an actual preference inconsistent with that hypothetical preference, which will be asymmetric because the instrumental claim didn't express an actual preference at all. Our theory explains Thomson's Observation without the absurd consequences of the absolutist interpretation.

While this discussion has barely scratched the surface of a complicated problem, we've seen that the end-relational theory supports a pragmatic solution for both information- and end-relativity that accommodates ordinary intuitions about disagreement, including some intuitions that are anomalous on rival expressivist and absolutist theories despite their alleged superiority.

8.8. Speech Reports and Truth Evaluations

A remaining objection to this quasi-expressivist account as an analysis of actual disagreement arises from speech or thought *about* normative speech or thought, or how it's reported and evaluated.[53] To illustrate, in *Two-Gun Roulette* it seems Bertie could appropriately say (e.g., to another captive, before he can advise Angie),

> B: 'Angie said/believes that she ought to use L. But that's false. She ought to use R and not L.'

Our account explains how his third sentence expresses (instrumental and outright, but not rational) disagreement with Angie's utterance, but it doesn't obviously accommodate his first two sentences.

To illustrate the problem for fundamental disagreement, suppose Dora says,

> D: 'Frank said/believes that he ought to continue felling the tree. But that's false. He ought to respect his neighbor's property.'

We have an explanation for how the third sentence expresses (this time fundamental) normative disagreement with Frank, but the first two sentences again pose a problem. As usual I'll focus primarily on speech reports.

Our theory apparently predicts that Bertie's first sentence reports that Angie asserted that *in order to survive unharmed she ought relative to her information to use L*, since that's the propositional content we've assigned to her utterance. But then Bertie's second, evaluating sentence would be transparently false and unjustified. Presumably his use of 'that' must refer to whichever proposition he's just referred to. (He could instead say simply, 'What she said/believes is

---

[53] E.g., Weatherson 2008, Schroeder 2009b.

false', and couldn't say, 'She *knows* she ought to use L.') But that proposition, which is relativized to Angie's information, plainly isn't false.

Suppose we tackle the problem from the opposite direction. In Bertie's context, the only obvious candidate for an end-relational proposition he can relevantly evaluate as false is roughly that *in order to escape unharmed Angie ought relative to Bertie's information to use L*. After all, that's the proposition we've interpreted his third sentence as rejecting. (This sentence is naturally read as expanding on the second.) But then his use of 'that' would suggest that this is also the proposition his first sentence reports Angie as asserting. Since Angie obviously didn't assert or believe that proposition, now it's the report that would be transparently false and unjustified. Partners in guilt are again plentiful, as similar problems arise for many other kinds of apparently rela-tivistic terms, but perhaps all guilty parties should be convicted alike in favor of truth-relativist, expressivist, or absolutist theories. I'll argue that our theory suggests a pragmatic solution, beginning with speech reports.

The conversational purpose of these speech or belief reports is evidently to share information about others' speech acts or mental states. By our theory, Angie asserted a proposition relativized both to an end and to some informa-tion. But Bertie doesn't say, 'Angie said that *in order to survive unharmed* she ought *given her information* to use L'; like the speaker herself he omits mention of end or information. This can't be explained merely by the fact that it was omitted in the speech being reported, since this is an indirect rather than a direct report; that is, Bertie doesn't say, 'Angie said, "I ought to use L."' When reporting speech indirectly, a reporter must use words that convey *in his context* what the speaker said in hers, which is of course why Bertie uses 'she' rather than 'I'. Suppose B hears A say on the phone from an unknown location, 'It's raining here'; to report this, he would say something like 'A said it's raining *where she is*.' Since the features of Angie's context that make her end and infor-mation salient don't obtain in Bertie's context, his ellipsis can't be licensed on the same basis, and requires a different explanation.[54]

That explanation isn't hard to find, however. By default, reporting a per-son's speech or thought makes her context or perspective salient instead. In reporting an epistemic modal statement or belief, for example (e.g., 'Angie said/believes she might survive if she uses L'), the default reading involves possibil-ity relative to the original speaker's information rather than the reporter's.[55] We've also seen that unrelativized normative claims would be interpreted by default as relativized to both the speaker's contextually preferred end and her

---

[54] In this case the end may be salient on the same basis, though not the information. But this doesn't hold in general; e.g., Sadie could also say simply, 'Angie said she ought to use L', or Frank could say, 'Dora said I ought to stop.'

[55] The parallel doesn't hold for indexicals like 'I' and 'she' because the context-relativity here is semantic rather than pragmatic.

available information (as simpliciter). So by our pragmatic principles, Bertie can be interpreted as reporting that Angie said, *of her preferred end e and her fullest available information i*, that in order that *e* and given *i* she ought to use L.

This is only half the story, however. By simpliciter use of 'ought' a speaker also pragmatically expresses a preference, as Angie expresses her preference to use L. By indicating that a reported utterance was simpliciter, the reporter also indicates that the speaker expressed that preference. By contrast, if Bertie were to report, 'Angie said/believes that *in order to survive* she ought *given her information* to use L', he wouldn't obviously indicate that this was her preferred end, or that she expressed the preference to use L. Additionally, since a simpliciter use could be reported with a more efficient sentence, the more verbose report rather tends to pragmatically indicate (by the maxim of manner) that the statement *wasn't* simpliciter or expressive of the speaker's preference. As this would be misleading, a nonrelativized report would often be not only permissible, but expected.

The same goes for information. Explicitly reporting the statement as "given her information" doesn't indicate that the speaker believed this the best available basis for a decision, as leaving it implicit would indicate, and therefore tends to indicate instead that she doesn't consider it best. Saying 'Angie knows she ought to use L, *given her information*' pragmatically suggests she is aware of or hopeful for a better basis for making her decision.[56]

Communicating a speaker's indication of preference will be essential for the reporter's conversational purposes in most contexts. While reporting the implicit ends explicitly *can* be felicitous if it's relevant exactly what end the speaker had in mind (especially if there are other indications it was a context of direct interest; e.g., it is common ground that Angie was deliberating),[57] it will be infelicitous if the reporter needs to indicate such a context or simpliciter use— and especially if the identity of the end isn't particularly relevant. We saw that in contexts of direct interest like Angie's (*Deliberation*) and Bertie's (*Advice*), what is of primary interest isn't the particular (end- and information-relative) proposition asserted, but what the speaker prefers on the basis of believing it to be most likely relative to whatever is the fullest available information, and given that whatever is the contextually most preferred end will obtain. This holds for most other contexts too; our usual interest in people's normative speech or thought essentially involves its implications for their preferences (actual or hypothetical) and dispositions; hence we found that intuitions of normative

---

[56] This may seem in tension with my claim that agents always prefer to act on the *fullest information available to them*, but that claim depends on the particular reading we stipulated.

[57] These seem to be the cases where we reverse the sentential order, e.g., 'Angie believes she ought to use L, in order to survive unharmed'. Putting the relativizer last allows the first clause to indicate simpliciter use.

disagreement are at least as sensitive to inconsistency in preference as to inconsistency in belief.

The primary purpose of normative speech or belief reports is commonly to indicate what the speaker or judge was disposed to do (recommend, approve, etc.) on the basis of her normative beliefs, in which case it needn't be particularly relevant what end she prefers: what is relevant is that she prefers that *p* on the basis of believing that whichever end she most prefers is most likely if *p*. (Recall also from Chapter 6 that in many contexts the speaker's exact ends or information are opaque, sometimes even to herself.) On our theory, most reports therefore aim to indicate the speaker's end-relational beliefs relative to her preferred ends (and fullest available information) whatever they might be, and thereby her dispositions.[58] For Bertie to make the relativization of Angie's statement explicit in his report would therefore be not merely misleading but counterproductive: by indicating that Angie's normative claim wasn't simpliciter he would convey the opposite of what he intends.

Reports therefore don't present any difficulty for our theory by themselves, but they still create the problem observed for evaluations, since (e.g.) the proposition Angie asserted is true. I'll now show that this pragmatics of normative speech and belief reports provides a solution.

We've seen that normative utterances and beliefs are generally of interest primarily on account of the preferences they express or support, whereas the particular propositions asserted or believed are only of secondary and derivative interest. So it better serves conversational purposes to respond to a normative claim by expressing agreement or disagreement with those preferences than by evaluating the truth of the propositions, as we observed for advisers' response to deliberators (e.g., Bertie's response to Angie). But to "evaluate" a claim just is to express agreement or disagreement with it, so our pragmatic principles therefore predict that the felicitous kind of evaluation of normative claims or beliefs is often to express disagreement in preference. Pragmatically, Bertie would be expected not to bother addressing the truth of the proposition we've interpreted Angie as asserting. When he says, 'That's false', we should expect him to be expressing his disagreement in preference, somehow.

The puzzle is therefore to explain why evaluators would use words like 'true', 'false', and 'knows' in responding to normative claims. Because of how these evaluations are linked to speech and belief reports demonstratively (e.g., 'That's false') and descriptively (e.g., 'What she said/believes is false'), this puzzle also extends to the use of propositional attitude verbs like 'said' and 'believes', and the individuation of normative claims and beliefs (what is it to have the "same" normative belief?). By our theory, uses of normative language communicate

---

[58] While my discussion here focuses on direct interest, analogous points hold (mutatis mutandis) for alienated contexts where the salient preferences aren't the speaker's, as in amoralism.

preferences pragmatically, but talk of what is "said" (as opposed to merely "implied") is a standard indicator of what is asserted, and what is "believed" contrasts with what is "desired".

One option is to follow the lead of expressivists, whose "quasi-realist" project interprets all this language in congenial ways: the "belief that p" is just whatever attitude would be expressed by declarative use of 'p', to "say that p" is just to express that attitude, to evaluate something as "true" or "false" is just to express an agreeing or disagreeing attitude, and to say that somebody "knows that p" involves both attributing him the "belief that p" in the previous sense and expressing an agreeing attitude.[59] When Bertie reports Angie's "belief" he would really be reporting her preference to use L, and when he evaluates it as "false", he would just be expressing his disagreement in preference. But this threatens to surrender the field to expressivism: if reports and evaluations of normative claims are really reports and evaluations of preferences rather than of asserted propositions, the advantages of descriptivism become less clear. Our theory suggests a different solution that is more conservative with respect to semantics, truth, and logic.

On the end-relational theory, declarative normative speech does assert descriptive propositions and express ordinary beliefs that are true or false in the ordinary correspondence way. Similarly, normative disagreement in preference is based on such beliefs. A speaker like Bertie isn't just expressing an inconsistent preference, but importantly, expressing it on the basis of a normative belief. So plausibly, the natural use of words like 'belief', 'said', 'knows', 'true', and 'false' in these reports and evaluations is due somehow to awareness that these sentences have descriptive contents and express real beliefs. When Bertie says, 'That's false', there is a salient proposition that Bertie relevantly rejects as false—that Angie ought to use L relative to *his* information—and it's on the basis of believing this false that he disagrees in preference. So perhaps when Bertie says, 'That's false', he's expressing his disagreement in preference *by* directly rejecting this other proposition, which is made relevant in his context by his fuller information.

One hypothesis, which Gunnar Björnsson and I previously defended, is that an evaluator might be able to respond felicitously by intentionally addressing a proposition related but distinct from the one the speaker asserted, by virtue of its greater relevance in the context.[60] But I now think this solution may be too cavalier about the role of the demonstrative 'that', or talk about what the

---

[59] Lennertz 2014 applies this kind of quasi-expressivist solution to parallel problems for contextualism about epistemic modals.

[60] E.g., the proposition the sentence would have asserted if used in the evaluator's context (Bjornsson & Finlay 2010). On one variation, 'that' refers to something subpropositional like *A ought to use L* (which approximates truth-relativism), or a linguistic string like 'A ought to use L.'

speaker "said" or "believed". The end-relational theory suggests alternatively that many evaluations could be expected to involve a benign kind of confusion.

If our analysis is correct, it wouldn't be surprising if an evaluator (like Bertie) were disposed to assume mistakenly that the speaker asserted the same proposition he rejects as false (so that Bertie and Angie express inconsistent beliefs). First, even competent speakers of a language needn't be fully conscious of the role played by parameters left implicit in ordinary speech, like preferred ends or available information in simpliciter claims. So in responding to Angie, Bertie may overlook the way her claims and his are implicitly relativized to their own respective information, leading him to assume that the proposition he rejects is the same one she asserted. (As an analogy, it might be argued that the ordinary concept of motion has always been relational, given how it is applied, although commonly mistaken for absolute as a result of overlooking the ubiquitous role of Earth's surface.)[61]

This conjecture might seem inconsistent with my claim that disagreement intuitions are highly sensitive to quality of information, and with the premise that the end-relational semantics captures ordinary competence, but these contexts of evaluation are special in two further ways. A second factor is that these evaluations involve minding two different, conflicting perspectives at once, which pose much greater cognitive demands. Consider the difficulty of steering a vehicle (e.g., in an arcade game) when you are viewing it head-on and so have to turn the wheel to *your* left to make the vehicle turn to *its* left (your right), or similarly, of backing a trailer.[62] Attending to one's own perspective makes it difficult to mind contrary perspectives; as Bertie is attending to the fact that Angie ought to use R relative to his information, this makes it difficult for him to be simultaneously sensitive to the relativity of her claim to her different information.

A third factor is that by our theory, Bertie does disagree with Angie on the basis of the normative beliefs they respectively express—although in *preference* rather than belief. But the belief and preference elements are tightly entwined, and ordinary speakers would seem unlikely to discriminate them clearly.[63] (The venerable philosophical debates between cognitivists and noncognitivists are evidence of how difficult distinguishing such elements can be.) Recognizing that he and the speaker intuitively disagree on the basis of their normative beliefs, an evaluator may reasonably assume that this is because the beliefs themselves are inconsistent.

---

[61] See Finlay 2008b; cf. Harman 1996: 13.

[62] By contrast, it's easy to steer a vehicle by wheel if it is moving upwards, left, or right in your visual field, because you need only mind a single perspective of left/right.

[63] Consider analogously pain, thirst, and hunger, which involve close connections between particular sensations and characteristic motivation. Ordinary talk about these topics frequently seems to overlook that two factors are involved.

Together these three factors provide a reasonable explanation why evaluators would commonly overlook ways in which normative speech or belief was relativized differently, and so why (e.g.) Bertie responds to Angie's statement by saying, 'That's false', and why Freddie may say that Angie "knew" she ought to use L or that he "believes the same thing". This provides a simultaneously quasi-expressivist and quasi-absolutist solution: words like 'said' and 'believes' are used to communicate others' (belief-based) preferences, as if they were just beliefs toward nonrelational propositions.[64] Evaluative words like 'true', 'false', and 'knows' are used to express normative agreement and disagreement in preference, as if this were simply disagreement in belief over nonrelational propositions.

This quasi-expressivist solution again has some significant advantages over expressivism proper. It doesn't require any radical revisions to naive semantics for 'say', 'believe', 'know', 'true', 'false', etc., or to our theories of assertion, belief, knowledge, and truth. We saw above that it avoids the expressivist's problem with negation, or of explaining the difference between believing *not-ought(p)* and not believing *ought(p)*. It also suggests an explanation why conflicts of preference expressed in normative language are more naturally described as "disagreements" than bare conflicts of preference are: they are a kind of (or easily confused with) disagreements in belief.[65]

It is fair to object that these "advantages" come at the cost of an error theory about some parts of the ordinary practice of evaluating and individuating normative claims or judgments, which is radical in rejecting the ordinary assumptions behind that practice.[66] But first, common sense is actually ambivalent here, and it isn't hard to find intuitions supporting the diagnosis of error, especially when evaluators are able to turn attention away from their own perspectives, and reflect. Once attention is drawn to the role of informational backgrounds in normative speech or thought, intuitions about truth and falsity often change.

Suppose that at some later time, when Angie's survival is no longer at issue, Bertie is pressed as follows:

"You said that Angie's claim was false. But she can't have meant to say that on the basis of all the facts (or all *your* information) she ought to use L, because she knew it was possible that using L was objectively the worst

---

[64] To have what is commonly called "the belief" that it ought to be that *p* is then to have some end-relational belief related in the right way to an end-preference; this resembles the *relational expressivism* of Toppinen 2013, Schroeder 2013.

[65] I previously acknowledged that saying, 'If I were you I'd φ' can intuitively express normative disagreement, but this seems to depend on pragmatically implying a basis of fuller information. Otherwise these utterances seem deceptive (A: 'If I were you I'd choose the vanilla'; B: 'The chocolate tastes fine to me. What's wrong with it?'; A: 'I didn't mean anything was wrong with it; I just personally prefer vanilla').

[66] Olson 2011, Joyce 2011.

choice. She must have been talking merely about what she ought to do in her subjective position. Surely she wasn't wrong about that."

Bertie plausibly should concede to this, concurring with Connie's hindsight claim: 'Okay, I guess what she said was true. But I knew that she *really* ought to use R.' These are just the considerations that prompted us to reject *Inconsistent Belief* earlier in this chapter.

Observe also that in many cases saying 'That's false' seems odd as an evaluation of normative speech. It seems more natural and felicitous for Bertie to say to Angie, 'No, don't do that!', which obviously rejects the preference she expressed rather than the proposition she asserted. This indicates intuitive discomfort about evaluating as 'false' those normative claims with which (according to our theory) one disagrees only in preference, which is evidence supporting our diagnosis.

Additionally, this error is highly *useful*, and so needn't be attributed entirely to confusion. By our theory, what simpliciter uses of normative language communicate and how they communicate it are both complex. It's convenient to simply use 'say' and 'believe' in the quasi-expressivist way to report these complex speech acts and judgments, and to simply use 'true', 'false', and 'knows' to express normative agreement or disagreement with them.[67] By our pragmatic principles, therefore, reporters and evaluators shouldn't be expected to modify their practice or correct others even when recognizing the error. Pressing advisers in this way would be exceptionally pedantic; for example, if Angie replied to Bertie by saying, 'Thank you for your helpful advice, but you're confused about what I actually said, which was that I ought to use L *given my information*. So what I said was actually true.' Since this would be an understandable and useful error that can't usually be felicitously corrected, such language may sometimes be used felicitously as a convenient fiction.[68]

These moves admittedly don't seem as natural for reports and evaluations of peculiarly *moral* speech or thought, or where differences in preferred ends are involved. Responding with 'What you said/believe is false' seems more appropriate for moral or fundamental disagreements (e.g., between Frank and Dora) than for instrumental disagreements (e.g.. Bertie to Angie). And it strains credulity (and moral decency) to claim that by saying, reprehensibly, 'We ought to use our chemical weapons on the Kurds', Saddam Hussein might actually say something true. However, in these cases there is both an additional factor

---

[67] As Mackie observes (1977: 44), suppressing relativization helps to "facilitate conceptual moves from one such demand relation to another". Pragmatic Generalization (from Chapter 7) might also be invoked here.

[68] Fictionalism rather about *moral* language has been proposed both as a theory of what speakers are doing (Kalderon 2005) and of what they ought to be doing (Joyce 2001).

contributing to confusion about the relational character of these claims, and additional reasons why it would be a useful (and even obligatory) error.

First, in Chapter 7 we analyzed paradigmatic moral and categorical uses of normative language as involving a kind of rhetorical objectivity, suppressing the end-relativization as if one set of normative facts were of shared concern to all parties, in order to convey prescriptive force. Here speakers are not only omitting the relativization but *suppressing* it. This can be predicted to dispose people even more strongly toward absolutist assumptions about moral semantics, and to make them slower to recognize moral claims as relativized to ends than to recognize (e.g.) deliberative claims as relativized to information.

Second, and for the same reason, acknowledging the end-relativity of normative propositions undermines the characteristic purposes of moral practice, and so this reticence needn't be attributed entirely to confusion. By our theory, rhetorical objectivity is essential to using normative language with morally prescriptive force, so to acknowledge relativization is to step outside moral practice. But "moral" ends are precisely those for which people are (morally) "expected" to have overriding preference, and so there is strong pressure not to step outside moral practice; in ordinary (nonphilosophical) contexts, people will seldom do so. Denying the relativization of moral propositions is therefore both an extension of moral practice itself, and also the counsel of social prudence.

This pressure also extends to philosophical practice, since moral ends are expected to be preferred even to philosophical ends of objective truth. If I am asked, 'So, do you think that Hussein said something true?', I feel trapped in a dilemma. To say that I do is, by virtue of moral pragmatics, infelicitously to indicate that I lack a certain "warmth in the cause of virtue". By "what he said/ believed", we commonly think of the overall mental state expressed thereby, and evaluating it as "true" is naturally interpreted as expressing agreement in attitude. So I can felicitously (and even honestly, if a bit cravenly) say, 'No, I think he said something false', intending this response to be understood in the normal, quasi-expressivist way.

But this moral pressure may be neutralized by moving to more technical language that doesn't have a normally quasi-expressivist pragmatic association. I'm not hesitant to say that Hussein may have asserted a true proposition (or that the informational content of the sentence he asserted may correspond to the facts), and then continue by explaining that I vehemently repudiate the moral stance and the preferences he more saliently expressed by asserting it. Pressuring me to assent to the question 'Do you think what he said/believes is true?' is from this perspective just a rhetorical ploy aimed at morally shaming me into disowning what I believe to be the philosophical truth. We'll address these issues further in the final chapter.

Whereas the extent of normative disagreement is a feature of the objectivity of normative speech and thought widely considered to be fatal to relational semantics and to require either an absolutist or expressivist semantics, the end-relational theory accommodates disagreement intuitions pragmatically, in jointly quasi-expressivist and quasi-absolutist ways. Despite its descriptivism, it explains intuitions of normative disagreement as sensitive to inconsistencies either in belief or in preference. The complexity of this account might seem to give an advantage to either absolutist or expressivist accounts; however, these results follow from our maximally simple and unifying semantics together with our basic pragmatic principles. Additionally, our theory explains data that confounds its rivals, and explains why normative disagreement resists analysis either exclusively in terms of inconsistent beliefs (e.g., the interaction of deliberation and advice, asymmetries in disagreement), or exclusively in terms of inconsistent preferences (e.g., negation). I conclude that the end-relational theory can only be supported by the ordinary practice and sense of normative disagreement, as with all the other challenges we've considered.

{ 9 }

Conclusion

Following the evidence from language led in Chapters 2–4 to a unifying end-relational semantics for 'good', 'ought', 'reason' (and related words) across a wide range of normative and non-normative uses, setting aside the specifically moral and deliberative uses of particular interest to moral philosophers. Although the possibility of such a theory accounting for these uses has been dismissed due to their special features of practicality and objectivity, Chapters 5–8 found that the end-relational semantics systematically generates solutions to these challenges on the basis of the single, intuitive principle of pragmatics that people always speak as they consider best for their ends.

Having scrupulously searched for the most inconvenient data about the use of normative language and finding nothing that can't be explained, we should accept this theory so long as we're justified in considering it the *best* explanation. As we are unable to compare every possible alternative, my primary case has been that it's a maximally simple and conservative explanation across all relevant dimensions as a whole: linguistically, metaphysically, psychologically, epistemologically, and ethically. I'll conclude by briefly addressing its commitments and implications for each of these dimensions.

9.1. Linguistics

The end-relational theory has been motivated primarily by the desideratum of a maximally simple and conservative *linguistic* treatment of the semantics and grammar of normative language. It provides a maximally unifying semantics, assigning a single meaning to each of these words not only in different normative uses, but also in non-normative uses (of 'ought' and 'reason'), though philosophers have usually dismissed these as due to lexical ambiguities. It is also compositional, generating the meanings of sentences systematically from the meanings of their components by simple and general rules of grammatical syntax, given only a systematic appeal to ellipsis. Our analyses of these lexical meanings were simple too; for example, we accounted for normative modal verbs like 'must' and 'may' with a single index, by contrast with the multiple indices required by the standard Kratzerian semantics.

The theory is also linguistically conservative, especially in comparison to expressivism, which looks like an attempt to fit a square peg into a round hole. On its surface, normative language seems to behave like all uncontroversially descriptive language, and unlike all uncontroversially nondescriptive language. 'Good', 'ought', and 'reason' are respectively an adjective, a verb, and a noun, grammatical categories that are naively taken as semantically functioning to refer respectively to properties, relations, and objects. Normative sentences are usually in the indicative mood, semantically indicating declarative or interrogative force, which are naively taken to consist in the giving and requesting of information. This contrasts with uncontroversial examples of words with semantically expressive or practical force: words like 'hooray', 'oops', and 'ouch' are nonsensical in indicative sentences, while expressives like 'alas' and imperatives have respectively a distinct grammatical category and mood.

Normative sentences are naturally evaluated as "true" or "false" like all uncontroversially descriptive sentences, and unlike uncontroversial imperatives (e.g., 'Do what I say!') and pure expressives or performatives like 'hello' and 'ouch'. Accordingly, like all descriptive sentences but unlike obviously nondescriptive expressions, normative sentences can be embedded grammatically in more complex sentences by negation, conjunction, disjunction, and in conditionals and attitude reports using words like 'believes' and 'knows'.[1]

While expressivists challenge naive assumptions about the significance of grammatical categories, moods, truth-aptness, and embedding, there has been broad consensus that normative language is descriptive on its face[2]—this is part of its apparent objectivity—and so expressivism's leading proponents have either pursued the "quasi-realist" project of attempting to explain away the descriptive appearances of normative speech and thought by appeal to purely expressivist resources, or have advanced hybrid theories combining expressivist with descriptivist semantic conventions.[3] By contrast, the end-relational theory respects these appearances in a simpler and more conservative way.

Expressivists typically offer one principal reason for rejecting pure descriptivism: that only an expressivist semantics can accommodate the practicality of this language. But the end-relational semantics systematically accommodates and explains this practicality pragmatically, given only a single, conservative

---

[1] Imperatives can be imbedded in conjunctions, disjunctions, and as the consequents of conditionals, but not in negations ('Don't φ' means *Do: not φ*, not *Not: do φ*), attitude reports, or as antecedents of conditionals.

[2] Recently some expressivists have begun to challenge this consensus (e.g., Sinclair 2012), but we need only observe how late this stance has appeared to see that descriptivism is the conservative view.

[3] E.g., Hare 1952, Slote 1968, Dreier 1990, Barker 1999, Copp 2001, Ridge 2006, Boisvert 2008.

principle of pragmatics. By providing quasi-expressivist pragmatic solutions
to puzzles about practicality we avoided any need to posit distinct expressivist
semantic conventions; similarly, by providing quasi-absolutist pragmatic solutions to puzzles about moral objectivity we avoided any need to posit distinct
absolutist semantics for moral terms.

While it's impossible to consider all relevant linguistic data here, presumably no rival theory could explain so much with such simple and conservative
resources. These results stand in stark contrast to most metaethical theorizing, which ignores or dismisses evidence from the surface form of language.
They also vindicate the much-maligned method of reductive semantic analysis
in metaethics.[4]

9.2. Metaphysics

As a form of descriptivism, the theory interprets normative language as having
the semantic function of referring to properties, relations, and facts. Here it
is less ontologically simple than expressivism or error theory, but as a metaphysically *reductive* account it makes no appeal to mysterious primitive normative properties, rather analyzing normative facts as consisting in probabilistic
relations already recognized by a common-sense and broadly scientific world-
view. Consequently, it also explains the supervenience of the normative on the
non-normative, which primitivists posit as a brute metaphysical necessity mysteriously holding between two entirely distinct kinds of properties and facts.

It may however be queried whether an analysis in terms of probability really
is an explanatory reduction, as the interpretation of probability is itself a controversial philosophical issue. If probability itself is ultimately to be analyzed
in normative terms (e.g., by 'the probability of *p*' is meant roughly *the degree
of credence one ought rationally to have that p*) then our analyses may turn out
to be circular, and if this normative definition itself requires an expressivist
analysis then they may fail to identify any real descriptive content for normative speech and thought after all, or any real normative properties. While we
can't settle these issues about the order of explanation here, normative analyses
of probability seem to put the cart before the horse: intuitively, an agent ought
to have a particular credence in a proposition because of its probability relative

---

[4] A caveat: we've agreed with expressivists that paradigmatically (and essentially, on one available sense of the qualifier 'moral'), to make a moral claim isn't simply to assert a proposition, but
to perform a speech act with a practical illocutionary force. It follows that the significance and
force of such claims isn't adequately captured by merely identifying some descriptive content, so
if this is all that a philosopher means by rejecting analytic reductionism about moral speech and
thought then we have no quarrel. This thesis is trivial, however, since even the force of ordinary
assertion isn't captured by identifying a content.

to her information, and not vice versa. So I conclude that the theory presumptively supports a metaphysical reduction of normative facts and properties.

Are these genuinely *normative* facts and properties? Expressivists might here complain that this mislocates the normativity, which emerges only in the quasi-expressivist part of the story. Contrast an instrumental conditional like 'If you're going to enjoy a long life, you'll have to quit smoking', for example, with 'If the tornado is going to destroy our house, it'll have to veer north.' The theory interprets these as referring to the same kinds of facts, but one might balk at describing the latter as "normative", as it doesn't characteristically have a practical force such as recommendation, or express the speaker's attitudes. Taking the concept of normativity to be essentially practical, it might then be supposed that on the end-relational theory it is properly speech or thought that is described as "normative", rather than facts or properties.

Even if so, we should still reject expressivism as a semantic theory about the conventional meaning of the language used in normative speech and thought, for committing the pragmatic fallacy of confusing what these words are commonly used to do with what they mean. But if "expressivism" were taken instead to be either a *speech act* theory about what it is to make a normative claim, or a *psychological* theory about what it is to hold a normative judgment, then our analyses may seem to provide less grounds for objection.[5]

Since 'normative' is a philosopher's term of art of recent origin, and we've found that the paradigms of normative speech and thought involve a complex mix of different elements, its meaning may just be indeterminate and contestable. But if I'm right to take *guidance* of actions or attitudes to be at its conceptual core, then these other kinds of "expressivism" are importantly mistaken too. Our analyses suggest that this guiding role is played neither by our desires and preferences nor by their expression, but instead by the end-relational information that our semantics identifies as the descriptive content of normative speech and thought.[6] In deliberation agents don't generally attend *to* their desires and preferences, but rather attend *from* them, to relevant end-relational information.

As primitivists often insist, normativity isn't the same thing as psychological force.[7] Our theory accommodates this observation: the "normative force" of end-relational facts isn't the psychological force of desires, but the equal and opposite reactive force of the world pushing back against them. To offer

---

[5] Such definitions are preferred in Ridge 2014; I believe they yield a less useful taxonomy, as arguably proponents of any metaethical theory (even primitivism) can and should be "hybrid expressivists" in these senses.

[6] Even conceptual role semantics, sometimes invoked in support of expressivism (Gibbard 2003, Chrisman 2015), may therefore ultimately support descriptivism (cf. Wedgwood 2001, 2007, Kalderon 2005).

[7] E.g., Parfit 2011b, Enoch 2011, and see Joseph Butler's contrast between "authority" and "power" (1726/1827).

another metaphor, normativity is the shadow cast by our desires in the external world, and is no more a part of our psychology than our shadows are parts of our bodies. So it would be fair to say that on the end-relational theory no properties or facts are normative per se (or absolutely), but only relative to agents or motivated perspectives.[8]

9.3. Psychology

We accommodated and explained the use of normative language by appealing only to the simple and conservative resources of a common-sense, Humean folk psychology appealing to ordinary, contingent beliefs and desires. No appeal was needed to hybrid attitudes, to beliefs that motivate intrinsically or necessarily, or to desires that every agent necessarily shares. The end-relational theory provides a quasi-expressivist explanation of why normative speech and thought is practical to just the extent it is, and of the efficacy of categorical and moral uses as a form of psychosocial influence. It is fully consistent with the conservative, naturalistic view of human beings as simply social animals using our intellectual capacities to pursue varying ends.

In the introduction I suggested that a basic goal of metaethical enquiry is to discover the nature of normativity and its relationship to us, particularly the relative priority of normativity and desire. Semantic analysis has led to a descriptivist account of normative language as referring to properties, relations, and facts in the world. These facts guide our deliberations and motivate us to action, identifying an important element of truth in the objectivist answer to the Euthyphro Question that gives normativity priority over desire: we are indeed motivated toward things because we judge them to be good, what we ought/have most reason to do, etc.

But this may be a merely Pyrrhic victory for the realist tradition in metaethics, as these are simply facts about probabilistic relations to ends, which guide and motivate only contingently upon a concern for those ends. We've apparently found a deeper truth in the subjectivist answer that gives desire priority over normativity: we judge things to be good, simpliciter (i.e., in a practically relevant way) because of what we more fundamentally desire.

Whereas "robust" moral realism is absolutist, interpreting everybody's moral speech and thought as addressed to common properties, our analysis is broadly relativist. The most fundamental disagreements don't involve inconsistent beliefs at all, but only inconsistent preferences and conflicts of will. Even if

---

[8] This might seem to imply that categorical claims may apply inescapably to an agent without being normative for that agent. But 'normative' might itself be taken as a normative term (e.g., as *ought to guide*), like 'moral' (and 'important', discussed below), in which case it too can be expected to have both "hypothetical" and "categorical" uses.

each party is asserting and guided by supposed facts, they are concerned with different facts: a kind of ethical "confusion of tongues". Normative speech and thought therefore appear to be just manifestations of our human, all too human nature as intelligent animals pursuing the varying and incompatible ends we contingently happen to care about, vindicating the viewpoint of Protagoras, Hume, and Nietzsche against that of Plato, Kant, and Moore.

This conclusion may seem too hasty, however. In developing my pragmatic account I have assumed a simple and conservative Humean psychological model without any argument, but this model is controversial among philosophers, and the end-relational semantics are broadly consistent with alternative psychological models that would give priority to normativity. These accounts can be described as assigning the roles I've assigned to desire and preference instead to cognition of some more fundamental normative facts, but they might rather be described as giving non-Humean accounts of desire and preference. On these views, to desire that *p* in the relevant sense isn't simply to have a noncognitive attitude or motivation toward *p*, but to either *judge* or *perceive* that *p* has some more basic normative property and be motivated toward it on that basis.[9]

My rationale for assuming the Humean model has been its relative simplicity and conservatism: in metaphysics, epistemology, and psychology (i.e., not needing any account of what these properties are, how we perceive them, or why this perception is necessarily or reliably motivating). All else being equal it therefore should enjoy the presumption of truth, but as it faces objections we haven't considered here, settling these issues would require delving further into moral psychology than we can in this book.[10]

To claim that the end-relational theory *establishes* the priority of desire over normativity would therefore overreach, and possibly beg the question. But it *supports* the priority of desire, because it refutes the central argument against the common-sense psychological model. The primary philosophical case against the Humean view and in favor of the more complex and radical psychology with its metaphysical and epistemological commitments has always been the role of normative speech and thought in human life, as observed in the introduction. Allegedly, human beings can't be mere animals motivated entirely by desire, *because* we can act instead on the basis of judgments or perceptions of what is good, etc. But I've argued that these practices of normative speech and thought can be fully accommodated and explained by the simpler and more conservative psychological theory.

More can be said, however, because our theory can accommodate the intuition that desires and preferences involve cognitions of normative properties.

---

[9] E.g., Stampe 1987, Millgram 1997, Scanlon 1998, Wedgwood 2007. For objections see especially Stocker 1979, Velleman 1992.

[10] My initial efforts in this direction can be found in my 2001, 2007a, 2008a, 2009c.

Usually our actions are directly aimed at ends that aren't the ultimate objects of desire, but are rather things we're derivatively motivated toward on the basis of seeing them as means to our ultimate or final ends. By our theory, this is indeed to be motivated by a perception of their value, or of reasons (relative to our ends). Extrinsic or derivative motivation therefore is a response to judged or perceived properties of value.

Additionally, even our own psychology is often opaque to us, and the ultimate objects of our desires are difficult to identify. This means that we are commonly unable to distinguish between the ordinary, derivative motivations which are responses to value, and the fewer intrinsic desires which aren't. It can be expected, therefore, that people would have a tendency to overgeneralize from the ordinary cases, and mistakenly take their intrinsic desires also to involve perceptions of some kind of value property. The Humean model can therefore account for the intuitive plausibility of perception or judgment theories of desire.

While cognitivist theories of desire commonly appeal to perceptions or judgments of what is "good" (or of "reasons" etc.), this is incompatible with the end-relational semantics for those words. So these views must either postulate a distinct absolutist semantics and lexical ambiguities, or else appeal to a different normative concept that isn't end-relational. Of course, in this book we've only examined a few central words, and normative vocabulary is much richer.[11] So for all our investigations have shown, perhaps analysis of other normative words or concepts would reveal a different, absolutist character—if they aren't simply primitive.

While there are many candidates, perhaps none are more promising than the concept of *importance*, or of what *matters*.[12] It's natural to say that an end is preferred or most salient in a context in case it's judged to be the *most important* end in that context. So end-relational speech and thought about what is "good", simpliciter, might be claimed to owe its normativity to implicit relativization to ends that are important, rather than to those that are *merely* desired or preferred.

As observed in Chapter 8, these sensible-sounding claims only support the priority of normativity over desire if they are interpreted in an absolutist way as referring to a common property of importance. But other interpretations are

---

[11] Some philosophers counsel abandoning study of "thin" normative terms like 'good' and 'ought' for study of "thick" terms like 'courage', 'honesty', 'sin', 'justice', etc. (e.g., Anscombe 1958, MacIntyre 1984, Williams 1985, Anderson 1993). But while study of thin terms will miss the rich detail of the normative, it seems appropriate for the important task of exploring its essential nature. Thick terms plausibly only count as normative at all because of their implications about what is good or bad, or agents' reasons for actions or attitudes. This counsel is often due to pessimism about the conceptual coherence of thin terms.

[12] Cf. Frankfurt 1982, Parfit 2011. Perhaps the most glaring omissions here are the thin terms 'right' and 'wrong', or 'correct'. Other candidates include *desirable* (e.g., Anscombe 1957), *choiceworthy* (e.g., Wedgwood 2007), and on a subjective account of normativity, *rational* (e.g., Smith 1994).

available: for example, we could rather opt for an expressivist analysis.[13] A more consistent response here is simply to extend the end-relational semantics to these other words too. Claims about "importance" can be explicitly relativized in the same ways as claims about what is "good": for example, important *for us* (patient-relativity) or important *for winning the game* (end-relativity). I suggest that to be "important" or "matter" for some end e and to some degree d is to *affect the probability of e to degree d*. Whereas speech or thought about what is "good" or "bad" addresses whether the probability of the end is increased or decreased, speech and thought about what is "important" addresses rather the degree to which the probability is changed: accordingly we can distinguish between what is importantly good and what is importantly bad.

Of course, the word 'important' is used in a variety of absolutist ways that challenge this analysis, for example, talk about what is *all-things-considered, categorically*, or *intrinsically* important (for its own sake), and people disagree fundamentally over these things. But these are obviously just the same kinds of use already observed for 'good', 'ought', and 'reason', which we accommodated pragmatically in Chapters 5–8. To claim that something is important or that it matters, simpliciter, would then be to express the belief that it affects the probability of the saliently preferred end to a contextually significant degree, and thereby to express a correspondingly high degree of concern about it.

The Humean model remains the simpler explanation, especially since the rival view needs to account for the special practicality of these alleged normative perceptions or judgments in order for them to support a version of our instrumental law of pragmatics and thereby have the same explanatory power: *why* would agents be expected always to do what they consider best for ends possessing one single, common property? It's far more plausible that desire is prior to normativity in the way I've suggested.

9.4. Epistemology

Our theory makes few demands on epistemology, and we've said little on the subject in this book, though it often occupies chapters of rival accounts. Normative speech or thought refers to ordinary facts about probabilistic relationships between states of affairs; as central objects of scientific enquiry these facts are in general known empirically, by inference from ordinary experience of the world. However, "fundamental" normative speech or thought, about intrinsic or final value, rather concerns propositions that are analytically true and therefore knowable a priori. The end-relational theory therefore appeals only to propositions that are synthetic a posteriori or analytic a priori, and not

---

[13] In this vein, Gibbard 1990 advances an expressivist theory of 'rational'.

to mysteriously synthetic a priori propositions. Unlike primitivism, it therefore doesn't postulate any controversial and mysterious ability to learn information about the world independent of experience of it, or to perceive primitive properties that don't causally influence our senses.

Nonetheless, we can accommodate and explain the intuition that basic moral or normative knowledge is both synthetic and a priori. By quasi-expressivism, saying or believing that something is good, simpliciter, isn't merely to assert or believe a proposition but also to express a preference for the implicit end and thereby a favorable attitude toward the object itself. As having a preference for any particular end isn't entailed by semantic competence with normative or any other kinds of words or concepts involved in these claims, the attitudes expressed by simpliciter uses aren't trivial but substantively informative, making these claims and attitudes "synthetic", in a way. But at least in the case of claims and judgments about intrinsic or final value, the *proposition* asserted or believed may be a priori (because analytic), which explains why somebody making such a claim may want to insist it is "self-evident". Additionally, experience of a particular kind of state of affairs isn't necessary for having preferences regarding it, which can arise spontaneously from our psychology rather than inferred from experience of the world, so one can truthfully claim to *know* that an event, situation, or object would be good, for its own sake, without having prior experience of things of that kind.[14]

In contrast to many rivals, the end-relational theory therefore provides an explanation of the characteristic features of moral epistemology, and with only simple and conservative resources. But this explanation has significant implications for normative ethics.

9.5. Ethics

The end-relational theory is conservative with regard to the content of first-order normative or ethical theory. Unlike error theoretic views, it vindicates our general confidence that we have normative or moral knowledge. It accommodates the intuitive truth conditions of a wide range of ordinary normative claims, and doesn't itself have substantive implications for which moral claims are appropriately judged "true" or "false", being neutral about which are the "moral" ends. It is therefore compatible with major moral theories including utilitarianism, Kantianism, contractualism, and Divine Command.

It might be supposed that an "end-relational" theory would at least be committed to some kind of teleology, and so incompatible with deontological theories like Kantianism. However, so-called teleological moral theories identify

---

[14] Cf. Blackburn 1985 on how expressivism explains why the supervenience of the moral on the nonmoral is a priori.

a single kind of value that is to be maximized, while our semantics is neither maximizing nor committed to identifying any general moral ends. Consider our analysis of 'Friends are good' as meaning roughly that *it's good for one's happiness, that one has friends*—which doesn't imply incorrectly that the more friends the better. Deontological "side constraints", such as an absolute moral prohibition on telling a lie, are accommodated by appeal to ends-in-action: for example, *in any circumstance you ought not to lie, in order that you thereby act in that circumstance only on a maxim you can will to be a universal law*. The end-relational semantics is flexible enough to accommodate any first-order moral views.

However, it therefore may have significant metaethical implications about the nature of normative or ethical theory. In Chapter 7 I tentatively proposed a quasi-expressivist analysis of (nonalienated) moral judgments, as expressing a speaker's peremptorily preferred ends. This implies that the philosophical hope that normative ethics might be a science, like mathematics, is in vain. Although there is plenty for philosophers to say about morality and moral issues (clarifying distinctions, identifying inconsistencies, drawing implications), to make either a moral or an all-things-considered normative claim, like 'One ought always to maximize happiness', is fundamentally to express a contingent and subjective preference. Claims of basic moral principles are little more than coercive expressions of preference.

As maintained by early expressivists like A. J. Ayer and R. M. Hare, fundamental first-order moral theorizing is therefore not properly the business of academic philosophy, understood as the pursuit of truth (as opposed to Nietzsche's conception of "legislating philosophy"), any more than it is the business of science to investigate first-order claims about what objects are to the *left* or *right* of others, or which people are *tall* or *rich*. Science or philosophy ought not to take up the cause of one subjective perspective on the world over others—if they are to be what they purport to be.

None of us are merely philosophers or scientists, of course. By the lights of this theory, the issue of what philosophy ought to be *all things considered* is subject to moral pressures, and the pure pursuit of truth (or the pursuit of pure truth) might sometimes be morally indecent. Perhaps as moral agents we ought all things considered to continue the rhetorical practice of moralism in the service of moral ends even when practicing moral philosophy. But even if philosophy is answerable to moral ends, it may yet be that, all things considered, there oughtn't be so much moralizing going on. Arguably we'd manage our conflicts better by openly acknowledging—to others as well as to ourselves—when they may involve brute inconsistencies in preference. Our pragmatic principles imply that people use the device of rhetorical objectivity because they consider it best for their purposes. But people can be mistaken, and this is an empirical question. From any perspective, moralism is a device that can be used either for Good or for Bad ends, and perhaps in balance we'd be Better off without it.

The grand philosophical ambition to resolve normative disagreements by the use of reason alone would seem futile. This could turn out to be unduly pessimistic, of course. Perhaps human nature is at base sufficiently homogeneous that if all distinctions were clarified, all inconsistencies identified, all implications drawn, and all factual errors corrected, we'd find convergence in moral perspective, as philosophers have often hoped. This wouldn't make our moral claims any less perspectival, but would diminish the influence of factors beyond the jurisdiction of philosophy or science. However, to me as to many others this looks like wishful thinking, and so I believe the end-relational theory justifies skepticism toward normative ethical theory about "first principles".

9.6. Metaethics

It is complained that even if the end-relational theory is ethically conservative in avoiding an error theory about first-order moral claims, it should be rejected on account of being unacceptably *metaethically* radical, attributing widespread error to ordinary reflective beliefs about our own moral practice.[15] Many people consider it evident on reflection that their moral speech and thought aims at reference to absolute moral properties, for example, and that fundamental moral disagreement does involve inconsistent beliefs; in discussing the absolutist challenges from categoricity, finality, and disagreement I appealed to such assumptions myself.

Certainly the end-relational theory is philosophically controversial, but this is true of every metaethical theory, none of which can lay claim to being *the* view of common sense. The objection exaggerates the degree to which reflection supports metaethical absolutism. Many people besides myself find some kind of relativist or relational theory more plausible, and so necessarily any theory violates many people's philosophical intuitions. A case can be made that the evidence from ordinary reflection overall lends greater support to relativism, though I won't attempt to make it here.[16]

As we've also just observed, espousal of metaethical absolutism may sometimes be explicable as an extension of moral practice,[17] which may be reason to question its credibility. Admitting that normative claims are relativized to ends undermines the prescriptive point of moralizing, and so those unwilling to step outside their moral practice for the sake of metaethical reflection will have a strong motive for denying anything but an absolutist theory. Some

---

[15] E.g., Joyce 2001, 2011, Olson 2011.

[16] See, e.g., Huemer 2005: xxii, Finlay 2008b, Beebe 2010, and empirical evidence in Sarkissian et al. 2011.

[17] Cf. Dworkin 1996, Blackburn 1998: 295, Kramer 2009, and see discussion in (e.g.) Bloomfield 2009.

moral philosophers freely admit to being motivated in part by a fear that the force or authority of morality would be diminished if metaethical absolutism isn't true.[18] My purpose here isn't to advance an ad hominem argument against absolutism (probably no philosophers are motivated purely by a "love of truth", each having our own agendas), but merely to observe defensively that the end-relational theory suggests alternative explanations for why absolutist intuitions would be so widely professed. As we've seen, it also predicts that reflection on the use of normative language is likely to incline people toward an absolutist theory. Without a theoretical appreciation of the rich pragmatics of these practices, the features of categoricity, finality, and disagreement are naturally taken as evidence that nonrelational concepts are being employed. So I've argued that the puzzles of metaethics are largely the result of philosophers' failure to understand these pragmatics, a metaethical "confusion of tongues".

We should of course be hesitant to accuse others either of not really believing their own theories, or of being wrong about the meaning of their own speech and thought.[19] It might seem that a better and more charitable explanation of the extent of metaethical disagreement is that different people employ different normative or moral concepts. Especially given my armchair method of consulting my own linguistic intuitions, this might be thought the most reasonable conclusion. In this vein, a reader with absolutist sympathies might respond that while I may be taken at my word that I use normative language with an end-relational meaning, he knows that he himself uses the same words in genuinely and not merely quasi-absolutist ways.

However, attributing cognitive failures is unavoidable, and the only question is where to attribute them. If it's true that some people use these words with primitivist concepts, then either their claims are systematically untrue (as I would conclude), or else the rest of us are blind to a significant dimension of reality—which strikes me as no less uncharitable a conclusion. It is much more charitable, and plausible, to locate the errors in reflective understanding somewhere, to what Nietzsche aptly described as our "weakest organ".

Attributing widespread metaethical error is unavoidable in any case, since it's almost universally assumed that there are genuine first-order moral agreements and disagreements between people who espouse different metaethical theories, and therefore that normative and moral concepts are shared (at least by those assenting to or dissenting from the same moral sentences in our society). These metaethical disagreements arise between members of a common community, using seemingly the same words in the same contexts. It strains

---

[18] E.g., Scanlon 1995, Enoch 2007. To be clear, I am not questioning the sincerity of their absolutism: simply admitting this motivation is itself a display of honesty unfavorable to the cause of morality.

[19] Although some primitivists haven't lately been shy about doing so; e.g., Parfit 2011a: 93, 2011b: 361, Enoch 2014.

credulity to suppose that this common lexicon, grammar, and usage could conceal what are effectively two different languages. On the other hand, concepts are often opaque and their analysis can be difficult, so the simpler and more plausible hypothesis is that some people just have mistaken theories about the meanings of their own words and the nature of their own practices of normative speech and thought.

Who is right and who is wrong? While I've mostly employed an armchair method, I'm confident that the linguistic intuitions to which I've appealed are widely shared by other speakers of English regardless of their metaethical inclinations. (This is of course subject to empirical verification). Primitivists, expressivists, and others don't differ significantly in which 'good', 'ought', and 'reason' sentences they use or accept in various ordinary contexts. We are justified in concluding that everybody's normative speech and thought employ end-relational concepts because we've found that this provides the best explanation of this first-order practice, even of those who accept or espouse different semantic theories. It explains why primitivists hold the first-order normative beliefs they do, for example, unlike primitivism itself, which doesn't even purport to explain how people come to have normative beliefs or knowledge, and it also explains the grammatical construction of the sentences by which they express those beliefs.

In this conclusion I've argued that the end-relational theory provides the best explanation of normative speech and thought, all else being equal, because of its maximal simplicity and conservatism. But I believe the preceding chapters also make a good case for the bolder claim that all else isn't equal and that no other theory is able to explain so much of the data, as we've also found the theory naturally suggesting solutions to many metaethical puzzles that otherwise remain unexplained, like the detachment problem for instrumental conditionals, the "moral problem" of reconciling practicality with objectivity, and the asymmetry of normative disagreement. By accommodating intuitions on both sides of many issues—like descriptivism versus expressivism, motivational internalism versus externalism, the Euthyphro Question, absolutism versus relativism—it also offers explanations for why these disputes have arisen and persisted. If some other theory can do better then we should embrace it instead, but I think this is unlikely.

{ REFERENCES }

Alvarez, Maria (2010). *Kinds of Reasons: An Essay in the Philosophy of Action.* Oxford: Oxford University Press.

Anderson, Alan Ross (1958). "A Reduction of Deontic Logic to Alethic Modal Logic." *Mind* 67: 100–103.

Anderson, Elizabeth (1993). *Value in Ethics and Economics.* Cambridge, MA: Harvard University Press.

Anscombe, G. E. M. (1957). *Intention.* Oxford: Blackwell.

Anscombe, G. E. M. (1958). "Modern Moral Philosophy." *Philosophy* 33(124): 1–19.

Åqvist, Lennart (1967). "Good Samaritans, Contrary-to-Duty Imperatives, and Epistemic Obligations." *Noûs* 1(4): 361–79.

Audi, Robert (1986). "Acting for Reasons." *Philosophical Review* 95(4): 511–46.

Bach, Kent (2002). "Semantic, Pragmatic." In J. Keim Campbell, M. O'Rourke, and D. Shier (eds.), *Meaning and Truth.* New York: Seven Bridges Press, 284–92.

Bach, Kent (2009). "Perspectives on Possibilities: Contextualism, Relativism, or What?" In A. Egan and B. Weatherson (eds.), *Epistemic Modality.* New York: Oxford University Press, 19–59.

Bar-Hillel, Yehoshua (1971). "Out of the Pragmatic Wastebasket." *Linguistic Inquiry* 2(3): 401–7.

Bar-On, Dorit and Chrisman, Matthew (2009). "Ethical Neo-Expressivism." In R. Shafer-Landau (ed.), *Oxford Studies in Metaethics*, 4. New York: Oxford University Press, 133–65.

Barker, Stephen (1999). "Is Value Content a Component of Conventional Implicature?" *Analysis* 60: 268–79.

Beardman, Stephanie (2007). "The Special Status of Instrumental Reasons." *Philosophical Studies* 134(2): 255–87.

Bech, Gunnar (1955). *Studien über das Deutsche Verbum Infinitum.* Tübingen: Niemeyer.

Beebe, James (2010). "Moral Relativism in Context." *Noûs* 44(4): 691–724.

Behrends, Jeff and DiPaolo, Joshua (2011). "Finlay and Schroeder on Promoting a Desire." *Journal of Ethics & Social Philosophy.* http://www.jesp.org/articles/download/promotingadesire.pdf.

Belnap, Nuel and Horty, John F. (1995). "The Deliberative STIT: A Study of Action, Omission, Ability, and Obligation." *Journal of Philosophical Logic* 24(6): 583–644.

Björnsson, Gunnar and Finlay, Stephen (2010). "Metaethical Contextualism Defended." *Ethics* 121(1): 7–36.

Blackburn, Simon (1985). "Supervenience Revisited." In I. Hacking (ed.), *Exercises in Analysis: Essays by Students of Casimir Lewy.* Cambridge: Cambridge University Press, 47–67.

Blackburn, Simon (1993). *Essays on Quasi-Realism.* New York: Oxford University Press.

Blackburn, Simon (1998). *Ruling Passions.* Oxford: Oxford University Press.

Bloomfield, Paul (2001). *Moral Reality*. Oxford: Oxford University Press.

Bloomfield, Paul (2009). "Archimedeanism and Why Metaethics Matters." In R. Shafer-Landau (ed.), *Oxford Studies in Metaethics*, 4. New York: Oxford University Press, 283–302.

Boghossian, Paul (2011). "The Maze of Moral Relativism." *New York Times*, July 24. http://opinionator.blogs.nytimes.com/2011/07/24/the-maze-of-moral-relativism/.

Boisvert, Daniel (2008). "Expressive-Assertivism." *Pacific Philosophical Quarterly* 89(2): 169–203.

Boyd, Richard (1988). "How to Be a Moral Realist." In G. Sayre-McCord (ed.), *Essays on Moral Realism*. Ithaca, NY: Cornell University Press, 181–228.

Bradley, Ben (1998). "Extrinsic Value." *Philosophical Studies* 91(2): 109–26.

Brandt, Richard (1979). *A Theory of the Good and the Right*. New York: Oxford University Press.

Brink, David (1989). *Moral Realism and the Foundations of Ethics*. Cambridge: Cambridge University Press.

Broome, John (1999). "Normative Requirements." *Ratio* 12(4): 398–419.

Broome, John (2001). "Normative Practical Reasoning." *Aristotelian Society Supplementary Volume* 75(1): 175–93.

Broome, John (2002). "Practical Reasoning." In J. Bermùdez and A. Millar (eds.), *Reason and Nature: Essays in the Theory of Rationality*. New York: Oxford University Press, 85–111.

Broome, John (2004). "Reasons." In J. Wallace, M. Smith, S. Scheffler, and P. Pettit (eds.), *Reason and Value: Themes from the Moral Philosophy of Joseph Raz*. New York: Oxford University Press, 28–55.

Broome, John (2005). "Does Rationality Give Us Reasons?." *Philosophical Issues* 15(1): 321–37.

Brunero, John (2013). "Reasons as Explanations." *Philosophical Studies* 165(3): 305–24.

Butler, Joseph (1726/1827). *Fifteen Sermons Preached at the Rolls Chapel*. Cambridge, MA: Hilliard, Gray, Little, and Wilkins.

Cappelen, Herman and Hawthorne, John (2009). *Relativism and Monadic Truth*. Oxford: Oxford University Press.

Cariani, Fabrizio (2013). "'Ought' and Resolution Semantics." *Noûs* 47(3): 534–58.

Carnap, Rudolf (1950). *Logical Foundations of Probability*. Chicago: University of Chicago Press.

Casebeer, William (2003). *Natural Ethical Facts*. Cambridge, MA: MIT Press.

Chisholm, Roderick (1964). "The Ethics of Requirement." *American Philosophical Quarterly* 1(2): 147–53.

Chrisman, Matthew (2008). "Ought to Believe." *Journal of Philosophy* 105(7): 346–70.

Chrisman, Matthew (2012). "'Ought' and Control." *Australasian Journal of Philosophy* 90(3): 433–51.

Chrisman, Matthew (2015). *The Meaning of Ought: Beyond Descriptivism and Expressivism in Metaethics*. New York: Oxford University Press.

Coffey, Brian (2014). *In Defense of a Relational Theory of Goodness*. Ph.D. dissertation, University of California-Davis.

Cohen, Jonathan (1982). "Are People Programmed to Commit Fallacies? Further Thoughts about the Interpretation of Experimental Data on Probability Judgment." *Journal for the Theory of Social Behaviour* 12(3): 251–74.

Collins, Arthur (1997). "The Psychological Reality of Reasons." *Ratio* 10(2): 108–23.

Comrie, Bernard (1976). *Aspect*. Cambridge: Cambridge University Press.

Condoravdi, Cleo (2002). "Temporal Interpretation of Modals." In D. Beaver, L. Casillas Martinez, B. Clark, and S. Kaufmann (eds.), *The Construction of Meaning*. Stanford, CA: CSLI Publications, 59–87.

Condoravdi, Cleo and Lauer, Sven (2014). "Preference-Conditioned Necessities: Detachment and Practical Reasoning." *Pacific Philosophical Quarterly* 95(4): 584–621.

Copley, Bridget (2006). "What Should *Should* Mean?" http://copley.free.fr/copley.should.pdf.

Copp, David (1997). *Morality, Normativity, and Society*. Oxford: Oxford University Press.

Copp, David (2001). "Realist-Expressivism: A Neglected Option for Moral Realism." *Social Philosophy and Policy* 18(2): 1–43.

Copp, David (2009). "Realist-Expressivism and Conventional Implicature." In R. Shafer-Landau (ed.), *Oxford Studies in Metaethics*, 4. New York: Oxford University Press, 167–202.

Cosmides, Leda and Tooby, John (2008). "Can a General Deontic Logic Capture the Facts of Human Moral Reasoning?" In W. Sinnott-Armstrong (ed.), *Moral Psychology*. Volume 1. Cambridge, MA: MIT Press, 53–119.

Darwall, Stephen (1983). *Impartial Reason*. Ithaca, NY: Cornell University Press.

Dancy, Jonathan (1977). "The Logical Conscience." *Analysis* 37(2): 81–84.

Dancy, Jonathan (2000). *Practical Reality*. New York: Oxford University Press.

Dancy, Jonathan (2004). *Ethics Without Principles*. Oxford: Clarendon Press.

Dancy, Jonathan (2005). "Nonnaturalism." In D. Copp (ed.), *The Oxford Handbook of Ethical Theory*. New York: Oxford University Press, 121–44.

Davidson, Donald (1963). "Actions, Reasons, and Causes." *Journal of Philosophy* 60(23): 685–700.

Davidson, Donald (1984). "Communication and Convention." In *Inquiries into Truth and Interpretation*. New York: Oxford University Press.

Davis, Wayne (2003). *Meaning, Expression, and Thought*. Cambridge: Cambridge University Press.

Dennett, Daniel (1995). *Darwin's Dangerous Idea*. New York: Simon & Schuster.

Dewey, John (1939). *Theory of Valuation*. Chicago: University of Chicago Press.

Dietz, Richard (2008). "Epistemic Modals and Correct Disagreement." In M. García-Carpintero and M. Kölbel (eds.), *Relative Truth*. Oxford: Oxford University Press, 239–62.

Dowell, Janice (2008). "Empirical Metaphysics: The Role of Intuitions about Possible Cases in Philosophy." *Philosophical Studies* 139(1): 91–110.

Dowell, Janice (2012). "Contextualist Solutions to Three Puzzles about Practical Conditionals." In R. Shafer-Landau (ed.), *Oxford Studies in Metaethics*, 7. New York: Oxford University Press, 271–303.

Dowell, Janice (2013). "Flexible Contextualism about Deontic Modals: A Puzzle about Information-sensitivity." *Inquiry* 56(2–3): 149–78.

Dreier, James (1990). "Internalism and Speaker Relativism." *Ethics* 101(1): 6–26.

Dreier, James (2006). "Negation for Expressivists." In R. Shafer-Landau (ed.), *Oxford Studies in Metaethics*, 1. Oxford: Oxford University Press, 217–33.

Dreier, James (2009). "Practical Conditionals." In D. Sobel and S. Wall (eds.), *Reasons for Action*. Cambridge: Cambridge University Press, 116–33.

Durrant, R. G. (1970). "Identity of Properties and the Definition of Good." *Australasian Journal of Philosophy* 48(3): 360–61.

Dworkin, Ronald (1996). "Objectivity and Truth: You'd Better Believe It." *Philosophy and Public Affairs* 25(2): 87–139.

Edwards, Paul (1955). *The Logic of Moral Discourse*. Glencoe, IL: Free Press.

Enoch, David (2007). "An Outline of an Argument for Robust Metanormative Realism." In R. Shafer-Landau (ed.), *Oxford Studies in Metaethics*, 2. New York: Oxford University Press, 21–50.

Enoch, David (2011). *Taking Morality Seriously: A Defense of Robust Realism*. New York: Oxford University Press.

Enoch, David (2014). "Why I Am an Objectivist about Ethics (and Why You Are Too)." In R. Shafer-Landau (ed.), *The Ethical Life*, 3rd ed. New York: Oxford University Press.

Evers, Daan (2009). "Humean Agent-Neutral Reasons?" *Philosophical Explorations* 12(1): 55–67.

Evers, Daan (2010). "The End-Relational Theory of 'Ought' and the Weight of Reasons." *Dialectica* 64(3): 405–17.

Evers, Daan (2011). "Subjectivist Theories of Normative Language." DPhil dissertation, Oxford University.

Evers, Daan (2013). "Weight for Stephen Finlay." *Philosophical Studies* 163(3): 737–49.

Ewing, A. C. (1953). *Ethics*. London: English Universities Press.

Finlay, Stephen (2001). "What Does Value Matter? The Interest-Relational Theory of the Semantics and Metaphysics of Value." Ph.D. dissertation, University of Illinois, Urbana-Champaign.

Finlay, Stephen (2004). "The Conversational Practicality of Value Judgement." *Journal of Ethics* 8(3): 205–23.

Finlay, Stephen (2005). "Value and Implicature." *Philosophers' Imprint* 5(4): 1–20.

Finlay, Stephen (2006). "The Reasons That Matter." *Australasian Journal of Philosophy* 84(1): 1–20.

Finlay, Stephen (2007a). "Responding to Normativity." In R. Shafer-Landau (ed.), *Oxford Studies in Metaethics*, 2. New York: Oxford University Press, 220–39.

Finlay, Stephen (2007b). "Too Much Morality." In P. Bloomfield (ed.), *Morality and Self-Interest*. New York: Oxford University Press, 136–54.

Finlay, Stephen (2008a). "Motivation to the Means." In D. Chan (ed.), *Moral Psychology Today: Values, Rational Choice, and the Will*. Berlin: Springer, 173–91.

Finlay, Stephen (2008b). "The Error in the Error Theory." *Australasian Journal of Philosophy* 86(3): 347–69.

Finlay, Stephen (2009a). "Oughts and Ends." *Philosophical Studies* 143(3): 315–40.

Finlay, Stephen (2009b). "The Obscurity of Internal Reasons." *Philosopher's Imprint* 9(7): 1–22.

Finlay, Stephen (2009c). "Against All Reason? Skepticism about the Instrumental Norm." In C. Pigden (ed.), *Hume on Motivation and Virtue*. New York: Palgrave Macmillan, 155–78.

Finlay, Stephen (2010a). "Normativity, Necessity, and Tense: A Recipe for Homebaked Normativity." In R. Shafer-Landau (ed.), *Oxford Studies in Metaethics*, 5. New York: Oxford University Press, 57–85.

Finlay, Stephen (2010b). "What 'Ought' Probably Means, and Why You Can't Detach It." *Synthese* 177(1): 67–89.

Finlay, Stephen (2011). "Errors upon Errors: A Reply to Joyce." *Australasian Journal of Philosophy* 89(3): 535–47.

Finlay, Stephen and Schroeder, Mark (2008). "Reasons for Action: Internal vs. External." *Stanford Encyclopedia of Philosophy*. http://plato.stanford.edu/entries/reasons-internal-external/.

Finlay, Stephen and Snedeger, Justin (2014). "One Ought Too Many." *Philosophy and Phenomenological Research* 89(1): 102–24.

von Fintel, Kai and Iatridou, Sabine (2005). "What to Do If You Want to Go to Harlem: Anankastic Conditionals and Related Matters." http://mit.edu/fintel/www/harlem-rutgers.pdf, accessed September 1, 2006.

von Fintel, Kai and Iatridou, Sabine (2008). "How to Say *Ought* in Foreign: The Composition of Weak Necessity Modals." In J. Guéron and J. Lecarme (eds.), *Time and Modality*. Studies in Natural Language and Linguistic Theory, 75. Dordrecht: Springer, 115–41.

Firth, Roderick (1952). "Ethical Absolutism and the Ideal Observer." *Philosophy and Phenomenological Research* 12(3): 317–45.

FitzPatrick, William (2008). "Robust Ethical Realism, Non-naturalism and Normativity." In R. Shafer-Landau (ed.), *Oxford Studies in Metaethics*, 3. New York: Oxford University Press, 159–205.

Foot, Philippa (1972). "Morality as a System of Hypothetical Imperatives." *Philosophical Review* 81(3): 305–16.

Foot, Philippa (1985). "Utilitarianism and the Virtues." *Mind* 94: 196–209.

Foot, Philippa (2001). *Natural Goodness*. New York: Oxford University Press.

Frankena, William (1973). *Ethics*. Englewood Cliffs, NJ: Prentice-Hall.

Frankfurt, Harry (1982). "The Importance of What We Care About." *Synthese* 53(2): 257–72.

Geach, P. T. (1956). "Good and Evil." *Analysis* 17(2): 33–41.

Geach, P. T. (1960). "Ascriptivism." *Philosophical Review* 69(2): 221–25.

Geach, P. T. (1982). "Whatever Happened to Deontic Logic?" *Philosophia* 11(1–2): 1–12.

Gensler, Harry (1985). "Ethical Consistency Principles." *Philosophical Quarterly* 35(139): 156–70.

Gert, Joshua (2003). "Requiring and Justifying: Two Dimensions of Normative Strength." *Erkenntnis* 59(1): 5–36.

Gibbard, Allan (1990). *Wise Choices, Apt Feelings*. Cambridge, MA: Harvard University Press.

Gibbard, Allan (2003). *Thinking How to Live*. Cambridge, MA: Harvard University Press.

Gibbons, John (2010). "Things That Make Things Reasonable." *Philosophy and Phenomenological Research* 81(3): 335–61.

Goldman, Alan (2009). *Reasons from Within: Desires and Values*. New York: Oxford University Press.

Greenbaum, Sidney (1996). *The Oxford English Grammar*. New York: Oxford University Press.

Greenspan, Patricia (1975). "Conditional Oughts and Hypothetical Imperatives." *Journal of Philosophy* 72(10): 259–76.

Grice, H. P. (1961). "The Causal Theory of Perception." *Proceedings of the Aristotelian Society*. Supplementary Volume 35: 121–52.

Grice, H. P. (1968). "Utterer's Meaning, Sentence Meaning, and Word Meaning." *Foundations of Language* 4: 225–42.

Grice, H. P. (1989). *Studies in the Way of Words*. Cambridge, MA: Harvard University Press.

Griffin, James (1992). "Values: Reduction, Supervenience, and Explanation by Ascent." In D. Charles and K. Lennon (eds.), *Reduction, Explanation, and Realism*. Oxford: Clarendon Press, 297–322.

Grosz, Barbara J. and Sidner, Candace L. (1986). "Attention, Intentions, and the Structure of Discourse." *Computational Linguistics* 12(3): 175–204.

Hacking, Ian (1983). *Representing and Intervening*. Cambridge: Cambridge University Press.

Hacquard, Valentine (2011). "Modality." In C. Maienborn, K. von Heusinger, and P. Portner (eds.), *Semantics: An International Handbook of Natural Language Meaning*. Berlin: de Gruyter, 1484–515.

Hájek, Alan (2011). "Interpretations of Probability." *Stanford Encyclopedia of Philosophy*. http://plato.stanford.edu/entries/probability-interpret/.

Hampton, Jean (1998). *The Authority of Reason*. Cambridge: Cambridge University Press.

Hare, R. M. (1952). *The Language of Morals*. Oxford: Oxford University Press.

Harman, Gilbert (1973). "Review of Wertheimer's *Significance of Sense*." *Philosophical Review* 82: 235–39.

Harman, Gilbert (1975). "Moral Relativism Defended." *Philosophical Review* 84(1): 3–22.

Harman, Gilbert (1976). "Practical Reasoning." *Review of Metaphysics* 29(3): 431–63.

Harman, Gilbert (1996). "Moral Relativism." In G. Harman and J. J. Thomson, *Moral Relativism and Moral Objectivity*. Malden, MA: Blackwell, 1–64.

Harsanyi, John C. (1977). "On the Rationale of the Bayesian Approach." In R. Butts and J. Hintikka (eds.), *Foundational Problems in the Special Sciences*. Dordrecht: Reidel, 381–92.

Hay, Ryan (2013). "Hybrid Expressivism and the Analogy between Pejoratives and Moral Language." *European Journal of Philosophy* 21(3): 450–74.

Henning, Tim (2014). "Normative Reasons Contextualism." *Philosophy and Phenomenological Research* 88(3): 593–624.

Hieronymi, Pamela (2005). "The Wrong Kind of Reason." *Journal of Philosophy* 102(9): 437–57.

Hill, Thomas E. Jr. (1973). "The Hypothetical Imperative." *Philosophical Review* 82(4): 429–50.

Hobbes, Thomas (1651/1994). *Leviathan*. Indianapolis, IN: Hackett.

Horgan, Terence and Timmons, Mark (1992). "Troubles on Moral Twin Earth: Moral Queerness Revived." *Synthese* 92(2): 221–60.

Horn, Larry (1972). "On the Semantic Properties of Logical Operators in English." Ph.D. dissertation, University of California–Los Angeles.

Hornsby, Jennifer (2011). "A Disjunctive Conception of Acting for Reasons." In A. Haddock and F. Macpherson (eds.), *Disjunctivism: Perception, Action, Knowledge*. Oxford: Oxford University Press, 244–61.

Horty, John F. (2001). *Agency and Deontic Logic*. New York: Oxford University Press.

Hubin, Donald (1999). "What's Special about Humeanism." *Noûs* 33(1): 30–45.

Huemer, Michael (2005). *Ethical Intuitionism*. Houndmills: Palgrave Macmillan.

Huitink, Janneke (2005). "Anankastic Conditionals and Salient Goals." In E. Maier, C. Bary, and J. Huitink (eds.), *Proceedings of Sinn und Bedeutung* 9, 140–54.

Humberstone, I. L. (1991). "Two Kinds of Agent-Relativity." *Philosophical Quarterly* 41(163): 144–66.

Jackson, Frank and Pargetter, Robert (1986). "Oughts, Options, and Actualism." *Philosophical Review* 95(2): 233–55.

Jackson, Frank (1985). "On the Semantics and Logic of Obligation." *Mind* 94: 177–95.

Jackson, Frank (1991). "Decision-Theoretic Consequentialism and the Nearest and Dearest Objection." *Ethics* 101(3): 461–82.

Jackson, Frank (1997). "Which Effects?" In J. Dancy (ed.), *Reading Parfit*. Oxford: Blackwell, 42–53.

Jackson, Frank (1998). *From Metaphysics to Ethics: A Defence of Conceptual Analysis*. Oxford: Oxford University Press.

Johnson, Rachel (2013). "What Are Practical Reasons? Explaining the Counting in Favor of Relation." Ph.D. dissertation, University of California–Los Angeles.

Joyce, Richard (2001). *The Myth of Morality*. Cambridge: Cambridge University Press.

Joyce, Richard (2006). *The Evolution of Morality*. Cambridge, MA: MIT Press.

Joyce, Richard (2011). "The Error in 'The Error in the Error Theory.'" *Australasian Journal of Philosophy* 89(3): 519–34.

Kahneman, Daniel and Tversky, Amos (1988). "Prospect Theory: An Analysis of Decision under Risk." In P. Gärdenfors and N. E. Sahlin (eds.), *Decision, Probability, and Utility*. Cambridge: Cambridge University Press, 183–214.

Kalderon, Mark Eli (2005). *Moral Fictionalism*. New York: Oxford University Press.

Kanger, Stig (1957). *New Foundations for Ethical Theory*. Stockholm: Almqvist & Wiksell.

Kaplan, David (1989). "Demonstratives." In J. Almog, J. Perry, and H. Wettstein (eds.), *Themes from Kaplan*. New York: Oxford University Press, 481–563.

Kearns, Stephen and Star, Daniel (2008). "Reasons: Explanations or Evidence?" *Ethics* 119(1): 31–56.

Kearns, Stephen and Star, Daniel (2009). "Reasons as Evidence." In R. Shafer-Landau (ed.), *Oxford Studies in Metaethics*, 4. New York: Oxford University Press, 215–42.

Kelly, Thomas (2003). "Epistemic Rationality as Instrumental Rationality: A Critique." *Philosophy and Phenomenological Research* 66(3): 612–40.

Kennedy, Christopher (2007). "Vagueness and Grammar: The Semantics of Relative and Absolute Gradable Adjectives." *Linguistics and Philosophy* 30(1): 1–45.

Kiesewetter, Benjamin (2011). "'Ought' and the Perspective of the Agent." *Journal of Ethics and Social Philosophy* 5(3): 1–24.

King, Jeffrey (1998). "What Is a Philosophical Analysis?" *Philosophical Studies* 90(2): 155–79.

Knight, Frank H. (1921). *Risk, Uncertainty, and Profit*. Boston: Houghton Mifflin.

Kölbel, Max (2002). *Truth without Objectivity*. London: Routledge.

Kolnai, Aurel (1961–62). "Deliberation Is of Ends." *Proceedings of the Aristotelian Society* 62: 195–218.

Kolodny, Niko (2005). "Why Be Rational?" *Mind* 114: 509–63.

Kolodny, Niko and MacFarlane, John (ms). "Ought: Between Subjective and Objective." Unpublished manuscript.

Korsgaard, Christine (1983). "Two Distinctions in Goodness." *Philosophical Review* 92(2): 169–95.

Korsgaard, Christine (1996). *The Sources of Normativity*. Cambridge: Cambridge University Press.

Korsgaard, Christine (1997). "The Normativity of Instrumental Reason." In G. Cullity and B. Gaut (eds.), *Ethics and Practical Reason*. Oxford: Clarendon Press, 215–54.

Kramer, Matthew (2009). *Moral Realism as a Moral Doctrine.* Malden, MA: Blackwell.

Kratzer, Angelika (1977). "What 'Must' and 'Can' Must and Can Mean." *Linguistics and Philosophy* 1(3): 337–55.

Kratzer, Angelika (1979). "Conditional Necessity and Possibility." In R. Bäuerle, U. Egli, and A. v. Stechow (eds.), *Semantics from Different Points of View.* New York: Springer, 117–47.

Kratzer, Angelika (1981). "The Notional Category of Modality." In H. J. Eikmeyer and H. Rieser (eds.), *Words, Worlds, and Contexts: New Approaches in Word Semantics.* Berlin: de Gruyter, 38–74.

Kratzer, Angelika (1986). "Conditionals." In A. M. Farley, P. Farley, and K. E. McCollough (eds.), *Papers from the Parasession on Pragmatics and Grammatical Theory.* Chicago: Chicago Linguistics Society, 115–35.

Kratzer, Angelika (2012). *Modals and Conditionals.* New York: Oxford University Press.

Kraut, Richard (2007). *What Is Good and Why: The Ethics of Well-Being.* Cambridge, MA: Harvard University Press.

Kripke, Saul (1980). *Naming and Necessity.* Oxford: Blackwell.

Langford, C. H. (1942). "The Notion of Analysis in Moore's Philosophy." In P. A. Schilpp (ed.), *The Philosophy of G. E. Moore.* La Salle, IL: Open Court, 321–42.

LaPlace, Pierre-Simon (1814). *Essai philosophique sur les probabilités.* Paris: Courcier.

Lennertz, Benjamin (2014). "Reasoning with Uncertainty and Epistemic Modals." Ph.D. dissertation, University of Southern California.

Lewis, David (1975). "Adverbs of Quantification." In E. Keenan (ed.), *Formal Semantics of Natural Language.* Cambridge: Cambridge University Press, 3–15.

Lewis, David (1979). "Scorekeeping in a Language Game." *Journal of Philosophical Logic* 8(3): 339–59.

Lewis, David (1989). "Dispositional Theories of Value." *Proceedings of the Aristotelian Society* 63: 113–37.

Lewy, Casimir (1964). "G. E. Moore on the Naturalistic Fallacy." *Proceedings of the British Academy* 50: 251–62.

MacFarlane, John (2007). "Relativism and Disagreement." *Philosophical Studies* 132(1): 17–31.

MacIntyre, Alasdair (1984). *After Virtue.* 2nd edition. South Bend, IN: University of Notre Dame Press.

Mackie, J. L. (1977). *Ethics: Inventing Right and Wrong.* Harmondsworth: Penguin.

McNamara, Paul (2006). "Deontic Logic." *Stanford Encyclopedia of Philosophy.* http://plato.stanford.edu/entries/logic-deontic/.

McNaughton, David (1988). *Moral Vision: An Introduction to Ethics.* Malden, MA: Blackwell.

Mele, Alfred (2003). *Motivation and Agency.* New York: Oxford University Press.

Millgram, Elijah (1997). *Practical Induction.* Cambridge, MA: Harvard University Press.

Moore, G. E. (1903). *Principia Ethica.* Cambridge: Cambridge University Press.

Moore, G. E. (1912). *Ethics.* London: Williams & Norgate.

Nagel, Thomas (1970). *The Possibility of Altruism.* Oxford: Clarendon Press.

Nagel, Thomas (1986). *The View from Nowhere.* New York: Oxford University Press.

Ninan, Dilip (2005). "Two Puzzles about Deontic Necessity." In J. Gajewski, V. Hacquard, B. Nickel, and S. Yalcin (eds.), *New Work on Modality.* MIT Working Papers in Linguistics 51.

Nissenbaum, Jon (2005). "Kissing Pedro Martinez: (existential) anankastic conditionals and rationale clauses." In E. Georgala and J. Howell (eds.), *Proceedings of Semantics and Linguistic Theory XV*, Ithaca, NY: CLC publications, 134–51.

Nordlinger, Rachel, and Traugott, Elizabeth (1997). "Scope and the Development of Epistemic Modality." *English Language and Linguistics* 1(2): 295–317.

Nozick, Robert (1974). *Anarchy, State, and Utopia*. New York: Basic Books.

Oddie, Graham and Milne, Peter (1991). "Act and Value: Expectation and the Representability of Moral Theories." *Theoria* 57(1–2): 42–76.

Oddie, Graham (2005). *Value, Reality and Desire*. New York: Oxford University Press.

Olson, Jonas (2011). "In Defense of Moral Error Theory." In M. Brady (ed.), *New Waves in Metaethics*. New York: Palgrave Macmillan, 62–84.

Palmer, F. R. (1986). *Mood and Modality*. Cambridge: Cambridge University Press.

Parfit, Derek (1997). "Reasons and Motivation." *Aristotelian Society* Supplementary Volume 71: 99–130.

Parfit, Derek (2001). "Reasons and Rationality." In D. Egonsson, B. Petersson, J. Joselfsson, and T. Rønnow-Rasmussen (eds.), *Exploring Practical Philosophy: From Action to Values*. Aldershot: Ashgate, 17–39.

Parfit, Derek (2006). "Normativity." In R. Shafer-Landau (ed.), *Oxford Studies in Metaethics*, 1. New York: Oxford University Press.

Parfit, Derek (2011a). *On What Matters*, Volume 1. Oxford: Oxford University Press.

Parfit, Derek (2011b). *On What Matters*, Volume 2. Oxford: Oxford University Press.

Perry, Ralph Barton (1926). *General Theory of Value*. New York: Longmans, Green.

Peters, Stanley and Westerståhl, Dag (2006). *Quantifiers in Language and Logic*. New York: Oxford University Press.

Pettit, Philip and Smith, Michael (1990). "Backgrounding Desire." *Philosophical Review* 99(4): 565–92.

Phillips, David (1998). "The Middle Ground in Moral Semantics." *American Philosophical Quarterly* 35(2): 141–55.

Piaget, J. and Inhelder, B. (1951/1975). *The Origin of the Idea of Chance in Children*. London: Routledge & Kegan Paul.

Pigden, Charles (2007). "Desiring to Desire: Russell, Lewis and G. E. Moore." In S. Nuccetelli and G. Seay, *Themes from G. E. Moore: New Essays in Epistemology and Ethics*. Oxford: Oxford University Press, 244–60.

Pigden, Charles (2011). "Identifying Goodness." *Australasian Journal of Philosophy* 90(1): 93–109.

Piller, Christian (2001). "Normative Practical Reasoning." *Aristotelian Society* Supplementary Volume 75: 195–216.

Portner, Paul (2009). *Modality*. New York: Oxford University Press.

Price, A. W. (2008). *Contextuality in Practical Reason*. New York: Oxford University Press.

Prior, Arthur N. (1949). *Logic and the Basis of Ethics*. Oxford: Clarendon Press.

Pritchard, H. A. (1949). "Duty and Ignorance of Fact." In W. D. Ross (ed.), *Moral Obligation*. Oxford: Clarendon Press, 18–39.

Putnam, Hilary (1975). *Mind, Language and Reality*. Cambridge: Cambridge University Press.

Railton, Peter (1986). "Moral Realism." *Philosophical Review* 95(2): 163–207.

Railton, Peter (1989). "Naturalism and Prescriptivity." In *Social Philosophy and Policy* 7(1): 151–74.

Raz, Joseph (1999). *Engaging Reason: On the Theory of Value and Action*. New York: Oxford University Press.

Regan, Donald (1980). *Utilitarianism and Cooperation*. Oxford: Oxford University Press.

Richard, Mark (2011). "Relativistic Content and Disagreement." *Philosophical Studies* 156(3): 421–31.

Ridge, Michael (2006). "Ecumenical Expressivism: Finessing Frege." *Ethics* 116(2): 302–36.

Ridge, Michael (2008). "Moral Non-Naturalism." *Stanford Encyclopedia of Philosophy.* http://http://plato.stanford.edu/entries/moral-non-naturalism/.

Ridge, Michael (2014). *Impassioned Belief*. Oxford: Oxford University Press.

Robinson, Denis (2009). "Moral Functionalism, Ethical Quasi-Relativism, and the Canberra Plan." In D. Braddon-Mitchell and R. Nola (eds.), *Conceptual Analysis and Philosophical Naturalism*. Cambridge, MA: MIT Press, 315–48.

Ross, Jacob (2006). "Acceptance and Practical Reason." Ph.D. dissertation, Rutgers University.

Ross, Jacob (2009). "How to Be a Cognitivist about Practical Reason." In R. Shafer-Landau (ed.), *Oxford Studies in Metaethics*, 4. New York: Oxford University Press, 243–81.

Ross, Jacob and Schroeder, Mark (2013). "Reversibility or Disagreement." *Mind* 122: 43–84.

Ross, W. D. (1939). *Foundations of Ethics*. Oxford: Oxford University Press.

Rubinstein, Aynat (2014). "On Necessity and Comparison." *Pacific Philosophical Research* 95(4): 512–54.

Russell, Bertrand (1944). "Reply to Criticisms." In P. A. Schilpp (ed.), *The Philosophy of Bertrand Russell*. Evanston, IL: Northwestern University Press, 679–741.

Sæbø, Kjell Johan (2001). "Necessary Conditions in a Natural Language." In C. Féry and W. Sternefeld (eds.), *Audiatur Vox Sapientiae: A Festschrift for Arnim von Stechow*. Berlin: Akademie Verlag, 427–49.

Sarkissian, H., Park, J., Tien, D., Wright, J. C., and Knobe, J. (2011). "Folk Moral Relativism." *Mind and Language* 26(4): 482–505.

Scanlon, T. M. (1995). "Fear of Relativism." In R. Hursthouse, G. Lawrence, and W. Quinn (eds.), *Virtues and Reasons: Philippa Foot and Moral Theory*. Oxford: Clarendon Press, 219–45.

Scanlon, T. M. (1998). *What We Owe to Each Other*. Cambridge, MA: Belknap Press.

Scanlon, T. M. (2001). "Thomson on Self-Defense." In R. Stalnaker, A. Byrne, and R. Wedgwood (eds.), *Fact and Value: Essays on Ethics and Metaphysics for Judith Jarvis Thomson*. Cambridge, MA: MIT Press, 199–214.

Schroeder, Mark (2004). "The Scope of Instrumental Reason." *Philosophical Perspectives* 18(1): 337–64.

Schroeder, Mark (2007). *Slaves of the Passions*. Oxford: Oxford University Press.

Schroeder, Mark (2008a). "How Expressivists Can and Should Solve Their Problem with Negation." *Noûs* 42(4): 573–99.

Schroeder, Mark (2008b). *Being For: Evaluating the Semantic Program of Expressivism*. Oxford: Oxford University Press.

Schroeder, Mark (2008c). "Having Reasons." *Philosophical Studies* 139(1): 57–71.

Schroeder, Mark (2009a). "Means-End Coherence, Stringency, and Subjective Reasons." *Philosophical Studies* 143(2): 223–48.

Schroeder, Mark (2009b). "Hybrid Expressivism: Virtues and Vices." *Ethics* 119(2): 257–309.

Schroeder, Mark (2011). "*Ought*, Agents, and Actions." *Philosophical Review* 120(1): 1–41.

Schroeder, Mark (2013). "Tempered Expressivism." In R. Shafer-Landau (ed.), *Oxford Studies in Metaethics*, 8. New York: Oxford University Press, 283–314.

Searle, John R. (1962). "Meaning and Speech Acts." *Philosophical Review* 71(4): 423–32.

Searle, John R. (1983). *Intentionality: An Essay in the Philosophy of Mind.* Cambridge: Cambridge University Press.

Searle, John R. (2001). *Rationality in Action.* Cambridge, MA: MIT Press.

Setiya, Kieran (2007). "Cognitivism about Instrumental Reason." *Ethics* 117(4): 649–73.

Shafer-Landau, Russ (2003). *Moral Realism: A Defence.* New York: Oxford University Press.

Shah, Nishi (2006). "A New Argument for Evidentialism." *Philosophical Quarterly* 56(225): 481–98.

Shanklin, Robert (2011). "On Good and 'Good'." Ph.D. dissertation, University of Southern California.

Sidgwick, Henry (1874). *The Methods of Ethics.* London: Macmillan.

Siegel, Muffy (2006). "Biscuit Conditionals: Quantification over Potential Literal Acts." *Linguistics and Philosophy* 29(2): 167–203.

Sinclair, Neil (2012). "Moral Realism, Face-Values and Presumptions." *Analytic Philosophy* 53(2): 158–79.

Sinnott-Armstrong, Walter (1984). " 'Ought' Conversationally Implies 'Can'." *Philosophical Review* 93(2): 249–61.

Sinnott-Armstrong, Walter (2008). "A Contrastivist Manifesto." *Social Epistemology* 22(3): 257–70.

Skorupski, John (2010). *The Domain of Reasons.* Oxford: Oxford University Press.

Skyrms, Brian (1980). "Higher Order Degrees of Belief." In D. H. Mellor (ed.), *Prospects for Pragmatism.* Cambridge: Cambridge University Press, 109–37.

Sloman, Aaron (1970). " 'Ought' and 'Better'." *Mind* 79: 385–94.

Slote, Michael (1968). "Value Judgments and the Theory of Important Criteria." *Journal of Philosophy* 65(4): 94–112.

Slote, Michael (2010). *Moral Sentimentalism.* New York: Oxford University Press.

Smith, Michael (1994). *The Moral Problem.* London: Blackwell.

Snedegar, Justin (2012). "Contrastive Semantics for Deontic Modals." In M. Blaauw (ed.), *Contrastivism in Philosophy: New Perspectives.* New York: Routledge, 116–33.

Snedegar, Justin (2013a). "Contrastive Reasons." Ph.D. dissertation, University of Southern California.

Snedegar, Justin (2013b). "Reason Claims and Contrastivism about Reasons." *Philosophical Studies* 166(2): 231–42.

Soames, Scott (2004). *Reference and Description: The Case against Two-Dimensionalism.* Princeton, NJ: Princeton University Press.

Sobel, D., Tenenbaum, J. and Gopnik, A. (2004). "Children's Causal Inferences from Indirect Evidence: Backwards Blocking and Bayesian Reasoning in Preschoolers." *Cognitive Science* 28(3): 303–33.

Stalnaker, Robert (1972). "Pragmatics." In D. Davidson and G. Harman (eds.), *Semantics of Natural Language.* Dordrecht: Reidel, 389–408.

Stalnaker, Robert (1999). *Context and Content: Essays on Intentionality in Speech and Thought.* New York: Oxford University Press.

Stampe, Dennis (1987). "The Authority of Desire." *Philosophical Review* 96(3): 335–81.

von Stechow, A., Krasikova, S., and Penka, D. (2005). "Anankastic Conditionals." http://vivaldi.sfs.nphil.uni-tuebingen.de/~arnim10/Aufsaetze/NEC.COND.7.pdf.

von Stechow, A., Krasikova, S., and Penka, D. (2006). "Anankastic Conditionals Again." http://folk.uio.no/torgriso/fs/files/stechowetal.pdf.

Stevenson, Charles L. (1937). "The Emotive Meaning of Ethical Terms." *Mind* 46: 14–31.

Stevenson, Charles L. (1944). *Ethics and Language*. New Haven, CT: Yale University Press.

Stocker, Michael (1971). "'Ought' and 'Can'." *Australasian Journal of Philosophy* 49(3): 303–16.

Stocker, Michael (1979). "Desiring the Bad: An Essay in Moral Psychology." *Journal of Philosophy* 76(12): 738–53.

Strandberg, Caj (2012a). "A Dual Aspect Account of Moral Language." *Philosophy and Phenomenological Research* 84(1): 87–122.

Strandberg, Caj (2012b). "Expressivism and Dispositional Desires." *American Philosophical Quarterly* 49(1): 81–91.

Sturgeon, Nicholas (1985). "Moral Explanations." In D. Copp and D. Zimmerman (eds.), *Morality, Reason, and Truth*. Totowa, NJ: Rowman Allenheld, 49–78.

Svavarsdóttir, Sigrun (1999). "Moral Cognitivism and Motivation." *Philosophical Review* 108(2): 161–219.

Szabo, Zoltan (2001). "Adjectives in Context." In R. M. Harnish and I. Kenesei (eds.), *Perspectives on Semantics, Pragmatics, and Discourse*. Amsterdam: Benjamins, 119–46.

Talbot, Brian (2009). "How to Use Intuitions in Philosophy." Ph.D. dissertation, University of Southern California.

Thomson, Judith Jarvis (1986). "Imposing Risks." In W. Parent (ed.), *Rights, Restitution, and Risk*. Cambridge, MA: Harvard University Press, 173–91.

Thomson, Judith Jarvis (1990). *The Realm of Rights*. Cambridge, MA: Harvard University Press.

Thomson, Judith Jarvis (1992). "On Some Ways in Which a Thing Can Be Good." *Social Philosophy and Policy* 9(2): 96–117.

Thomson, Judith Jarvis (1997). "The Right and the Good." *Journal of Philosophy* 94(6): 273–98.

Thomson, Judith Jarvis (2001). *Goodness and Advice*. Princeton, NJ: Princeton University Press.

Thomson, Judith Jarvis (2008). *Normativity*. Chicago: Open Court.

Timmons, Mark (1999). *Morality without Foundations*. Oxford: Oxford University Press.

Toppinen, Teemu (2013). "Believing in Expressivism." In R. Shafer-Landau (ed.), *Oxford Studies in Metaethics*, 8. New York: Oxford University Press, 252–82.

Toulmin, Stephen (1950). *An Examination of the Place of Reason in Ethics*. Cambridge: Cambridge University Press.

Tresan, Jon (2006). "De Dicto Internalist Cognitivism." *Noûs* 40(1): 143–65.

Tversky, Amos and Kahneman, Daniel (1986). "Rational Choice and the Framing of Decisions." *Journal of Business* 59(4): 251–78.

Unwin, Nicholas (1999). "Quasi-Realism, Negation and the Frege-Geach Problem." *Philosophical Quarterly* 50(196): 337–52.

Unwin, Nicholas (2001). "Norms and Negation: A Problem for Gibbard's Logic." *Philosophical Quarterly* 51(202): 60–75.

van Roojen, Mark (ms). "Consequents of True Practical Conditionals Detach." Unpublished manuscript.

Velleman, J. David (1989). *Practical Reflection*. Princeton, NJ: Princeton University Press.

Velleman, J. David (1992). "The Guise of the Good." *Noûs* 26(1): 3–26.

Velleman, J. David (1996). "The Possibility of Practical Reason." *Ethics* 106(4): 694–726.

Vermazen, Bruce (1977). "The Logic of Practical 'Ought'-Sentences." *Philosophical Studies* 32(1): 1–71.

Wallace, R. Jay (2001). "Normativity, Commitment, and Instrumental Reason." *Philosophers' Imprint* 1(4): 1–26.

Watson, Gary (1975). "Free Agency." *Journal of Philosophy* 72(8): 205–20.

Way, Jonathan (2010). "Defending the Wide-Scope Approach to Instrumental Reason." *Philosophical Studies* 147(2): 213–33.

Weatherson, Brian (2008). "Attitudes and Relativism." *Philosophical Perspectives* 22(1): 527–44.

Wedgwood, Ralph (2001). "Conceptual Role Semantics for Moral Terms." *Philosophical Review* 110(1): 1–30.

Wedgwood, Ralph (2006). "The Meaning of 'Ought'." In R. Shafer-Landau (ed.), *Oxford Studies in Metaethics*, 1. New York: Oxford University Press, 127–60.

Wedgwood, Ralph (2007). *The Nature of Normativity*. Oxford: Oxford University Press.

Wertheimer, Roger (1972). *The Significance of Sense: Meaning, Modality, and Morality*. Ithaca: Cornell University Press.

Wheeler, Samuel C. III (1974). "Inference and the Logical "Ought"." *Noûs* 8: 233–58.

Wheeler, Samuel C. III (2013). *Neo-Davidsonian Metaphysics: From the True to the Good*. New York: Routledge.

White, Alan (1975). *Modal Thinking*. Ithaca, NY: Cornell University Press.

Williams, Bernard (1979). "Internal and External Reasons." In R. Harrison (ed.), *Rational Action*. Cambridge: Cambridge University Press, 17–28.

Williams, Bernard (1981a). "*Ought* and Moral Obligation." In *Moral Luck*. Cambridge: Cambridge University Press, 114–23.

Williams, Bernard (1981b). "Persons, Character and Morality." In *Moral Luck*. Cambridge: Cambridge University Press, 1–19.

Williams, Bernard (1985). *Ethics and the Limits of Philosophy*. Cambridge, MA: Harvard University Press.

Williams, Bernard (1989). "Internal Reasons and the Obscurity of Blame." *Logos* 10: 1–11.

Williams, Bernard (2001). "Postscript: Some Further Notes on Internal and External Reasons." In E. Millgram (ed.), *Varieties of Practical Reasoning*. Cambridge, MA: MIT Press, 91–97.

Williamson, Timothy (2000). *Knowledge and Its Limits*. Oxford: Oxford University Press.

Williamson, Timothy (2007). *The Philosophy of Philosophy*. Malden, MA: Blackwell.

Wittgenstein, Ludwig (1930/1996). "Lecture on Ethics." In S. Darwall, A. Gibbard, and P. Railton (eds.), *Moral Discourse and Practice*. New York: Oxford University Press, 65–70.

Wong, David (1984). *Moral Relativity*. Berkeley: University of California Press.

von Wright, G. H. (1963). *Norm and Action*. New York: Humanities Press.

Ziff, Paul (1960). *Semantic Analysis*. Ithaca, NY: Cornell University Press.

{ INDEX }

CPSIA information can be obtained at www.ICGtesting.com
Printed in the USA
BVOW04s0534221016

465755BV00003B/7/P